Leibold/Probst/Gibbert   Strategic Management in the
Knowledge Economy

Strategic Management in the Knowledge Economy

New Approaches and Business Applications

By Marius Leibold,
Gilbert J. B. Probst
and Michael Gibbert

 PUBLICIS

WILEY

Bibliographic information published by Die Deutsche Bibliothek
Die Deutsche Bibliothek lists this publication in the Deutsche Nationalbibliografie;
detailed bibliographic data is available in the Internet at http://dnb.ddb.de.

http://www.publicis-erlangen.de/books
http://www.wiley-vch.de

ISBN 3-89578-168-1

A joint publication of Publicis Corporate Publishing and Wiley-VCH-Verlag GmbH & Co KGaA

Printed in Germany

Preface

Why this book now?

This book is based on the premise that from about the middle of the 1990s onward the global environment has been causing "revolutionary" changes in traditional industries, corporations and business models. Extant strategic management approaches and tools cannot adequately cope with the scope and thrusts of these dynamic knowledge-enhanced changes. We have entered a knowledge society and our companies are increasingly becoming knowledge-based entities, without giving enough thought to the impact of knowledge dynamics on strategic management.

Strategy approaches have to be changed, companies need new competencies, and the business logic and models have to be revisited. Companies are realizing that the competitive, information-based method of strategically managing enterprises in the previous century is fundamentally changing in a knowledge-based, networked society in which *strategic collaboration* is becoming as important as *competitive strategy* mindsets and practices.

What this book is about?

This book provides understanding of the dramatic shifts in the knowledge economy and the resulting significant implications for traditional strategic management theory and application. It furthermore helps the reader to learn and discover pre-eminent writings as well as methods and tools for strategic management in the knowledge society. Strategy innovation in the knowledge economy requires a new mindset, rooted in a systemic (networked, interactive) view and not a traditional (mechanistic) value-chain, industry-bound, or an existing resource capability orientation. Companies should no longer only focus on efficient intra-organizational knowledge creation and sharing, but should also include the inter-organizational realm, as well as other relevant stakeholders in its ecosystem and relevant socio-cultural networks.

The *key message is that the new knowledge-networked economy requires a totally different strategic management mindset and toolbox.* The traditional approaches are not completely obsolete, but used on their own they are inappropriate for sustainable organizational performance and survival in today's knowledge-networked economy.

Step by step, each chapter leads the reader towards a better understanding of the environment, the need for a new approach and the tools available today. Per chapter the authors furthermore offer a brief introduction and theoretical overview, followed by selected research papers and viewpoints, which are concluded by clearly related and embedded case studies, developed by the editing authors.

Who should read this book and how should it be used?

The book is aimed primarily for use at MBA-level and PMD-executive courses, as well as for capstone undergraduate courses in strategic management. In addition, strategists and top managers will find it an effective aid in understanding the shifts and impacts of the knowledge society on strategic management, as well as the need for new tools and methods. The book originated from a realization that students and business leaders cannot be educated/oriented in strategy by simply reviewing extant strategic management theory and applications. Our approach is not to teach theory or cases, but to understand the evolution of strategic management thought, related to historical timeframes and contexts, and the difficulties of extant strategic management approaches and tools in dealing with current "discontinuities" in the environment. Additionally, we provide integrated substantiation for a new approach by corporate leaders and strategists to strategic management in the knowledge economy – *systemic strategic management*.

The contents and style of the book are significantly different from the usual strategic management textbooks. The content is a unique combination of theory, published articles, and case studies, all designed to make key points and bring across messages that substantiate the proposals for new and complementary strategic management approaches and applications. The style of the book is easily readable by advanced students and business executives alike. Case vignettes are provided to amplify key points, and a list of questions are provided at the end of each chapter to stimulate further review, comparison and debate.

The overall learning objective is to provide a strong basis (aptly argued and substantiated) for the acceptance of new strategic management approaches and tools to be used complementary to extant strategy approaches and tools. The purpose is not to make a case that extant approaches and tools are obsolescent or invalid in the "knowledge economy", but that they are inadequate if used on their own.

The book's major new (or additional) conceptual contributions to the field of strategic management are:

- The concept of *systemic strategic management*, in contrast to the traditional concept of analytical strategic management.

- The concept of *business socio-cultural network dynamics* – including business ecosystems perspectives – in contrast to the traditional industry or internal business value chain perspective.

- The concept of *systemic scorecard* (*SSC*) in contrast to the traditional balanced scorecard (BSC). The latter focuses more on single enterprise strategy dynamics, while the SSC emphasizes stakeholder systems dynamics in an increasingly collaborative, knowledge-networked environment.

The writing of the book

This book became reality due to stimulating personal meetings and an intensive virtual knowledge exchange between the authors. The common systems-oriented background, dynamic teaching and practical experiences, and learning-based, corporate case writing allowed the authors to make it happen. But many other people's contributions have made this book possible. First of all, we are indebted to Gerhard Seitfudem for his incisive and thoughtful editorial assistance. Many thanks are due to Liisa Valikangas, Ellen Enkel, Carlos Jarillo, Barry Nalebuff, Georg von Krogh and Johann Kinghorn. Our discussions with them, their queries and comments helped us greatly in shaping our ideas. Johann Kinghorn made an important contribution with his article on organizational sense making for strategic leadership. Our gratitude to Eva DiFortunato, research assistant at HEC, University of Geneva for her most helpful work in the fine-tuning of the cases and her valuable comments. Special thanks to Ms Jo-Marie Pretorius for the word processing of the chapter texts, and to Mr Solomon Habtay, research assistant at Stellenbosch University, for reading and commenting ably on the draft chapters. Gunhilt and Wolfram Elwert allowed us to communicate easily by sharing their telephone lines and creating a great working environment. And last but not least we thank Ilse Evertse for her editorial magic. Her disarming criticism, infinite patience and imperturbable personality are more than any author could wish for.

Marius Leibold, Stellenbosch, South Africa
Gilbert Probst, Geneva, Switzerland
Michael Gibbert, New Haven, USA

September 2002

Contents

IV New Strategic Management Approaches and Processes

V A New Strategic Management Toolbox

VI Strategic Management – The Challenging Road Ahead

I Introduction

Chapter 1:
Fundamental Impacts of the Global Knowledge Economy on Strategic Management

An Emerging New Era

The global economic landscape and business world are changing rapidly. Strategic management in turbulent conditions needs to be pro-active. Just when managers think they have developed a strategy for future success, a new technology, process, competitor or customer behavioral pattern emerges. While a sharp focus and "sticking to the knitting" are sometimes the key to success in more stable conditions, the turbulent, knowledge-driven markets of today require dynamic new strategic management approaches and tools.

In the fast-changing, network-innovative, knowledge-driven global economy that mainly gained momentum in the last decade of the 20th century, the deficiencies of the traditional, relatively static strategic management approaches, tools and processes are becoming evident. The stakes in global business are too high to continue to rely on inappropriate strategic management practices, and this book offers a platform for sensible, new strategic management approaches and tools in a today's environment. A sound understanding of the dramatic, even revolutionary, *shifts* that the knowledge economy is causing in the business competitive landscape, and a resulting grasp of the *implications* of these shifts, are both essential in order to realize the necessity of new strategic management practices, and the relevance of the proposed strategic management concepts, approaches and tools in this book.

Table 1.1 Environmental Turbulence, Knowledge and Strategy

Time Environment	Short term	Long term
Unstable, chaotic, knowledge-networked	Reactive, myopic strategy	Dynamic, "shaping", robust strategy
Stable, orderly, information-focused	Static "fire-fighting"	Strategic planning and "adaptation"

The relationships between levels of environmental turbulence and types of strategy are indicated in Table 1.1.

The key issue illustrated in Table 1.1 is the types of response companies make to the increasingly unstable, chaotic, knowledge-networked nature of the business environment – either short-term reactive responses, resulting in partial and myopic strategy, or longer-term dynamic, shaping, robust strategy resulting in sustainable organizational fitness and survival. While all four strategy types could be valid in particular situations, the focus today is shifting to the upper right hand box – strategy that is dynamic, robust and "shaping" new customer value, and leading to major changes in and even reinvention of industries. What are the major shifts leading to this development?

Dramatic Shifts Due to the Global Knowledge Economy

In the final decade of the 20th century we witnessed the end of the Cold War, a new appreciation of the value of freedom and diversity, dramatic changes in the way we work, and the emergence of a globally networked society accelerated by computer and communications technology. We are at a juncture in the era of organizational leadership in which the traditional Sloan, Taylor and Ford approaches can no longer cope with the exploding opportunities afforded in a global economy in rapid transition. Enterprises across all sectors of the economy have experienced excruciating measures during reengineering, downsizing, outsourcing, total quality standards, cost-cutting and productivity improvements. In many respects, creativity and innovation have been squeezed out of the system, and the real value of creativity and intellectual capability in sound inter-relationships have been neglected.

Since the late 1980s a major turning period in the world's economic, political and social history has occurred. The walls seem to have collapsed – between nations, between industries, between sectors of the economy, between organizations, and between functions inside an organization. Linkages, networks and symbiosis are becoming the order of the day, as evidenced in the increasing incidence of alliances, mergers, joint ventures, cross-functional project teams and communities of practice. *Inside* organizations, enterprises are realizing the value of *interdependencies,* rather than differences and independencies, through initiatives such as simultaneous development processes, concurrent engineering, agile manufacturing and resource management networks; and *outside* organizations the need for value system management (as opposed to value chain management), and business ecosystem influencing are now starting to be realized.

What has been happening, is that the speed and *complexity* of decision making have increased, as well as the acceleration of technological change and rapid acceptance of computer and electronic communications. Industries and markets are being shaped, reshaped and invented as niche-market vendors capitalize on connecting products, services, and businesses in ways unimagined a few years ago. Larger (incumbent) companies experiment with radical diversification and alliances of all forms, including those with archrivals, while smaller and "start-up" companies often upset industry traditions through innovative new business models, often by circumventing traditional industry channels. The notion of independent, competitive strategies – although still prominent in business and government rhetoric – is being diluted by the intense need to *collaborate* in order to survive and prosper through the creation of significant new customer value propositions, enabled by new technologies.

There are at least *six major forces*[1] causing significant shifts in strategic management thinking and implementation. These are forces causing a shift from:

- information to knowledge and wisdom.
- bureaucracies to networks.
- training/development to learning.
- local/national to transnational/global and metanational.
- competitive to collaborative thinking.
- single connections to multi-connectivity to biocorporate systems in relationships among individuals, organizations and nature.

These forces are strongly interrelated, and there are numerous other forces, but for purpose of overall understanding, these suffice. The assumptions are that these shifts are fundamental and that organizations have to be able to make sense of them and develop appropriate strategic approaches and practices. Let's look into each of these forces.

Forces causing a shift from information to knowledge and wisdom

In the information technology profession, there has been a natural evolution of computing. *Data* are elements of analysis. *Information* is data with context. *Knowledge* is information with meaning. *Wisdom* is knowledge plus insight and sound judgement. When applied to any community, these concepts refer to the sum total experience and learning residing within an individual, group, enterprise, or nation. The new source of wealth is knowledge, not labor, land, or financial capital. It is the intangible, intellectual assets that must be managed.

The shift in orientation from information to knowledge is not a cosmetic change. It requires an entirely new lens through which the world is viewed. But what in people is important? What constitutes value-added? The answer, naturally, is the *knowledge* they have to contribute to the business and their innate capability to continue to do so. Moreover, it is the ability of groups to learn from one another and contribute collectively to the solution of a problem and/or the identification of a new business opportunity.

Professionals have found themselves experiencing "information overload" and being starved for knowledge – the downside of a technologically sophisticated society. The challenge, then, is to develop mechanisms to ensure that time – the most precious commodity of all – is spent on genuine value-added, knowledge-creating and knowledge-utilizing activities. More important, mechanisms need to be established to be able to project viable businesses in future, while current practices track only past trends, resulting from static and incremental strategy thinking. This in turn involves risk and options analysis, requiring wisdom – knowledge with foresight and sound judgment, based on both experience and experimentation with strategy innovation and robust new business models.

Shift from bureaucracies to networks

The traditional hierarchical designs that served the Industrial Era are not flexible enough to harness the full intellectual capability of an organization. Much more unconstrained, fluid, networked organizational forms are needed for effective modern decision-making. The *strategic business units* (SBUs) of the Alfred P. Sloan era have given way to the creation and effective utilization of *strategic business networks* (SBNs) by a given enterprise. Progressive organizations establish *strategic business systems* (SBSs) with multiple networks, interdependent units, and dual communications.

Another new lens from which the organization should be viewed, is the shift from hierarchical authority to a system based on new organization-wide ideas – and the performance thereof. A marketplace reliant on the flow of new ideas cannot place restrictions on the origin of those ideas. By definition, boundaries are shattered. Organizations seek valuable contributions both inside and external to the firm. The *strategic business system* (SBS) now includes partners, suppliers, and other stakeholders, including customers and sometimes competitors.

The reality is that effective organizations are neither hierarchical nor networked, but a blend of both. Based on a company's traditions and values, different priorities would be placed on the management spectrum. The important thing is that there is flexibility built into the managerial system to capitalize on opportunities, while simultaneously ensuring proper responsibility and accountability. This notion of *constrained freedom* is more complex than it appears, but holds significant creativity and innovation benefits for the enterprise.

Shift from training/development to learning

The role of education has become paramount in all organizations – public and private. However, the change has been from a passive orientation with a focus on the trainer and the curriculum, to an active perspective that places the learner at the heart of the activity. In fact, learning must occur real-time in both structured and informal ways. Detailed curriculums have given way to action research by teams as the best way to advance the knowledge base.

The new lens requires one to realize the real-time value of learning – in the classroom, on the job, and in all customer and professional interactions. Learning is the integral process for progress. It is an investment rather than perceived expense to the organization. The knowledge that one creates and applies is more important than the knowledge one accumulates. New techniques, such as collaborative teams and action research, can be easily incorporated into the culture.

Naturally, issues such as learning for responsible competition, creativity and innovation need to be addressed, which are often the spur to enhanced development and

15

progress. In effect, moral issues such as the definitions of "progress", "value", and "purpose" of the enterprise, should form part of new strategic management approaches and "toolkits".

Trust is a concept of increasing value in the knowledge-networked economy. With the emergence of an interdependent, global economy, collaborative faith is essential. Beyond the obvious advantages of shared resources is an understanding that there must be a more effective way to increase the standard of living of all countries, regions and communities simultaneously.

Shift from local/national to transnational/global and metanational

No longer can enterprises rely on purely regional approaches to maintain their profitable growth. More and more, companies and industries of all types are necessitated to globalize in order to optimize their profitability. The fact is that every national business strategy must be created within an international and cross-national context – thus, the term *transnational*. After World War II, there was a need to create mechanisms (e.g., the World Bank and the IMF) to move capital around the world. During the post-Cold War era, there is a need to create the equivalent for *"the world trade of ideas"*.

This is the new managerial lens that may require the greatest adjustment of all. For most companies experiencing productivity measures, one of the first expenses to be eliminated is international travel, exactly when an understanding of multiple cultures is essential to future global business success. This is the lens that begs a strategy of collaboration versus competition. It is the same lens that demands a view of the whole in order to understand the interrelationship of the parts. While most organizations are still rooted in their home country, some are now moving towards a transcending of their historical home boundaries, adopting a truly *metanational* approach in terms of location, resources and processes.

Acceleration of communication technology has expanded the definition of potential business. Transnational alliances of all forms are necessary in order to enter and survive in the global playing field. There is no way that an organization can easily survive without an integral relationship with partners, suppliers, and other cross-border stakeholders. Cultural differences should harmonize and the leveraging of distinctive competencies is a major recipe for survival.

Shift from competitive to collaborative thinking

We live in an era dominated by competitive strategy thinking – one that produces only win/lose scenarios. Even in a cooperative environment, parties divide up the wealth to create a win/win situation. The pie, however, often remains the same. With a collaborative approach, symbiosis creates a larger pie to share or more pies to divide. Alliances of every dimension are the natural order of the day in the realization that go-it-alone strategies are almost always suboptimal.

The last decade has been bursting with institutionalized examples of competitive strategy. It is time to remove the barriers to progress and to establish mechanisms of communication, collaboration and partnership that transcend current practice.

The emerging collaborative practices among traditional competitors, e.g. supply chain collaboration between GM, Ford and DaimlerChrysler in the automotive industry, illustrate this shift to collaborative learning and strategy.

Shift from single and multi-connective relationships to biocorporate relationships

The thinking, logic and language that surrounded our past assumptions are based on a view that the world works like a machine and that it is, to a considerable degree, predictable and understandable. This way of thinking was a perfect match for the Industrial Era and it allowed us to function with ease and effectiveness throughout that era. In fact, this way of thinking "created" the Industrial Era. Only under rare circumstances do we approach anything in a way that is not linear, mechanistic, reductionist or analytic. For most of us, this is the only way we know of approaching action, organization and events.

The Industrial Era and its approaches are now rapidly being displaced and a new way of thinking about the world is emerging – one that is far too different from that of the past for mere adaptation. This new way of thinking, and the theories and approaches that accompany it, are emerging out of our awakening to new levels of understanding in the areas of *ecosystems, intelligence, organization, information* and *language*. Our understanding of these areas is spawning new network technologies that are now sweeping the commercial world. These new technologies are demanding changes in every aspect of our organizational structures and management practices. Innovative ways of working together, utilizing information and spreading knowledge are being employed by associates and competitors in ways that are taking and creating new market territory.

The major deficiency of current educational practices is that they are intended to create a learning ability (i.e., the capacity to create new ideas). Indeed, new ideas are usually generated in the process. But there are no institutionalized mechanisms to capture those ideas, nurture them, and create new products and processes. They tend to be "lost" in the system. Most evaluation systems measure the "quality" of the training instruments rather than assessing the actual "value" of the process itself.

Biology has become a new place to look for organizational inspiration, in which organizations mutate into organism, markets to ecologies, and mechanical metaphors to biological analogies. With the rapid spread of global knowledge, sciences are starting to cross-pollinate and learn from one another, and the biological concepts of self-organizing systems, emergence and coherence are now also starting to be applied in today's business organizations. From traditional, *systematic*, multi-connectivity thinking, the shift to *systemic* thinking, i.e. organizations as part of global ecosystems, is now becoming accepted. Various authors are now emphasizing the need for "robust adaptive strategies"[2], based on *biocorporate* metaphors, supported by increasing evidence of successful businesses utilizing these concepts.

When reviewing the above forces, the interrelationships among them are clearly evident. For purpose of summary, three (combined) forces are driving significant impacts for strategic management:

a) The impact of knowledge and learning on customer value propositions.

b) The impact of global and metanational thinking on the purpose of the organization.

c) The impact of the shift in mindset from individual organizations, bureaucracies and competitive value chains, to networked organizations, meritocracies and collaborative bio-corporate value systems.

Table 1.2 (on the following page) illustrates the transition from industrial to knowledge age organizations, due to the shift in emphasis to knowledge and learning, global thinking, and networked organizations and systems.[3]

Implications for Strategic Management

What are the implications of these shifts for strategic management? What can we learn from these shifts, and, in particular, how do they interact with established strategic management approaches?

In the past twenty years, many strategic management thinkers have been drawn into the search for new approaches to make sense of the increasingly turbulent environment, and to develop tools to identify new sources of value and sustainable exploitation of that value. The major themes of the previous decade – shareholder value maximization, resource-based theory, and dynamic organizational capabilities – continue to influence strategic management theory and research. Whereas the 1980s were dominated by aggressive competitive strategic thinking that was reflected in market share gains, economies of experience, and business portfolio optimization, the 1990s were characterized by a focus on efficiencies as a principal source of increased profitability: restructuring, refocusing, cost cutting, unbundling, downsizing, outsourcing and reengineering.

The critical strategic management challenge in the first decade of the 21st century now becomes how organizations can continually adapt, shape, change, innovate, create and network to survive and prosper in global market environments that are quickly becoming more unpredictable, with organizations that have become more virtual, mobile and porous, with technologies that are becoming revolutionary and integrative, and with people that are more independent, knowledgeable, assertive and mobile. A new overall organizational purpose, or strategic thrust, seems to emerge: unlocking the mystery of organizational self-renewal, resulting from knowledge-based creativity and innovation.

This task is daunting, as the major shifts in environmental forces seem to challenge deeply held strategic management ideas, beliefs, orientations, approaches and tools. Table 1.3 indicates these challenges to strategic management orthodoxy.

In the current turbulent world, traditional approaches and structured processes to strategic management can no longer cope with the complexity of new demands. New problems are being confronted, requiring new solutions that involve fundamental transformation of strategic management thinking and practices.

Table 1.2 Industrial Age Business Transitioning to Knowledge Age Business

	Industrial Age Business	**Knowledge Age Business**
Focus	Bulk-material manufacturing	Design and use of technology & information
Goal	Commodity & differentiated products	Knowledge-based & innovative products
Domain	Regional, local	Global, transnational, metanational
Future	Predictability, deterministic	Uncertainty, probability, possibility
Change	Periodic, steady rate, digestible	Accelerating, overwhelming, fluctuating
Rules	Linear cause and effect	Nonlinear complex interaction
Game plan	Five-year strategic plans	Three-year probability scenarios
Leader	Manages strategic plan to end-state	Envisions and guides on direction
Power	Centralized decision-making and responsibility	Distributed decision-making and responsibility
Challenge	Demand versus capacity to deliver	Demand versus capacity for change
Resources	Material and financial capital	Knowledge and intellectual capital
Knowledge Base	Highly specialized knowledge base resulting in single-skilling	Interdisciplinary knowledge base resulting in multi-skilling
Risk	Moving too quickly – out of control	Moving too slowly – out of the running
Approach	Quality, low cost of production Branding, emergent price standards Diminishing returns	Be first – best if possible, high-cost R&D Market lock-on, high margins Increasing returns
Role of the Managerial Team	Optimization of quality and productivity Application of raw energy Repetitive day-to-day operations Processing of resources & information Separation and specialization of work and organization	Quality = productivity = adaptability and response Application of ideas Quest for innovation Processing of knowledge & capabilities Holistic approach and integration to work and organization
Process Perspective	Parts interact in sequence of steps End-to-end efficiency; standardization the answer Hierarchical, linear information flows	Whole emerges from interacting parts Micro-to micro-integrity key; feedback the answer Multiple, boundary-less knowledge networking

Source: Adapted from Kelly, S. & Allison, M.A. (1999), The Complexity Advantage, New York: Business Week Books, McGraw-Hill.

Table 1.3 Challenges to Strategic Management Orthodoxy

	From	**To**
Ideas & Values	• Classical/neo-classical strategy (Orthodox)	• Multiple changing paradoxes
	• Organization as systematic machine	• Organization as systemic organism
Strategic Orientation	• Strategic planning and "fit"	• Strategic emergence and "shaping" strategy
	• Rational strategy	• "Fuzzy" strategy
	• Resources & competencies	• Capabilities & innovation
Market Environment	• Local/national/regional	• Global, transnational, metanational, glocal
Organization & Control	• Bureaucratic	• Meritocratic
	• Direction, control	• Guiding, cohering, focusing
	• Value chain; single organization	• Value system; multiple organizations
Performance measures	• Shareholder value	• Stakeholder value
	• Financial performance	• Non-Financial performance (besides Financial)
Objectives	• Profit/growth/control	• Self-renewal/sustainable enterprise/innovation

When organizations fail to make this leap into new strategic management thinking, they quickly find themselves supplemented by new entrepreneurs who are not encumbered by the technology, structures and assumptions of traditional players. This has indeed been happening in computer software, telecommunications, airlines, beverages, financial services, life sciences and a host of other industries.

Implications for Strategy Dimensions: Context, Content and Process

Three dimensions of strategy, and thus strategic management, are usually identified: *context, content* and *process*. The implications of the major shifts due to the global knowledge economy on these strategic management dimensions are subsequently reviewed.

a) Strategy context: international, industry and organization

Strategy researchers, writers and practitioners largely agree that every strategy context is unique, and amenable to analysis in terms of boundaries, borders, structures, systems and policies. With increasing globalization, emergence of virtual corporations, and breakdown of traditional industry boundaries, the traditional ways of approaching strategy context are being challenged. Analytical approaches alone are unable to capture the multidimensionality and heterogeneity of the global environment, for example:

- *Globalization*
  The world market for capital and human capital have few barriers at the moment, and manufacturing capacity is also becoming increasingly mobile. More enterprises are entering global markets as multinationals, transnational and metanational organizations. Traditional classifications according to country, industry and organizational type are consequently becoming increasingly irrelevant. The major reason for this is that knowledge moves quickly and easily across traditional boundaries and industries.

- *Innovation*
  Traditionally, innovation has been seen as the domain of R&D, marketing (e.g. product development) and processes/technology. Today, entire new industries are being created due to rapid and widespread innovations in customer value propositions and value system configurations (disintermediation, reintermediation, convergence etc.) that "leapfrog" traditional industries, due to the knowledge economy.

- *Customization*
  This refers to the new focus on customers as the real "drivers" of organizations, even co-creators of value, rather than something external and ancillary to the organization. Knowledge-driven technologies enable this occurrence.

b) Strategy content: functional, business, corporate and network levels

The product of a strategy process is referred to as the strategy content – what is, and what should be, the strategy for the enterprise and each of its constituent units. Four levels of strategy content are usually discerned, i.e. functional, business, corporate and network levels.

- *Functional level*
  This involves strategies for different activities within an organization, linked to specialization skills such as marketing strategy, financial strategy, operations strategy etc. This traditional categorization often results in internal organizational barriers, "silos" of knowledge, and resistance to change. In a turbulent environment, such functional strategy content results in the inability to respond rapidly and innovatively in a coherent, integrated way.

- *Business Level*
  Strategy at business level requires the grouping of functional level strategies for a distinct set of products and/or services, intended for a specific group of customers. Often termed strategic business units (SBUs), these organizations focus narrowly on their own industry and market share, and consequently suffer from a lack of agility and adaptability, not to mention a lack of pro-active innovation of its core businesses.

- *Corporate Level*
  Many enterprises are in two or more distinctly differentiated types of businesses,

i.e. multibusinesses (several (SBUs) or multi-industry activities, requiring corporate level strategy. A well-known technique is to consider a corporation as a "portfolio" of discrete businesses, each in a separate industry, but logically synergizing in terms of technologies, processes or markets. The challenge of turbulent, knowledge-enhanced environments is that traditional synergy measurement tools (such as core competencies) and traditional opportunity evaluation tools (such as market opportunity analysis) are unable to cope with the dynamic nature of knowledge-networked environments. Corporate portfolio tools have often been devised for relatively static industry and market conditions.

- *Network Level*
  Most multi-company organizations consist of a few parties, such as strategic alliances, joint ventures and consortia. When a strategy is developed for a group of such firms, which may number from a few to hundreds, it is called a network level strategy. The difficulty with this approach is that today network strategies are not only on multi-company levels, but also on process, business and corporate levels of organizations. Vertical and horizontal knowledge networking is proliferating on a formal and informal basis (e.g. "communities of practice"), and traditional strategy content approaches are unable to handle this.

c) Strategy process: analysis, formulation, implementation and change

Traditionally, most strategic management textbooks have portrayed the strategy process as a basically linear progression through several distinct steps. A differentiation is usually made between *strategy analysis, strategy formulation, strategy implementation* and *strategy change.*

In the analysis stage, a SWOT-analysis (strengths-weaknesses-opportunities-threats analysis) of the organization is usually made. Next, in the formulation stage, strategists determine which strategic options are available to them, evaluate each of the so-called "generic" or "grand" strategy options, and choose one or more of them. Subsequently, in the implementation stage, the selected strategic option(s) is translated into a number of concrete activities/programs that are then started. Finally, in the strategy change stage, the documented strategy (or strategic plan) is periodically reviewed, results are compared, and changed if required.

This view of the strategy process is now being seriously challenged due to the realities of the global knowledge economy and its major forces. Three significant deficiencies can be highlighted:

- *The emphasis on rationality*
  The true nature of strategic thinking is now emerging as more holistic, intuitive and creative than analytical and rational. Strategizing is about envisioning opportunities and threats, perceiving strengths and weaknesses, and creating or shaping the future, for which sense making, imagination and judgment are more important than analysis and logic. This constitutes a fundamental shift in the view of cognitive processes of the strategist.

- *The presumption of linearity of processes*
  The division of the strategy process into a number of sequential steps is fallacious,

because, in reality, the strategy process is fuzzier, with analysis, formulation and implementation activities on-going and intertwined. Strategies are usually formed incrementally through various forms of interaction, including inter-related processes, as managers continually think and act, letting strategies emerge as they progress.

- *The assumption of comprehensiveness of the strategy process*
  The assumption of the traditional strategy process is that strategy is made for the entire organization and everything can be radically changed all at once. Yet it is almost impossible to get the various aspects of an organization lined up to go through change at the same time. The rate and direction of any change are seriously limited by the cultural, political and cognitive history of the firm, and strategic change has often not been revolutionary. In the knowledge economy, organizations are able to experiment with a radical new business model alongside a gradually changing existing business model. Experimenting is now often necessitated by radical changes in the environment.

Conclusion

Due to the global knowledge-networked economy, dramatic shifts have been experienced in the business environment since the last decade of the 20th century in particular. Under these circumstances, the challenge to strategic management is to identify, access and utilize new sources of profitable opportunities, and, if necessary, to help reinvent their enterprises.

Six major forces causing shifts in strategic management thinking and implementation due to the global knowledge economy were reviewed, and the implications for strategic management practice were highlighted. The challenges to orthodox strategic management were illustrated, especially orthodox strategy ideas and values, orientation, market views, organization and control, performance measures, and strategic objectives. Finally, the deficiencies in the traditional application of strategy dimensions of context, content and process in coping with a knowledge-networked economy were indicated. The next chapter (Chapter 2) reviews the traditional approaches to, and difficulties in existing strategic management approaches and tools in the knowledge economy in more detail.

Innovating Our Way to the Next Industrial Revolution*

By Peter M. Senge and Goran Carstedt

What's so new about the New Economy? Our real future lies in building sustainable enterprises and an economic reality that connects industry, society and the environment.

Much of what is being said about the New Economy is not all that new. Waves of discontinuous technological change have occurred before in the industrial age, sparked by innovations such as the steam engine in the 18th century; railroads, steel, electrification and telecommunications in the 19th century; and auto and air transport, synthetic fibers and television in the first half of the 20th century. Each of those technologies led to what economist Joseph Schumpeter called "creative destruction", in which old industries died and new ones were born. Far from signaling the end of the industrial era, these waves of disruptive technologies accelerated and extended it.

What would constitute the beginnings of a truly postindustrial age? Only fundamental shifts in how the economic system affects the larger systems within which it resides – namely, society and nature. In many ways, the industrial age has been an era of harvesting natural and social capital in order to create financial and productive capital. So far there is little evidence that the New Economy is changing that.

The industrial-age assault on natural capital continues. Vague hopes about "bits for atoms" and "demassification" are naive at best, echoes of talk about "paperless offices" 20 years ago. The rate of losing species has not slowed.

Most New Economy products end up where Old Economy products do: in increasingly scarce landfills. Globalization is destroying the last remnants of stewardship for natural resources in industries such as forest products: Today, buy-and-sell decisions are executed by faceless agents living on the other side of the world from the people and ecosystems whose futures they decide. Moreover, New Economy growth stimulates related growth in Old Economy industries – along with the familiar pattern of suburban sprawl, pollution, loss of habitat and competition for natural resources.

The New Economy's effects on social capital are more complex but no less disturbing.[1] Industrial progress has tended to destroy cultural as well as biological diversity,

---

* Taken with permission from MIT Sloan Management Review, Winter 2001, pp. 24-38

despite the protests of marginalized groups like the Provençal farmers who oppose the globalization of food production. Likewise, although changes in traditional family and community structures have brought greater freedom for women and many ethnic groups, the past decade also has brought worldwide increases in divorce rates, single-parent families and "street" children. Global markets, capital flows and e-commerce open up new opportunities for emerging economics, but they also create new generations of technological haves and have-nots. According to the World Bank, the poorest quartile of humankind has seen its share of global income fall from 2.5% to 1.25% over the past 25 years. More immediately, eroding social capital manifests in the isolation, violence and frenzy of modern living. Individuals and small circles of friends carve out increasingly private lives amidst increasingly distrustful strangers, preferring to "bowl alone". We

The challenge today is to develop sustainable businesses that are compatible with the current economic reality. Innovative business models and products must work financially, or it won't matter how good they are ecologically and socially.

almost take for granted road rage, deaths of spectators at sporting matches and kids, shooting kids at school.[2] The "24-7" job has become the norm in many industries, the latest step in subjugating our lives to the clock, a process begun with the mechanization of work at the outset of the industrial era.

Judged by its impact on natural and social capital, so far the New Economy looks more like the next wave of the industrial era than a truly postindustrial era. Why should we care? Because the basic development patterns of the industrial era are not sustainable. At U.S. National Academy of Sciences home secretary Peter Raven says, quoting the Wildlife Conservation Society's George Schaller, "We cannot afford another century like the last one." Plus, there are other possibilities.

Corporate Heretics

"Is genuine progress still possible? Is development sustainable? Or is one strand of progress – industrialization – now doing such damage to the environment that the next generation won't have a world worth living in?"[3]

Those are not the words of the Sierra Club or Greenpeace, but of BP chairman John Browne. In 1997, Browne broke rank with the oil industry to declare, "There is now an effective consensus among the world's leading scientists and serious and well-informed people outside the scientific community that there is a discernible human influence on the climate." Moreover, he argued that "the time to consider the policy dimensions of climate change is not when the link between greenhouse gases and climate change is conclusively proven, but when the possibility cannot be discounted."[4]

Equally important, BP looks at the situation as a business opportunity. "There are good commercial reasons for being ahead of the pack when it comes to issues to do with the environment," says Bromme. Since 1997, the company has become active in public forums on global climate, has begun to reduce emissions in exploration and production, has started to market cleaner fuels and has invested significantly in alternative sources of energy (such as photovoltaic power and hydrogen). All the while, Browne has led an effort to build a more performance-oriented culture, and company profits have been at an all-time high.

The Dimensions of Sustainability

Rationalism, the belief in reason, has dominated society throughout modern times. It remains the dominant perspective in business and education. Yet it has limits. It cannot explain the passion that motivates entrepreneurs committed to a new product idea nor the imagination of scientists testing an intuition. Nor does it explain why a quiet walk on a beach or a hike into the mountains may inspire both. These can only be understood by seeing how naturalism, humanism and rationalism infuse one another. Naturalism arises from our innate sense of being part of nature. Humanism arises from, the rich interior life that connects reason, emotion and awareness – and ultimately allows us to connect with one another. Epochs in human history that have nurtured all three have stood out as golden ages.

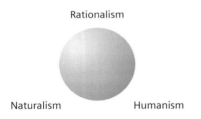

Rationalism

Naturalism   Humanism

Three Worldviews Required
for Building Sustainable Enterprises

BP is but one example of the shift in thinking that is becoming evident in many companies and industries. Appliance maker Electrolux uses water- and powder-based paints (rather than hazardous solvent-based paints), prioritizes the use of recycled materials, and has introduced the world's first family of refrigerators and freezers free of the chlorofluorocarbons that contribute to ozone depletion. In 1999, Toyota and Honda began selling hybrid cars that combine internal combustion and electric propulsion, perform comparably to competitors – and can achieve up to 70 miles per gallon today, with prospects for two to three times that mileage in a few years.[5] In 1998, Xerox introduced its first fully digitized copier, the Document Centre 265, which is more than 90% remanufacturable and 97% recyclable. The product has only about 200 parts, an order of magnitude less than its predecessor. Its sales have exceeded forecasts. According to Fortune, remanufacturing and waste reduction saved Xerox $250 million in 1998. Some firms, such as Interface Inc., a $1.3 billion manufacturer of commercial carpet tiles, which saved about $140 million in sustainable waste reductions from 1995 to 1999, are even rethinking their basic business model. Interface's goal is to stop selling product altogether. Instead, it will provide floor-covering services, leasing products and later taking them back for 100% recycling. Assessing the environmental impact of the carpeting industry, chairman Ray Anderson says bluntly, "In the future, people like me will go to jail."[6]

These examples are all just initial steps, as each of these companies – panics would readily admit. Ultimately, sustainability is a challenge to society as a whole. Nonetheless, business can play a legitimate leadership role as a catalyst for larger changes. We believe that a new environmentalism is emerging, driven by innovation, not regulation – radical new technologies, products, processes *and* business models. More and more businesses are recognizing the opportunities this creates. "Sustainability not only helps improve the world, but also energizes the company," says ABB's GEO Goran Lindahl.

The good news is that change through market-driven innovation is the type of change our society understands best. The problem is that much in today's business climate appears to run in the opposite direction. Short-term financial pressures, the free-agent work force, dramatic opportunities to start new companies and get rich quickly, often cynical mass media, and industrializing countries aspiring to catch up to the industrialized world's consumption standards – these hardly seem like the conditions for increasing stewardship of the earth.

The challenge today is to develop sustainable businesses that are compatible with the current economic reality. Innovative business models and products must work financially, or it won't matter how good they are ecologically and socially. To explore how to achieve this, the SoL Sustainability Consortium was formed to bring together like-minded corporate executives experienced in organizational learning who also see sustainability becoming a cornerstone of their business strategy.[7] Together, we are asking. Can organizations committed to sustainability work with the forces propelling most of the New Economy in the opposite direction? And, can organizational-learning principles and tools help in realizing the changes that this will require?

Between Two Stories

The first reality confronting businesses that are serious about sustainability is ambiguity, starting with the question: What do we mean by *sustainability*? The ambiguity inherent in sustainability has deep cultural roots.

"We are in trouble just now because we do not have a good story," says cultural historian Thomas Berry. "We are in between stories. The old story, the account of how the world came to be and how we fit into it … sustained us for a long period of time. It shaped our emotional attitudes, provided us with life purposes and energized our actions. It consecrated our suffering and integrated our knowledge. We awoke in the morning and knew where we were. We could answer the questions of our children.[8] In a sense, sustainability requires letting go of the story of the supremacy of the human in nature, the story that the natural world exists as mere "resources" to serve human "progress". But most of us grew up with this story, and it is still shared by the vast

Living Systems Follow Cycles

Industrial-Age Systems Do Not

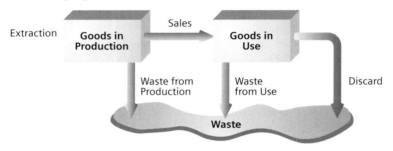

majority of modern society. It is not easy to let it go, especially when we are uncertain about what the new story will be. Businesses seeking sustainability can easily feel like a trapeze artist suspended in the air. They have let go of a secure worldview without knowing what they can hang on to.

Yet the dim outlines of a new story are emerging. At its root are two elements: a new picture of the universe and a new sense of human possibility. "We are just beginning to explore what it means to be part of a universe that is alive … not just cosmos but cosmogenesis," in the words of Barry and physicist Brian Swimme. Moreover, the new universe story "carries with it a psychic-spiritual dimension as well as a physical-materialistic dimension. Otherwise, human consciousness emerges out of nowhere … an addendum [with] no real place in the story of the universe."[9] Echoing Barry, Roger Saillant, former Ford executive and now Visteon vice president, says, "The new story will have to do with personal accountability… new communities in business and elsewhere based on knowing that there is no parent to take care of us and that we have a stewardship responsibility for future generations." Saillant adds that gradually "a larger intelligence will emerge. Those special moments when we glimpse that our actions are informed by a larger whole will become more frequent." Interface marketing vice president Joyce LaValle foresees a similar shift: I think this will actually get easier as we proceed. But first we must go through a kind of eye of the needle."

According to John Ehrenfeld, president of the International Society for Industrial Ecology, the challenge arises because sustainability "is a radical concept that stretches our current ideas about rationality. It has often been framed as environmentalists against business. But this generates polarization and misses the three very different worldviews needed to move forward: rationalism, naturalism and humanism." Only by embracing all three can we begin to understand what sustainability actually means. (See "The Dimensions of Sustainability.")

Naturalism: Biomimicry and the Logic of Natural Systems

The diverse innovations that created the first Industrial Revolution sprang from the same guiding image that inspired the preceding scientific revolution – the image of the machine. "My aim", wrote 17th-century scientist Johannes Kepler, "is to show that the celestial machine is to be likened not to a divine organism but rather to a clock-work."[10] The assembly line became the prototypical organization – with managers as controllers and workers operating in rigid routines, all coordinated by bells, whistles and production schedules. The assembly line was so successful it became the model for other types of organizations, including the 19th-century urban school system. Although the machine-age organization achieved previously unimaginable productivity, it also created a mechanized organizational environment that dehumanized and fragmented how people worked together.

If the machine inspired the industrial age, the image of the living system may inspire a genuine postindustrial age. This is what life sciences writer Janine Benyus calls "biomimicry", innovation inspired by understanding how living systems work "What is consistent with life is sustainable," says Benyus. For example, in nature there is no waste. All byproducts of one natural system are nutrients for another. Why should industrial systems be different? We would not ask engineers to build bridges that defy the laws of gravity nor chip designers to violate laws of physics. Why should we expect businesses to violate the law of zero waste?

All living systems follow cycles: produce, recycle, regenerate.

By contrast, industrial-age systems follow a linear flow of extract, produce, sell, use, discard – what "Ecology of Commerce" author Paul Hawken calls "take-make-waste".

Focusing on ecoefficiency may distract companies from pursuing radically different products and business models – changes that require shifts in mental models. This is unlikely to occur without mastering the human dimensions of learning and change.

Indeed, the primary output of today's production processes is waste. Across all industries, less than 10% of everything extracted from the earth (by weight) becomes usable products. The remaining 90% to 95% becomes waste from production.[11] Moreover, what is sold creates still more waste – from discard and from use (for example, from auto exhaust). So, while businesses obsess over labor and financial capital efficiency, we have created possibly the most inefficient system of production in human history.

What would industrial systems that conform to natural principles look like? First, they would be circular rather than linear, with significant reductions in all waste flows. (See "How Industry Can Reduce Waste.") This implies three specific waste-reduction strategies: resource productivity, clean products, and remanufacturing, recycling and composting.[12]

Strategy 1. Resource productivity reduces waste from production through ecoefficient production technologies and the design of production processes in which wastes from one process become nutrients for another.

Strategy 2. Clean products (say, hybrid cars) reduce waste from goods in use through nonpolluting product technologies.

Strategy 3. Remanufacturing and recycling (creating "technical nutrients") and designing more products that are biodegradable (creating "natural nutrients") reduce waste from discard.

Architect William McDonough and chemist Michael Braungart summarize the three strategies with the simple dictum: "Waste equals food".

Second, companies would invest in nature's regenerative processes. They would do fewer things that compromise regeneration, such as paying over wetlands, and would invest some surpluses in restoring natural capital – for example, companies like Interface plant trees to match business miles traveled because increasing forest cover reduces greenhouse gases.

Third, following Buckminster Fuller's dictum, companies would "learn how to live on our energy income [solar, wind, hydrogen] rather than off our principal [oil and gas]." Living on our income would not only reduce resource extraction, but also eliminate the side effects of using minerals, like auto emissions.

Thinking in more systemic terms may appear simple, but it raises important questions about current corporate environmentalism. For example, ecoefficiency has become a goal for companies worldwide, with many realizing significant cost savings from eliminating waste from production. That is good in some ways, but troubling in others. Thinking about the larger system shows that ecoefficiency innovations alone could actually worsen environmental stresses in the future.

Ecoefficiency innovations reduce waste from production, but this does not alter the number of products produced nor the waste generated from their use and discard. Indeed, most companies investing in cost-reducing ecoefficiency improvements are doing so with the aim of increased profits and growth. Moreover, there is no guarantee that increased economic growth from ecoefficiency will come in similarly ecoefficient ways. In today's global capital markets, greater profits show up as investment capital that could easily be reinvested in old-style eco-inefficient industries.

To put it another way, nature does not care about the industrial system's efficiency. Nature cares about its impact in *absolute terms.* If a vastly more ecoefficient industrial system grows much larger, it conceivably could generate more total waste and destroy more habitat and species than a smaller, less ecoefficient economy.

The answer is not necessarily zero growth. The implications of naturalism are more subtle: We can sustain growth only by reducing total material throughput and total accumulated waste. Ecoefficiency gains are laudable but dangerously incomplete, as is any strategy that fails to consider the industrial-natural system as a whole. A systemic approach would reduce all sources of waste: from production, use and discard.

Managers' faith in ecoefficiency also illustrates the power of mental models. Industrial-age managerial practice has always been about increasing efficiency. Increased natural-resource productivity that translates directly into lower costs offers a compelling business case, one that does not challenge established thinking deeply. However,

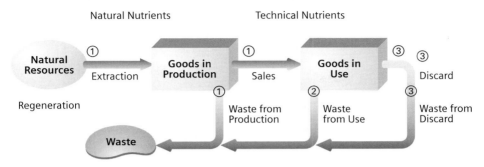

Natural Nutrients   Technical Nutrients

① Resource Productivity

② Clean Products

③ Remanufacture, Recycle, Compost

How Industry Can Reduce Waste: A Cyclic Industrial System That Mimics Nature

focusing on ecoefficiency may distract companies from pursuing radically different products and business models – changes that require shifts in mental models, not just shifting attention within existing mental models.

This is unlikely to happen without mastering the human dimensions of learning and change.

Humanism: The Logic of Learning

"The prevailing system of management has destroyed our people," said total-quality pioneer W. Edwards Deming. "People are born with intrinsic motivation, self-esteem, dignity, curiosity to learn, joy in learning." Echoing Deming, anthropologist Edward Hall declares, "Humans are learning organisms *par excellence. The drive to learn is as strong as the sexual drive – it begins earlier and lasts longer.*" The premise of work on learning organizations has been that thriving in today's knowledge-based market-places means reversing the destructiveness that Deming speaks about and cultivating people's drive to learn.

In fall 1999 the sustainability consortium was hosted by the Xerox "Lakes" team that had developed the Document Centre 265 copier. Already aware of the team's innova-tions in design for remanufacture (more than 500 patents came from the Lakes project) and the product's success in the marketplace, we learned about how the team's Zero waste vision translated into a manufacturing facility with virtually no waste and eventually became embraced by many of the team's suppliers. But it still wasn't clear *how* the team had achieved those accomplishments.

Late in the day, Rhonda Staudt, a young engineer who was one of the lead designers, was talking about the team's innovations when she was interrupted by David Berdish, veteran of many organizational-learning projects at Ford. "Rhonda," Berdish said, "I

31

understand what a great opportunity this was for you and how exciting it was. I work with engineers, and I know the excitement of pushing the technological envelope. But what I really want to know is why you did this. What I mean is: 'What was the stand you took and who were you taking that stand for?'"

Rhonda looked at David for a long time in silence and then, in front of many peers and a few superiors, began to cry. "I am a mom," she answered. We had all heard the Lakes motto, "Zero to landfill, for the sake of our children." But now we were in its presence. Roger Saillant of Visteon turned to Peter and whispered, "Seamlessness". Peter knew exactly what he meant: when what we do becomes inseparable from who we are.

We have all spent much of our lives in institutions that force us to be someone we are not. We commit ourselves to the company's agenda. We act professionally. After a while, we have lived so long in the house of mirrors that we mistake the image we are projecting for who we really are. The poet David Whyte quotes an AF&T manager who wrote, "Ten years ago, I turned my face for a moment ... and it became my life."

Over the past decade, many companies have attempted to build learning organizations with little grasp of the depth of the changes required. They want to increase imagination and creativity without unleashing the passion that comes from personal vision. They seek to challenge established mental models without building real trust and openness. They espouse systems thinking, without realizing how threatening that can be to established "quick fix" management cultures. There is a difference between building more-sustainable enterprises because there is profit in it and because it is one's life's work. The journey ahead will require both.

If understanding natural systems establishes the guiding ideas for sustainability innovations, then learning provides the means to translate ideas into accomplishments. But, just as the logic of natural systems conflicts with take-make-waste industrial systems, so too does the logic of a learning culture conflict with traditional, control-oriented organizational cultures. To a controlling culture, a learning culture based on passion, curiosity and trust appears to be out of control. But, in fact, it is based on a different type of control. "We are not trying to eliminate control and discipline in our organizations," says retired CEO William O'Brien, formerly with Hanover Insurance Co. "We are trying to substitute top-down discipline based on fear with self-discipline. This does not make life easier for people in organizations. It makes it more demanding – but also more exciting."

These two tensions – between natural systems and industrial systems on the one hand and between learning and controlling on the other – may appear to make sustainable enterprises impossible. However, deeper currents in the New Economy could also cause those tensions to become immutable forces transforming traditional industrial-age management.

A New Business Logic

Kevin Kelly, editor at large of Wired, observes that the "emerging new economic order ... has three distinguishing characteristics. It is global. It favors intangibles – ideas, information and relationships. And it is intensely interlinked." Kelly sees electronic networks generating new patterns of "organic behavior in a technological matrix". But he suggests that the real changes are not ultimately about technology but communication. According to Kelly, in the world that is emerging, "Communication is the economy".[13]

Today, perhaps the earth as a living system is communicating to us through increasingly turbulent weather patterns. Perhaps our frayed social structures are communicating to us through increasing acts of child violence. Are we listening? If the New Economy is revolutionizing communication, can it enable deeper listening. If so, we may discern a new business logic emerging, one that starts with rethinking how firms create value and continues by redefining "customers", "employees", "suppliers" – and ultimately the company itself.

From Things to the Value provided by Things

"Production is increasingly not where value is created," says Ting Ho, vice president of strategy for global-logistics Internet startup Zoho. "The traditional company produced something that it then had to sell. Today, we must understand a customer and serve a genuine need."

At the heart of the industrial-age growth machine was a kind of mass hypnosis – convincing consumers that happiness meant owning a new thing. A new washing machine. A new computer. A new car. However, people do not want a hunk of steel in the driveway. They want the benefits it provides – whether they are tangible benefits like transport or intangible benefits like freedom or fun.

What does it mean to create new business models on the basis of that understanding? For Interface, it means shifting from selling carpets to providing floor-covering services, automatically taking back worn carpet tiles or replacing entire sections if a customer wants a different color. For Dow Chemical, it means leasing "dissolving services" then reusing the solvents. For Carrier, the world's leading manufacturer of air-conditioning equipment, it means renting cooling services rather than selling air conditioners. For IKEA, according to its published mission

Providing services rather than just selling products creates a potential new alignment between what is sound economically and what is sound environmentally.

statement, it means providing services to help people "make a house or apartment into a home" rather than selling furniture. All these firms believe that "higher profits will come from providing better solutions rather than selling more equipment", in the words of "Natural Capitalism" authors Amory and Hunter Lovins and Paul Hawken.

From the standpoint of sustainability, providing services rather than just selling products creates a potential new alignment between what is sound economically and what

Organizational Learning's Ten-Year March

To attain sustainability, executives should ponder Senge's earlier writings and the experiences of those who have attempted to build learning organizations.

By Patrick L. Porter

Ten years ago Ford Motor Company executive Nick Zeniuk inherited the unenviable task of turning around the company's storied Lincoln Continental franchise. Zeniuk, the business and launch leader for the Continental line, was asked to redesign the product, while cutting costs, improving quality and speeding time to market. Plagued by political infighting and disagreements among 1,000 engineers and managers, the billion-dollar project was four months behind schedule and falling on every measure.

Zeniuk's transformation efforts might nave ended then had he not learned about Peter Senge's work on organizational learning. Zeniuk read Senge's then new book, "The Fifth Discipline", as well as a paper Senge had published at about the same time in MIT Sloan Management Review, "The leader's New Work: Building Learning Organizations" (fall 1990, pp. 7-23; reprint 3211). "I had an epiphany," recalls Zeniuk. "Everything I needed was there."

A year-long effort ensued in which Zeniuk, program manager Fred Simon and the leadership team practiced the now familiar techniques that foster organizational learning – systems thinking, personal mastery, surfacing and testing mental models. and building shared vision. Slowly, the ideas gained credence among rank-and-file engineers who began to use the learning tools in their work groups. "At first they thought it was a boondoggle." says Zeniuk. "But then they noticed that we were beginning to behave differently. We had started asking them questions. We would stop and actually listen to them. We began to encourage them to do things in a different way."

It took nearly three years, but Zeniuk and his colleagues completely transformed the troubled project. "We saved a couple of hundred million dollars in expenditures, including 560 million of a $92 million launch budget for the 1995 Lincoln," says Zeniuk, who today travels the world teaching others about organizational learning. "We launched the car two weeks ahead of schedule. And we were the first Ford program to produce a prototype that was almost product-ready. Many of the learning practices carried over to the highly successful 1998 Continental."

Stories like Zeniuk's abound. Since Senge's 1990 writings on organizational learning, scores of companies, nonprofits, government agencies – even entire school districts – have used his learning tools to move away from industrial-age, command-and-control work environments to ones founded on individual commitment.

Senge is the first to admit that his work on organizational learning has many antecedents, including Jay Forrester's groundbreaking work on systems dynamics, W. Edwards Deming's half-century evocation of quality management, and the work of Chris Argyris on the impact of mental models on shared work. But it was Senge who pulled these and other threads together and connected them to organizational learning in a way that captured the imagination of business and government leaders.

What have we learned during the past decade about the value of Organizational learning? Richard Teerlink, the recently retired chairman and CEO of Harley-Davidson, believes that it is the only way to build a lasting company that can adjust to changing times. "As Eric Hoffer, the longshoreman philosopher said, 'in times of change it is the learners who will inherit the earth, while the dullards are beautifully equipped for a world that no longer exists.'" says Teerlink. "If you believe as I do that people are the only sustainable competitive advantage, then leaders have to view their responsibility differently. They must create an environment in which groups of people voluntarily come together around a shared vision and work toward shared goals. And that's what Peter Senge's learning tools enable you to do." Dave Meador, treasurer of DTE Energy in Detroit, Michigan, is using Senge's learning tools to help the utility company profit from deregulation. "We're going through a lot of change as the industry transforms says Meador. These tools help us avoid getting stuck in an old mind-set. They help us stay open-minded to a changing marketplace, which enables us to build the internal capacity to learn and adapt."

Meador first learned of Senge's work a decade ago at Chrysler Corp., where he used organizational learning to engage line managers in activity-based costing. "We shifted from an environment of compliance to one of commitment, in which people acted because they really believed it would help them accomplish their business objectives," says Meador. "And I went from extreme frustration and fear of failure to really making a contribution and adding value to the enterprise."

Today, Meador cannot imagine working for a company that fails to embrace organizational learning. "At DTE, we're creating an environment in which people can raise questions and recommend alternative ideas, and do that in the spirit of learning and trying to grow the business. But we can engage many more people in solving complex issues, which avoids putting the burden of decision making on a handful of senior executives."

If you were to take the time, you could find hundreds of stories like Dave Meador's. Zeniuk says he knows dozens of teams that have transformed themselves with these methods. "But there aren't a lot of stories about a whole company transforming itself into a learning organization," he adds. "The immune system in big companies tends to resist this work. And the resistance is not necessarily conscious. It's simply the inertia that's naturally there. Ford continues to use these methods. Visteon does so too at very high levels. Shell is building a learning organization. And even the U.S. government is starting to use them. But I can't tell you that a whole company has transformed itself using these tools."

Perhaps someday a large company will institutionalize organizational learning to the point that it becomes part of the companywide cultural fabric. But many obstacles stand in the way, says Senge. Some groups master organizational learning only to backslide, ending up where they began when learning champions retire or move on. At other companies, short-term thinking makes managers and employees unwilling to tackle fundamental change.

Says Senge, "The number one impediment in this work is that it takes time, patience, perseverance and dedication. Most people in most organizations are not geared for that. Most management groups want things to happen quickly, because they're planning to be in the job for only a short time and they tend to think that they'd better reap the benefits on their watch. This has been and continues to be the main reason that Deming's work didn't get applied and that our organizational-learning work still struggles."

Patrick L. Porter is a contributing editor to MIT Sloan Management Review is sound environmentally. A company's business model no longer requires designed-in obsolescence to push customers into buying new products. Instead, producers have an incentive to design for longevity, efficient servicing, improved functioning, and product take-back. Such design allows for maintaining relationships with customers by continually ensuring that products are providing the services that people desire – at the lowest cost to the provider.

The shift from "the value is in the stuff" to "the value is in the service the stuff provides" also may lead to a radical shift in the concept of ownership. Swiss industry analyst Walter Stahel and chemist Braungart have proposed that, in the future, producers will own what they produce forever and therefore will have strong incentives to design products to be disassembled and remanufactured or recycled, whichever is more economical. Owning products forever would represent a powerfull step toward changing companies' attitudes about product discard.

Such ideas signal a radical shift in business models, one that will not come easily. It starts with how a company thinks of itself in relation to its customers: as a producer of things people buy or a provider of services through products made and remade? Marketing strategist Sandra Vandermerwe argues that such a view is essential to true customer focus, providing value *for* customers as well as obtaining value from customers.[14] It also shifts producers' time horizons. As Volvo discovered years ago, when a company is only selling cars, its relationship with the customer ends with the purchase. When it is providing customer satisfaction, it just begins.

From Producers and Consumers to Cocreators of Value

Focusing on the services provided by products also shifts the very meaning of "customer". Customers are no longer passive; they are cocreators of value. Thirty years ago, futurist Alvin Toffler coined the term "prosumer", people who actively participate in generating the value they derive from any product.[15] "Today, prosumers are everywhere," says Kelly, "from restaurants where you assemble your own dinner to medical self-care arenas, where you serve as doctor and patient." As Kelly says, the essence of prosumerism today is that "customers have a hand in the creation of the product."[16]

Prosumerism is infiltrating diverse marketplaces, especially those where internet technology is strong. One of Amazon.com's most popular Web-site features is customer reviews of books, CDs and other products. The five-year-old magazine Fast Company now rivals Business Week, Fortune and Forbes, partly because of its "Company of Friends", a Web-site feature that allows subscribers to get together to discuss common concerns, form support networks for projects, or tell the magazine their interests. "I can go to our Web site and determine which are the 10 most frequently forwarded articles," says editor Alan Webber. "Our readers are no longer just an audience but cocreators of product."

How does that shift to prosumers relate to sustainability? It starts with activist customers who think for themselves. And activist customers are organizing themselves. "Thanks largely to the Internet," say C. K. Prahalad and V. Ramaswamy, "consumers have increasingly been engaging themselves in an active and explicit dialogue with manufacturers of products and services."[17] They add, "The market has become a forum." Or, as the popular "Cluetrain Manifesto" puts it, the market is becoming "a community of discourse."[18] With the inmates running the asylum, will they start to change the rules? What if people start talking to one another? What if they talk about the state of the world and how different types of products affect the quality of people's lives?

Leading Web-based companies, because they relate to their customers differently, also gain a different sense of what truly concerns customers. "Without a doubt, sustainability of our current lifestyle – personally and environmentally – matters to a lot of our readers," says Webber. "These were among the concerns that motivated us to start the magazine, and we've seen nothing to persuade us otherwise".

At this stage, it is speculation whether self-organizing networks of customers will unearth the deeper values essential to building sustainable societies. But it is no speculation that shifts in consumer behavior will be essential in creating such societies. One of the most significant concentrations of power in the industrial era has been the growth of a massive advertising industry applying psychological savvy to manipulate consumer preferences. "Soap operas" acquired their name because they were devised by Procter & Gambler and other consumer-goods companies to market soap. Could this be another form of centralized control that becomes history, the victim of the freer flow of information and interaction that allows people to know more and learn faster?

Homo sapiens has been around longer than *Homo consumer.* People still care deeply about the world their children will live in. Building sustainable enterprises will require tapping and harnessing that caring.

Many market-oriented companies sense just such a shift emerging in consumer preferences. For example, Nike has a host of recycled and recyclable products coming to market. For a company that sells the image of fitness, it is not surprising that Darcy Winslow, general manager of sustainable products and services, says: "Corporations in the 21st century cannot be fit if we don't prioritize and neutralize our impact on the environment."

From Compliant Employment to Committed Members of Social Networks

There are few companies today that do not struggle with the implications of the free-agent work force. The traditional employment contract based on good pay and benefits in exchange for loyalty is vanishing in many industries. Entrepreneurial opportunities are enticing, especially to young people. Most companies respond by trying to rework the old contract. They increase salary and benefits. They offer stock. They invent creative new perks. But in so doing, they miss entirely die change that might make the greatest difference: a mission worthy of people's commitment.

In 1991, IKEA faced the daunting challenge of extending its European business success to North America, the "graveyard of European retailers". It was clear from the outset that IKEA managers could not say "Here's how we do it in Sweden", and expect much enthusiasm. Achieving strong returns for a distant corporate office was not enough. Being part of a proud and widely imitated European firm had limited meaning. It became clear that IKEA's North American management team had to find ways to truly engage people.

It turned out that North Americans, like Europeans, were concerned about the environment. Eventually, some 20,000 IKEA employees in North America and Europe participated voluntarily in a two-day training session on "The Natural Step", an intuitive introduction to the system conditions that must be met by a sustainable society. Not only did that engage people in selling the company's environmentally oriented products and creating related product and service ideas, it engaged them in working for IKEA. From 1990 through 1994, North American sales increased 300%.

Most companies respond by trying to rework the old contract. They increase salary and benefits. They offer stock. They invent creative new perks. But in so doing they miss entirely the change that might make the greatest difference: a mission worthy of people's commitment.

The free-agent image connotes to many employers lack of commitment, people seeking a purely transactional relationship with a company. Perhaps the opposite is true. It may be a unique opportunity for organizations that truly value commitment. If we actually thought of people as free, we would have to approach them with respect, knowing that they can choose where to work. "It is amazing the commitment that people feel toward our focus on sustainability and the environment," says Vivienne Cox, BP vice president for marketing. "In a very tough business environment, it really matters to people who have many options in their lives".

Most industrial-age companies wanted what *they* regarded as committed employees. Today, the definition of commitment is changing, and paternalism is giving way to more-adult relationships. "People stay with a firm, in many instances, because they see an alignment between their personal values and those they perceive the firm to be committed to," says Ged Davis, who is Shell's vice president for global business environment. If enterprises are not committed to anything beyond making money, why should managers be surprised that workers make transactional commitments?

Kelly also notes that in the competitive labor markets found in fast-growing industries, people change companies but maintain their loyalty "to advancing technology or to the region".[19] And to trusted colleagues. One key person may take groups of people from employer to employer like the Pied Piper.[20] Project teams form, un-form and then re-form like the teams of writers, actors and technical specialists that make movies. Yet larger social networks remain intact. Increasingly, such networks are the keepers of values and commitments and the subtle know-how that makes winners and losers. Longer-term relationships embedded in fluid but enduring social networks are a new phenomenon that most companies have not yet understood.

"Companies have felt that workers needed them more than they needed workers," says Peter Drucker. "This is changing in ways that most companies still do not seem to grasp."[21]

From Separate Businesses to Ecological Communities

"The great benefits reaped by the New Economy in the coming decades," says Kelly, "will be due in large part to exploring and exploiting the power of decentralized and autonomous networks," which in many ways now resemble "an ecology of organisms, interlinked and coevolving, constantly in flux, deeply entangled, ever expanding at its edges."

"In traditional businesses, everything was piecework," says Zoho's Ho. "Now we are all part of larger system and our success depends on understanding those systems." For example, the traditional relationship between producer and supplier was neat and tidy. Producers wanted reliable supply at the lowest possible cost. Today, cost maybe only one of several criteria that shape successful producer-supplier relationships. "Both as a supplier and with our suppliers, we are continually codesigning and co-innovating," says Ho. "There is no other way to keep pace with rapid changes and expanding knowledge."

Paradoxically, the realization that all enterprises are part of complex, evolving systems imparts new meaning to relationships and trust. As Webber has said, "The New Economy starts with technology and ends with trust."[22] People who are co-innovating must know each other and trust each other – in ways unnecessary in traditional relationships between providers and customers. That leads to the question: Can partners in complex supply networks co-innovate more-sustainable practices?

For example, Nike has programs in place with six of its material suppliers to collect 100% of their scrap and recycle it into the next round of products. The goal is to scale this up to all material suppliers. Similarly, all the big steps in design for remanufacture require intense cooperation up and down supply chains. "If you don't have suppliers hooked in, the whole thing will fail," says former Lakes chief engineer John Elter. The Xerox team hosted "supplier symposiums" where "we taught suppliers what remanufacturing means and gave them the basic tools for remanufacture," says Elter. Even more important, they assured suppli-

Can organizations committed to sustainability work with the forces propelling most of the New Economy in the opposite direction?

ers that they would share in the cost savings – because used parts would go back to the suppliers for remanufacture. "The key is that suppliers participate in the economic benefit of remanufacturing because they don't have to make everything new. "This is a big deal. Plus, they are developing new expertise they can apply with other customers."

Building the necessary alignment for product take-back among networks of wholesalers, retailers and customers is equally daunting. "Without doubt, one of the biggest challenges with our 'Evergreen Service Contract' [Interface's model for selling floor-covering services rather than carpeting]," says chairman Ray Anderson, "is transforming mental models built up over generations" – such as those of purchasing departments in big companies whose incentives are based purely on cost of purchase, rather than on lifetime costs and aesthetic benefits.

Intense cooperative learning will never occur unless companies view their fates as linked. That is why the shift from seeing a world of suppliers and customers to one in which "we are all part of larger systems" is essential. Companies that do not recognize their interdependence with suppliers, distributors and customers will never build the trust needed to shift established mental models.

"Tennyson had it only half right when he said nature was 'red in tooth and claw,'" writes Janine Benyus. "In mature ecosystems, cooperation seems as important as competition. [Species cooperate] in order to diversify and … to fully use the habitat." Companies that see one another only as competitors may likewise find their habitat disappearing as the world around them changes.

From Closed Doors to Transparency

The world in which key corporate decisions could be made behind closed doors is disappearing. In 1995, Shell encountered a dramatic and unexpected reaction to its plans to sink in the North Sea its Brent Spar oil platform, which was approaching the end of its productive lifetime. Despite the fact that the company had gone through a three-year process to identify the best environmental option and had the concurrence of the U.K. government, the situation became a public-relations nightmare when other governments objected to the plan. Shell had failed to realize that its private decision had become a public one, a harsh lesson learned by many other companies, from Nike to Ford to Microsoft in recent years.

There is an old saying in the field of ecology: "There is no 'away.'" The old world of corporate inner sanctums isolated managers from many of their decisions' social and environmental consequences, distant in time and space from those who made the decisions. As transparency increases, these feedback loops are closing, and consequences must be faced. In this sense, transparency is a powerful ally to naturalism and may drive many of the changes needed to implement more-naturalistic, circular business processes and models.

The world in which key corporate decisions could be made behind closed doors is disappearing

Growing transparency already has led to the inclusion of voices traditionally outside the inner circle. Several years ago, Greenpeace objected to the chlorides IKEA used in the printing of catalogs. Few in the industry thought there was any cost-effective alternative. But working together, Greenpeace and IKEA found a Finnish printing company that could produce catalogs without chlorides. IKEA presented its chloride-free catalog at an environmental conference in Washington and set a new industry standard. This experience showed that Greenpeace and IKEA could work together productively by focusing on tangible problems and by believing that breakthroughs were possible. Such trust can only be built over time.

Growing transparency is also leading to new accounting and performance-management practices. Shell and others are moving toward "triple-bottom-line" accounting – assessing economic, environmental and social performance in a balanced way. The Global Reporting Initiative provides practical guidelines for such changes. "Adopting GRI guidelines and triple-bottom-line practices is an enormously difficult step," says

New Competencies

The challenges of building sustainable enterprises describe a strange new world few firms are equipped to understand, let alone navigate. The members of the SoL Sustainability Consortium came together, believing that their preceding work with organizational-learning principles and tools might make a difference in meeting these challenges.

Today, Consortium members are engaged in projects on sustainability frameworks (from which the ideas on naturalism and humanism came), new energy sources, implementing new business models, and nurturing new leadership networks embodying competencies that build upon the leadership skills for learning organizations (published in the MIT Sloan Management Review 10 years ago[1]):

- building shared vision.
- surfacing and testing mental models, and
- systems thinking.

Research on mental models and dialogue[2] needs to be scaled up to allow strategic conversations that involve hundreds and even thousands of people. As Juanita Brown, founder of Whole Systems Associates, says, "The questions we are facing will require members of organizations to learn together at an unprecedented rate, often on a global scale." Starting in 1999, Brown's colleagues Bo Gyllenpalm and David Isaacs helped several large Swedish organizations convene conversations on "Infocom (information and communications services) and the Environment." Convening and

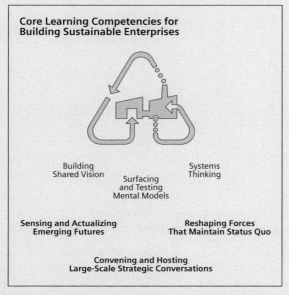

Core Learning Competencies for Building Sustainable Enterprises

Building Shared Vision

Surfacing and Testing Mental Models

Systems Thinking

Sensing and Actualizing Emerging Futures

Reshaping Forces That Maintain Status Quo

Convening and Hosting Large-Scale Strategic Conversations

hosting such large-scale conversations require particular methodologies. But Brown believes that the key lies in "questions that challenge current experiences and assumptions, while evoking new possibilities for collective discovery." For example, "How can infocom technology and services support the evolution of a sustainable and renewable environment?"

Most attempts at large-scale change fail because otherwise competent leaders do not understand the complex forces maintaining the status quo. Getting a CEO to support sustainability is not enough. Bottom-up environmental innovations also often fail. Leaders at all levels must understand the multiple "balancing processes" that on the one hand, make any complex organization viable, but on the other, consistently defeat large-scale change. Leadership strategies must address these balancing forces. For example: relevance (people asking, "What does sustainability have to do with my job?"), believers vs. nonbelievers (the Polarization that passionate advocates for social and environmental causes can create), the tyranny of established metrics (most current metrics reflect take-make-waste mental models, and new metrics aimed at life-cycle costs are useless without changes in mental models), and purpose (if the company's core purpose is perceived as making money, people's commitment may be below the threshold required to lead significant change).[3] All meaningful work on shared vision rests on distinguishing "creating" from "problem solving". Problem solving seeks to make things we don't like go away. Creating seeks to make things we care about come into being. This is a vital distinction for innovation. When problem solving dominates an organizational culture, life is about survival rather than about bringing into reality things that people care about. Recent research on leadership among entrepreneurs and scientists reveals a particular creative capacity – sensing and actualizing emerging futures. Successful leaders see the world as "open, dynamic, interconnected and full of possibilities."[4] They are both committed and "in a state of surrender" as cognitive scientist Francisco Varcia expresses it. Economist W. Brian Arthur adds that "cognizing" in business today follows three stages:

- "Observe, observe, observe: become one with the world."
- "Reflect and retreat: listen from the inner place where knowing comes to the surface."
- "Act in an instant: incubate and bring forth the new into reality."

[1] P.M. Senge, "The Leader's New Work: Building Learning Organizations", MIT Sloan Management Review 32 (fall 1990): p. 7-23.

[2] W. Isaacs, "Dialogue: The Art of Thinking Together" (New York: Doubleday/Currency, 1999).

[3] These are four of 10 basic challenges to sustaining deep change addressed in P. Senge et al., The Dance of Change: The Challenges to Sustaining Learning Organizations' (New York: Doubleday/Currency, 1999).

[4] J. Jaworski and O. Scharmer, "Leadership in the New Economy: Sensing and Actualizing Emerging Future", SoL working paper, www.SoLonline.org/Resources/working_papers.html

consultant John Elkington. "But companies like Shell, Ford and many others feel they must do this if they want to lead, rather than just react to change."

But the path toward broader accountability is fraught with perils. Last spring, Ford's first "Corporate Citizenship Report", based loosely on GRI guidelines, was greeted with as much cynicism as appreciation. The New York Times ignored most of the report (which included lengthy sections on reducing emissions and radical redesign of manufacturing processes) to announce that "Ford Is Conceding SUV Drawbacks."[23] The article focused on a three-page section of the 98-page report that discussed the dilemma of having a profitable product line that had environmental and safety problems. The Wall Street Journal was more personal, suggesting that chairman William Clay Ford was a hypocrite for both making and criticizing SUVs, a "guilt-ridden rich kid" who should either embrace his customers' preferences or leave the business to those who do.[24]

Ultimately, transparency is about awareness. With increasing awareness will come pressures for greater accountability for social and natural capital as well as financial capital. Gradually, this will lead to innovations in the larger social context as well.

It is impossible to predict the range of social innovations that growing transparency will ultimately foster. Perhaps new collaborative action-research networks will create the right climate of objectivity and compassion, tough standards and fair reporting combined with a spirit of learning together. Perhaps more-participative media, building on successful experiments such as those of Fast Company, will enable new levels of collaborative innovation. It may even be time to question the traditional limited-liability status of corporations, which uniquely favors owners of financial capital. Today's world of abundant financial capital and limited natural and social capital differs profoundly from the world of a century ago, when there was a need to protect individual investors. "In a world where learning and knowledge generation are the basis for corporate survival and wealth creation, managers must see a company as a living being, a human community," says writer and former Shell executive Arie de Geus. "Yet, today's managers inherit a very different worldview, focused on the optimism of financial capital. Is it not inconsistent to emphasize knowledge creation, on the one hand, and then treat a company as a machine for producing money, which is owned by its financial investors on the other?"

Perhaps when we are able to rediscover "company" (from the Latin *com-panis,* sharing of bread), as "living community", we will also rediscover its place within the larger community of living systems where it rightfully resides.

The Logic of Revolutions

The New Economy is both not new and new. It continues industrial-age patterns, yet it also may hold the seeds for a truly postindustrial world. As such, it brings us to a crossroads. We can either continue moving ever more rapidly in a direction that cannot be sustained, or we can change. Perhaps, no time in history has afforded greater possibilities for a collective change in direction.

"Creative engineers understand the role of constraints," says Elter of his Lakes experience. "Design engineers always deal with constraints: time, weight, operability. These are all real. The extraordinary creativity of [our] team had its source in recognizing a different constraint – the constraint of nature, to produce no waste. Zero to landfill is an uplifting constraint. It's worth going after. It's not manmade" Constraint and creativity are always connected. No artist paints on an infinite canvas. The artist understands that rather than just being limits, constraints can be freeing, especially when those constraints that have genuine meaning are recognized. What if product and business designers everywhere recognized that their constraints came from living systems? What if they adhered to the simple dictums: waste equals food; support natures regenerative processes; live off energy income, not principal, and, borrowing

43

from Elter's team, do it for the children. As occurred with the Lakes engineers, might this tint free everyone's creativity in previously unimaginable ways?

Such rethinking will not happen all at once. It will not arise from any central authority. It will come from everywhere and nowhere in particular. The first Industrial Revolution, according to author Daniel Quinn, was "the product of a million small beginnings. [It] didn't proceed according to any theoretical design [and] was not a utopian undertaking."[25] Likewise, the next Industrial Revolution, if it is to happen, will have no grand plan and no one in charge. It will advance, in Quinn's words, on the basis of "an outpouring of human creativity", innovations not just in the technological but in the human landscape as well – the only way a new story can arise.

Resource and Knowledge Transfer at the Château Lafite-Rothschild Wine Estate

The Estate and its Wines

The wines that the well-known wine guide "Johnson" describes as "wines for million-aires with intelligence and taste", are cultivated on a 100 ha wine-growing area in Pauillac at the Château Lafite-Rothschild. This is one of the best-known wine estates of the Bordeaux region, producing the highest valued wines in the world. The subscription price of a bottle of the 2000 vintage, for example, costs approximately $115, while a bottle of the 2001 vintage is already going for $170. These are, please note, subscription prices – the true prices can be much higher.

The Secret of the Success

The secret of the success of the estate lies in the specific knowledge of the harvesters, the cellar master and the oenologists. A qualified harvest team, who always produces a professional and quality-oriented vintage, ensures that only the best grapes reach the wine cellar. There they are crushed, are removed from the stem and are further ministered to by highly qualified oenologists and cellar masters. However, not only the specific knowledge of the employees of the Château Lafite-Rothschild is responsible for the production of one of the most renowned wines of the world, but also the use of state-of-the-art cellar techniques supports the special quality of the wines.

The Los Vascos Wine Estate

Lafite-Rothschild wished to establish itself on the South American soil as well and to this end acquired the 180 ha Vina los Vascos wine estate in Chile. Both the vine cultivation as well as the entire harvesting process, up to and including the wine pressing, follows the French pattern. In order to guarantee that their wines in Chile maintain the same high quality as those in France, exactly similar technical equipment to that in France was installed. Furthermore, since the harvest is at different times of the year in the two hemispheres, the entire staff of French harvesters is set to work in the Chilean vineyards during the South American harvest.

Resource Transfer as a Business Strategy

This interesting business strategy of personnel transfer, know-how transfer and the transfer of technical equipment installation offers Lafite-Rothschild enormous competitive benefits in Chile. They decreased the Chilean production costs considerably and succeeded in transferring the image and culture of a French wine estate to a South American one. According to the wine guide "Johnson", the Los Vascos wines have become known as one of the best red wines of South America. These wines have become firm favorites with all over the world wine lovers.

Product Differentiation as a Business Strategy

The wines of Lafite-Rothschild are in the high price category where market growth is hardly possible. Concomitantly, similar wine estates are mostly unobtainable. For this reason Lafite-Rothschild is with equal success expanding its presence in the medium price category of wines. This is only possible through the resource transfer strategy with its resultant decrease in costs as described above.

The Effect of the Resource Transfer Business Strategy

The resource transfer strategy therefore has two effects for Lafite-Rotschild: on the one hand the quality and image of first class wines could be transferred to other wine estates, which meant that market share could be gained in the high price category. On the other hand, this resource transfer led to cost benefits, which in turn gave also rise to a successful entrance in the market for more moderately priced wines.

ShareNet – the Next Generation Knowledge Management[*]

By Michael Gibbert, Stefan Jenzowsky, Claudia Jonczyk,
Michael Thiel & Sven Völpel

Background

Kuala Lumpur, Friday afternoon. Two intensive weeks of hard work awaited Martin Wong. As the Manager at Siemens ICN Malaysia, he was responsible for the telecommunications business with Malaysia Telecom, one of Siemens' most important Asian clients. Martin needed to complete a comprehensive proposal for a voice-over IP network solution for Malaysia Telecom within two weeks. This was the first proposal of its kind for Siemens Malaysia's business unit.

While working on this proposal, Martin had to come up with answers to questions like:

- Which technical solution would suit this situation the best?
- Should Siemens immediately offer an existing service package?
- How exactly could he demonstrate to this specific customer that, in a very competitive environment, the Siemens solution would best fit his needs?
- Where could he get hold of a business plan, at short notice, that would show the customer how soon the Siemens solution would be profitable?

In the past, finding these answers alone might have taken him many weeks, or even months.

Today, the answers are just a mouse-click away for an expert salesman like Martin Wong: His company's intranet offers him access to the Siemens ICN ShareNet – a global knowledge database that provides him answers to those tough questions. In ShareNet he will find similar customer solutions with their accompanying sales arguments, descriptions of successful projects, presentations, relevant business plan, as well as several contact persons who could help him with questions on technical issues, or financial concepts. The crucial proposal can be compiled quite quickly and Martin will be able to focus on his core competence – developing strategic solutions with the customer.

---

[*] Taken from T.H. Davenport, G.B. Probst, *"Knowledge Management Case Book"*, 2nd ed. (Erlangen/Weinheim: Publicis/Wiley-VCH, 2002)

ShareNet is an example of how practical knowledge management within Siemens has had a substantial effect on its business success. ShareNet links the salespeople of Siemens Information and Communication Networks (ICN) worldwide, making each salesperson's accumulated learning experiences accessible to the entire sales force. This facilitates sales, helps to save valuable time and money, and leads to increased revenue with higher profit margins.

With the telecommunication industry's strategic context characterized by great flux (as described later) the codifying and sharing of relevant knowledge through database-media has become much more difficult. Recognizing the risk of being saddled with codified knowledge in obsolete data graveyards, ICN ShareNet went beyond the mere hoarding of information in data repositories. It focused on orchestrating an interactive web of knowledge and expert networks on a global scale.

The shifting context in telecommunications

The changing landscape in telecommunications

From the inception of the telephone service until the 1980s, customers of telecommunication equipment around the world had mostly been of one type: the monolithic, integrated telephone company. The entire range of activities involved in providing telephone and data services to the end-user, i.e. the entire value chain, starting with the planning of the network to its implementation (including customer acquisition and care), was concentrated in a single, large entity. Being less cost-sensitive by nature these telecommunication monopolies usually focused on long-term business relations with just a few telecommunications suppliers. The integration of the telecommunication equipment was normally handled by the monopolists themselves.

Previously the main business of a telecommunications-equipment supplier, such as Siemens ICN, was to manage the long-term relationship with its customer and to supply a range of well-engineered equipment. Time-to-market and pricing were of secondary concern. Consequently, the telecommunication-equipment suppliers of the past came to mirror their monopolistic customers: They also became vertically integrated, less sensitive to costs and oriented to the needs of a few, stable customers. Decision-making was centralized which, in turn, resulted in the flow of information following suit.

Times changed. Over the past two decades, governments worldwide have been deregulating the telecommunications-services market to provide consumers and end-users with more competitive pricing and better service. This led to the various telecommunication markets being at a different stage of their economic development. To complicate matters, technological advances in electronics and computer science led to an explosion of new products and services in the telecommunication services market. The end-result was a previously unknown diversity of telecommunication demands from all over the world.

Another consequence of this worldwide deregulation of telecommunication was the unbundling of the integrated, monolithic telephone companies. The large few were replaced by a variety of companies, often offering services in specialized market segments, such as telecommunication to certain foreign destinations, or specifically to business customers. The new, competitive landscape also led to the disintegration of traditional value chains. Once it was possible for a company to shift costs between services, for example by charging much more for long-distance calls that actually cost very little to supply, and using the margins on this lucrative service to subsidize residential services. Today, competing long-distance service companies, with no residential business to subsidize, can provide that same service much cheaper. Cost shifting is no longer possible.

The change in the telecommunication industry led to a radical change in the nature of the telecommunications-equipment business. Siemens ICN, a leading telecommunication-equipment provider, active in over 160 countries with 60,000 employees and a revenue of US$ 13 billion, served a variety of customers with very different needs. The CEO of Siemens ICN, Dr. Roland Koch, anticipated the new rules of the game: The new entrants to the telecommunication market would be competing on grounds of costs and innovative services and would be very sensitive to equipment prices. It was therefore of crucial importance that providers of such equipment bring new innovations to the market as quickly as possible.

The result was a highly complex and competitive telecommunications-equipment supply business with all processes accelerated. This, in turn, required decentralized decision-making and a flow of globally networked knowledge. While this situation certainly threatened many incumbents, it represented vast opportunities for agile companies.

Challenges and new opportunities for business

As Siemens ICN faced the tremendous increase in the complexity of its business, all telecommunication companies, both the new entrants to the telecommunications market, and the incumbents, brought new challenges. The emphasis was often on highly customized product and service packages. ICN therefore had to lower costs and develop innovative products and services simultaneously – at a pace not previously experienced.

Yet the new telecommunications landscape also brought opportunities: While the new reality threatened profit margins, it also opened up new business with higher profit margins for Siemens ICN. A case in point was the complex product and service packages that the new types of customers required. Additionally, they were often innovative and quite lean organizations with a relatively small technical staff and thus required more technical services. These ranged from systems integration and network planning to the provision, integration, tuning, and implementation of services. The new entrants needed fresh business analysis and planning to accommodate the rapidly changing markets in which they operated but many did not have the resources or experience to handle this. Most of them were also start-up ventures without sufficient

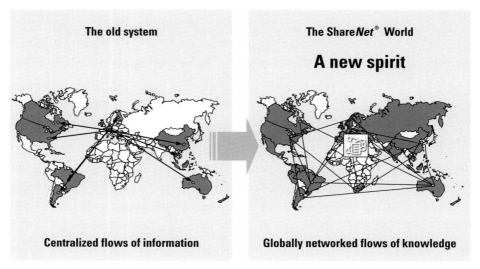

Figure 1.1 Old system / new system

capital to make cash equipment purchases, which led to their demanding new terms of financing and innovative contracts.

In the deregulated telecommunications market, a customer could therefore expect a supplier like ICN to provide most of the services involved in running a telecommunications-service business, including financing, business planning, engineering, and operation. These complex service and product packages that a telecommunications-services provider wishes to sell to his end-user, have become known as "solutions". The individual conceptual elements constituting a solution are shown in Figure 1.1.

Naturally, the material components, such as switches or routers, still form an important part of a solution. Another important part of a complete customer solution is the

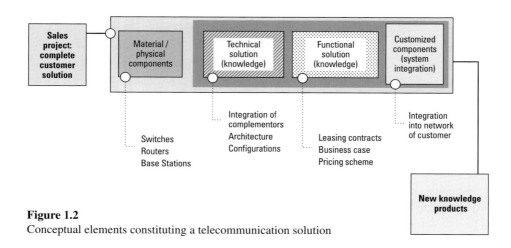

Figure 1.2
Conceptual elements constituting a telecommunication solution

customization of the delivered components. Components, for example, often require country-specific, or customer-specific, customization for implementation in a network.

To meet the demands of these new customers, components offering the technical and functional know-how are highly important – and highly reusable as well. A so-called technical-solution component consists of a service such as network planning, or performance optimization, and is, therefore, based on technical knowledge. Functional solutions include such components as leasing contracts, or the development of customer-specific business cases, and are often based on commercial practices, or knowledge about the customer's business.

While many of the new entrants to the market were seeking solutions from telecommunications businesses, other elements of this business were yielding significantly lower profit margins. The high value-added aspect of the telecommunications-solution selling business, contributed significantly to its importance, leading to solution creation and solution selling becoming key competitive levers for ICN.

Orchestrating a global network of knowledge sharing

The need for new competencies

The changing rules of the game in telecommunications have had a significant impact on sales people like Martin Wong.

In the past, it had been the customer who formulated a demand that was then forwarded to the telecommunication supplier's ordering system by the salesperson. In the new landscape, Martin himself often has to proactively present a business idea to customers, helping them to develop innovative business strategies. His new clients do not want just a product, but complex solutions. There are no shortcuts to these solutions, as the customers often articulate their intentions and needs in broad terms only. It takes time, meetings, and negotiations before a project aim and some milestones can be defined.

Martin and his sales colleagues all over the world had to face new challenges regarding competency development. The new demands, differing so entirely from those their customers required in the "old days", require sales staff whose competency portfolios are aligned accordingly. Furthermore, the shifts in the competitive landscape have greatly increased most businesses' knowledge intensity. This means that sales personnel at ICN require comprehensive knowledge of both the individual components of solutions as well as the integration of these components. This again represented new challenges to be mastered.

One industrial relationship manager reasoned:

"We will have to unlearn thinking in packaged products and applications. The way we work together is the most important clue to success. Once we start negotiations about a new project with the customer, we have to immediately identify internal and external qualified people to build and operate these new businesses jointly with the customer.

Because of the multifaceted knowledge needed, we have to learn how to source our knowledge from convenient sources. We have to get used to integrating internal and external know-how".

It had been clear to Martin that he and his colleagues could no longer rely just on former product knowledge. Where, in the past, they had often anticipated customer needs even before they had been articulated, they now had to guess, try to assess and discuss the complex needs of the new entrants to the telecommunications market. By doing this proactively, the salesperson had to gather information about the new clients and develop in-depth knowledge about the customer's way of doing business – beforehand. Unlike their established customers, who had placed orders in a relatively predictable way, these new customers had latent wishes, which had to be served.

The industrial relationship manager illustrated this as follows:

"What we need most is intimate customer knowledge, especially knowledge about the customer's economic branch. We have to make pro-active suggestions about where our customer's business may go and in which field he may be operating the next years. Up to now, we have only become involved in the sales process once it reached the stage of ordering products and applications. The challenge is to start discussions much earlier: We have to play the role of a strategy-management consultant who is able to interpret trends and to design new business opportunities together with the customer".

Martin knew how time-consuming, difficult, and complicated this consulting role could be. Successful solutions selling requires an organizational set-up which is geared towards the rapid, purposeful identifying and sharing of relevant information and knowledge, across markets around the world, and a continual refining of competencies, to keep pace with market developments. This implied identifying best practices quickly, sharing them on a global scale, and ensuring that they were reused for profit in similar settings. The objective was to detect local innovations and leverage them on a global scale.

A prerequisite for this global reuse of local innovations was the ability to transfer the explicit elements of knowledge that could be easily transferred, or stored in databases, as well as the more tacit elements of knowledge that arise from joint business development with a customer. Each of these types of knowledge elements demand a fundamentally different transfer and management mechanism. Personalized knowledge, bound to the individual mind, cannot be transferred easily without actually transferring the person. Knowledge codified in databases, manuals, and project debriefings, however, can be transferred with relative ease. And yet, both are needed to make true knowledge sharing happen on a global level. How could this gap be bridged?

Bridging the gap

The shift to solutions selling greatly increased the impact of knowledge on the competitive success of ICN. To succeed in providing solutions, the individual sales person had, in effect, to act like a consultant. He or she had to consider a wide array of aspects concerning the telecommunications-business offering, including financing, business analysis, and network planning. This included substantial amounts of tacit and, therefore, highly personalized knowledge together with important elements of codified knowledge.

Tacit knowledge is usually transferred by people exchanging knowledge through social interaction, e.g. during meetings, videoconferences, or in discussion groups. Transferring codified knowledge by means of a codification strategy is realized by capturing and storing knowledge in documents and transferring it via databases or similar means. Both types of knowledge have to be transferred to make true knowledge sharing happen. An over-reliance on personalized knowledge at the expense of codified forms would sacrifice the leverage that can be gained from conveniently transferring codified knowledge. Likewise, an overemphasis on codified knowledge can miss out on important tacit elements that constitute an integral component of the added value that solution selling provides.

Bridging this gap was often described as a dilemma, where the one could not be achieved without negatively affecting the other. And yet, the solution to this dilemma would be fundamental to the way in which ICN was to operate in a global environment – where added value emanates less from selling products than from providing complex integrated solutions.

The solution was found in the development of a tool and conceptual apparatus that provides the salesperson with convenient access to the two fundamental building blocks of all solutions. The orchestration of a global network of shared knowledge, using both a personalization and a codification strategy, has become the heart of ICN's competitive strategy.

ShareNet – leveraging local innovations globally

Dr. Roland Koch, CEO of Siemens ICN, was quick to recognize the opportunities that the reuse of knowledge would provide. Having decided to focus on the selling of complex solutions, ICN developed a practical approach that leveraged what had developed into a key factor in competitiveness in the new telecommunications landscape – sales knowledge and innovation. In order to stimulate and encourage empowerment, creativity, and innovation, Dr. Koch assigned the department Business Transformation Partners (BTP) the challenge of developing, rolling out and monitoring ICN ShareNet.

ShareNet is an interactive knowledge-management tool through which a global network of shared knowledge could be established. It was developed in close co-operation with the ICN board members, with Joachim Doering, the head of BTP and ICN Vice President, actively promoting the initiative in the different local companies.

The initial development of ShareNet

To ensure that ShareNet would be relevant to the day-to-day work of the sales people, the first step was to assemble a selection of the company's most successful sales people in a hands-on, knowledge-mapping process. Members of this core ShareNet

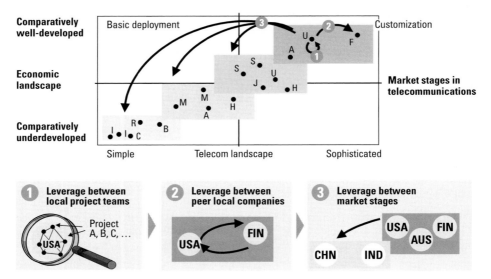

Figure 1.3 Types of sharing

team included sales representatives and local company heads from markets around the world, covering the full spectrum of business situations faced by the company. The question that this team addressed was "How do we sell solutions?"

The team developed a map of the solutions-selling process and identified broad categories of business-relevant knowledge for each aspect of this process. This rigorous approach also helped the sales people to realize how much they had to learn from one another. A key insight gained through this mapping process was that not only the software and hardware building blocks of different solutions, but virtually every activity enabling a telecommunication service for the end-user, constituted a potential solution element that could be leveraged and re-deployed.

It soon became clear that knowledge sharing between the local project teams within a country – focusing on the same market, facing the same competitors, and therefore challenged by the same problems – could lead to a substantial competitive advantage. This type of knowledge sharing is called *leverage between local project teams (process 1)*.

However, a fundamental question still remained to be answered: What would be the benefit of leveraging knowledge globally? Telecommunications markets were in different stages of development, leading to differing demands in these markets. The market stage depended on a country's economic development, as well as on the development of the telecom landscape.

Each country could be positioned on a two-dimensional graph by determining:

- its economic development – ranging from comparatively underdeveloped to comparatively well-developed – by means of its GNP

- its telecom landscape development – ranging from a simple landscape to a sophisticated one – by means of most important influencing factor, namely the degree of deregulation in the market.

Based on its position on this graph, a country's market stage in telecommunications could be determined. The market stage, in turn, determined the kinds of solutions demanded in the market.

Why then should solutions be leveraged across countries? The mapping of the sales process suggested that countries in the same market stage often addressed similar needs and therefore tended to seek similar solutions. By the same token, evolving telecommunication markets often encountered problems or upgrade pressures engendered by their more demanding end-users. These problems and upgrade pressures, again, tended to be similar to those previously encountered by markets that had now evolved to a more sophisticated stage.

This suggested that a solution sold in one country could be leveraged to another country at the same market stage, forming a so-called peer group. This type of knowledge sharing is called *leverage between local peer companies (process 2)*.

As markets develop, solutions of the next market stage become more and more relevant to customers' market success. To allow customers to develop ahead of their competition, Siemens ICN leveraged solutions of higher market stages to those of the lower stages. This type of knowledge sharing is called *leverage between market stages (process 3)*.

These three types of knowledge sharing do not require three types of systems. Leveraging between local project teams in itself leads to a significant competitive advantage, therefore installing a system to allow this kind of sharing should be profitable. If the same kind of system were installed all over the world, the system's interoperability would be guaranteed and knowledge would be reused. This would not only enable knowledge sharing between local project teams but also knowledge sharing between peer local companies and between market stages. By utilizing a single worldwide tool for knowledge sharing within one country (process 1), two additional byproducts are also obtained, virtually gratis – knowledge sharing between peer countries (process 2) and between market stages (process 3) – making it a very attractive prospect.

ShareNet – a business application system

The knowledge management initiative ShareNet was launched early in 1999 to provide sales people, worldwide, with relevant knowledge about solutions and applications, sales processes, and projects. With its aim to leverage knowledge and innovation globally, it was explicitly designed to foster the emergence of best-practice sharing, thus enabling a powerful learning process.

In this context, ShareNet nurtures the changed role of local Siemens companies throughout the world. In the face of new customer demands, these local companies evolve from mere outlets to companies with full responsibility for customer manage-

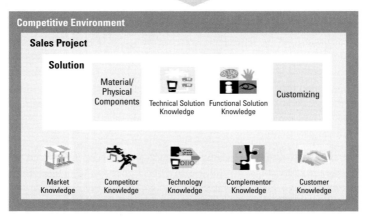

Figure 1.4 Value creation chain

ment. At the local-company level, the goal is to detect local innovations and leverage them on a global scale.

ShareNet avoids the problem of too great an emphasis being placed on information technology at the expense of in-depth business understanding that has proved to be a pitfall of many similar knowledge-management systems. Unlike traditional, often intranet-based, knowledge-management systems that have primarily been conceived as "document repositories", ShareNet provides a network that has been explicitly designed as an interactive medium. Instead of functioning as an infrastructure that exists alongside people's actual work, ShareNet functions as a business application, seamlessly dovetailing with employees' ways of solving customer problems. It covers both the explicit and tacit knowledge of the sales value-creation process, including project know-how, technical- and functional-solution components, and knowledge about the business environment (e.g. customer, competitor, market, technology, and partner knowledge). The emphasis here is on experience-based knowledge. As shown in Figure 1.4, knowledge about the different steps of the value-creation chain was transferred to ShareNet solution objects (e.g. technical- or functional-solution knowledge) and ShareNet environment objects (e.g. customer or market knowledge). Share-Net's focus is less on "brochureware", than on personal statements, comments, the "field experience" of sales employees, or the real-life tested pros and cons of a solution.

In addition to structured "questionnaires" on the above-mentioned topics, ShareNet provides less structured spaces, such as chat rooms, community news, discussion groups on special issues, and so called urgent requests. Urgent requests are basically forums for asking all kinds of urgent questions, such as, "My customer needs a business case for implementing the new technology X by next Monday. Who can help me?" or "Does anybody have a list of recent network projects by competitor Y?" These are, in other words, questions that do not have a defined organizational owner. As ShareNet works independently of time zones and organizational boundaries, members usually receive answers within hours. In many cases, the right answers are "harvested" and made available for later use in a FAQ (Frequently Asked Questions) section. Thus, unlike traditional knowledge-management systems, ShareNet is based on an interactive approach and mobilizing knowledge and innovation in sales.

Mobilizing global knowledge sharing

Identifying areas of intervention

An important concern in the development of ShareNet was the adequate positioning of initiative as a true value-adder that helps to solve relevant problems in employees' day-to-day work. It was critical to emphasize this to prevent ShareNet from being portrayed as yet another headquarters project that would be demanding precious resources. This was the goal from the onset. It started with ShareNet's development as a joint effort of a core team of sales people from all over the world who recognized that local sales and marketing people felt that they too had a vested interest in the development of such a system. This was mainly achieved by addressing four interrelated areas of intervention.

1. Cognitive knowledge – or know-what – is defined as basic technical mastery and is achieved through extensive training and certification. For ShareNet this means technical knowledge, for example in the form of pricing concepts, represents an essential, but not complete, aspect to ensure commercial viability.

2. Skills – or know-how – refers to the effective execution and application of abstract rules and regulations in the real-world context. ShareNet achieves this through the feedback given by sales professionals in de-briefing projects.

3. Systems understanding – or know-why – refers to a deep understanding of cause-and-effect-relationships underlying an experience. In a global-sales-and-marketing context, this enables professionals to anticipate subtle aspects in their interaction with a customer. This understanding is especially important in view of the increased complexity of the sales process. For example, an experienced key account manager will instinctively know which components of a solution can be developed further, be leveraged and re-deployed in other countries, or even re-invented to suit different requirements. The Systems understanding therefore represents a particularly important area of intervention.

4. Self-motivated creativity – or care-why – refers to an active and caring involvement in a given cause. For ShareNet this means systematically identifying and promoting highly motivated and creative groups of employees. Indeed, such groups often outperform other groups with greater resources.

These four areas of intervention together ensured that a user-friendly, accessible tool with authentic added value was developed for the sales and marketing staff. In the words of a senior key account manager:

"Offering a user-friendly tool, which can be accessed via the Intranet is not enough. You have to care for the people who are actually using it. You need a deep understanding of their ways of doing business and the problems they encounter. Ultimately, this ensures that you get the right attention and co-operation".

Critical success factors for global knowledge sharing

Designing a user-friendly tool was one thing but what it would look like in practice was another. In order to make knowledge sharing happen on a world-wide level, potential barriers obstructing the free flow of knowledge within Siemens ICN had to be anticipated and systematically eliminated. Joachim Doering and his ShareNet team identified five critical success factors that had to be considered, namely (1) leadership, (2) organizational structure, (3) motivation and reward systems, (4) organizational culture, and (5) a viable business case.

Leadership

Perhaps the most important critical success factor to making global knowledge sharing happen is the unconditional support of top management. In the words of Roland Koch, CEO of Siemens ICN:

"ShareNet is about collaboration beyond all existing organizational barriers. Our future lies in the creation of a net of knowledge spanning between all our employees".

Top management's support enhanced the value and strategic quality of the knowledge-management initiative and sent a signal to channel organizational resources and individual commitment towards this element. Management helped to communicate the idea of ShareNet across organizational levels and functional departments to ensure its added value was understood and appreciated.

The responsibility for the ShareNet initiative was given to the ShareNet Committee, the highest decision-making body of the unit. It was responsible for the strategic development of ShareNet worldwide. The committee was composed of eleven members: One member served on the ICN board, two members came from ICN Business Transformation Partners BTP, but the majority of the members were local company representatives. This guaranteed that the opinions of the local users of ShareNet would be heard and that they would be actively involved in the initiative. The size of the committee was deliberately kept small to enable its members to develop consistent decision-making competency and to react quickly to stimuli and suggestions from the field.

Organizational structure and rollout

The concept of ShareNet is probably more concerned about the managerial system and processes than about the technical platform itself. These managerial processes have been managed carefully from the first emergence of ShareNet. They cover the input of valuable knowledge as well as the elevation of this knowledge to more reusable (and thereby: abstract) knowledge. This task of making the knowledge inside the ShareNet system richer and more general and reusable is the prime task of the content editors, which are part of the ShareNet organization. This organization also contains country-specific consultants, IT-support, and a telephone and email hotline, providing answers and help for all users worldwide.

The ShareNet committee is the highest decision body of ShareNet. It consists of several heads of the Siemens ICN local companies and a few high-ranking headquarter managers, including the CEO himself. This committee was of utmost importance for the ShareNet rollout – which demanded devoting resources from all local companies. Local ShareNet managers are these resources. They are facilitators and trainers, ensuring the roll-out and support in their respective countries. Without the network of the ShareNet managers, the rollout of ShareNet would not have been possible. The ShareNet managers were trained, prepared, and outfitted for their task at one worldwide ShareNet bootcamp, organized by the ICN Business Transformation Partners organization.

The backbone of the ShareNet organization are – of course – the users, which are contributors at the same time. They are the main driving force behind the system, and they form the network of friends and colleagues that make knowledge management work for Siemens ICN.

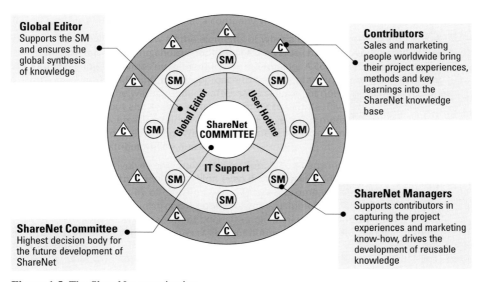

Global Editor
Supports the SM and ensures the global synthesis of knowledge

Contributors
Sales and marketing people worldwide bring their project experiences, methods and key learnings into the ShareNet knowledge base

ShareNet Committee
Highest decision body for the future development of ShareNet

ShareNet Managers
Supports contributors in capturing the project experiences and marketing know-how, drives the development of reusable knowledge

Figure 1.5 The ShareNet organization

While technology can certainly act as a facilitator for global knowledge creation and sharing, especially in the case of explicit knowledge, it is erroneous to believe that high-volume, quantitative data repositories can significantly improve organizational knowledge assets. Since knowledge is not static, but subject to continuous modification, it cannot be frozen into depositories. In recognition of this, ShareNet had to ensure adequate levels of interactivity in order to conserve the dynamic nature of knowledge.

To make knowledge sharing happen, interactivity was also required on an inter-departmental, inter-divisional, and inter-functional level. It is often difficult to accept and adopt another person's knowledge, especially if this person is from another division or department. An account manager at ICN commented on this "not invented here" syndrome:

"Sometimes knowledge, which has been brought in from external sources, such as another Siemens departments or divisions, raises defense reactions. People often do not use it for the simple and stupid reason that they did not invent it. We have to develop people who can integrate suggestions from different origins and make a successful project out of it. In short, make things happen, even if a project is composed of external inputs only".

Motivation and reward system

It was necessary to systematically identify and eliminate any organizational structures that could prevent knowledge from being shared, leveraged, and enriched by different functions and departments – and across organizational levels. A critical success factor, therefore, was firstly the establishment of a targeting and compensation system for top managers (see the "Bonus on Top Case").

But a targeting and compensation system for top managers was not enough. On the level of the employees actually using ShareNet, a motivation and reward system was developed that removed the fears and anxieties that could prevent the exchange of knowledge across divisions and departments. Knowledge in general, and sales knowledge in particular, is bound to a person. It cannot be shared with others against a person's will. This raises questions about motivating people to share their knowledge. Getting a person to enhance other people's knowledge by voluntarily contributing his or her own does not happen easily. A further constraint is that it is considered a time-consuming and tedious exercise. In fact, the individual contributor might wonder how he or she could possibly benefit. An important benefit for the individual contributor is to portray the individual concerned as an expert in a certain field. The drawback is that once this reputation had been gained, others may often solicit this expert's opinion, leading to time lost for the individual's own projects.

The need to motivate and reward such sharing is equally important for both the contributor (or "giver of knowledge"), and the re-user (or "taker of knowledge"). The contributor, who receives no direct reward for making experiences available, has to be specifically rewarded for the time invested in sharing his or her knowledge. The main reward for the re-user is the knowledge itself, which facilitates daily work. Yet, rewarding individual performance can lead to another counterproductive result. Dur-

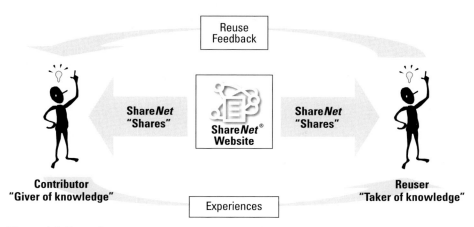

Figure 1.6 Reward system

ing the ShareNet implementation people were reluctant to adopt knowledge from others. The "not invented here"-syndrome described in the organizational structure, is closely related to this. The willingness to re-use existing knowledge became crucial for this initiative to fully succeed.

For the re-user to benefit and thus gain the reward, ShareNet had to ensure that the available knowledge was truly useful. This was done through stringent quality control. Nevertheless, a reward beyond that of gaining knowledge, significantly improved the re-user's motivation to re-use knowledge. The ICN ShareNet Quality Assurance and Reward System is designed analogous to frequent flyer mile systems found in the airline industry. As shown in Figure 1.6, contributing and re-using knowledge is rewarded by ShareNet "shares". Depending on the number of shares accumulated during a year, employees are awarded with several incentives, such as conference participation or telecommunication equipment. The number of shares given to the contributor depends on the re-use feedback of the taker of knowledge, thus rewarding the usefulness of the transferred knowledge. The higher the usefulness of the knowledge, the higher the reward is. The feedback mechanism is an important part of the quality-assurance system, too. The quality of available knowledge can be quantified through re-use feedback from several knowledge re-users. Based on this feedback, knowledge of an inferior quality can be removed from ICN ShareNet, whereas high-quality knowledge can be identified and developed further. This leads to a constant improvement of the quality of the available knowledge.

Organizational culture

Organizational culture as a set of beliefs, attitudes, and assumptions is mainly concerned with the unwritten, less visible part of the organization. Symbols, ceremonies, office settings, and dress code are examples of organizational culture. Additionally, it determines the way in which people interact and work together, and also prescribes rules and regulations about what is considered acceptable.

Organizational culture has vast implications for the implementation of knowledge management at Siemens ICN. To a large extent, knowledge sharing depends on the quality of the relationship between employees, as well as their relationship with management. A culture of openness, mutual respect and the absence of ambiguity is fundamental for fostering knowledge sharing.

A strong hierarchy often counteracts such an atmosphere since it promotes individual performance at the expense of team performance. Promoters of ShareNet, like Joachim Doering, worked hard to spread the ShareNet message that "unlike in school, copying is not only allowed – it is required". Another barrier was that the strong hierarchy naturally directed responsibility towards the top, whereas a culture conducive to knowledge sharing is built on empowerment.

A viable business case

A viable business case was a key factor for a successful knowledge-sharing project. The IT system, the motivation and reward system, the change of organizational structure and culture all contributed to making ICN ShareNet expensive. ShareNet, therefore, had to illustrate its benefits with a realistic business case.

Of course a knowledge-sharing system is expensive – but so is the continual labour of rediscovering solutions. The costs of sharing knowledge are quite obvious, the benefits are less so. There are three types of somewhat quantifiable ShareNet benefits:

- The saving of costs, e.g. by re-using tenders or re-using knowledge on how to simplify processes.
- Increased revenues, e.g. by increasing the quality of tenders by re-using knowledge of the success factors of tenders, or by simply being faster than the competition by re-using documents.
- The alignment with customer needs, by recognizing important trends and developments worldwide.

Perspectives

Since the beginning of this millennium, ICN ShareNet has become an integral part of the strategy of Siemens ICN. Dr. Koch, CEO of Siemens ICN, remarked:

"This [ShareNet] network will be of key importance to the success of ICN's solutions business because the company that can make use of existing experiences and competencies quickest has a distinct competitive edge over other players. We need to be among the first to realize this strategic competitive advantage through efficient knowledge management".

ShareNet can be improved further. With the community of 7,000 sales, marketing, and business-development people at Siemens ICN worldwide who actually comprise ShareNet, the use of ShareNet has reached a critical mass. Within its first year of existence, it has developed into a tool of practical knowledge management, enabling improved sales and marketing processes, faster action in the marketplace, and knowledge-based competition. The ambitious target of earning 250 million Euro in additional revenue in the first year of ShareNet's implementation has still to be met.

Joachim Doering, vice president of Siemens ICN, believes that ShareNet has an even greater potential to realize a measurable business impact through the creation of new business opportunities. As a next step, new communities, such as the worldwide service units and R&D, have to "come on board" to develop ShareNet into a knowledge portal that integrates the expertise of the whole enterprise in virtual workspaces.

Broadening the focus of ShareNet internally to include other functions is not the only task ahead. Joachim has a clear vision of what the next steps should be. He envisages expanding ShareNet across organizational boundaries to integrate customer knowledge into the system. In this context, new questions arise, such as, How can customers be motivated to participate in the ShareNet initiative? What exactly is the critical knowledge ICN expects to gain from its customers? And last, but not least, the broadening of ShareNet across ICN boundaries gives rise to a whole range of completely new issues, such as security and confidentiality concerns.

Finding the answers to these questions is the key to leveraging the potential of ShareNet in particular, and Siemens ICN's future, in general.

Kuala Lumpur, Two weeks later. Martin Wong moves his chair back with a sigh of satisfaction. It has been an extremely long two weeks. ShareNet has not left him twiddling his thumbs, but it has made his job so much easier. After receiving input from around the globe, he is certain that the proposal which he has just completed will sweep the opposition aside. This weekend he needs to reward himself! Now, what would he like to do ...?

Conclusive remark

Because of the high interest the ShareNet concept affectuated at the Siemens divisions and outside Siemens, a startup company called The Agilience Group headed by the former Siemens manager Dr Christian Kurtzke was chosen to leverage the key success factors of ShareNet to the world outside Siemens ICN.

Questions

1. Major forces causing shifts in strategic management thinking and practice were highlighted. Are these forces really "new", why did these forces arise, and why at this particular point in history?

2. Some observers disagree with the view that there is a "knowledge economy" or even a "new economy". Analyze these views and their counterparts, and provide your own opinion.

3. What is the concept of "increasing returns"? Does this mean that the "economic law of diminishing returns" is now obsolete?

4. Contrast the concepts of organizational "reengineering" with organizational "reinvention". What are the similarities and dissimilarities between these concepts?

5. Select any enterprise of your choice and provide a logical review of why the traditional (analytical) strategy dimension of context, content and process are inadequate to cope with the current turbulent environment.

6. In how far is a major winery such as Lafite-Rothschild, renowned for its terroir and tacit skills, an international/metanational enterprise that is affected by the shifts as outlined here?

7. Discuss the three most important strategic drivers that forced Siemens Information Communication Networks (ICN) to implement an international knowledge sharing platform in the 1990s. Where does Siemens ICN stand today? Are the three strategic drivers still relevant? Why? Why not?

References

Chapter 1: Fundamental Impacts of the Global Knowledge Economy on Strategic Management

[1] Various authors have reviewed, emphasized and motivated the impacts of the global knowledge economy for industries and organizations. This section is a synthesis of several authors' views. One of the most insightful reviews is by Amidon, D.M. (1977), *Innovation Strategies for the Knowledge Economy: The Ken Awakening*, Oxford: Butterworth-Heinemann, from which pertinent thoughts were drawn.

[2] Beinhocker, E.D. (1999), "Robust Adaptive Strategies", *Sloan Management Review*, Spring, 95-106.

[3] Kelly, S. and Allison, M.A. (1999), *The Complexity Advantage*, New York: BusinessWeek Books, McGraw-Hill.

Innovating Our Way to the Next Industrial Revolution

[1] Social capital refers to "connections among individuals – social networks and the norms of reciprocity and trustworthiness that arise with them". See: F.D. Putnam, "Bowling Alone" (New York: Simon & Schuster, 2000). p. 19. It is also the necessary context for developing human capita. – skills and knowledge embedded in people. See: J.S. Coleman, "Social Capital and the Creation of Human Capital", American Journal of Sociology 94 (1988): 95-120.

[2] "Why Is Everyone So Short-Tempered?" USA Today, July 18, 2000, sec. A, p. 1.

[3] J. Browne. "Respect for the Earth!" a 2000 BBC Reith Lecture, available from BP, London.

[4] J. Browne, "Rethinking Corporate Responsibility", Reflections 1.4 (summer 2000): p. 48-53.

[5] See www.rmi.org/sitepages/pid175.asp for Rocky Mountain Institute publications about the hypercar.

[6] E.P. Gunn, "The Green CEO", Fortune, May 24, 1999, pp. 190-200.

[7] The SoL (Society for Organizational Learning) Sustainability Consortium was established by BP and Interface and now includes established SoL members Royal Dutch/Shell, Ford, Xerox. Harley-Davidson, Detroit-Edison, Visteon and the World Bank, along with new members Nike and Northeast Utilities. The group's current projects – on product development, innovation across complex supply networks, new energy sources, and leadership and cultural change – are described at www.SoLonline.org and are being studied through a National Science Foundation grant.

[8] T. Berry, "The Dream of the Earth" (San Francisco: Sierra Club Books, 1990), pp. 123.

[9] Ibid., pp. 131-132.

[10] D. Boorstin, "The Discoverers: A History of Man's Search To Know His World and Himself (New York. Randorn House, 1985), pp. 108-109.

[11] See P. Hawken, A.B. Lovins and L.H. Lovins, "Natural Capitalism" (New York: Little Brown and Co., 1999), p. 14; R.U. Ayers, "Industrial Metabolism", in J.S. Ausubel and H.E. Sladovich, eds., "Technology and Environment" (Washington, D.C.: National Academy Press, 1989); and A.B. Lovins, L.H. Lovins and P. Hawken, "A Road Map for Natural Capitalism", Harvard Business Review 77 (May-June 1999): pp. 145-158.

[12] These three strategies, in concert with ideas below, relate closely to the four strategies of "natural capitalism", three of the four "system conditions' of "the natural step" described in J. Holmberg and K.-H. Robert, "Backcasting From Nonoverlapping Sustainability Principles – A Framework for Strategic Planning", International Journal of Sustainable Development and World Ecology 7 (2000): 1-18; and William McDonough, "Hannover Principles: Design for Sustainability" (New York: William McDonough Architects, 1992). Available through McDonough Braungart Design Chemistry, Charlottesville, Virginia (info@mbdc.com) or downloadable from www.mcdonough.com/principles.pdf.

[13] K. Kelly, "New Rules for the New Economy" (New York: Penguin Books, 1999), pp. 2, 5, 31.

[14] S. Vandermerwe, "How Increasing Value to Customers Improves Business Results", MIT Sloan Management Review 42 (fall 2000): p. 28.

[15] A. Toffler, "The Third Wave" (New York: William Morrow, 1980).

[16] Kelly, "New Rules", pp. 121-122.

[17] C.K. Prahalad and V. Ramaswamy, "Cc-Opting Customer Competence", Harvard Business Review 78 (January-February 2000): pp. 79-87.

[18] R. Levine, C. Locke, D. Seads and D. Weinberger, "The Cluetrain Manifesto: The End of Business as Usual" (Cambridge, Massachusetts: Perseus Press, 2000), xiv.

[19] Kelly, "New Rules", p. 28.

[20] B. Wysocki Jr., "Yet Another Hazard of the New Economy: The Pied Piper Effect", Wail Street Journal, March 30, 2000, sec. A, p. 1.

[21] P.F. Drucker and P. Senge, "Becoming a Change Leader", video conversations, Peter E. Drucker Foundation for Nonprofit Management, New York, and SoL (the Society for Organizational Learning), Cambridge, Massachusetts, forthcoming.

[22] A. Webber, "What's So New About the New Economy?" Harvard Business Review 71 (January-February 1993): pp. 24-42.

[23] K. Bradsher, "Ford Is Conceding SUV Drawbacks", New York Times, May 12. 2000, sec. A, p. 1.

[24] B. Yates, "On the Road: Pecksniffs Can't Stop SUV", Wall Street Journal Europe, May 19, 2000, sec. A, p. 26.

[25] D. Quinn, "My Ishmael" (New York: Bantam Books, 1997), pp. 200-201.

II Traditional Strategic Management Approaches and Tools, and their Deficiencies

Chapter 2:
Traditional Strategic Management Approaches, and their Deficiencies

What is Wrong with Traditional Approaches to Strategic Management?

Business strategy and strategic management have long been viewed as the concept and process that link an organization and its environment. The current turbulence and significant shifts in the environment mean that traditional ways of articulating strategy and practicing strategic management have to be seriously reconsidered. Since the 1950s, various approaches to strategic management have been popularized, and some have served very well in their particular eras. With a significant new era of massive, revolutionary change – the era of the knowledge economy – having been entered during the late 1990s, it is becoming evident that all of the traditional approaches to strategic management are showing serious deficiencies in dealing with the discontinuous links between an organization and the environment. The conventional approaches simply cannot comprehensively deal with the richness and diversity of creativity, innovation and inventions now enabled by the knowledge-networked economy, and causing rapid shifts in traditional industry boundaries, the rise of significant new industries, and a plethora of new business models being devised and implemented.

This chapter reviews the evolution of traditional approaches to strategic management in their various eras, and subsequently categorizes them into major groups – the "outward-in" approaches vs. the "inward-out" approaches, and the prediction approaches vs. the learning approaches. The difficulties (or deficiencies) of these approaches in dealing with the new environmental realities are highlighted and discussed, offering practical business examples.

The Evolution of Traditional Approaches to Strategic Management

The traditional approaches to strategic management are predicated on an emphasis on analysis, reason and periods of stability. This is very much in keeping with Newton's mechanistic model of the universe, and Fayol's analytical view of the management function. There is a presumption that a combination of analysis, experience and

Table 2.1 The evolution of strategic management

Period / Issue	1950 – 1960s	1970s	1980s	1990s
Dominant Focus	*Planning:* Business and Budgetary planning	*Balancing:* Optimizing corporate entities and functions	*Positioning:* Industry, market and firm "adapting", and unique "fit"	*Resources & Capabilities:* Resource-based view for competitive advantage
Main Concerns	Planning growth Capital and operational budgeting Financial control	Balancing a portfolio of SBU's/firms/products Synergy of resources and functions	Choosing industries and markets, and positioning within them Adapting and fitting to the environment	Sources of competitive advantage within the firm Responding to hyper-competition
Principal Concepts and Tools	Investment planning Financial budgeting Economic forecasting Linear programming	Portfolio planning matrices (e.g. BCG, GE, Shell directional policy) SWOT analyses	Industry analysis (e.g. "5 Forces" model) Competitor analyses Value Chain analyses PIMS analyses	Resource analyses Core competency analyses Capability analyses BPR (Business Process Reengineering) BSC (Balanced Scorecard) TQM (Total Quality Management)
Organizational & Implementation Issues	Formal structures and procedures Financial management predominant	Multidivisional structures Diversification Quest for market share growth	Industry restructuring Value chain configuration Positioning evaluations	Restructuring around key resource competence Focus on building core competencies Outsourcing Alliances

insight can lead to reliable predictions regarding the future – an environment "out there" which has to be adapted to.

Table 2.1 illustrates the various eras in strategic management approaches, with each era depicting the respective major focus of strategic management.

The above table is of necessity a generalization, i.e. in reality the eras are not strictly limited to a particular decade (or number of decades). Furthermore, many prominent authors such as Grant, Mintzberg, and Collis & Montgomery depict these eras in more elaborate or different ways.[1] Nevertheless, there seems to be general consensus regarding the dominant focus of these eras, evolving from business and budgetary planning in the 1950s/60s, to a focus on firm resources and capabilities in the 1990s.

The evolution of strategic management has been driven more by the practical needs of business than by the development of theory. The emergence of the *planning* approach was associated with the problems faced by managers in the 1950s and 1960s in coordinating decisions and maintaining control in increasingly large and complex enterprises. The emphasis on longer-term planning during the 1960s reflected concern with achieving coordination and consistency in investment planning during a period of stability and expansion. The typical format was a five-year business planning document that set goals, objectives, forecast key economic trends, established priorities in each business area, and allocated capital expenditure. Ansoff, widely regarded as one of the founding figures of the new discipline of corporate strategy, defined strategy as follows:

"Strategic decisions are primarily concerned with external rather than internal problems of the firm, and specifically with the selection of the product-mix that the firm will produce and the markets to which it will sell".[2]

During the 1970s, attention shifted towards strategic management in a quest for performance based on a *balancing* of sources of profitability. This was the result of the oil industry shocks of 1973/4 and 1979, that ushered in a new era of macro-economic instability. Businesses simply could no longer forecast five years ahead, with the resultant shift from *planning* to *balancing* market opportunities and threats with various business strengths and weaknesses (the so-called SWOT analysis). At the Boston Consulting Group (BCG), the determinants of profitability differences within industries were the focus of investigation – studies pointing to the critical role of market share and economies of experience.[3] Various types of portfolio planning matrices, such as the BCG, GE (General Electric) and SDP (Shell Directional Policy matrix) became popular.

During the 1980s the focus shifted towards competitive *positioning* of the firm through analysis of industry structure and competition. Michael Porter of Harvard Business School pioneered the application of industrial organization economics to analyze the determinants of firm profitability.[4] The emphasis of strategic management was a quest for optimal positioning (or "fit") – companies needed to locate within the most attractive industries or markets where they had to endeavor to become market leaders. Porter made the point that "competitive strategy is about being different – it means deliberately choosing a different set of activities to deliver a unique mix of value".[5] The principal concepts and tools of the positioning era became industry analysis (the so-called "5-forces" model), competitor analysis, market analysis, value chain analysis and PIMS (profit impact of market strategy) analysis.

In the late 1980s and early 1990s, the intensifying competition to achieve market share leadership led to a shift in strategic management focus on internal firm *resources and capabilities* – the difference between companies' resources and the need to develop core competencies for the establishment of unique positions of competitive advantage. Various authors, such as Grant[6], pointed to the firm's resources and capabilities, and its unique leveraging thereof as a primary source of profitability and the basis for formulating its longer-term strategy. Resource analysis, core competency analysis, and capability analysis, and business process reengineering (BPR) became popularly known as the RBV (resource-based view), and organizational emphasis on restructuring, reengineering, outsourcing and alliancing to build unique capabilities was evidenced. In the middle to late 1990s, the dimension of dynamic capabilities was added to the RBV due to high-velocity industry and market changes. Hyper-competition and high-velocity strategies contend that one firm will outperform another if it is more adept at rapidly and repeatedly disrupting the current situation by creating unprecedented and unconventional dynamic capabilities, i.e. repeatedly forming new, albeit temporary, competitive advantages based on different resource combinations than those of the existing pattern. Authors such as D'Aveni, Chakravarthy, Eisenhardt & Brown, and Eisenhardt & Martin identified various principles of hyper-competition and dynamic capabilities, and proposed that corporate strategy should center on managing strategic processes rather than on strategic positioning.[7]

To discuss the current deficiencies of the above-mentioned traditional approaches to strategic management, they are grouped into two categories, namely "outward-in" vs. "inward-out" approaches, and "prediction" vs. "learning" approaches.

"Outward-in" vs. "inward-out" approaches

The *planning, balancing* and *positioning* approaches to strategic management can be grouped as "outward-in" approaches, i.e. first analyzing the external (macro, industry, market etc.) environment and then analyzing and competitively gearing the internal (firm) environment. This is based on implicit assumptions of periods of relatively stable (or static) environmental conditions, relevance of forecasting and prediction, and achievement of particular industry positioning objectives over an extended period of time.

In the knowledge economy, with its high rate of environmental discontinuities due to the disruptive impact of networking technologies, speed of globalization, and rate of product and industry innovation, environmental forecasting and prediction are impossible in many, if not most, industries. Companies that continue to focus on "the competition", on leveraging and extending current capabilities to retain or extend their positions in the "existing industry", and striving for periodic optimum "fit with their environment", are faced with major dilemmas. A focus on matching and beating the competition leads to reactive, incremental and often imitative strategic actions – not what is required in the fast-changing knowledge economy. Even in relatively stable or slow-changing industries (which are increasingly difficult to find) the concepts and tools of the "outward-in" approaches are becoming deficient.

The *resources and capabilities* approach to strategic management can be termed an "inward-out" approach, i.e. first focusing on the firm's internal resources and capabilities and their leveraging possibilities, thereafter incorporating the "realities" of the external environment. An inwardly driven focus on resources and capabilities within a company, however, significantly limits a company's opportunity horizon and introduces resistance to change if the market is evolving away from a company's forté. It also leads to an emphasis on existing customers – the conventional focus on retaining and better satisfying existing customers tends to promote hesitancy to challenge the competency status quo for fear of losing or dissatisfying them. Some authors, such as Leonard-Barton[8], have pointed to the possibility of core competencies turning into "core rigidities", emphasizing the potential of an inwardly-driven focus on capabilities to lead to resistance to change (see also the mini case study on Encyclopaedia Britannica on the following page).

"Prediction" vs. "learning" approaches

The *planning, balancing, positioning* and *resource-based* approaches can also be termed *"predictive"* approaches, as they all attempt to predict a particular environment and probable position or fit of a company within that environment through its strategic thrusts. With the increasing inability to predict the future, the focus of strategic management has to change fundamentally. Plans have now come to be seen not as descriptions of future performance, but as a basis for initiating flexible and speedy responses to a changing present. GE's Jack Welch shifted his attention in the 1990s from sophisticated strategic plans to the pressing, current strategic issues that his company faced. Some Japanese companies, such as Matsushita, have explicitly adopted a philosophy that views strategic management not as a grand plan based on forecasts and insights about the future, but as a "design of experiments" to provide a basis for learning and adaptation.[9]

Mintzberg is well-known for his criticism of "predictive" approaches, which he terms the "fallacy of prediction", as well as for declaring that strategy making cannot be organized, formalized or detached from operational issues.[10] He also distinguishes between strategy formation as either "deliberate" or "emergent", i.e. either a process of prediction, planning and formalization, or as an on-going "emergent" process resulting from various (on-going) external impacts and internal decisions. "Emergent" strategies are the result of a learning approach to strategic management, as reflected in the dynamic capabilities view that became especially prevalent during the latter part of the 1990s (see Table 2.1).

The *"learning"* approach to strategic management changes the character of the concepts and techniques commonly utilized in the "prediction" approach. The task of strategic management becomes one of managing adaptation, with the proposition that the only sustainable competitive advantage for an organization is the ability to learn faster than its competition. The "learning" approach seems to have emanated from the seminal work of Peter Senge[11] on organizational learning, which enjoyed considerable popularity during the 1990s. The learning approach has proved its value to many organizations and intuitively makes sense in the knowledge economy. Kaplan and Norton[12] have incorporated this approach in a model of strategic management termed the "balanced scorecard" (BSC), which indicates the dynamics and managerial requirements between learning, organizational processes, customer value and profitability.

The "learning" approach has a serious deficiency, however, which renders it inadequate to cope with major discontinuities of the knowledge economy. The learning

The Encyclopaedia Britannica saga

In 1768, three Scottish printers began publishing an integrated compendium of knowledge – the earliest and most famous in the English-speaking world. They called it Encyclopaedia Britannica. Since then, Encyclopedia Britannica has evolved through fifteen editions and to this day it is regarded as the world's most comprehensive and authoritative encyclopaedia. In 1920, Sears, Roebuck and Company, an American mail-order retailer, acquired Britannica and moved its headquarters from Edinburgh to Chicago. Ownership passed to William Benton in 1941, who then willed the company in the early 1970s to the Benton Foundation, a charitable organization whose income supports the communications programs at the University of Chicago.

Under its American owners Britannica grew into a serious commercial enterprise, while sustaining its reputation as the world's most prestigious and comprehensive encyclopaedia. The content was revised every four or five years. The company built one of the most aggressive and successful direct sales forces in the world. By 1990, sales of Britannica's multivolume sets had reached an all-time high of about US$650 million. Dominant market share, steady if unspectacular growth, generous margins, and a two-hundred year history all testified to an extraordinarily compelling and stable brand. Since 1990, however, sales of Britannica, as of all printed encyclopaedias in the United States, have collapsed by over 80 percent. Britannica was under serious threat from a new competitor: the CD-ROM.

The CD-ROM came from nowhere and destroyed the printed encyclopaedia business. Whereas Britannica sells for $1,500.00 to $2,200.00 per set (depending on the quality of the binding), CD-ROM encyclopaedias sell for $50 to $70. But hardly anybody pays even that: the vast majority of copies are given away to promote the sale of computers. With a marginal manufacturing cost of $1,50 per copy, the CD-ROM as a freebie makes economic sense. The marginal cost of Britannica, in contrast, is about $250 for production plus about $500 to $600 for the salesperson's commission.

Judging from their inaction, Britannica's executives initially seemed to have viewed the CD-ROM encyclopaedia as an irrelevance: a child's toy, one step above video games. As revenues plunged, it became obvious that regardless of the quality, CD-ROM encyclopaedias were serious competition. Britannic executives reluctantly considered manufacturing their own CD-ROM product. Months passed, and sales continued to plummet. In response, the company eventually put together their own CD-ROM version of the encyclopaedia.

The CD-ROM version engendered yet another crises: a revolt by the sales force. Even if priced at a significant premium over its CD-ROM competitors such as Encarta, the CD-ROM version of Britannica could not possibly produce the $500 to $600 sales commission its traditional counterpart produced, and from which it would obviously detract sales. Indeed, a CD-ROM version would have demanded a completely different channel. To avoid a revolt by the sales force, Britannica executives decided to bundle the printed product with its digital counterpart. The CD-ROM was given free to buyers of the multivolume set. Anyone who wanted to buy just the CD-ROM would have to pay $1,000.00. The decision appeased the sales force briefly, but did nothing to stem the continuing collapse of sales. Losses mounted. In 1995, the Benton Foundation finally put the company up for sale. For nearly eighteen months, investment bankers tried to find a buyer. Microsoft declined, as did Technology Media and information companies. Finally, in 1996, financier Jacob Safra agreed to buy the company, paying less than half of the book value. In less then five years, one of the greatest brand

73

names in the English-speaking world, with a heritage of more than 200 years, was nearly destroyed by a cheap, shiny disk.

(Adapted from Evans and Wurster, 1997, 2000: 1-21)

approach works well in evolutionary periods, and when focused on a single organization. When revolutions occur, blurring the boundaries between industries and firms, and various new forms of knowledge networking arise or exist, the learning approach is ineffective. Fundamental strategic remodeling (or new business models), and not strategic repositioning is necessary when a major discontinuity impacts on an organization. Organizations are only now becoming aware of the notion of how disruptive change occurs in living, organic and open systems, and biologists and economists, among others, expect periods of equilibrium to be interrupted by major disruptions – so-called "punctuated equilibrium".

When evolution is replaced by revolution, or the potential for revolution, both the predictive and learning paradigms are ineffective. The existing strategic management system – including defined purpose (vision, mission, objectives etc.), organizational structure, planning processes, measurement practices, core competency focus, human resource management, cultural norms, and evaluation and reward systems – is more likely to be a source of organizational inertia than a proactive force for dynamic change. Prior experiences, business process reengineering, balancing and "mapping" strategic processes, and historic "formulas" for success increasingly become an impediment to the innovative strategic management required for dealing with a turbulent knowledge economy. Large incumbent firms in an industry, and those very successful in the past, are especially susceptible to becoming victims of traditional strategic management approaches.

Challenges faced by Conventional Strategic Management Wisdom

Four significant challenges to the conventional strategic management wisdom can be identified.

- The dramatic shift from visible assets and invisible customers to invisible assets and visible customers.
- The reality that vertical and horizontal organizations are being displaced by networks of intrafirm, extrafirm and interfirm relationships.
- Displacement of the focus on competition (and competitive "outperformance") to a focus on collaboration (and "unique performance" and sustainability).
- Descriptive and reactive traditional strategic management mindsets being forced to shift to creative, proactive strategic mindsets.

Towards invisible assets and visible customers

Until recently, the most important assets in production of new societal value (products, services) have been land and capital in the form of machinery, raw materials and cash. The financial statements of companies still mirror the value of these visible, tangible assets. In the field of strategic management, the focus has been on managing these visible assets in such a way that shareholder value, i.e. return on shareholders' funds, is maximized. In the global knowledge economy of today, it is tangible capital that is becoming pre-eminent for improved performance and organizational fitness in a turbulent environment.

By having superior intellectual resources, an organization can exploit and develop its traditional visible resources better and differently from those of competitors, even if some or all of those traditional resources are not unique. Therefore, knowledge can be considered the most important (invisible) strategic resource of any company today, and the ability to identify, acquire, integrate, store, share, apply and protect it, among other objectives, has significant implications for strategic management. The nature of visible assets, and their sources and performance measurements, are radically different from those of visible assets, and require completely different strategic management approaches and tools.

Concomitant with the above-mentioned shift, there is also a dramatic shift from invisible, group-segmented customers to visible, individualized customers. Developments in e.g., technology and knowledge diffusion are empowering both customers and organizations, with individual customer profiles, interactions and customized satisfaction now possible. Customers are increasingly being treated as individuals, not as objects belonging to a constructed segment or class of customer, which leads to closer connections and a richer diversity of innovate customer value propositions through formal arrangements, informal co-option techniques, monitoring techniques, and individualization/customization of products and services.

The change from customers as markets to customers as individuals represents a dramatic change from mass production to mass customization in an increasing number of industries. This shift means that conventional strategic management approaches and tools are significantly challenged – customers, industries and competitors are not just "out there" or given, and amenable to quantitative analysis, based on the ideal of objectivity. Focusing on individualization and co-evolution in the knowledge-networked economy calls for changing the philosophy, approaches and tools of strategic management.

Towards cross-boundary networks

Vertical and horizontal organizational structures are based on traditional thinking on how organizations allocate resources to achieve superiority and success. They display mechanistic, often one-directional "funnels" or "chains" of value-adding activities and relationships. A view of organizations as latent processes, influenced and activated on request by empowered customers and empowered human resources inside and outside the organization, fundamentally changes the strategic management perspective. As a consequence, we see that markets, functions and hierarchies are being supplanted by network structures of multi-dimensional nature, in other words, not only vertical and horizontal, but on multidimensional levels.

Increasingly diverse networks of intrafirm relationships (inside organizations), extrafirm relationships (inside the firm's value system of suppliers, distributors etc.), and interfirm relationships (with all relevant stakeholders in its ecosystem) are necessary. For example, customized production starts and ends with the customer, and the organization has to activate appropriate processes (inside and outside) rapidly in order to fulfill individual customer needs. The stable organizing element is not found in the structure of the organization, but in the structure of the evoked processes, and the traditional strategy-structure continuum becomes a meaningless relation as a dimension for determining the fit between an organization and the environment.

In effect, the tremendous shift to networking and nurturing relationships in the knowledge economy points firstly, to the necessity of a new strategic management mindset in which organizational structure is a variable, rather than a given or stable element. Traditional strategic management approaches are unable to cope with the need for flexible organizational designs, and redesigns, the need to respond to changes but also to inevitably stimulate changes. Secondly, assets are becoming part of the environment and aren't under sole company control or "ownership". In many industries today, companies can access the same assets, machinery, engineers, marketers, knowledge and capital, and it is becoming very difficult to develop unique assets as a competitive "weapon". Instead, there is an increased focus on the human capital of an organization as a firm-specific resource base. The difference between organizations can no longer be effected by strategies controlled by an ideal type of hierarchical machine, but rather by the uniqueness of how they organize customers and human capital, and how they continuously improve these relationships.

Towards collaboration

Competitive advantage, as displayed by all traditional strategic management approaches, reflects the underlying rationale of attempting to achieve an edge over rivals. A resource-based logic asserts that competitive advantage is the root of value creation, is sustainable, and can be achieved by exceptional scarce, valuable, inimitable and non-substitutable assets. More recently, the dynamic capabilities approach contends that sustained competitive advantage is impossible in situations of hyper-competition and high-velocity environmental changes. According to this theory, firms should be enabled to repeatedly form new, albeit temporary, competitive advantages based on asset combinations that differ from the existing pattern.

The purpose of the traditional approach is to be faster, better, cheaper or more special than the competition. In the global knowledge economy, the concept of competitive advantage is now being seen differently: the firm's potential relative to the overall processes and resources in business ecosystems and organizational networks, with a balancing of competitive advantage with collaborative co-evolution. A sustained competitive advantage is regarded as a misplaced objective, even a possibly self-defeating one, in a dynamic, nonlinear systems context. Thus, a firm's real "competitive advantage" is both its contributions to the ecosystem and systemic enterprise, and acting as an essential "attractor", shaping ecosystem patterns of behavior. The traditional focus on competition carries the inherent dangers of a myopic view of the existing "industry", "market" and "competitors".

In many industries, the shift to both competitive and collaborative activity is evident, especially in collaborative enterprise resource management (ERM) and supply chains. The automobile industry is one prominent example, with collaboration at the one end of the automobile industry "value chain", and intense competition at the other end (the customer end). In a global context, a focus on collaboration in geographical industry clusters, such as a country's wine industry, is becoming prominent. For example, the Australian wine industry competes with the Californian wine industry through increasing internal collaboration, as well as external value system collaboration. Even the fiercest of competitors often find themselves acting in consortia to create new opportunities – witness Kodak and Fuji in developing the advanced photo system, and GM and Toyota in the context of the Numi plant.

Towards creative & proactive strategic mindsets

Traditional strategic management approaches reflect a mindset to mirror the world in a descriptive sense – a complex and turbulent world "out there". This indicates a strategic imagination that identifies the patterns in the environment, labels the regularities that associate the images necessary to cut through and perceive the mass of data generated by analysis, and to utilize judgment and action based on experience. Roos and Victor[13] indicate that a descriptive imagination manifests itself in the perceived need to "see" five industry forces during a strategy-making process, and a range of diagnostic and forecasting techniques whereby the world is programmed, "mapped" and profiled. Value chains, 2-by-2 matrices, portfolio matrices, competitive "diamonds", and scorecards all belong to this mindset.

The major fallacy of the descriptive strategic mindset is a continuously expanding range of new descriptions, such as different industry analyses, different SWOT analyses, different competence analyses, different portfolio analyses, different scenario analyses, different value chain and scorecard mapping etc. All of these attempts are aimed at searching for a "perfect" strategy based on ever-increasing complex analyses, descriptions and alternative reaction scenarios. Both the prediction and learning approaches to strategic management focus on analytical activities and gathering of experience, which, like data and information, are arguably essential resources for strategy making. Authors such as Hamel as well as Roos and Victor, call for a new theory of strategic management that would enable the field to develop creative, proactive strategic mindsets.[14]

Are Traditional Strategic Management Approaches Irrelevant?

In closing, it should be emphasized that traditional strategic management approaches and tools are not entirely irrelevant or obsolete. There are situations in which prediction or learning approaches can be appropriate, but the key issue is that these approaches when used on their own are likely to be ineffective in a turbulent, knowledge-network economy. New forms of strategic management approaches that are proactive, collaborative and systemic are necessary to bridge the disruptions and discontinuities in the environment at the beginning of the 21st century. Acquiring a new strategic mindset, as a basis for understanding the nature and application of new strategic management approaches appropriate in the knowledge economy, is the theme of the next chapter.

Strategy and the Internet[*]

By Michael E. Porter

Many have argued that the Internet renders strategy obsolete. In reality, the opposite is true. Because the Internet tends to weaken industry profitability without providing proprietary operational advantages, it is more important than ever for companies to distinguish themselves through strategy. The winners will be those that view the Internet as a complement to, not a cannibal of, traditional ways of competing.

The Internet is an extremely important new technology, and it is no surprise that it has received so much attention from entrepreneurs, executives, investors, and business observers. Caught up in the general fervor, many have assumed that the Internet changes everything, rendering all the old rules about companies and competition obsolete. That may be a natural reaction, but it is a dangerous one. It has led many companies, dot-coms and incumbents alike, to make bad decisions – decisions that have eroded the attractiveness of their industries and undermined their own competitive advantages. Some companies, for example, have used Internet technology to shift the basis of competition away from quality, features, and service and toward price, making it harder for anyone in their industries to turn a profit. Others have forfeited important proprietary advantages by rushing into misguided partnerships and outsourcing relationships. Until recently, the negative effects of these actions have been obscured by distorted signals from the marketplace. Now, however, the consequences are becoming evident.

The time has come to take a clearer view of the Internet. We need to move away from the rhetoric about "Internet industries", "e-business strategies", and a "new economy" and see the Internet for what it is: an enabling technology – a powerful set of tools that can be used, wisely or unwisely, in almost any industry and as part of almost any strategy. We need to ask fundamental questions: Who will capture the economic benefits that the Internet creates? Will all the value end up going to customers, or will companies be able to reap a share of it? What will be the Internet's impact on industry structure? Will it expand or shrink the pool of profits? And what will be its impact on strategy? Will the Internet bolster or erode the ability of companies to gain sustainable advantages over their competitors?

---

[*] Taken with permission from Harvard Business Review, March 2001, pp. 63-78

In addressing these questions, much of what we find is unsettling. I believe that the experiences companies have had with the Internet thus far must be largely discounted and that many of the lessons learned must be forgotten. When seen with fresh eyes, it becomes clear that the Internet is not necessarily a blessing. It tends to alter industry structures in ways that dampen overall profitability, and it has a leveling effect on business practices, reducing the ability of any company to establish an operational advantage that can be sustained.

The key question is not whether to deploy Internet technology – companies have no choice if they want to stay competitive – but how to deploy it. Here, there is reason for optimism. Internet technology provides better opportunities for companies to establish distinctive strategic positionings than did previous generations of information technology. Gaining such a competitive advantage does not require a radically new approach to business. It requires building on the proven principles of effective strategy. The Internet per se will rarely be a competitive advantage. Many of the companies that succeed will be ones that use the Internet as a complement to traditional ways of competing, not those that set their Internet initiatives apart from their established operations. That is particularly good news for established companies, which are often in the best position to meld Internet and traditional approaches in ways that buttress existing advantages. But dot-coms can also be winners – if they understand the trade-offs between Internet and traditional approaches and can fashion truly distinctive strategies. Far from making strategy less important, as some have argued, the Internet actually makes strategy more essential than ever.

Distorted Market Signals

Companies that have deployed Internet technology have been confused by distorted market signals, often of their own creation. It is understandable, when confronted with a new business phenomenon, to look to marketplace outcomes for guidance. But in the early stages of the rollout of any important new technology, market signals can be unreliable. New technologies trigger rampant experimentation, by both companies and customers, and the experimentation is often economically unsustainable. As a result, market behavior is distorted and must be interpreted with caution.

That is certainly the case with the Internet. Consider the revenue side of the profit equation in industries in which Internet technology is widely used. Sales figures have been unreliable for three reasons. First, many companies have subsidized the purchase of their products and services in hopes of staking out a position on the Internet and attracting a base of customers. (Governments have also subsidized on-line shopping by exempting it from sales taxes.) Buyers have been able to purchase goods at heavy discounts, or even obtain them for free, rather than pay prices that reflect true costs. When prices are artificially low, trait demand becomes artificially high. Second, many buyers have been drawn to the Internet out of curiosity; they have been willing to conduct transactions on-line even when the benefits have been uncertain or limited. If Amazon.com offers an equal or lower price than a conventional bookstore and free or subsidized shipping, why not try it as an experiment? Sooner or later, though, some customers can be expected to return to more traditional modes of commerce, especially if subsidies end, making any assessment of customer loyalty based on conditions so far suspect. Finally, some "revenues" from on-line commerce have been received in the form of stock rather than cash. Much of the estimated $450 million in revenues that Amazon has recognized from its corporate partners, for example, has come as stock. The sustainability of such revenue is questionable, and its true value hinges on fluctuations in stock prices.

If revenue is an elusive concept on the Internet, cost is equally fuzzy. Many companies doing business on-line have enjoyed subsidized inputs. Their suppliers, eager to affiliate themselves with and learn from dot-com leaders, have provided products, services, and content at heavily discounted prices. Many content providers, for example, rushed to provide their information to Yahoo! for next to nothing in hopes of establishing a beachhead on one of the Internet's most visited sites. Some providers have even paid popular portals to distribute their content. Further masking true costs, many suppliers – not to mention employees – have agreed to accept equity, warrants, or stock options from Internet-related companies and ventures in payment for their services or products. Payment in equity does not appear on the income statement, but it is a real cost to shareholders. Such supplier practices have artificially depressed the costs of doing business on the Internet, making it appear more attractive than it really is. Finally, costs have been distorted by the systematic understatement of the need for capital. Company after company touted the low asset intensity of doing business on-line, only to find that inventory, warehouses, and other investments were necessary to provide value to customers.

Signals from the stock market have been even more unreliable. Responding to investor enthusiasm over the Internet's explosive growth, stock valuations became decoupled from business fundamentals. They no longer provided an accurate guide as to whether real economic value was being created. Any company that has made competitive decisions based on influencing near-term share price or responding to investor sentiments has put itself at risk.

Distorted revenues, costs, and share prices have been matched by the unreliability of the financial metrics that companies have adopted. The executives of companies conducting business over the Internet have, conveniently, downplayed traditional measures of profitability and economic value. Instead, they have emphasized expansive definitions of revenue, numbers of customers, or, even more suspect, measures that might someday correlate with revenue, such as numbers of unique users ("reach"), numbers of site visitors, or click-through rates. Creative accounting approaches have also multiplied. Indeed, the Internet has given rise to an array of new performance metrics that have only a loose relationship to economic value, such as pro forma measures of income that remove "nonrecurring" costs like acquisitions. The dubious connection between reported metrics and actual profitability has served only to amplify the confusing signals about what has been working in the marketplace. The fact that those metrics have been taken seriously by the stock market has muddied the waters even further. For all these reasons, the true financial performance of many Internet-related businesses is even worse than has been stated.

One might argue that the simple proliferation of dot-coms is a sign of the economic value of the Internet. Such a conclusion is premature at best. Dot-coms multiplied so rapidly for one major reason: they were able to raise capital without having to demonstrate viability. Rather than signaling a healthy business environment, the sheer number of dot-coms in many industries often revealed nothing more than the existence of low barriers to entry, always a danger sign.

A Return to Fundamentals

It is hard to come to any firm understanding of the impact of the Internet on business by looking at the results to date. But two broad conclusions can be drawn. First, many businesses active on the Internet are artificial businesses competing by artificial means and propped up by capital that until recently had been readily available. Second, in periods of transition such as the one we have been going through, it often appears as if there are new rules of competition. But as market forces play out, as they are now, the old rules regain their currency. The creation of true economic value once again becomes the final arbiter of business success.

Economic value for a company is nothing more than the gap between price and cost, and it is reliably measured only by sustained profitability. To generate revenues, reduce expenses, or simply do something useful by deploying Internet technology is not sufficient evidence that value has been created. Nor is a company's current stock price necessarily an indicator of economic value. Shareholder value is a reliable measure of economic value only over the long run.

Internet technology provides better opportunities for companies to establish distinctive strategic positionings than did previous generations of information technology.

In thinking about economic value, it is useful to draw a distinction between the uses of the Internet (such as operating digital marketplaces, selling toys, or trading securities) and Internet technologies (such as site-customization tools or real-time communications services), which can be deployed across many uses. Many have pointed to the success of technology providers as evidence of the Internet's economic value. But this thinking is faulty. It is the uses of the Internet that ultimately create economic value. Technology providers can prosper for a time irrespective of whether the uses of the Internet are profitable. In periods of heavy experimentation, even sellers of flawed technologies can thrive. But unless the uses generate sustainable revenues or savings in excess of their cost of deployment, the opportunity for technology providers will shrivel as companies realize that further investment is economically unsound.

So how can the Internet be used to create economic value? To find the answer, we need to look beyond the immediate market signals to the two fundamental factors that determine profitability:

- *industry structure,* which determines the profitability of the average competitor; and

- *sustainable competitive advantage,* which allows a company to outperform the average competitor.

These two underlying drivers of profitability are universal; they transcend any technology or type of business. At the same time, they vary widely by industry and company. The broad, supra-industry classifications so common in Internet parlance, such as business-to-consumer (or "B2C") and business-to-business (or "B2B") prove meaningless with respect to profitability. Potential profitability can be understood only by looking at individual industries and individual companies.

The Internet and Industry Structure

The Internet has created some new industries, such as on-line auctions and digital marketplaces. However, its greatest impact has been to enable the reconfiguration of existing industries that had been constrained by high costs for communicating, gathering information, or accomplishing transactions. Distance learning, for example, has existed for decades, with about one million students enrolling in correspondence courses every year. The Internet has the potential to greatly expand distance learning, but it did not create the industry. Similarly, the Internet provides an efficient means to order products, but catalog retailers with toll-free numbers and automated fulfillment centers have been around for decades. The Internet only changes the front end of the process.

Whether an industry is new or old, its structural attractiveness is determined by five underlying forces of competition: the intensity of rivalry among existing competitors, the barriers to entry for new competitors, the threat of substitute products or services, the bargaining power of suppliers, and the bargaining power of buyers. In combination, these forces determine how the economic value created by any product, service, technology, or way of competing is divided between, on the one hand, companies in an industry and, on the other, customers, suppliers, distributors, substitutes, and potential new entrants. Although some have argued that today's rapid pace of technological change makes industry analysis less valuable, the opposite is true. Analyzing the forces illuminates an industry's fundamental attractiveness, exposes the underlying drivers of average industry profitability, and provides insight into how profitability will evolve in the future. The five competitive forces still determine profitability even if suppliers, channels, substitutes, or competitors change.

Because the strength of each of the five forces varies considerably from industry to industry, it would be a mistake to draw general conclusions about the impact of the Internet on long-term industry profitability; each industry is affected in different ways. Nevertheless, an examination of a wide range of industries in which the Internet is playing a role reveals some clear trends, as summarized in the exhibit "How the Internet Influences Industry Structure". Some of the trends are positive. For example, the Internet tends to dampen the bargaining power of channels by providing companies with new, more direct avenues to customers. The Internet can also boost an industry's efficiency in various ways, expanding the overall size of the market by improving its position relative to traditional substitutes.

But most of the trends are negative. Internet technology provides buyers with easier access to information about products and suppliers, thus bolstering buyer bargaining power. The Internet mitigates the need for such things as an established sales force or access to existing channels, reducing barriers to entry. By enabling new approaches to meeting needs and performing functions, it creates new substitutes. Because it is an open system, companies have more difficulty maintaining proprietary offerings, thus intensifying the rivalry among competitors. The use of the Internet also tends to expand the geographic market, bringing many more companies into competition with one another. And Internet technologies tend to reduce variable costs and tilt cost structures toward fixed cost, creating significantly greater pressure for companies to engage in destructive price competition.

While deploying the Internet can expand the market, then, doing so often comes at the expense of average profitability. The great paradox of the Internet is that its very benefits-making information widely available; reducing the difficulty of purchasing, marketing, and distribution; allowing buyers and sellers to fred and transact business with one another more easily – also make it more difficult for companies to capture those benefits as profits.

We can see this dynamic at work in automobile retailing. The Internet allows customers to gather extensive information about products easily, from detailed specifications and repair records to wholesale prices for new cars and average values for used cars. Customers can also choose among many more options from which to buy, not just local dealers but also various types of Internet referral networks (such as Autoweb and AutoVantage) and on-line direct dealers (such as Autobytel.com, AutoNation, and CarsDirect.com). Because the Internet reduces the importance of location, at least for the initial sale, it widens the geographic market from local to regional or national. Virtually every dealer or dealer group becomes a potential competitor in the market. It is more difficult, moreover, for on-line dealers to differentiate themselves, as they lack potential points of distinction such as showrooms, personal selling, and service departments. With more competitors selling largely undifferentiated products, the basis for competition shifts ever more toward price. Clearly, the net effect on the industry's structure is negative.

That does not mean that every industry in which Internet technology is being applied will be unattractive. For a contrasting example, look at Internet auctions. Here, customers and suppliers are fragmented and thus have little power. Substitutes, such as classified ads and flea markets, have less reach and are less convenient to use. And though the barriers to entry are relatively modest, Companies can build economies of scale, both in infrastructure and, even more important, in the aggregation of many buyers and sellers, that deter new competitors or place them at a disadvantage. Finally, rivalry in this industry has been defined, largely by eBay, the dominant competitor, in terms of providing an easy-to-use marketplace in which revenue comes from listing and sales fees, while customers pay the cost of shipping. When Amazon and other rivals entered the business, offering free auctions, eBay maintained its prices and

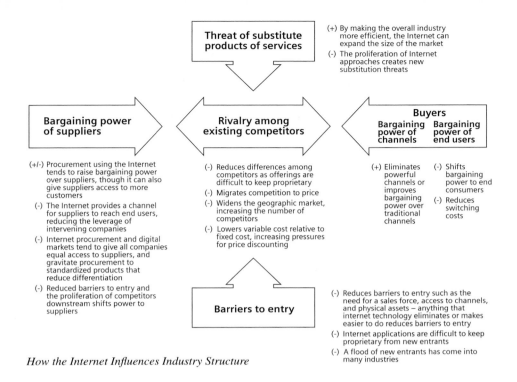

How the Internet Influences Industry Structure

pursued other ways to attract and retain customers. As a result, the destructive price competition characteristic of other on-line businesses has been avoided.

EBay's role in the auction business provides an important lesson: industry structure is not fixed but rather is shaped to a considerable degree by the choices made by competitors. EBay has acted in ways that strengthen the profitability of its industry. In stark contrast, Buy.com, a prominent Internet retailer, acted in ways that undermined its industry, not to mention its own potential for competitive advantage. Buy.com achieved $100 million in sales faster than any company in history, but it did so by defining competition solely on price. It sold products not only below full cost but at or below cost of goods sold, with the vain hope that it would make money in other ways. The company had no plan for being the low-cost provider; instead, it invested heavily in brand advertising and eschewed potential sources of differentiation by outsourcing all fulfillment and offering the bare minimum of customer service. It also gave up the opportunity to set itself apart from competitors by choosing not to focus on selling particular goods; it moved quickly beyond electronics, its initial category, into numerous other product categories in which it had no unique offering. Although the company has been trying desperately to reposition itself, its early moves have proven extremely difficult to reverse.

The Myth of the First Mover

Given the negative implications of the Internet for profitability, why was there such optimism, even euphoria, surrounding its adoption? One reason is that everyone tended to focus on what the Internet could do and how quickly its use was expanding rather than on how it was affecting industry structure. But the optimism can also be traced to a widespread belief that the Internet would unleash forces that would enhance industry profitability. Most notable was the general assumption that the deployment of the Internet would increase switching costs and create strong network effects, which would provide first movers with competitive advantages and robust profitability. First movers would reinforce these advantages by quickly establishing strong new-economy brands. The result would be an attractive industry for the victors. This thinking does not, however, hold up to close examination.

Consider switching costs. Switching costs encompass all the costs incurred by a customer in changing to a new supplier – everything from hashing out a new contract to reentering data to learning how to use a different product or service. As switching costs go up, customers' bargaining power falls and the barriers to entry into an industry rise. While switching costs are nothing new, some observers argued that the Internet would raise them substantially. A buyer would grow familiar with one company's user interface and would not want to bear the cost of finding, registering with, and learning to use a competitor's site, or, in the case of industrial customers, integrating a competitor's systems with its own. Moreover, since Internet commerce allows a company to accumulate knowledge of customers' buying behavior, the company would be able to provide more tailored offerings, better service, and greater purchasing convenience – all of which buyers would be loath to forfeit. When people talk about the "stickiness" of Web sites, what they are often talking about is high switching costs.

Another myth that has generated unfounded enthusiasm for the Internet is that partnering is a win-win means to improve industry economics.

In reality, though, switching costs are likely to be lower, not higher, on the Internet than they are for traditional ways of doing business, including approaches using earlier generations of information systems such as EDI. On the Internet, buyers can often switch suppliers with just a few mouse clicks, and new Web technologies are systematically reducing switching costs even further. For example, companies like PayPal provide settlement services or Internet currency – so-called e-wallets – that enable customers to shop at different sites without having to enter personal information and credit card numbers. Content-consolidation tools such as OnePage allow users to avoid having to go back to sites over and over to retrieve information by enabling them to build customized Web pages that draw needed information dynamically from many sites. And the widespread adoption of XML standards will free companies from the need to reconfigure proprietary ordering systems and to create new procurement and logistical protocols when changing suppliers.

What about network effects, through which products or services become more valuable as more customers use them? A number of important Internet applications display network effects, including e-mail, instant messaging, auctions, and on-line message boards or chat rooms. Where such effects are significant, they can create demand-side economies of scale and raise barriers to entry. This, it has been widely argued, sets off a winner-take-all competition, leading to the eventual dominance of one or two companies.

But it is not enough for network effects to be present; to provide barriers to entry they also have to be proprietary to one company. The openness of the Internet, with its common standards and protocols and its ease of navigation, makes it difficult for a single company to capture the benefits of a network effect. (America Online, which has managed to maintain borders around its on-line community, is an exception, not the rule.) And even if a company is lucky enough to control a network effect, the effect often reaches a point of diminishing returns once there is a critical mass of customers. Moreover, network effects are subject to a self-limiting mechanism. A particular product or service first attracts the customers whose needs it best meets. As penetration grows, however, it will tend to become less effective in meeting the needs of the remaining customers in the market, providing an opening for competitors with different offerings. Finally, creating a network effect requires a large investment that may offset future benefits. The network effect is, in many respects, akin to the experience curve, which was also supposed to lead to market-share dominance – through cost advantages, in that case. The experience curve was an oversimplification, and the single-minded pursuit of experience curve advantages proved disastrous in many industries.

Internet brands have also proven difficult to build, perhaps because the lack of physical presence and direct human contact makes virtual businesses less tangible to customers than traditional businesses. Despite huge outlays on advertising, product discounts, and purchasing incentives, most dot-corn brands have not approached the power of established brands, achieving only a modest impact on loyalty and barriers to entry.

Another myth that has generated unfounded enthusiasm for the Internet is that partnering is a win-win means to improve industry economics. While partnering is a well-established strategy, the use of Internet technology has made it much more widespread. Partnering takes two forms. The first involves complements: products that are used in tandem with another industry's product. Computer software, for example, is a complement to computer hardware. In Internet commerce, complements have proliferated as companies have sought to offer broader arrays of products, services, and information. Partnering to assemble complements, often with companies who are also competitors, has been seen as a way to speed industry growth and move away from narrow-minded, destructive competition.

But this approach reveals an incomplete understanding of the role of complements in competition. Complements are frequently important to an industry's growth-spreadsheet applications, for example, accelerated the expansion of the personal computer industry – but they have no direct relationship to industry profitability. While a close substitute reduces potential profitability, for example, a close complement can exert either a positive or a negative influence. Complements affect industry profitability indirectly through their influence on the five competitive forces. If a complement raises switching costs for the combined product offering, it can raise profitability. But if a complement works to standardize the industry's product offering, as Microsoft's operating system has done in personal computers, it will increase rivalry and depress profitability.

With the Internet, widespread partnering with producers of complements is just as likely to exacerbate an industry's structural problems as mitigate them. As partnerships proliferate, companies tend to become more alike, which heats up rivalry. Instead of focusing on their own strategic goals, moreover, companies are forced to balance the many potentially conflicting objectives of their partners while also educating them about the business. Rivalry often becomes more unstable, and since producers of complements can be potential competitors, the threat of entry increases.

Another common form of partnering is outsourcing. Internet technologies have made it easier for companies to coordinate with their suppliers, giving widespread currency to the notion of the "virtual enterprise" – a business created largely out of purchased products, components, and services. While extensive outsourcing can reduce near-term costs and improve flexibility, it has a dark side when it comes to industry structure. As competitors turn to the same vendors, purchased inputs become more homogeneous, eroding company distinctiveness and increasing price competition. Outsourcing also usually lowers barriers to entry because a new entrant need only assemble purchased inputs rather than build its own capabilities. In addition, companies lose control over important elements of their business, and crucial experience in components, assembly, or services shifts to suppliers, enhancing their power in the long run.

The Future of Internet Competition

While each industry will evolve in unique ways, an examination of the forces influencing industry structure indicates that the deployment of Internet technology will likely continue to put pressure on the profitability of many industries. Consider the intensity of competition, for example. Many dot-coms are going out of business, which would seem to indicate that consolidation will take place and rivalry will be reduced. But while some consolidation among new players is inevitable, many established companies are now more familiar with Internet technology and are rapidly deploying on-line applications. With a combination of new and old companies and generally lower entry barriers, most industries will likely end up with a net increase in the number of competitors and fiercer rivalry than before the advent of the Internet.

The power of customers will also tend to rise. As buyers' initial curiosity with the Web wanes and subsidies end, companies offering products or services on-line will be forced to demonstrate that they provide real benefits. Already, customers appear to be losing interest in services like Priceline.com's reverse auctions because the savings they provide are often outweighed by the hassles involved. As customers become more familiar with the technology, their loyalty to their initial suppliers will also decline; they will realize that the cost of switching is low.

A similar shift will affect advertising-based strategies. Even now, advertisers are becoming more discriminating, and the rate of growth of Web advertising is slowing. Advertisers can be expected to continue to exercise their bargaining power to push down rates significantly, aided and abetted by new brokers of Internet advertising.

Not ail the news is bad. Some technological advances will provide opportunities to enhance profitability. Improvements in streaming video and greater availability of low-cost bandwidth, for example, will make it easier for customer service representatives, or other company personnel, to speak directly to customers through their computers. Internet sellers will be able to better differentiate themselves and shift buyers' focus away from price. And services such as automatic bill paying by banks may modestly boost switching costs. In general, however, new Internet technologies will continue to erode profitability by shifting power to customers.

To understand the importance of thinking through the longer-term structural consequences of the Internet, consider the business of digital marketplaces. Such marketplaces automate corporate procurement by linking many buyers and suppliers electronically. The benefits to buyers include low transaction costs, easier access to price and product information, convenient purchase of associated services, and, sometimes, the ability to pool volume. The benefits to suppliers include lower selling costs, lower transaction costs, access to wider markets, and the avoidance of powerful channels.

From an industry structure standpoint, the attractiveness of digital marketplaces varies depending on the products involved. The most important determinant of a marketplace's profit potential is the intrinsic power of the buyers and sellers in the particular product area. If either side is concentrated or possesses differentiated products, it will gain bargaining power over the marketplace and capture most of the value generated. If buyers and sellers are fragmented, however, their bargaining power will be weak, and the marketplace will have a much better chance of being profitable. Another important determinant of industry structure is the threat of substitution. If it is relatively easy for buyers and sellers to transact business directly with one another, or to set up their own dedicated markets, independent marketplaces will be unlikely to sustain high levels of profit. Finally, the ability to create barriers to entry is critical. Today, with dozens of marketplaces competing in some industries and with buyers and sellers dividing their purchases or operating their own markets to prevent any one marketplace from gaining power, it is clear that modest entry barriers are a real challenge to profitability.

Competition among digital marketplaces is in transition, and industry structure is evolving. Much of the economic value created by marketplaces derives from the standards they establish, both in the underlying technology platform and in the protocols for connecting and exchanging information. But once these standards are put in place, the added value of the marketplace may be limited. Anything buyers or suppliers provide to a marketplace, such as information on order specifications or inventory availability, can be readily provided on their own proprietary sites. Suppliers and customers can begin to deal directly on-line without the need for an intermediary. And new technologies will undoubtedly make it easier for parties to search for and exchange goods and information with one another.

In some product areas, marketplaces should enjoy ongoing advantages and attractive profitability. In fragmented industries such as real estate and furniture, for example, they could prosper. And new kinds of value-added services may arise that only an independent marketplace could provide. But in many product areas, marketplaces may be superceded by direct dealing or by the unbundling of purchasing, information, financing, and logistical services; in other areas, they may be taken over by participants or industry associations as cost centers. In such cases, marketplaces will provide a valuable "public good" to participants but will not themselves be likely to reap any enduring benefits. Over the long haul, moreover, we may well see many buyers back away from open marketplaces. They may once again focus on building close, proprietary relationships with fewer suppliers, using Internet technologies to gain efficiency improvements in various aspects of those relationships.

The Internet and Competitive Advantage

If average profitability is under pressure in many industries influenced by the Internet, it becomes all the more important for individual companies to set themselves apart from the pack – to be more profitable than the average performer. The only way to do so is by achieving a sustainable competitive advantage – by operating at a lower cost, by commanding a premium price, or by doing both. Cost and price advantages can be achieved in two ways. One is operational effectiveness – doing the same things your competitors do but doing them better. Operational effectiveness advantages can take myriad forms, including better technologies, superior inputs, better-trained people, or a more effective management structure. The other way to achieve advantage is strategic positioning – doing things differently from competitors, in a way that delivers a unique type of value to customers. This can mean offering a different set of features, a different array of services, or different logistical arrangements. The Internet affects operational effectiveness and strategic positioning in very different ways. It makes it harder for companies to sustain operational advantages, but it opens new opportunities for achieving or strengthening a distinctive strategic positioning.

Operational Effectiveness

The Internet is arguably the most powerful tool available today for enhancing operational effectiveness. By easing and speeding the exchange of real-time information, it enables improvements throughout the entire value chain, across almost every company and industry. And because it is an open platform with common standards, companies can often tap into its benefits with much less investment than was required to capitalize on past generations of information technology.

But simply improving operational effectiveness does not provide a competitive advantage. Companies only gain advantages if they are able to achieve and sustain higher levels of operational effectiveness than competitors. That is an exceedingly difficult proposition even in the best of circumstances. Once a company establishes a new best practice, its rivals tend to copy it quickly. Best practice competition eventually leads to

The Six Principles of Strategic Positioning

To establish and maintain a distinctive strategic positioning, a company needs to follow six fundamental principles.

First, it must start with the *right goal:* superior long-term return on investment. Only by grounding strategy in sustained profitability will real economic value be generated. Economic value is created when customers are willing to pay a price for a product or service that exceeds the cost of producing it. When goals are defined in terms of volume or market share leadership, with profits assumed to follow, poor strategies often result. The same is true when strategies are set to respond to the perceived desires of investors.

Second, a company's strategy must enable it to deliver a *value proposition,* or set of benefits, different from those that competitors offer. Strategy, then, is neither a quest for the universally best way of competing nor an effort to be all things to every customer. It defines a way of competing that delivers unique value in a particular set of uses or for a particular set of customers.

Third, strategy needs to be reflected in a *distinctive value chain.* To establish a sustainable competitive advantage, a company must perform different activities than rivals or perform similar activities in different ways. A company must configure the way it conducts manufacturing, logistics, service delivery, marketing, human resource management, and so on differently from rivals and tailored to its unique value proposition. If a company focuses on adopting best practices, it will end up performing most activities similarly to competitors, making it hard to gain an advantage.

Fourth, robust strategies involve *trade-offs.* A company must abandon or forgo some product features, services, or activities in order to be unique at others. Such trade-offs, in the product and in the value chain, are what make a company truly distinctive. When improvements in the product or in the value chain do not require trade-offs, they often become new best practices that are imitated because competitors can do so with no sacrifice to their existing ways of competing. Trying to be all things to all customers almost guarantees that a company will lack any advantage.

Fifth, strategy defines how all the elements of what a company does *fit* together. A strategy involves making choices throughout the value chain that are interdependent; all a company's activities must be mutually reinforcing. A company's product design, for example, should reinforce its approach to the manufacturing process, and both should leverage the way it conducts after-sales service. Fit not only increases competitive advantage but also makes a strategy harder to imitate. Rivals can copy one activity or product feature fairly easily, but will have much more difficulty duplicating a whole system of competing. Without fit, discrete improvements in manufacturing, marketing, or distribution are quickly matched.

Finally, strategy involves *continuity* of direction. A company must define a distinctive value proposition that it will stand for, even if that means forgoing certain opportunities. Without continuity of direction, it is difficult for companies to develop unique skills and assets or build strong reputations with customers. Frequent corporate "reinvention", then, is usually a sign of poor strategic thinking and a route to mediocrity. Continuous improvement is a necessity, but it must always be guided by a strategic direction.

For a fuller description, see M.E. Porter, "What Is Strategy?"
(HBR November-December 1996).

competitive convergence, with many companies doing the same things in the same ways. Customers end up malting decisions based on price, undermining industry profitability.

The nature of Internet applications makes it more difficult to sustain operational advantages than ever. In previous generations of information technology, application development was often complex, arduous, time consuming, and hugely expensive. These traits made it harder to gain an IT advantage, but they also made it difficult for competitors to imitate information systems. The openness of the Internet, combined with advances in software architecture, development tools, and modularity, makes it much easier for companies to design and implement applications. The drugstore chain CVS, for example, was able to roll out a complex Internet-based procurement application in just 60 days. As the fixed costs of developing systems decline, the barriers to imitation fall as well.

Today, nearly every company is developing similar types of Internet applications, often drawing on generic packages offered by third-party developers. The resulting improvements in operational effectiveness will be broadly shared, as companies converge on the same applications with the same benefits. Very rarely will individual companies be able to gain durable advantages from the deployment of "best-of-breed" applications.

Strategic Positioning

As it becomes harder to sustain operational advantages, strategic positioning becomes all the more important. If a company cannot be more operationally effective than its rivals, the only way to generate higher levels of economic value is to gain a cost advantage or price premium by competing in a distinctive way. Ironically, companies today define competition involving the Internet almost entirely in terms of operational effectiveness. Believing that no sustainable advantages exist, they seek speed and agility, hoping to stay one step ahead of the competition. Of course, such an approach to competition becomes a self-fulfilling prophecy. Without a distinctive strategic direction, speed and flexibility lead nowhere. Either no unique competitive advantages are created, or improvements are generic and cannot be sustained.

Having a strategy is a matter of discipline. It requires a strong focus on profitability rather than just growth, an ability to define a unique value proposition, and a willingness to make tough trade-offs in choosing what not to do. A company must stay the course, even during times of upheaval, while constantly improving and extending its distinctive positioning. Strategy goes far beyond the pursuit of best practices. It involves the configuration of a tailored value chain – the series of activities required to produce and deliver a product or service – that enables a company to offer unique value. To be defensible, moreover, the value chain must be highly integrated. When a company's activities fit together as a self-reinforcing system, any competitor wishing to imitate a strategy must replicate the whole system rather than copy just one or two discrete product features or ways of performing particular activities. (See the sidebar "The Six Principles of Strategic Positioning".)

The Absence of Strategy

Many of the pioneers of Internet business, both dot-coms and established companies, have competed in ways that violate nearly every precept of good strategy. Rather than focus on profits, they have sought to maximize revenue and market share at all costs, pursuing customers indiscriminately through discounting, giveaways, promotions, channel incentives, and heavy advertising. Rather than concentrate on delivering real value that earns an attractive price from customers, they have pursued indirect revenues from sources such as advertising and click-through fees from Internet commerce partners. Rather than make trade-offs, they have rushed to offer every conceivable product, service, or type of information. Rather than tailor the value chain in a unique way, they have aped the activities of rivals. Rather than build and maintain control over proprietary assets and marketing channels, they have entered into a rash of partnerships and outsourcing relationships, further eroding their own distinctiveness. While it is true that some companies have avoided these mistakes, they are exceptions to the rule.

By ignoring strategy, many companies have undermined the structure of their industries, hastened competitive convergence, and reduced the likelihood that they or anyone else will gain a competitive advantage. A destructive, zero-sum form of competition has been set in motion that confuses the acquisition of customers with the building of profitability. Worse yet, price has been defined as the primary if not the sole competitive variable. Instead of emphasizing the Internet's ability to support convenience, service; specialization, customization, and other forms of value that justify attractive prices, companies have turned competition into a race to the bottom. Once competition is defined this way, it is very difficult to turn back. (See the sidebar "Words for the Unwise: The Internet's Destructive Lexicon")

Even well-established, well-run companies have been thrown off track by the Internet. Forgetting what they stand for or what makes them unique, they have rushed to implement hot Internet applications and copy the offerings of dot-coms. Industry leaders have compromised their existing competitive advantages by entering market segments to which they bring little that is distinctive. Merrill Lynch's move to imitate the low-cost on-line offerings of its trading rivals, for example, risks undermining its most precious advantage – its skilled brokers. And many established companies, reacting to misguided investor enthusiasm, have hastily cobbled together Internet units in a mostly futile effort to boost their value in the stock market.

It did not have to be this way – and it does not have to be in the future. When it comes to reinforcing a distinctive strategy, tailoring activities, and enhancing fit, the Internet actually provides a better technological platform than previous generations of IT. Indeed, IT worked against strategy in the past. Packaged software applications were hard to customize, and companies were often forced to change the way they conducted activities in order to conform to the "best practices" embedded in the software. It was also extremely difficult to connect discrete applications to one another. Enterprise resource planning (ERP) systems linked activities, but again companies were forced to adapt their ways of doing things to the software. As a result, IT has been a force for standardizing activities and speeding competitive convergence.

Internet architecture, together with other improvements in software architecture and development tools, has turned IT into a far more powerful tool for strategy. It is much easier to customize packaged Internet applications to a company's unique strategic positioning. By providing a common IT delivery platform across the value chain, Internet architecture and standards also make it possible to build truly integrated and customized systems that reinforce the fit among activities. (See the sidebar "The Internet and the Value Chain.")

To gain these advantages, however, companies need to stop their rush to adopt generic, "out of the box" packaged applications and instead tailor their deployment of Internet technology to their particular strategies. Although it remains more difficult to customize packaged applications, the very difficulty of the task contributes to the sustainability of the resulting competitive advantage.

The Internet as Complement

To capitalize on the Internet's strategic potential, executives and entrepreneurs alike will need to change their points of view. It has been widely assumed that the Internet is cannibalistic, that it will replace all conventional ways of doing business and over-turn all traditional advantages, That is a vast exaggeration. There is no doubt that real trade-offs can exist between Internet and traditional activities. In the record industry, for example, on-line music distribution may reduce the need for CD-manufacturing assets. Overall, however, the trade-offs are modest in most industries. While the Internet will replace certain elements of industry value chains, the complete cannibal-ization of the value chain will be exceedingly rare. Even in the music business, many traditional activities – such as finding and promoting talented new artists, producing and recording music, and securing airplay – will continue to be highly important.

The risk of channel conflict also appears to have been overstated. As on-line sales have become more common, traditional channels that were initially skeptical of the Internet have embraced it. Far from always cannibalizing those channels, Internet technology can expand opportunities for many of them. The threat of disintermedia-tion of channels appears considerably lower than initially predicted.

Frequently, in fact, Internet applications address activities that, while necessary, are not decisive in competition, such as informing customers, processing transactions, and procuring inputs. Critical corporate assets-skilled personnel, proprietary product tech-nology, efficient logistical systems – remain intact, and they are often strong enough to preserve existing competitive advantages.

In many cases, the Internet Complements, rather than cannibalizes, companies' tradi-tional activities and ways of competing. Consider Walgreens, the most successful pharmacy chain in the United States. Walgreens introduced a Web Site that provides customers with extensive information and allows them to order prescriptions on-line. Far from cannibalizing the company's stores, the Web site has underscored their value. Fully 90% of customers who place orders over the Web prefer to pick up their prescriptions at a nearby store rather than have them shipped to their homes. Wal-

Words for the Unwise:
The Internet's Destructive Lexicon

The misguided approach to competition that characterizes business on the Internet has even been embedded in the language used to discuss it. Instead of talking in terms of strategy and competitive advantage, dot-coms and other Internet players talk about "business models". This seemingly innocuous shift in terminology speaks volumes. The definition ora business model is murky at best. Most often, it seems to refer to a loose conception of how a company does business and generates revenue. Yet simply having a business model is an exceedingly low bar to set for building a company. Generating revenue is a far cry from creating economic value, and no business model can be evaluated independently of industry structure. The business model approach to management becomes an invitation for faulty thinking and self-delusion.

Other words in the Internet lexicon also have unfortunate consequences. The terms "e-business" and "e-strategy" have been particularly problematic. By encouraging managers to view their Internet operations in isolation from the rest of the business, they can lead to simplistic approaches to competing using the Internet and increase the pressure for competitive imitation. Established companies fail to integrate the Internet into their proven strategies and thus never harness their most important advantages.

greens has found that its extensive network of stores remains a potent advantage, even as some ordering shifts to the Internet.

Another good example is W.W. Grainger, a distributor of maintenance products and spare parts to companies. A middleman with stocking locations all over the United States, Grainger would seem to be a textbook case of an old-economy company set to be made obsolete by the Internet. But Grainger rejected the assumption that the Internet would undermine its strategy. Instead, it tightly coordinated its aggressive on-line efforts with its traditional business. The results so far are revealing. Customers who purchase on-line also continue to purchase through other means – Grainger estimates a 9% incremental growth in sales for customers who use the on-line channel above the normalized sales of customers who use only traditional means. Grainger, like Walgreens, has also found that Web ordering increases the value of its physical locations. Like the buyers of prescription drugs, the buyers of industrial supplies often need their orders immediately. It is faster and cheaper for them to pick up supplies at a local Grainger outlet than to wait for delivery. Tightly integrating the site and stocking locations not only increases the overall value to customers, it reduces Grainger's costs as well. It is inherently more efficient to take and process orders over the Web than to use traditional methods, but more efficient to make bulk deliveries to a local stocking location than to ship individual orders from a central warehouse.

Grainger has also found that its printed catalog bolsters its on-line operation. Many companies' first instinct is to eliminate printed catalogs once their content is replicated on-line. But Grainger continues to publish its catalog, and it has found that each time a new one is distributed, on-line orders surge. The catalog has proven to be a

The Internet and the Value Chain

The basic tool for understanding the influence of information technology on companies is the value chain – the set of activities through which a product or service is created and delivered to customers. When a company competes in any industry, it performs a number of discrete but interconnected value-creating activities, such as operating a sales force, fabricating a component, or delivering products, and these activities have points of connection with the activities of suppliers, channels, and customers. The value chain is a framework for identifying all these activities and analyzing how they affect both a company's costs and the value delivered to buyers.

Because every activity involves the creation, processing, and communication of information, information technology has a pervasive influence on the value chain. The special advantage of the Internet is the ability to link one activity with others and make real-time data created in one activity widely available, both within the company and with outside suppliers, channels, and customers. By incorporating a common, open set of communication protocols, Internet technology provides a standardized infrastructure, an intuitive browser interface for information access and delivery, bidirectional communication, and ease of connectivity – all at much lower cost than private networks and electronic data interchange, or EDI.

Many of the most prominent applications of the Internet in the value chain are shown in the figure at right. Some involve moving physical activities on-line, while others involve making physical activities more cost effective.

But for all its power, the Internet does not represent a break from the past; rather, it is the latest stage in the ongoing evolution of information technology.[1] Indeed, the technological possibilities available today derive not just from the Internet architecture but also from complementary technological advances such as scanning, object-oriented programming, relational databases, and wireless communications.

To see how these technological improvements will ultimately affect the value chain, some historical perspective is illuminating.[2] The evolution of information technology in business can be thought of in terms of five overlapping stages, each of which evolved out of constraints presented by the previous generation. The earliest IT systems automated discrete transactions such as order entry and accounting. The next stage involved the fuller automation and functional enhancement of individual activities such as human resource management, sales force operations, and product design. The third stage, which is being accelerated by the Internet, involves cross-activity integration, such as linking sales activities with order processing. Multiple activities are being linked together through such tools as customer relationship management (CRM), supply chain management (SCM), and enterprise resource planning (ERP) systems. The fourth stage, which is just beginning, enables the integration of the value chain and entire value system, that is, the set of value chains in an entire industry, encompassing those of tiers of suppliers, channels, and customers. SCM and CRM are starting to merge, as end-to-end applications involving customers, channels, and suppliers link orders to, for example, manufacturing, procurement, and service delivery. Soon to be integrated is product development, which has been largely separate. Complex product models will be exchanged among parties, and Internet procurement will move from standard commodities to engineered items.

In the upcoming fifth stage, information technology will be used not only to connect the various activities and players in the value system but to optimize its workings in real time. Choices will be made based on information from multiple activities and corporate entities. Production decisions, for example, will automatically factor in the capacity available at multiple facilities and the inventory available at multiple suppliers. While early fifth-stage applications will involve relatively simple optimization of sourcing, production, logistical, and servicing transactions, the deeper levels of optimization will involve the product design itself. For example, product design will be optimized and customized based on input not only from factories and suppliers but also from customers.

The power of the Internet in the value chain, however, must be kept in perspective. While Internet applications have an important influence on the cost and quality of activities, they are neither the only nor the dominant influence. Conventional factors such as scale, the skills of personnel, product and process technology, and investments in physical assets also play prominent roles. The Internet is transformational in some respects, but ma ny traditional sources of competitive advantage remain intact.

[1] See M.E. Porter and V.E. Millar, "How Information Gives You Competitive Advantage", (HBR July-August 1985) for a framework that helps put the Internet's current influence in context.

[2] This discussion is drawn from the author's research with Peter Bligh.

Firm Infrastructure
- Web-based, distributed financial and ERP systems
- On-line investor relations (e.g., information dissemination, broadcast conference calls)

Human Resource Management
- Self-service personnel and benefits administration
- Web-based training
- Internet-based sharing and dissemination of company information
- Electronic time and expense reporting

Technology Development
- Collaborative product design across locations and among multiple value-system participants
- Knowledge directories accessible from all parts of the organization
- Real-time access by R&D to on-line sales and service information

Procurement
- Internet-enabled demand planning; real-time available-to-promise/capable-to-promise and fulfillment
- Other linkage of purchase, inventory, and forecasting systems with suppliers
- Automated "requisition to pay"
- Direct and indirect procurement via marketplaces, exchanges, auctions, and buyer-seller matching

Inbound Logistics	Operations	Outbound Logistics	Marketing and Sales	After-Sales Service
• Real-time integrated scheduling, shipping, warehouse management, demand management and planning, and advanced planning and scheduling across the company and its suppliers • Dissemination throughout the company of real-time inbound and in-progress inventory data	• Integrated information exchange, scheduling, and decision making in in-house plants, contract assemblers, and components suppliers • Real-time available-to-promise and capable-to-promise information available to the sales force and channels	• Real-time transaction of orders whether initiated by an end consumer, a sales person, or a channel partner • Automated customer-specific agreements and contract terms • Customer and channel access to product development and delivery status • Collaborative integration with customer forecasting systems • Integrated channel management including information exchange, warranty claims, and contract management (versioning, process control)	• On-line sales channels including Web sites and marketplaces • Real-time inside and outside access to customer information, product catalogs, dynamic pricing, inventory availability, on-line submission of quotes, and order entry • On-line product configurators • Customer-tailored marketing via customer profiling • Push advertising • Tailored on-line access • Real-time customer feedback through Web surveys, opt-in/opt-out marketing, and promotion response tracking	• On-line support of customer service representatives through e-mail response management, billing integration, co-browse, chat, "call me now," voice-over-IP, and other uses of video streaming • Customer self-service via Web sites and intelligent service request processing including updates to billing and shipping profiles • Real-time field service access to customer account review, schematic review, parts availability and ordering, work-order update, and service parts management

←———— Web distributed supply chain management ————→

Prominent Applications of the Internet in the Value Chain

97

good tool for promoting the Web site while continuing to be a convenient way of packaging information for buyers.

In some industries, the use of the Internet represents only a modest shift from well-established practices. For catalog retailers like Lands' End, providers of electronic data interchange services like General Electric, direct marketers like Geico and Vanguard, and many other kinds of companies, Internet business looks much the same as traditional business. In these industries, established companies enjoy particularly important synergies between their on-line and traditional operations, which make it especially difficult for dot-coms to compete. Examining segments of industries with characteristics similar to those supporting on-line businesses-in which customers are willing to forgo personal service and immediate delivery in order to gain convenience or lower prices, for instance-can also provide an important reality check in estimating the size of the Internet opportunity. In the prescription drug business, for example, mail orders represented only about 13% of all purchases in the late 1990s. Even though on-line drugstores may draw more customers than the mail-order channel, it is unlikely that they will supplant their physical counterparts.

Virtual activities do not eliminate the need for physical activities, but often amplify their importance. The complementarity between Internet activities and traditional activities arises for a number of reasons. First, introducing Internet applications in one activity often places greater demands on physical activities elsewhere in the value chain. Direct ordering, for example, makes warehousing and shipping more important. Second, using the Internet in one activity can have systemic consequences, requiring new or enhanced physical activities that are often unanticipated. Internet-based job-posting services, for example, have greatly reduced the cost of reaching potential job applicants, but they have also flooded employers with electronic resumes. By making it easier for job seekers to distribute resumes, the Internet forces employers to sort through many more unsuitable candidates. The added back-end costs, often for physical activities, can end up outweighing the up-front savings. A similar dynamic often plays out in digital marketplaces. Suppliers are able to reduce the transactional cost of taking orders when they move on-line, but they often have to respond to many additional requests for information and quotes, which, again, places new strains on traditional activities. Such systemic effects underscore the fact that Internet applications are not stand-alone technologies; they must be integrated into the overall value chain.

Third, most Internet applications have some short-comings in comparison with conventional methods. While Internet technology can do many useful things today and will Surely improve in the future, it cannot do everything. Its limits include the following:

- Customers cannot physically examine, touch, and test products or get hands-on help in using or repairing them.
- Knowledge transfer is restricted to codified knowledge, sacrificing the spontaneity and judgment that can result from interaction with skilled personnel.
- The ability to learn about suppliers and customers (beyond their mere purchasing habits) is limited by the lack of face-to-face contact.

Strategic Imperatives for Dot-Coms and Established Companies

At this critical juncture in the evolution of Internet technology, dot-coms and established companies face different strategic imperatives. Dot-coms must develop real strategies that create economic value. They must recognize that current ways of competing are destructive and futile and benefit neither themselves nor, in the end, customers. Established companies, in turn, must stop deploying the Internet on a stand-alone basis and instead use it to enhance the distinctiveness of their strategies.

The most successful dot-coms will focus on creating benefits that customers will pay for, rather than pursuing advertising and click-through revenues from third parties. To be competitive, they will often need to widen their value chains to encompass other activities besides those conducted over the Internet and to develop other assets, including physical ones. Many are already doing so. Some on-line retailers, for example, distributed paper catalogs for the 2000 holiday season as an added convenience to their shoppers. Others are introducing proprietary products under their own brand names, which not only boosts margins but provides real differentiation. It is such new activities in the value chain, not minor differences in Web sites, that hold the key to whether dot-coms gain itive advantages. AOL, the Internet pioneer, recognized these principles. It charged for its services even in the face of free competitors. And not resting on initial advantages gained from its Web site and Internet technologies (such as instant messaging), it moved early to develop or acquire proprietary content.

Yet dot-coms must not fall into the trap of imitating established companies. Simply adding conventional activities is a me-too strategy that will not provide a competitive advantage. Instead, dot-coms need to create strategies that involve new, hybrid value chains, bringing together virtual and physical activities in unique configurations. For example, E*Trade is planning to install stand-alone kiosks, which will not require full-time staffs, on the sites of some corporate customers VirtualBank, an on-line bank, is cobranding with corporations to create in-house credit unions. Juniper, another on-line bank, allows customers to deposit checks at Mail Box Etc. locations. While none of these approaches is certain to be successful, the strategic thinking behind them is sound.

Another strategy for dot-coms is to seek out trade-offs, concentrating exclusively on segments where an Internet-only model offers real advantages. Instead of attempting to force the Internet model on the entire market, dot-coms can pursue customers that do not have a strong need for functions delivered outside the Internet – even if such customers represent only a modest portion of the overall industry.

In such segments, the challenge will be to find a value proposition for the company that will distinguish it from other Internet rivals and address low entry barriers.

Successful dot-coms will share the following characteristics:

- Strong capabilities in Internet technology
- A distinctive strategy vis-a-vis established companies and other dot-coms, resting on a clear focus and meaningful advantages
- Emphasis on creating customer value and charging for it directly, rather than relying on ancillary forms of revenue
- Distinctive ways of performing physical functions and assembling non-Internet assets that complement their strategic positions
- Deep industry knowledge to allow proprietary skills, information, and relationships to be established

Established companies, for the most part, need not be afraid of the Internet-the predictions of their demise at the hands of dot-coms were greatly exaggerated. Established companies possess traditional competitive advantages that will often continue to prevail; they also have inherent strengths in deploying Internet technology.

The greatest threat to an established company lies in either failing to deploy the Internet or failing to deploy it strategically. Every company needs an aggressive program to deploy the Internet throughout its value chain, using the technology to reinforce traditional competitive advantages and complement existing ways of competing. The key is not to imitate rivals but to tailor Internet applications to a company's overall strategy in ways that extend its competitive advantages and make them more sustainable. Schwab's expansion of its brick-and-mortar branches by one-third since it started on-line trading, for example, is extending its advantages over Internet-only competitors. The Internet, when used properly, can support greater strategic focus and a more tightly integrated activity system.

Edward Jones, a leading brokerage firm, is a good example of tailoring the Internet to strategy. Its strategy is to provide conservative, personalized advice to investors who value asset preservation and seek trusted, individualized guidance in investing. Target customers include retirees and small-business owners. Edward Jones does not offer commodities, futures, options, or other risky forms of investment. Instead, the company stresses a buy-and-hold approach to investing involving mutual funds, bonds, and blue-chip equities. Edward Jones operates a network of about 7,000 small offices, which are located conveniently to customers and are designed to encourage personal relationships with brokers.

Edward Jones has embraced the Internet for internal management functions, recruiting (2.5% of all job inquiries come via the Internet), and for providing account statements and other information to customers. However, it has no plan to offer on-line trading, as its competitors do. Self-directed, on-line trading does not fit Jones's strategy nor the value it aims to deliver to its customers. Jones, then, has tailored the use of the Internet to its strategy rather than imitated rivals. The company is thriving, outperforming rivals whose me-too Internet deployments have reduced their distinctiveness.

The established companies that will be most successful will be those that use Internet technology to make traditional activities better and those that find and implement new combinations of virtual and physical activities that were not previously possible.

- The lack of human contact with the customer eliminates a powerful tool for encouraging purchases, trading off terms and conditions, providing advice and reassurance, and closing deals.
- Delays are involved in navigating sites and finding information and are introduced by the requirement for direct shipment.
- Extra logistical costs are required to assemble, pack, and move small shipments.
- Companies are unable to take advantage of low-cost, nontransactional functions performed by sales forces, distribution channels, and purchasing departments (such as performing limited service and maintenance functions at a customer site).
- The absence of physical facilities circumscribes some functions and reduces a means to reinforce image and establish performance.

- Attracting new customers is difficult given the sheer magnitude of the available information and buying options.

Traditional activities, often modified in some way, can compensate for these limits, just as the shortcomings of traditional methods – such as lack of real-time information, high cost of face-to-face interaction, and high cost of producing physical versions of information – can be offset by Internet methods. Frequently, in fact, an Internet application and a traditional method benefit each other. For example, many companies have found that Web sites that supply product information and support direct ordering make traditional sales forces more, not less, productive and valuable. The sales force can compensate for the limits of the site by providing personalized advice and after-sales service, for instance. And the site can make the sales force more productive by automating the exchange of routine information and serving as an efficient new conduit for leads. The fit between company activities, a cornerstone of strategic positioning, is in this way strengthened by the deployment of Internet technology.

Once managers begin to see the potential of the Internet as a complement rather than a cannibal, they will take a very different approach to organizing their on-line efforts. Many established companies, believing that the new economy operated under new rules, set up their Internet operations in stand-alone units. Fear of cannibalization, it was argued, would deter the mainstream organization from deploying the Internet aggressively. A separate unit was also helpful for investor relations, and it facilitated IPOs, tracking stocks, and spin-offs, enabling companies to tap into the market's appetite for Internet ventures and provide special incentives to attract Internet talent.

But organizational separation, while understandable, has often undermined companies' ability to gain competitive advantages. By creating separate Internet strategies instead of integrating the Internet into an overall strategy, companies failed to capitalize on their traditional assets, reinforced me-too competition, and accelerated competitive convergence. Barnes & Noble's decision to establish Barnesandnoble.com as a separate organization is a vivid example. It deterred the on-line store from capitalizing on the many advantages provided by the network of physical stores, thus playing into the hands of Amazon.

Rather than being isolated, Internet technology should be the responsibility of mainstream units in all parts of a company. With support from IT staff and outside consultants, companies should use the technology strategically to enhance service, increase efficiency, and leverage existing strengths. While separate units may be appropriate in some circumstances, everyone in the organization must have an incentive to share in the success of Internet deployment.

The End of the New Economy

The Internet, then, is often not disruptive to existing industries or established companies. It rarely nullifies the most important sources of competitive advantage in an industry; in many cases it actually makes those sources even more important. As all companies come to embrace Internet technology, moreover, the Internet itself will be neutralized as a source of advantage. Basic Internet applications will become table stakes – companies will not be able to survive without them, but they will not gain any advantage from them. The more robust competitive advantages will arise instead from traditional strengths such as unique products, proprietary content, distinctive physical activities, superior product knowledge, and strong personal service and relationships. Internet technology may be able to fortify those advantages, by tying a company's activities together in a more distinctive system, but it is unlikely to supplant them.

Ultimately, strategies that integrate the Internet and traditional competitive advantages and ways of competing should win in many industries. On the demand side, most buyers will value a combination of on-line services, personal services, and physical locations over stand-alone Web distribution. They will want a choice of channels, delivery options, and ways of dealing with companies. On the supply side, production and procurement will be more effective if they involve a combination of Internet and traditional methods, tailored to strategy. For example, customized, engineered inputs will be bought directly, facilitated by Internet tools. Commodity items may be purchased via digital markets, but purchasing experts, supplier sales forces, and stocking locations will often also provide useful, value-added services.

The value of integrating traditional and Internet methods creates potential advantages for established companies. It will be easier for them to adopt and integrate Internet methods than for dot-coms to adopt and integrate traditional ones. It is not enough, however, just to graft the Internet onto historical ways of competing in simplistic "clicks-and-mortar" configurations. Established companies will be most successful when they deploy Internet technology to reconfigure traditional activities or when they find new combinations of Internet and traditional approaches.

Dot-coms, first and foremost, must pursue their own distinctive strategies, rather than emulate one another or the positioning of established companies. They will have to break away from competing solely on price and instead focus on product selection, product design, service, image, and other areas in which they can differentiate themselves. Dot-coms can also drive the Combination of Internet and traditional methods. Some will succeed by creating their own distinctive ways of doing so. Others will succeed by concentrating on market segments that exhibit real trade-offs between Internet and traditional methods – either those in which a pure Internet approach best meets the needs of a particular set of customers or those in which a particular product or service can be best delivered without the need for physical assets. (See the sidebar "Strategic Imperatives for dot-coms and Established Companies.")

These principles are already manifesting themselves in many industries, as traditional leaders reassert their strengths and dot-coms adopt more focused strategies. In the brokerage industry, Charles Schwab has gained a larger share (18% at the end of 1999) of on-line trading than E-Trade (15%). In commercial banking, established institutions like Wells Fargo, Citibank, and Fleet have many more on-line accounts than Internet banks do. Established companies are also gaining dominance over Internet activities in such areas as retailing, financial information, and digital marketplaces. The most promising dot-coms are leveraging their distinctive skills to provide real value to their customers. ECollege, for example, is a full-service provider that works with universities to put their courses on the Internet and operate the required delivery network for a fee. It is vastly more successful than competitors offering free sites to universities under their own brand names, hoping to collect advertising fees and other ancillary revenue.

When seen in this light, the "new economy" appears less like a new economy than like an old economy that has access to a new technology. Even the phrases "new economy" and "old economy" are rapidly losing their relevance, if they ever had any. The old economy of established companies and the new economy of dot-coms are merging, and it will soon be difficult to distinguish them. Retiring these phrases can only be healthy because it will reduce the confusion and muddy thinking that have been so destructive of economic value during the Internet's adolescent years.

In our quest to see how the Internet is different, we have failed to see how the Internet is the same. While a new means of conducting business has become available, the fundamentals of competition remain unchanged. The next stage of the Internet's evolution will involve a shift in thinking from e-business to business, from e-strategy to strategy. Only by integrating the Internet into overall strategy will this powerful new technology become an equally powerful force for competitive advantage.

What Makes a Strategy Brilliant?*

By Brian Huffman

"The art of war is simple; everything is a matter of execution."
  Napoleon Bonaparte

"If you're so smart, why aren't you rich?"
  Anonymous

Is strategy a joke? Does Napoleon's observation apply to business as well as war? Is business only a matter of "execution"? And if it is more than that, and if clever strategies really do win the day, then – seriously – why aren't all smart people rich?

"In many organizations," notes Hamel (1996), "corporate planning (strategy) departments are being disbanded ... [C]onsulting firms are doing less and less 'strategy' work and more and more 'implementation' work." Porter (1996), himself an ardent proponent of strategy, states that business has lost its faith in strategy, preferring to spend its time on "concrete" and "actionable" concerns such as operational effectiveness. Tom Peters has never had to pay the $100 he offered to the first manager who could demonstrate that a successful strategy had resulted from a planning process.

There are two possible explanations for the business world's disappointment with strategy. First, the science of strategy has not lived up to the expectation that it should provide us with strategy-making methods – a reasonable expectation since the very existence of strategy case courses presupposes those people who believe that such methods exist and can be taught. Still, there is little empirical evidence to suggest that strategies can be produced by teachable formal methods. In fact, brilliant strategies come from "beyond the box" thinking – beyond the box of tried and true methods, beyond the box of our current strategic paradigm.

Great works of art are produced without methods; so too are brilliant strategies. The secret lies in learning to recognize them and working hard to achieve them.

The second explanation is that business people know how often strategy can be overwhelmed by tactics. They are in a better position than ivory tower denizens to see the truth of Napoleon's words, to see that execution is critical. Wheeler (2000) describes two examples of strategies that were soundly defeated by tactics: Civil War General Joseph Hooker's "perfect plan" that

---

* Taken with permission from Business Horizons, July-August 2001, pp. 13-20

failed at Fredericksburg because of tactical actions on both sides; and a brilliant strategy at ABC that failed because of Ted Turner's bold tactical responses.

Although tactical actions generally flow from strategy, unexpected exigencies often call for tactics that radically depart from the strategic plan. A newly minted MBA does not generally expect the necessity of these departures nor appreciate the hard tactical work needed to make a strategy succeed.

Two points are to be made here. First, there are no methods for creating brilliant strategies; nonetheless, brilliant strategies can be produced in the absence of methods, and managers can at least learn to recognize them. Such an ability is important because true brilliance may come from organizational members who lack the political power to sell and implement it. Second, tactics are as important as strategy, and this importance needs to be emphasized.

Certain criteria can be used to help managers recognize brilliant strategy. Students should be taught to use these criteria in strategy-evaluating history courses (as opposed to the existing strategy-generating case courses). They must also be taught to appreciate the importance of tactics by the history course approach.

What's Wrong with Strategy?

A popular book on strategic management does not define the word *strategy* until page 127, the fourth page of the fourth chapter. It could be that students are not ready to understand that definition, which is fairly complex, until they have read the first 126 pages. But it could also be that the definition is overly complex. Strategy in business can be defined simply as the general statement of how a firm intends to win. Strategy is not specific; it is not a step-by-step plan. It is about the more distant future, whereas tactics are about the nearer future. Although strategy should be in place before the game begins, it may be modified, or even completely rewritten, by tactical actions as the game progresses.

Tactics can be defined simply as the competitive actions taken either to implement a strategy or to respond to a competitor's actions. Tactics are "strategy-in-process". If we have the initiative, our tactics are generally slave to our strategy; if the enemy has the initiative, our tactics are generally slave to his strategy.

Strategies do work. The success of the U.S. and allied forces in Operation Desert Storm was due in no small part to a clever end-run strategy. And strategies can be essential. In chess, states Gulko (1997), "everything hinges on the formulation of a long-term strategy."

Business strategy critics do not criticize strategy per se. No one would seriously maintain that companies would be better off running on instinct. However, there is still much to criticize. First there is serious doubt as to whether strategy-making can be taught at all. If one can strategize according to some method, then strategy-making can be taught; but if there is no method, then it cannot. Criticism can be classified according to the position the critic takes on the existence of a method. Critics maintain that the current strategic paradigm as outlined in the Figure:

1. is well suited as a method for generating strategies, if only it is applied correctly; or

2. can be used as a method for generating strategies after a recommended fix is made; or

3. cannot be used as a method for generating strategies no matter what changes are made and no matter how useful the paradigm may be for other purposes, such as evaluating strategy-because strategy-making methods cannot exist.

Three criticisms fall into the first category. Porter asserts that the strategic paradigm can be used to generate strategies, but that businesses have misused it and have become sidetracked into focusing on operational effectiveness rather than on strategy formulation. He believes that strategy is about "positioning", which requires trade-offs, and that most managers misunderstand the concept of trade-offs, incorrectly believing that they are unnecessary. Henderson (1989) accepts the strategic paradigm as a strategy generator, but states that more effort needs to be expended in understanding competitive behavior in the market. Brandenburger and Nalebuff (1995) also accept the paradigm as a strategy generator, but feel that Porter's Five Forces deserve more emphasis.

The criticisms of Courtney, Kirkland, and Viguerie (1997) and Hamel (1996) fit into the second category. Courtney et al. maintain that the current paradigm is useful only for generating strategies for businesses facing low levels of uncertainty, and offer an alternative approach for businesses facing higher levels of uncertainty. Hamel believes strategy must be revolutionary and points out that the current paradigm is about planning, not strategizing. He is especially critical of two of the key players in the current paradigm: top management and planning specialists (technocrats). Top management, he maintains, is often too vested in maintaining the status quo to allow the necessary revolution to take place. And asking planning technocrats to deliver a creative strategy, he says, is "like asking a bricklayer to create Michelangelo's Pieta." Nevertheless, Hamel's criticism belongs in the second category because he does not entirely give up the hope that a process does exist for generating strategy. In fact, he recommends a process in which strategy development is supposed to be "bottom-up" (or democratic) to achieve diversity of perspective and at the same time be "top-down" (or management-directed) to achieve unity of purpose. He does not, however, clarify how a process is supposed to begin at both ends of the organizational spectrum simultaneously.

Hamel and Prahalad (1989) fall somewhere between the second and third categories. They imply that no paradigm would be very useful for making strategy, and are "not comforted" by the thought that the current one "can be reduced to eight rules for excellence, seven S's, five competitive forces, four product life cycle stages, three generic strategies, and innumerable two-by-two matrices." They point out that even "reasonable strategic concepts" like the product life cycle often have "toxic side effects", such as creating a preference for selling businesses rather than defending

I. **Situation Analysis**
    A. General External Environment
        1. Political/Legal
        2. Sociocultural
        3. Technological
        4. Demographic
        5. Economic
        6. Global
    B. Industry Analysis
        1. Porter's Five Forces
    C. Competitive Environment Analysis
    D. Environmental Trends
    E. Strategic Analysis
        1. Key Success Factors
        2. Strategies
           a. Business Level
           b. Competitive Strategy
           c. Corporate Level
           d. Modes of Entry
        3. Core Competencies
           a. Resources
              i. Tangible
                 – Financial
                 – Physical
                 – Human
                 – Organizational
              ii. Intangible
                 – Resources for Innovation
                 – Reputation
           b. Capabilities (Value Chain)
              i. Operations
              ii. Marketing & Sales
              iii. Service
              iv. Human Resources
              v. Technology
    F. Performance Appraisal (Financial Ratios)

II. **SWOT Analysis** (Strength, Weakness, Opportunity, Threat)

III. **Strategy Formulation and Implementation**

The Strategic Paradigm (Source: Hitt, Ireland, Hoskisson, and Nixon 1997)

them. And they argue that using the current paradigm as a strategy generator results in predictable strategies that can easily be decoded by rivals.

Mintzberg's (1994) criticism fits into the third category. He points out that methods for generating strategies rest on three fallacies: that prediction is possible, that strategy can be developed by staff specialists who are not involved in the day-to-day operations of the business, and above all, that strategy-making can be formalized. He says that innovation, a necessary characteristic of a good strategy, has never been institutionalized "and likely never will be."

Mintzberg, as well as Campbell and Alexander (1997) and Freedman (1992), all reject the possibility of a methodology or formalized process for developing strategy, insisting that strategies can only come from experienced managers who intuitively understand key interrelationships that influence behavior in their businesses. In such a view, strategic planning specialists cannot hope to understand a business system the way managers do, so only experienced managers are capable of making the important big-picture observations necessary to formulate brilliant strategy. Mintzberg calls this capability "synthesis", Campbell and Alexander call it "insight", and Freedman calls it "systems thinking" or "seeing wholes" (terms he credits to Peter Senge).

In considering the question of what method companies should use to develop the insights they need to strategize, Campbell and Alexander admit, "The answer is, we don't know. Rival camps sell different solutions, but none has been able to demonstrate that its solutions are clearly the best. In fact, since strategy is about insights, almost by definition there is no best way."

Ohmae (1982) also rejects the notion that teachable methods exist for making brilliant strategy. He believes that strategies come from a particular state of mind rather than from rigorous analysis or some rote process. He also shows, an awareness of the political power issue, noting that in Japan "chief executives are typically over 60 – well past the age when they are likely to be able to generate dynamic strategic ideas."

Can Strategy Be Made by a Method?

If, as many believe, there are no methods for generating strategies, must we then give up the search? If the present strategic paradigm does not work as a method for developing strategies, does that mean a method cannot be found? Is it reasonable to expect that strategy-generating methods exist?

Strategy-making Methods and "Newness"

"Normal science ..., often suppresses fundamental novelties because they are necessarily subversive of its basic commitments ... No part of the aim of normal science is to call forth new sorts of phenomena; indeed, those that will not fit the box are often not seen at all. Nor do scientists normally aim to invent new theories, and they are often intolerant of those invented by others. Instead, normal-scientific research is directed to the articulation of those phenomena and theories that the paradigm already supplies."
   Kuhn (1996)

Kuhn's words apply to any normal science, including the social science of business strategy. Therefore, the science of business strategy does not involve a search for new phenomena any more than the normal science of classical physics involved a search for modern physics. The unpleasant and inescapable truth for all those involved in strategy research is this: If making strategy is essentially about making something "new" (and many argue that this is the case), then strategy-making is beyond normal science.

In the late 1970s and early 1980s, the Japanese taught American manufacturers a new strategic paradigm in the school of hard knocks. The Japanese strategy of manufacturing products that were simultaneously high in quality and low in cost was well beyond the box of the existing Western strategic paradigm (according to which those goals should have been mutually exclusive). Nothing about the normal practice of business strategy at that time would have led an American company to develop a strategy that could have protected itself against the Japanese attack, since that sort of attack was considered impossible.

Serious errors in the strategic paradigm of the 1970s became more and more obvious, and by the late 1980s strategy writers clearly had begun to smell a rat. As Hamel and Prahalad observed, "As 'strategy' has blossomed, the competitiveness of Western companies has withered. This may be a coincidence, but we think not."

But didn't the Japanese produce their strategy using a paradigm? Hardly. As Womack, Jones, and Roos demonstrated in their 1990 The Machine That Changed the World, the Japanese strategy of simultaneously pursuing high quality and low cost was not the result of strategic thinking on their part, but rather an evolutionary adaptation to the poverty they experienced after World War II. Whatever their implicit paradigm may have been, it was not written down and was not being taught as a method for creating strategy. Mintzberg and Lampel (1999) note that there are even strategy researchers who believe the Japanese have no strategic paradigm.

"Strategies may be the result of evolution or learning, rather than planning, more often than business leaders would like to admit."

Evolution (as opposed to any strategic paradigm) as the source of successful strategy has been recognized in the literature. Laudon and Laudon (1998), for example, note, "Studies of successful strategic systems have found that they are rarely planned but instead evolve slowly over a long time." Indeed, so many authors believe in evolution as a source of strategy that Mintzberg and Lampel have identified the "learning school" as one of the ten dominant schools of thought in business strategy.

Strategies may be the result of evolution or learning, rather than planning, more often than business leaders would like to admit. H. Edward Wrapp (1984), himself a business executive, saw evolution as the dominant process. He observed that corporate strategy is not the result of a planning process, but the outgrowth of day-to-day operating decisions by top-level managers who get involved in low-level decisions both to stay informed and to push the company in the direction they want it to move. Wrapp's work shows that, like Napoleon, top managers concentrate on tactics rather than on making sweeping policy decisions – which they seem to believe could straitjacket the organization.

"Newness", then, is not to be found in strategic paradigms. Normal science does not seek new phenomena, and the strategic paradigm is normal science. Therefore, if newness is a requisite of successful strategy (and authors such as Prahalad insist on this), then successful strategies cannot be generated by strategic paradigms.

Strategy-making Methods and Predictability

Despite what Prahalad and others say, maybe "newness" is not absolutely required for strategic success. There are not many truly new moves in chess, but chess matches are still won by using standard moves unpredictably. It is, after all, fairly rare that one faces an opponent like the Japanese, who have been spawned in an entirely different competitive ocean and who therefore play by a completely new set of rules. Even if a teachable strategic paradigm cannot be used to generate truly new strategies, might it not at least be capable of generating strategies that are unexpected and therefore successful?

"Rommel, you magnificent bastard, I read your book!"
> George C. Scott as General Patton in the motion picture Patton, when he was pummeling Rommel's forces after having studied Rommel's book and anticipated his strategy

"It should be noted that Japan has never preceded hostile action by a declaration of war. We have concluded that it is a possibility a fast-raiding Japanese carrier force might arrive in Hawaiian waters with no prior warning from our intelligence services. The most favorable time to the enemy would be dawn. He would probably employ a maximum of six carriers and strike on a weekend."
> U.S. Army/Navy Report accurately predicting Japanese attack on Pearl Harbor, 1941

"We're glad to find a competitor managing by the portfolio concept – we can almost predict how much share we'll have to take away to put the business on the CEO's sell list."
> Anonymous senior executive (Hamel and Prahalad 1989)

The above three quotes are witness to the fact that strategy-generating methods yield predictable strategies. Predictable strategies do not necessarily lose; the Japanese did very well with their "predictable" attack on Pearl Harbor. In fact, strategies often succeed precisely because they do conform to the common sense embedded in the prevailing paradigm. Nevertheless, they are expected by the enemy and will hardly catch him completely flatfooted. In spectacular upsets and stunning victories, one usually sees the unpredictable, the "revolution", such as in the Japanese business strategy of high quality and low cost.

Keegan (1973) states that between the first and second world wars, the highest echelons of the German military "formed the opinion that the tank could be discounted as a weapon of war … and not, as the British tank pioneers were beginning to perceive, of strategic, perhaps even war-winning significance." Fortunately for them, lower-ranking officers such as Heinz Guderian did not buy in to that. German victories in France at the beginning of WWII depended on the unpredictably swift advance of their army, which would not have been possible had Germany stuck to its outdated paradigm.

General Robert E. Lee also fought in an unpredictable manner by often running absolutely contrary to the accepted military strategic paradigm of his day, dividing his forces in the face of vastly larger enemy forces. He achieved his many victories not in spite of having divided his forces, but *because* he divided them.

Young and Bradley (1995) and Alexander (1993) both describe how a bad strategy (according to the existing paradigm) became a good one in the Inchon landing during the Korean War. General Douglas MacArthur proposed landing there knowing it was such a "terrible idea" that the North Koreans would never expect it.

The successes of MacArthur, Guderian, and Lee are not unique in history; winning strategies have often involved doing something completely unpredictable in that it is contrary to the existing strategic paradigm. This observation actually goes back to the very origins of Western strategic thought, to Heraclitus of Ephesus (ca. 500 BC), who delineated a concept known as "the coincidence of opposites." According to this concept, it is sometimes smart to avoid better ways of attacking because that is just what the enemy expects. Thus, "bad strategy" (that contrary to the paradigm) is good strategy because it is unpredictable.

So once again the strategic paradigm fails. Strategies generated by strategic paradigms are predictable, and predictable strategies are bad. But although we may never find methods to generate brilliant business strategies, all is not lost. Brilliance will still pop up. It will come about as it always has, either as part of an evolutionary process or as the product of an unknown anti apparently unknowable process inside the head of the experienced manager. Making brilliant strategy is not the problem; the problem is being able to recognize it when we see it. This is especially important because, again, the most creative strategies may come from those with the least power to promote them successfully.

Recognizing Brilliant Strategy

There are two problems with the way strategy is taught in universities vis-a-vis the way it is used in industry. The first is that the focus has been on developing strategies rather than on evaluating them. The second is that the importance of tactics has been badly understated. Here we focus on the first problem by suggesting a number of useful criteria to be used in recognizing brilliant strategy. It should be clear that even if a strategy is judged on the basis of the following criteria to be brilliant, it could nonetheless subsequently fail (although brilliant strategies should generally outperform the lesser ones).

> *"The successes of MacArthur, Guderian, and Lee are not unique in history; winning strategies have often involved doing something completely unpredictable in that it is contrary to the existing strategic paradigm."*

Evaluation Criteria from the Science of Business Strategy

The strategic paradigm outlined in Figure 1 is an obvious first place to look for criteria to evaluate business strategy. It may seem inconsistent to reject that paradigm for the purpose of making strategy while accepting it for the purpose of evaluation. But the tasks of making and evaluating are not the same. According to the paradigm, a business strategy should be judged good or bad based on the following:

1. How well does it fit the general external environment? Does it consider the political/legal, sociocultural, technological, economic, demographic, and global aspects of the outside world?
2. How well does it fit the industry in question (Porter's Five Forces)?
3. Does it consider environmental trends'?
4. How well does it identify key success factors and deal with their ramifications?
5. How well does it take advantage of the firm's current core competencies, or call for acquiring core competencies necessary for the strategy to succeed?

Evaluation Criteria from Military Science

Although articles on business strategy often refer to or derive from military strategy, it is often argued that the business and military worlds are too different for cross-fertilization. For one thing, much is usually made of the difference between their respective goals. In particular, business writers like Brandenburger note that business is not necessarily a zero-sum game. But neither is war. Neo-Clausewitzians, says Anatol Rapoport in his 1968 introduction to Clausewitz's *On War,* have "gone to great lengths to explain the limitations of the zero-sum game as a paradigm of conflict, and to point out that even enemies have some common interests."

Conversely, business, like most wars, can result in zero-sum. Strategy textbooks have begun to reflect the warlike, competitive nature of business by including chapters on competitive response, rather than leaving students with the naive assumption that our competitors will sit back and do nothing while we eat their lunch. Ohmae also stresses the more aggressive nature of business, stating that "without competition there would be no need for strategy."

If the military and business worlds are not that different, then criteria used to judge military strategy may be useful in judging business strategy as well. The U.S. Army uses two sets of criteria to evaluate strategy: the "Tenets of Army Operations" and the "Principles of War." The former is for an ex post analysis, whereas the latter is for evaluating a strategy a priori the time orientation we want to take in evaluating business strategy. Thus, a military or business strategy is judged brilliant if it is in accordance with the nine principles of war: it has a clear objective; it has an offensive orientation; it masses resources at one decisive place and time; it uses forces economically; it calls for maneuvers that give our forces the situational advantage; it institutes unity of command; it considers the security of our forces; it will surprise the enemy; and it is simple.

Evaluation Criteria from Art Criticism

Strategic thinking is an art, and thus a particular strategy is a work of art. So we should be able to judge a strategy the way we judge art. There are three basic questions in art criticism: What was the artist trying to do? Given that, how well was it done? And was it worth doing?

The film *Raiders of the Lost Ark* may not seem like great art, but it is nonetheless judged as great because it scored well on those three questions. The director tried to recreate the feeling of the old Saturday morning movie serials, that feeling was achieved (it was well done), and the result was a very entertaining film (it was worth doing).

The art criticism questions could easily be adapted for evaluating business strategy. A strategist should know what he is trying to do, so the first question is easily answered. Whether or not the strategy was worth doing will depend on the value the critic assigns to the task the strategist set for himself (for example, a strategy that is expected to increase the bottom line by 20 percent is certainly worth doing). The question of how well the strategy is done will depend on the critic's subjective judgment (which may be disconcerting to the strategist, but agreement among strategy critics may be fairly strong, as is often the case in art criticism).

Evaluation Criteria from Game Theory

Modern game theory was developed to help explain the complex web of natural competition. As in business, players in games of strategy have a choice of action, and their actions are interdependent. Surprisingly, the optimal strategy in game theory is based on the pessimistic assumption that one's opponent already knows one's strategy. A player with this degree of pessimism will only launch a strategy so good that it does not need secrecy to be successful. In games in which there is imperfect information (such as in poker as opposed to chess), the optimal strategy also requires players to distribute their bluffs irregularly on a controlled probability basis. Players who do not bluff telegraph perfect information to their opponents (forfeiting the benefit of imperfect information).

Two criteria for business strategy evaluation can be inferred here. First, business strategies that do not depend on secrecy can be judged superior to those that do. Second, strategies that effectively employ disinformation (bluffing) can be judged superior to those that either do not use disinformation or use it poorly.

Evaluation Criteria from Artificial Intelligence and Chess

The chess world was shocked when IBM's Deep Blue computer bested world chess champion Garry Kasparov 31/2 to 21/2. Krol (1999) even speculated that the world may have seen the first demonstration of a computer passing the Turing test – the acid test for demonstrating that artificial intelligence has been achieved. And in a *Time* article two weeks after his defeat in May 1997, Kasparov said that in Game 2 "we saw something that went well beyond our wildest expectations of how well a computer would be able to foresee the long-term positional consequences of its decisions." Kasparov even described Deep Blue in nearly human terms as "psychologically stable, undisturbed, and unconcerned."

On the other hand, Gulko (1997) maintains that Deep Blue was not playing according to any strategy, that "even after Kasparov found himself in a truly horrendous bind, the computer made an entirely pointless move", and that Deep Blue demonstrated many times that it was playing with no sort of discernible plan. "Deep Blue made senseless if typically computer-like moves," he says, "and was thus far from passing the Turing test for artificial intelligence." Moreover, Gulko notes, far from being "human-like", Deep Blue's play lacked creativity, imagination, intuition, and planning.

Two criteria for business strategy evaluation can be derived from these observations. First, good strategies need to be creative. Second, they must reflect a purpose. A strategy can be judged creative if, for example, it is a surprise to the evaluator. It can be judged as reflecting a purpose if it projects far into the future, anticipating several rounds of competitive moves, responses, and countermoves.

The Strategy Classroom

Anyone who has ever learned to play a game of strategy knows that the key to winning is experience. It would certainly be silly to expect someone who has just learned the rules of chess to play his first game with any measure of strategic creativity.

A Little League coach once attempted to teach baseball strategy to a group of fourth-graders. It was not a pretty picture. The players lay in a semicircle around the coach watching the clouds roll along while he engaged in an animated (but completely ignored) soliloquy about what a player should do when, say, there was one out and a runner on third. Even if the kids had had the temperament to listen, they would still have been unable even to understand, much less appreciate, the advice being given.

Coaches and college professors may like to talk about strategy, but unless they are talking to experienced players their message will be over the listeners' heads. Strategy-making is learned by playing, not by listening.

It may seem that solving cases in a case course is playing the game, and that the students should learn how to make strategies as they work through more and more cases. The problem with that argument, however, is that each business situation is so unique that each case is really a completely different game. The business student, in effect, plays only one game of baseball, one game of hockey, and so on.

Moreover, the strategy case study is a safe and "dumbed-down" version of the real game-safe because the situation is not real, dumbed down because it gives the student all the information necessary (presumably) to produce a winning strategy. This pre-packaging of salient information may lead students to assume that only information that is readily obtainable is relevant, or to become overconfident in their ability to recognize salient factors in the real world where they must actually hunt for them. Students may inadvertently be taught to believe that industry experience is not necessary – one need only breeze in, look at the facts, and put together a guaranteed winning strategy.

Finally, case studies are not always completely honest. They often direct students toward desirable conclusions. It is difficult to see how students could learn to produce truly "out of the box" solutions when cases are designed to push them into a box.

How else might business strategy courses be taught? They could be taught as history courses-the same approach the military uses in teaching strategy. Students could be told what strategy an unidentified business intended to pursue in a situation disguised so that they would not know whether or not the strategy was ultimately successful, and could therefore evaluate it without the benefit of 20/20 hindsight. Such histories would sometimes involve strategies that had been winners and sometimes those that had been losers. The goal would be to teach students to apply the evaluation criteria and recognize the winners.

Students could also evaluate subsequent tactical moves (again without the benefit of knowing whether or not those tactics succeeded). The goal would be to instill a respect for the hard work involved in making strategies succeed, then to create the awareness that strategies are not cast in stone – deviations sometimes must be made.

The military has found that generals, such as George Patton, who have a firm grasp of military history are the ones best able to recognize brilliant strategies. They are also the ones most capable of eventually learning what cannot be taught: how to create brilliant ones themselves.

It is unfortunate that neither the present approach to strategy education nor this new approach will produce students who can immediately create brilliant strategies. This recommended approach, however, at least recognizes that fact and focuses efforts on what can be done.

Max Planck, the father of quantum theory and therefore the father of modern physics, once said that his discoveries were so incredible he had a hard time believing them himself. Just as it was especially difficult for a physicist to see that classical physics was seriously flawed, it will be especially difficult for business strategists to see that business strategy is likewise flawed. Nevertheless, a change in the focus of strategy is needed.

The present focus on formalized processes for creating strategies needs to give way to a focus on criteria for evaluating them and an emphasis on the importance of tactics in making or breaking them. Strategy case courses need to be recast as strategy history courses, with an emphasis on evaluating strategies and being able to recognize brilliant ones when we see them. Universities and business trainers would not be producing strategists – but they aren't producing them now. They would, however, be producing students who may save good strategies from being overlooked and who have a healthy respect for both industry experience and the power of tactics.

Who's Who: Changing the Traditional Strategic Management Mindset[*]

The Electronic Revolution in Publishing

The electronic revolution and publishing have had a stormy relationship. They began with a passionate engagement, then became disenchanted when their wilder hopes failed to be fulfilled. As far back as the 1970s, electronic typesetters developed stand-alone applications that they offered to publishers in the hope of enhancing their services. These applications evolved into desk-top publishing (DTP) systems, and the typesetters were disappointed to find they were losing work rather than gaining it as a result, because the publishers started to do their own typesetting in-house. In non-fiction publishing, only the large-scale, text-heavy publishers, for reference, academic and professional books, continued to depend on typesetters as they had done in the past.

The second phase in the relationship came as illustrated non-fiction publishers saw the promise of a new electronic publishing age in the form of CD-ROMs, which proved outrageously expensive to produce, and found little or no market from which the investment could be recovered.

The third phase saw publishers being much more cautious about the online revolution, although their former enthusiasm was more than made up for by the delirium of others who lacked publishing experience in the content communication trade. Publishers, after all, have been finding ways to make content management pay since the invention of moveable type, about half a millennium ago.

In practice, for information and reference publishers of all kinds – educational texts, dictionaries, directories, handbooks or manuals, archived resources, and so on – the business of publishing has involved finding or creating raw content, manipulating this into a readable style (i.e. editing), presenting this in a readable way (i.e. design and typesetting), and then trying to sell it as effectively as possible, where possible re-selling it in various forms to different markets as opportunities arise. The publishers' editorial skills were particularly useful in this respect because they enabled something manipulated once to be manipulated again, differently, several more times, in a process now called, politely and perhaps euphemistically, "re-versioning" or "re-packaging".

In contrast to the ongoing electronic revolution in text manipulation and presentation, where publishers and software businesses continue their fluid and tempestuous dance,

---

[*] © 2002, Hal Robinson and Librios Ltd.

another electronic revolution has been embraced much more effectively by other areas of business than by publishers.

This other revolution is the development of database technology since the 1960s. Any business with the need for a mailing list or a stock control system operates some kind of database. Publishers do as well, in these commercial areas. But, for reasons that are hard to fathom, they have not been quick to combine their profound, inherent knowledge of content management with the power, control and enormous potential for cost savings that a database can bring.

Issues for Reference Publishers

The issue for reference publishers is a common one. There is a need to acquire content inexpensively, develop it cost-effectively, and sell it as profitably as possible. As with other products, some of the results are sold with a high margin in relatively small quantities, and some are sold with a low margin in high quantities. Only occasionally does a high-margin product sell in high quantities, and a publisher's success and commercial longevity are usually assured when this occurs. (Such is the case with *Who's Who*, published by A&C Black). This success allows the brand to be defined not only by the publisher's name, but also by the product itself. In the case of the most successful products, their identity will come to overshadow the publisher's.

For many reference publishers, however, there is a commercial inertia in the process of acquiring, developing and selling a product. If an acquired product doesn't sell well, it is likely to be written off as a failure, and allowed to languish. On the other hand, if it does sell well, there is a strong tendency to enjoy the fruits of success and otherwise leave it alone. Neither circumstance encourages innovation and, in each case, assets (all carefully acquired and potentially valuable) are likely to be left as they are, apart from updating where necessary.

The probable cause of the inertia is the idea that the product, traditionally a book, and its content, are the same thing. With the electronic revolution, this equation has been challenged, because it is becoming clear that the book itself is not the only significant product, merely a version of it. The important product is the content, which can be used and re-used in various products. The more modular the content, and the more amenable it is to modification, the more potential for re-use it will have.

While this theory seems straightforward, the greatest inhibitor of re-versioning and re-packaging has been the fear of difficulties with the logistics, and the associated cost. The logistics of diverting human resources from the established acquire-develop-sell process, or of setting up parallel teams, combined with the time such re-development could take, as well as the intellectual difficulty of reinventing success, are all discouraging factors. But the opportunities presented by multiple markets, which electronic publishing generates, have begun to alter the balance.

Owners of good content resources such as a dictionary or a directory – marketable, re-marketable when updated, modular, and potentially suitable for re-versioning in subsidiary forms – were attracted by the opportunity to earn easy revenue from electronic versions in addition to conventional print. But in most cases earning the revenue was not easy, because an additional cost factor came into play, which was the high charge they would face when converting the content into an electronically accessible form. Even where the content itself was being re-used without modification, there appeared to be a need to reform it entirely for each new medium. A CD-ROM required one approach, this perhaps being SGML (an acronym for Standard Generalized Mark-up Language), which tags bits of content to define their style and function, but which is complex to use and difficult to apply. A website required another, namely HTML (HyperText Mark-up Language), which is a severely simplified and restricted implementation of SGML. Syndication might require a third. Even re-typesetting could not be done "at the press of a button". And the charges for each conversion were high.

The emergence of XML (eXtensible Mark-up Language) provided a much more usable, flexible and adequately powerful alternative to both SGML and HTML, and is being widely adopted as an industry standard. This simplified the situation for publishers, because they could decide on just one conversion, and a minor industry has sprung up offering XML conversion services. But the question still remains: what to do with the content when it is converted? The fear among publishers is that, as with CD-ROMs, the market simply isn't there.

A&C Black, the owners of *Who's Who*, decided that there might be a market for such a well-known and prestigious source of information if they could process the content cheaply enough. But to make the exercise worthwhile, they wanted a "one-stop" solution that would not only achieve this, but would also allow updating, re-versioning, and typesetting within the same electronic environment. Beyond this, the solution also had to generate content for publishing on the internet, and on CD-ROM as well, even if that medium were only used as a sales enhancement with no specific commercial value of its own. The solution also needed to be easy for the editors to use, affordable, and also accessible to others, without training, who might need to access the database from time to time. These same criteria can be applied to almost any other reference-publishing product as well.

Combining all these points within a fast, networked, flexible and powerful database is the obvious solution. But most database software is not especially flexible, nor does it allow the familiar functions of word processing, let alone typographic design, to be carried out within a common electronic environment. This is where Librios and its XML-based, database software, came into the frame.

Who's Who

Who's Who is the leading source book of British biographical information about people of influence and interest, in all areas of national life. It has been published annually since 1849 and sells worldwide. Many other "Who's Who" directories echo its name and have followed its model, but this publication is regarded as the progenitor and leader of this genre.

The 2002 edition of *Who's Who* has more than 2,000 pages, closely typset, and contains more than 30,000 biographies. In each edition, approximately one thousand of these biographies make their first appearance in the publication. Each year all entries are carefully updated, both from information supplied by biographees, who amend and update proof copies of their entries, and from independent sources of reference. As a result, tens of thousands of amendments are made, because the majority of the entries require some degree of change.

Electronic versions of the biographies are published online and on CD-ROM.

All biographies remain in *Who's Who* until their subject's death, are then archived and form a database of more than 100,000 biographies, dating back to 1897. This archive collection is known as *Who Was Who*, and is published volume by volume as sufficient material becomes available. Currently it makes up ten volumes with the most recent, published in 2001, covering those who have died between 1996 and 2000.

What Librios Does

Librios software combines a powerful relational database, developed with Borland's Delphi development tools in conjunction with Microsoft's SQL Server 2000 operating system, with XML-based tagging for optimal flexibility, and with a wordprocessor-like interface that is so intuitive that most users are barely aware they are using a database at all.

The power of a database is that it can link modules of information in a multiplicity of ways, so these can be grouped, sorted, retrieved, standardized, organized and generally managed as effectively as the users and the computer will allow. Our minds naturally make such associations or links all the time, and the aim of the design of the Librios interface has been to make the process of association seem as natural as possible… not least because editors need to be thinking about the content and designers need to be thinking about how it looks, rather than struggling with the idiosyncrasies of the software they are using.

Although publishing was not the first industry for which Librios developed the software – much of the earliest development was done with corporate knowledge management in mind – reference publishing in general and dictionary publishing in particular provided what seemed to be the toughest and most rigorous test-bed available. By fulfilling a reference publisher's requirements, the software can answer almost any content or knowledge management needs.

In practice, for *Who's Who*, the Librios software:

- Ensures details such as punctuation don't need double-checking;
- Avoids the need for expensive staff training or for extra staff;
- Maintains continuity of presentation to the biographees, so they can remain unaware of the new technology, as this could alienate them;
- Facilitates the administration of the enormous amount of collateral information associated with more than 30,000 current biography files;

- Helps the editorial and production teams keep to schedule while also implementing technological change;
- Improves the effectiveness, and therefore the cost-savings, of employing out-of-house staff.

In addressing the principle concerns of the management team, the verdict was that: *"Implementing change is very difficult when you have a tight schedule, and when you also depend on optimal cost-benefits staffing. Librios helped us achieve this change by making the transition possible without adding significantly to the team's workload."*

The context of change

Before using Librios, the process of research, commissioning, checking, updating, correcting, proofing and preparing for press used conventional typesetting and proof-correcting techniques. This involved marking changes and corrections manually on paper proofs of the previous edition, and sending these to a typesetter who would supply corrected proofs. These would also be supplied as individual versions of each entry, with the biographees' address added to it, so copies could be sent conveniently to biographees by post for review, updating and approval. Amendments would be collated by in-house editors and then sent to the typesetter who would generate revised proofs and ultimately provide the printer with the definitive typeset content for printing.

This work was carried out by a team of editors who had refined the process so that the minimum number of people were required to meet the schedule for each year's publication. However, a disadvantage of this process was that new demands associated with electronic media, such as the desirability of publishing on CD-ROM or on the internet, could not be met by a team already fully occupied.

Other disadvantages of this procedure included:

- high costs for preparing electronic material for CD-ROM, online use, or syndication, because this needed to be prepared by converting electronic typesetting files;
- a significant cost for typesetting corrections;
- a relatively slow typesetting and proofing cycle, which allowed only the minimum time for editing within the annual publication schedule;
- no easy facility for re-using material in different forms, such as *Who's Who in Politics*, or *Who's Who in Education*, unless this was done manually by the editors;
- the need for an extensive card-file and paper proof storage archive;
- no in-house electronic database;
- the difficulty and cost of training new members of the team;

While none of these factors threatened the profitability of the publication itself, so cost-reduction was not a primary driver in the need for change, the inability of the process to adapt to new opportunities was perceived as the over-riding limitation, and prompted the search for alternative procedures.

Specific requirements for the new system that were identified by the *Who's Who* team included:

- maintaining data integrity as effectively as at present;
- achieving a data granularity that would be flexible enough to allow the creation of new data sets and subsets;
- promoting greater consistency in data and presentation;
- bringing together in a single system as much as possible of the data currently held in different internal (paper-based) systems and the typesetter's system.

The system was also expected to meet obvious criteria such as adaptability, flexibility, speed, potential for growth, ease of use, importing from other electronic sources, searching, representative "live" output on screen, on paper and for electronic products, availability for external editing, security and, last but not least, the reinforcement of morale within the team, in order for the business to benefit from the dedication and productivity of editorial and production staff – in other words, the team had to like it.

Managing Change

The need for change was to meet opportunities and demands presented by electronic publishing, without the high conversion costs that would render such opportunities pyrrhic.

This need translated into a commercial requirement to create a database that could store all the working material involved in creating *Who's Who*, including editors' notes, in a format suitable for both typesetting and for syndication. The ability to store themed information would also improve the quality of material for syndication, as well as provide the potential for cross-cuts – i.e. the extraction of a coherent subset of content. Letters, proofs, and page-layouts should all be produced in-house in order to save both time and costs. The system should be able to track changes and generally provide tools to improve the editorial workflow. The system should also be able to support additional editors working out of house.

The *Who's Who* production process was required to change from paper-based to electronic without disrupting the annual production cycle. As in-house electronic publishing skills only extended as far as word-processing, the system needed to be easy for an editor to use since key deadlines might otherwise be jeopardized. "Intelligence" should exist within the software so that as many editorial chores as possible could be removed. This should also be seen as a way of expanding the commercial potential of the content. For example, the system would be required to generate many of the labels and punctuation within an entry automatically, so reducing the need for checking many parts of the entry. In addition, by separating typeset formatting, labels and punctuation from the core data, there should be the potential to give the content different form (such as a different appearance for publishing online), which would also increase the opportunities for repurposing.

Because the latest version of the content of *Who's Who* existed only in typeset form, readable only by professional typesetting systems and not by in-house editorial systems, there was also the requirement to convert the existing material into structured content for the database. This would involve interpreting the formatting and punctuation of the typeset material so it could generate semantically structured content in XML format.

Finally, the database was required to store notes and also hold material for the archives of *Who Was Who*.

Solutions in Practice

The first stage of the process for converting the existing content into Librios software was to set up typographic and semantic styles within the database corresponding to conventional database fields, but with full typographic control integrated with the content. A sample of the typesetting files was used for this purpose, and Librios programmers worked with *Who's Who* editors to ensure the styles and their significance were correct.

When converting a large project into XML, the industry standard electronic tagging for controlling the style and function of modules of content, there is a need for a series of conversion stages to establish definitive rules. There are two reasons for this. The first is that to optimize the assessment and evaluation process, the early conversion stages focus on a limited sample of the content, and this sample is unlikely to include all variables found in the whole. The second reason is that even in the best-edited typescript there are likely to be minor stylistic inconsistencies, which will be standardized in the XML system. The result is a process of refinement, which takes longer the more complicated the structure of the resource is.

When the content had been brought into the database, Librios editors worked with the Who's Who editors to make the content suit the latter's accustomed ways of working as closely as possible. In effect, this process involved training too, but "collaborative training", in which both sides learned, would be a more accurate description. This approach also served to familiarize both sides with each other's working practices, which provided significant benefits in terms of both project management and support when the process was fully operational.

The purpose of this collaborative training was to enable *Who's Who* editors and in-house production and IT staff to operate all aspects of the system fluently. Librios support continued to be available, but any reduction in the need for support reduces the on-going costs, and this was one explicit objective of the agreement.

The software's design and interface have been developed to be as intuitive as possible for writers and editors, and this also helps reduce the time needed for training, as well as the difficulty of answering questions and meeting requests when the software is in use.

The aim of the set-up process was that the complete *Who's Who* directory was data-based in Librios during the normal research period, when editing requirements are fewest, in the annual *Who's Who* publishing cycle. The *Who's Who* team were provided with a system that could produce typeset output simply and quickly and, above all, do this directly from the equipment used in-house. This equipment was not expensive, and consisted of standard business-level networked PCs and a fast, high-volume A3/A4 monochrome office laser printer.

To take printed content from Librios into a print-ready typeset form, page make-up software from Adobe was chosen. FrameMaker+SGML is a stand-alone boxed product with a power and quality that compares well with professional typesetting systems. For this to be used, Librios exports databased content via an inbuilt export conversion to SGML, so this can be run in FrameMaker templates with all structured information and styles intact. The Librios team prepared these templates and refined them to meet the requirements of the *Who's Who* team. The result was that the need for further manual intervention in the typesetting process was avoided.

To ensure that individual copies of entries could be sent out to all biographees, Librios also provided a mechanism for automatically merging the person's name and address with his or her entry on A4 format. These could be folded and inserted into standard envelopes with a window in which the address would appear.

In setting up the system, security issues had to be considered. Any level of security can be applied, but it is normal to look for an approach that combines adequate security with ease of use. In the *Who's Who* system, users log on to the system, and the software tracks any changes they make. Previous versions are retained for comparison. Because each database entry (in conventional terms, each database record) may contain confidential information, such as the biographees' confidential home address, or editor's notes, mechanisms are also built in to control and restrict the information that is output at the different stages of the process.

The result was that, from the date of the contract at the beginning of 2001 through to the end of the publication cycle at the end of 2001, the new edition (called *Who's Who 2002*) was held in and operated in Librios software, typeset in-house, and most important of all, produced on schedule with an identical appearance to the previous edition so that a seamless transition had been achieved.

Commercial Benefits and Opportunities Delivered

The commercial benefits of using the Librios database can be separated into short-, medium- and long-term, or immediate, evolving and potential.

Short-term
In the short term, the immediate benefits were

- reduced costs;
- greater flexibility in the choice of suppliers;

- increased ability to exploit the potential of the data;
- reduced compilation workload;
- greater internal control and monitoring of costs and time;
- greater flexibility in scheduling;
- greater control of design, quality and publishing requirements.

The learning process was quick, minimizing the investment of time and cost relating to this. In practice it proved possible to convert both the content of *Who's Who* from the old form to the new, and also to convert the skills of the team to operate the new system without jeopardizing the on-going production process. There was with only a minor need for additional help with keyboarding to ensure the schedule of the annual cycle was adhered to.

The advantages of software that combines word processing and database technology, which is one of Librios' unique features, became increasingly apparent to the *Who's Who* team as the work progressed. This also applied to the benefits of working with Librios staff, who have a thorough working knowledge of the practical requirements of content management in general and of reference publishing in particular.

Medium-term

The evolving medium-term benefits include:
- the ability to provide licensed content, selectively, and at negligible cost, in a suitable format (XML) for syndication for online use, to an organization that perceives the value of it as an enhancement of their own online services;
- the ability to provide some or all of the content on CD-ROM, at very low cost, if a market for this is found;
- the ability to provide subsets of content, modified or unchanged, to related publications, and also to develop related publications, such as *Who's Who in the Theatre*, that have additional biographies but also overlap with the content of *Who's Who*, and by integrating the content of each help build up the resource as a whole;
- the ability to generate subsets of content for "spin-off" publications, such as *Who's Who in Government*;
- the ability to streamline the production process, by using outsource suppliers who can work directly on the database software, with it installed remotely (i.e. at the suppliers' offices), or potentially with it made accessible online, with corrections and new entries synchronized with the master database;
- a theming/taxonomic/classification structure is being introduced to improve the quality of the syndicated material (for instance, by adding power to online searches) as well as enhancing the potential to create book products based on cross-cut information.

Long-term

The potential long-term benefits are principally the integration of the content and the users' skills into a Knowledge Management system, which can grow as the business grows. This can materially assist the development of the business by improving internal management information so that organizational limits to growth are reduced, and by facilitating production processes so that they lead to economies of scale rather than increased administrative needs.

- Librios delivers the organizational benefit because it not only has the inbuilt workflow and version control features of an established Content Management system, but also has information tracking and analysis tools, combined with the potential for testing new process scenarios in a "what if?" manner. Pattern learning, content weighting, context management, and taxonomic browsing are also available when their knowledge management functions are required.

- The software delivers benefits for evolving production processes because it can be adapted easily to new requirements, in a way that encourages management to think of improvements rather than inhibiting decisions as many other systems do on the grounds of cost, disruption, and uncertainty of result. In Librios, for instance, a desired change can be implemented quickly in a trial form so it can be tested and evaluated before being applied to the main system, again with minimal or even no disturbance to the ongoing process. Training requirements in the updated system would normally be minimal, because the overall system design is generic and special features are used only when required – which makes them not only easy to understand but also intuitive to use.

Looking Ahead

The two fundamental requirements for a cost-effective solution to the content management issues faced by the *Who's Who* team related to cost and to effectiveness. The cost had to be low enough, not only in terms of license and support costs but also in terms of in-house costs such as editorial and management time, to avoid the need for net investment in change. And the effectiveness of the new system had to be high enough to deliver all the requirements without compromise.

In the words of a senior manager: *"We set the hardest target, and Librios assured us that they could achieve both low cost and high effectiveness. I'm pleased to say that they have proved as good as their word."*

The principles underlying this solution are not just relevant to this particular case, even though it appears to be a highly specific one. The detail may cloud the broader issue, which is that people have a long history of communication in different media. Once upon a time only words and pictures were used. Then handwriting and typography standardized the forms. Now electronic media are also used.

The underlying principle, however, is that information is essentially modular – we think in bits. We organize these bits in the way we think, and also – more significantly here – in the way we communicate. The media we use – voice, images, words, printed pages, on-screen visuals, audio sound-bites, and so on – sometimes help and sometimes seem to hinder the message we aim to convey. But whatever that message or that medium is, organization of the content can only assist the process of sharing it.

The management model then extends further, beyond manipulating the content itself to monitoring and refining the whole creative and commercial process. In psychology, this could be called self-awareness but, in communication, content management or knowledge management would be a more appropriate term.

These functions are currently being implemented by the *Who's Who* team, as they continue to combine the new technology with the tried and tested management techniques of the former system. But, as the technology opens up opportunities for expanding the core resource, developing subsidiary products, adding partially new and partially overlapping content, maintaining multiple parallel product lines drawing on common resources, expanding the team without increasing overheads, and reporting developments to their parent company, Bloomsbury plc, additional requirements and more knowledge-based functionality built into the core system will come into its own. As far as possible, intelligent technology – like intelligent management – should build with the future in mind. Without being prescient, this is what the Librios technology and the *Who's Who* strategic planning have done.

Questions

1. Some prominent authors, such as Michael Porter, contend that traditional strategic management approaches are adequate in any environment, and do not require any significant change, renewal or complementation. Review the various viewpoints in this "debate", and make your own (motivated) conclusions.

2. Why did the decade of the 1990s witness an emphasis on BPR (business process reengineering), TQM, outsourcing, downsizing and unbundling in strategic management? Are these techniques still relevant today?

3. Review the major analytical approaches to external environmental interpretations, and give your view on the need for additional/new environmental "sense-making" approaches and tools.

4. Some observers contend that an organization should not strive for a "fit" with its environment, but an intentional "misfit". Provide a logical review of this contention, and give your own opinion.

5. The traditional strategic management approaches are often contrasted as dichotomies of "prediction" vs. "learning", or "deliberate" vs. "emergent", or "outward-in" vs. "inward-out", or "design/configuration" vs. "incremental". Are the ends of the continuum necessarily "wrong"? What are the advantages and disadvantages inherent in each approach?

6. To what extent do the Encyclopaedia Britannica and Who's Who case studies reflect the shifts in traditional strategic management? Which of the shifts are more accentuated in each case study? Does this emphasis apply equally to other industries? Why/why not?

References

Chapter 2: Traditional Strategic Management Approaches, and their Deficiencies

[1] Grant, R.M. (2002), *Contemporary Strategy Analysis*, Fourth Edition, Oxford: Blackwell Publishers; Mintzberg, H. (1994), "The Rise and Fall of Strategic Planning", *Harvard Business Review,* January-February, 107-114; Collis, D.J. and Montgomery, C.A. (1995), "Competing on Resources: Strategy in the 1990's", *Harvard Business Review*, July-August, 118-128.

[2] Ansoff, H.I. (1965), *Corporate Strategy*, New York: McGraw-Hill Inc.

[3] Boston Consulting Group (1978), *Perspectives on Experience*, Boston: Boston Consulting Group.

[4] Porter, M.E. (1980), *Competitive Strategy*, New York: The Free Press.

[5] Porter M.E. (1996), "What is Strategy?", *Harvard Business Review*, November-December, 64.

[6] Grant, R.M. (1991), "The Resource Based Theory of Competitive Advantage: Implications for Strategy Formulation", *California Management Review*, 33, Spring, 114-135.

[7] D'Aveni, R.A. (1974), *Hypercompetition: Managing the Dynamics of Strategic Maneuvering*, New York: Free Press; Chakravarthy, B. (1997), "A New Strategy Framework for Coping with Turbulence", *Sloan Management Review*, Winter, 69-82; Eisenhardt, K.M. and Martin, J.A. (2000), "Dynamic Capabilities: What Are They?", *Strategic Management Journal*, 21, 1105-1121; Eisenhardt K.M. and Brown, S.L. (1999), "Patching: Restitching Business Portfolios in Dynamic Markets", *Harvard Business Review*, May-June, 72-82.

[8] Leonard-Barton, D. (1995), *Wellsprings of Knowledge,* Boston: Harvard Business School Press.

[9] Camillus, J. (1997), "Shifting the Strategic Management Paradigm", *European Management Journal*, 15 (1), 1-7.

[10] Mintzberg, H. (1994), *op.cit.*

[11] Senge, P. (1990), *The Fifth Discipline*, London: Century.

[12] Kaplan, R.S. and Norton D.P. (1996), *The Balanced Scorecard,* Boston: Harvard Business School Press.

[13] Roos, J. and Victor, B. (1999), "Towards a New Model of Strategy-Making as Serious Play", *European Management Journal*, 17(4), 348-355.

[14] Hamel, G. (1998), "Strategy Innovation and the Quest for Value", *Sloan Management Review*, 39(2): 7-14; Roos, J. and Victor, B. (1999), *op. cit.*

What Makes a Strategy Brilliant?

Bevin Alexander, *How Great Generals Win* (New York: Norton, 1993).

Adam Brandenburger and Barry J. Nalebuff, "The Right Game: Use Game Theory to Shape Strategy", *Harvard Business Review,* July-August 1995, pp. 57-71.

Andrew Campbell and Marcus Alexander, "What's Wrong with Strategy?" *Harvard Business Review,* November-December 1997, pp. 42-51.

Carl von Clausewitz, *On War,* ed. and intro. by Anatol Rapoport (Baltimore: Penguin Books, 1968).

Hugh Courtney, Jane Kirkland, and Patrick Viguerie, "Strategy Under Uncertainty", *Harvard Business Review,* November-December 1997, pp. 67-79.

David H. Freedman, "Is Management Still a Science?" *Harvard Business Review,* November-December 1992, pp. 26-38.

Russell W. Glenn, "No More Principles of War?" *Parameters: U.S. Army War College Quarterly,* Spring 1998, pp. 48-66.

Boris Gulko, "Is Chess Finished?" *Commentary,* July 1997, pp. 45-47.

G. Hamel, "Strategy as Revolution", *Harvard Business Review,* July-August 1996, pp. 69-82.

G. Hamel and C.K. Prahalad, "Strategic Intent", *Harvard Business Review,* May-June 1989, pp. 63-76.

Headquarters, Department of the Army, *FM 100-5: Operations* (Washington, 1993).

Bruce D. Henderson, "The Origin of Strategy", *Harvard Business Review,* November-December 1989, pp. 139-143.

Michael A. Hitt, R. Duane Ireland, Robert Hoskisson, and Robert D. Nixon, *Strategic Management: Competitiveness and Globalization,* 2nd ed. (Minneapolis/St. Paul: West Publishing, 1997).

Garry Kasparov, "IBM Owes Mankind a Rematch", *Time,* May 26, 1997, pp. 66-67.

John Keegan, *Guderian* (New York: Ballantine, 1973).

Marina Krol, "Have We Witnessed a Real-Life Turing Test?" *Computer,* March 1999, pp. 27-30.

Thomas S. Kuhn, *The Structure of Scientific Revolutions,* 3rd ed. (Chicago: University of Chicago Press, 1996).

Kenneth C. Laudon and Jane P. Laudon, *Management Information Systems,* 5th ed. (Upper Saddle River, NJ: Prentice-Hall, 1998).

John McDonald, *Strategy in Poker, Business and War* (New York: Norton, 1989).

Henry Mintzberg, "The Fall and Rise of Strategic Planning", *Harvard Business Review,* January-February 1994, pp. 107-114.

Henry Mintzberg and Joseph Lampel, "Reflecting on the Strategy Process", *Sloan Management Review,* Spring 1999, pp. 21-30.

Kenichi Ohmae, *The Mind of the Strategist: The Art of Japanese Business* (New York: McGraw-Hill, 1982).

Michael E. Porter, "What Is Strategy?" *Harvard Business Review,* November-December 1996, pp. 61-78.

Tom Wheeler, *Leadership Lessons from the Civil War* (New York: Currency Doubleday, 2000).

James P. Womack, Daniel T. Jones, and Daniel Roos, *The Machine That Changed the World* (New York: Rawson Associates, 1990).

H. Edward Wrapp, "Good Managers Don't Make Policy Decisions", *Harvard Business Review,* July-August 1984, pp. 8-21.

Peter Young and Omar Nelson Bradley, *Great Battles of the Modern World* (New York: Barnes & Noble Books; London: Bison Books, 1995).

III   A Systemic Approach to Business Models and Strategic Management

Chapter 3:
A New Mindset:
Systemic Strategic Management

Another New Evolutionary Era in Strategic Management?

The question inevitably arises if one is not just looking for another new evolutionary era (or strategic focus for a new decade) in strategic management. History is replete with many authors and researchers proposing a unique strategy management theory, and then looking for anecdotal evidence, often highly selective, to "validate" the different theory. The answer is an emphatic no, as the knowledge economy is causing a revolutionary shift, and not just another evolutionary emphasis in strategic management thinking. In Chapter 1 the challenges to strategic management orthodoxy due to the shift to the global knowledge economy were highlighted, and the revolutionary implications for strategy context, content and process indicated.

In Chapter 2, the inability of traditional strategic management approaches to deal with the revolutionary challenges posed by the knowledge economy were identified. These were challenges such as invisible assets no longer under organizational "control"; networks of relationships resulting in organizational structure becoming a variable and not a stable element; a focus on collaboration in ecosystems becoming as important for survival and performance as competition; and a descriptive strategy mindset that needs to shift to a creative strategy mindset.

Before reviewing specific new strategic management approaches and tools for the knowledge economy (the themes of Chapters 4 and 5) it is essential to provide a basis, or context, for adopting a additional strategic management mindset – a mindset of participating in and co-shaping social knowledge-based networks. This chapter firstly outlines the basis for strategic ecosystems thinking; secondly, makes a case for strategic management having to co-shape the environment; thirdly, indicates the emerging new dimensions of business behavior in networks; fourthly, summarizes the new revolutionary conceptual base of strategic management; and finally concludes by listing the new strategic management mindset "rules".

Business Ecosystems Thinking

A number of recent views are emerging of the firm not just as a legal, social and economic institution, but as a social organism that develops over time. De Geus,

Table 3.1 From Company Adaptation to Ecosystem Co-evolution

Issue	Company/Industry View	Ecosystem View
Boundaries	Boundaries are relatively fixed and stable	Boundaries are variable, often a matter of choice
Primary unit	Industry or company	The business ecosystem
Economic performance is a function of	Internal management and average profitability of industry	Value creation and stakeholders (especially customer) success (satisfaction, profitability etc.) in the business ecosystem
Central concern	Individual company growth	Development of, and position in, the ecosystem
Co-operation & Collaboration	Limited to direct suppliers and customers, to maintain existing boundaries	Includes all players relevant to the search for ideas, and unmet needs that can become part of the co-evolving business community
Competition	Seen as between products and between companies	Also seen as between ecosystems and for leadership within particular ecosystems
Strategy	Adaptation and out-Performing	Co-shaping and co-performing
Capabilities	Core competencies of the company	Distributed and co-opted capabilities in the ecosystem, often around new innovations

Wheatley, Moore, Sherman & Schultz, and Clippinger are among those that regard the firm as a social organism whose central characteristic is a knowledge system.[1] This approach proposes that a company be viewed not as a member of a single industry, but as a part of a *business ecosystem* that crosses a variety of industries, and is open to multidimensional knowledge impacts and influences. Table 2.1 provides an overview of the major differences between a company/industry adaptation view and an ecosystems view.

From Table 3.1 it can be seen that from an ecosystem perspective, the boundaries of the firm and industry are regarded as variable, and shaped by many actors in the business community. The strategy focus of an individual firm is to co-shape and co-perform with the other players in the business community and to build co-opted capabilities (including with customers) in the ecosystem, often around new innovations. The critical dimension of an ecosystem is that it spans a variety of industries, stakeholders, organizations, and markets and customers, not only those included in an organization's traditional industry, customer base and supply chain. This reflects current business reality, which displays a proliferation of new industries, "blurring" of traditional boundaries, deconstruction of "old" industries, and innovative new cross-industry linkages – witness e.g., "bankassurance". Examples are also Infotainment (information and entertainment industry boundaries blurring) and Lifesciences (pharmaceutical, agriculture, chemical, human wellness/fitness) as Novartis proves in its strategy.

In a business ecosystem, companies and customers co-evolve knowledge and capabilities around a new value proposition (or "product"): they work collaboratively and competitively to support development of new products, satisfy different customer needs, configure new value chains, and incorporate new rounds of innovations. The basic tension is between the parts and the whole – the emphasis on the parts has been called mechanistic, reductionistic, or atomistic; the emphasis on the whole is termed holistic, organismic or ecological. In 20th century science, the holistic perspective has become known as *systemic*, as opposed to *systematic*. Each part can be seen as an organ that shapes the other parts, thus being both an organized and self-organized being. In contemporary theories of living systems, the concept of organization has been refined to that of self-organization, and understanding the pattern of self-organization is regarded as the key to understanding the essential nature of life.

Business ecosystems thinking requires a grasp of the integrated whole of business within its environment, whose essential properties arise from relationships among its parts. "Systemic thinking" is the basis of this mindset, i.e. understanding of a phenomenon within the context of a larger whole. The recent great shock to strategic management has been that systems cannot be understood by analysis. The properties of the parts are not intrinsic properties, but can be understood only within the context of the larger whole. Accordingly, systems thinking does not concentrate on basic building blocks, but rather on basic principles of organization – it is the whole that determines the behavior of the parts. The business ecosystem concept can now be defined: a community of business and related organisms and their environment, interacting as an ecological unit.

Adopting new strategic management premises for ecosystem success

Ecosystems thinking recognizes that formal, hierarchical structures and their logic should be complemented, if not replaced, with self-organization, magnifying rather than obscuring individual differences, and focusing on business relationships, communities, patterns and relativism. Strategic success now becomes a function of a firm's talent for thriving in dynamic nonlinear systems that rely on network feedback and emergent relationships. The core premises[2] of new strategic management thinking are:

- Recognizing that individual, unit or organizational success requires a healthy ecosystem. Task-based, fragmented thinking is discarded in favor of workflows and process-based activity.
- Emphasizing the importance of unpredictable, nonlinear, natural consequences. While some strategic consequences are the result of deliberate intent, most are emergent results, i.e. behavior that spontaneously and unexpectedly follows a different set of rules or patterns.
- Influencing and co-shaping of the business ecosystem is achieved by managing initial conditions and the underlying forces ("attractors" or "coherence mechanisms") which organize and guide the system. Attractors, such as values and vision, create constraints on a firm's activities. Since behavior patterns can emerge

without being intended, i.e. in a chaotic way, influence through attractors (or coherence mechanisms) means shaping the basic elements that impose some regularity on a system. Strategic management now includes the manipulation of these concurrent and paradoxical elements to create and sustain a healthy, evolving ecosystem.

- Understanding that systemic change is a continuous, relentless process. Co-evolution results from interdependent webs or networks experiencing continuous waves of changes – complex systems constantly coalesce, decay, change and grow.

- Accepting the concept of self-organization that triggers transformation. This means that firms can generate intelligent, effective responses to the need for change without externally imposed direction or plans – they emerge naturally through the implementation of self-organizing principles. In effect, emergent strategies will be more important than intended strategies.

- Recognizing that cultural integrity is a basis for establishing relevant boundaries. Ecosystem-based strategies rely on shared values and common purposes. Whereas physical systems are shaped by unchanging natural laws, social systems are the result of interventions by individuals and groups, and cultural norms determine the limits on these interventions.

Strategically coping with more complex external and internal environments

The ecosystems approach to business life raises an important question. If everything is connected to everything else, how can we ever hope to understand the complexity of it all, let alone influence and shape it? The answer: the discovery of approximate knowledge and the principles of complexity theory makes this possible. The traditional strategic management approaches are based on the belief of the certainty of scientific knowledge and specific industry and world "views". In the new strategy management mindset it is recognized that all theories and knowledge are limited and approximate.

In resorting to concepts of self-organization and emergent behavior, we are acknowledging the limits to management as traditionally defined. If the environment of business is complex and unpredictable, we are unable to formulate strategy based on a rational, objective analysis of the firm and its environment, no matter how well trained we are in the art and science of strategic management. This challenge is addressed by complexity theory, evolving from research into complex adaptive systems (CAS). Complexity science is the name commonly used to describe a set of interdisciplinary studies that share the idea that all things tend to self-organize into systems, while complexity theory is based on the observation that in an enormous diversity of systemic patterns there are simple, underlying sets of rules.

Recently, authors such as Eisenhardt, Brown, Sull, Galunic, Martin, Kelly and Allison have applied the concepts of complexity theory to strategic management in turbulent environments.[3] Their research points to the advantages of business ecosystems that evolve to the "edge of chaos" – an area of business activity where the greatest potential for creativity and innovation resides, with astute management requiring a balance between "no rules" or boundaries (total chaos) and rigid norms and controls (total control). Such dynamic ecosystems are capable of both adaptations and reinventions, i.e. are able to make larger "leaps" towards higher "fitness peaks" such as "leapfrogging" competition to create a new business model or industry, while avoiding the danger of "falling off the fitness edge" into chaos.

In coping with more complex internal and external environments, i.e. locating at the edge of chaos and scaling new fitness and performance peaks, strategic management processes that guide the behavior of the organization can be introduced. These include:

- Establishing a few, *simple, robust rules* that provide general direction but do not confine activities and behavior. Companies such as Microsoft, Vodafone, Yahoo! and Cisco do not plan integrated strategies in any traditional sense – they are unable to do so because their markets are too chaotic. Rather than selecting a market position or focusing on a particular set of capabilities, they select a few strategically significant options and processes, and craft simple rules in areas such as product innovation, market entry, alliancing and experimentation. Five categories of simple rules are identified by Eisenhardt & Sull[4]:
  - *Boundary rules*: "rules of thumb", for example in screening opportunities.
  - *Activity rules:* "how-to" rules that designate a common approach for a company to approach and exploit opportunities.
  - *Priority rules*: rules to determine priorities in resource allocation.
  - *Timing rules*: rules for lead and scheduling times.
  - *Exit Rules*: termination and disengagement rules.
- Adopting a *co-evolutionary approach* for sharing resources and capabilities among businesses and organizational units. Rather than to try to manage business linkages from a structural perspective, it may be better for organizations to create a context within which businesses can co-evolve. Two elements of such a context are[5]:
  - Maintaining flexible, adaptive boundaries to each business to enable voluntary collaborations to thrive. For example, Disney's merchandising spin-offs from their movies, such as videos, theme park attractions, stage musicals and hundreds of merchandise items are not planned by corporate leadership, but emerge through voluntary cooperation across Disney's different divisions and alliance partners.
  - Linking rewards to individual business performance, rather than to reward collaborative efforts.

Applications of complexity theory to strategic management provide analytical support in favor of "emergent" rather than planned, intentional approaches to strategic management. With the emphasis on organizational processes rather than structures, there is a logical emergent focus on building and managing *dynamic capabilities*, not merely to compete better, but especially to co-evolve better, and to be careful to avoid possible core rigidities developing. According to Teece et al., dynamic capabilities are "the firm's ability to integrate, build and reconfigure internal and external competencies to address rapidly changing environments".[6] Specifying what these dynamic capabilities are, where they are located, and what their architecture looks like, represents a major challenge. Eisenhardt and Martin suggest that a critical feature is a

Microsoft's dynamic capabilities and robust strategies[7]

In the late 1980s, with the DOS operating system approaching the end of its useful life, Bill Gates focused on moving the industry to another Microsoft product, Windows. Appreciating the uncertainty of this development and its possible acceptance in the business ecosystem, he hedged his bets by also investing in Windows' competitors: Unix, OS/2 and the Apple Macintosh system. In addition, his company developed generic capabilities in object-oriented programming and graphical interface design – skills that would be useful no matter which system won in the ecosystem, even if it were a complete unknown. Gates's approach of pursuing several paths simultaneously is intrinsically complex, and also confusing to both existing customers and employees.

Robust strategy differs from traditional industry and scenario analysis in that it does not presuppose an ability to identify the most or least likely outcomes. Being robust calls for the ability to pursue a range of potentially conflicting strategies at the same time. In the case of Microsoft, it included major *shaping* bets such as Windows, *hedging* bets (support of OS/2), and *no-regrets* dynamic capability moves that are valid regardless of environmental outcome (building object-oriented programming skills). Microsoft operates more like a complex adaptive business system, with a range of strategies that cover a spectrum of possibilities and co-evolve with other organizations in its ecosystem over time.

process that allows the firm to alter its resource base.[8] In turbulent environments, dynamic capabilities rely extensively on new knowledge emerging for specific situations, requiring organizational routines to be simple, flexible and adaptable.

Traditional strategic management emphasizes a focused line of attack – a clear statement of where, how and when to compete. In a complex adaptive business ecosystem, a focused strategy to dominate a market or industry might be necessary for temporary survival, but is not sufficient in the long run. Given an uncertain, turbulent environment, strategies have to be robust – able to perform well in a variety of possible future environments. One company that has managed to be both focused and robust is Microsoft (see box).

New Organizing Structures to Enable Co-Shaping of Organizational Capabilities and Behavior

New organizing structures are necessary to enable co-shaping and co-evolving organizational capabilities and behavior to develop. This presents strategic management with a paradox, which cannot be resolved as simple trade-offs: having strategies that are both focused and robust; operating both conservatively and innovating radically; being efficient today while also adapting for tomorrow; maintaining diversity while establishing standards and routines; optimizing both the scale of a large organization, and the entrepreneurial flexibility and flair of an innovative start-up. The central strategic management challenge in a complex adaptive business ecosystem is to be both a competitor and an evolver, this also includes the implementation of structures that drive efficiencies but are also conducive to innovation. For example:

- Disney manages the tension between conservation and innovation by maintaining focused attention to detail and discipline, but simultaneously allowing experimentation and mistakes in the pursuit of innovation.
- General Motors started its Saturn division in a "greenfields" organization to free itself from the constraints of corporate bureaucracy of its established organization.
- AT & T split itself into three companies to create smaller organizations and reduce strategic conflict between established practices and entrepreneurial ventures.

The effects of the above strategy paradoxes present huge management challenges – we witness how many big (incumbent) organizations, despite their resources, are unable to respond to smaller, entrepreneurial competitors; likewise, many traditional small enterprises go out of business due to their inability to adapt to industry innovations. The fact is that traditional strategic management approaches and tools prepare companies well to be competitors, but not evolvers. Grant proposes a new strategy mindset in the design of organizations to a) develop and deploy multiple organizational capabilities; and b) design of organizations to permit rapid adaptability.[9]

a) Multiple structures for development and deployment of organizational capabilities

One solution to the strategic management paradoxes in turbulent environments is to simultaneously deploy different structures for different purposes and tasks. The principles of knowledge management provide one approach to understand how different capabilities require different types of structure. Knowledge management distinguishes between building the organization's stock of knowledge ("exploration") and deploying the existing stock of knowledge ("exploitation"). Separate (or "parallel") structures for pursuing both exploratory activities, e.g. for experimenting with new business models, and exploiting activities, e.g. optimizing existing value chain configurations, are necessary.

Examples of separate structures include:

- GE's "Work-Out" program is a classic example of a separate structure effecting change within the formal organization structure.
- Chevron's "Breakthrough Teams" were formed from multiple levels and functions in the company.
- Texaco's "Star Quality" program created a multiplicity of quality management groups in different organizational structures.
- 3M's innovative new products emerge from separate informal organization structures, which may ultimately form the basis for new business units within the formal structure.

Informal networks in which individuals share experience and expertise across organizational boundaries are called "communities of practice"[10] – a tool further elaborated on in Chapter 5. The move towards team-based, project-based and process-based structures indicates that the building of dynamic capabilities may be better undertaken by teams that self-organize, rather than relying on management direction. For example, processes that co-opt customer competence embrace the entirety of an organization's interactions with its customers, enabling co-shaping of innovations and new customer value propositions.

b) Organizational design for rapid adaptability

To successfully manage gradual evolutionary change with occasional revolutionary leaps requires an *ambidextrous* strategic management mindset – one rooted in "loosening" the formal organizational structure for rapid adaptability.[11] Welch's approach to management at GE involved a minimalist approach to formal control systems – its once elaborate strategic planning system was simplified to focus on a few issues with a minimal degree of direction and control. Slogans such as "boundaryless", "destroy-your-company-dot-com", "six-sigma" and "work-out" directly influenced the culture of GE and permitted more complex patterns of collaboration with resilience for rapid adaptability and innovation in the GE ecosystem.

In order to create an organization that can resolve the paradoxes between efficiency and creativity, management should be more concerned with developing and maintaining a social system guided by coherence mechanisms such as purpose, values and behavioral norms. Four concepts are useful in formulating coherence mechanisms: *identity, knowledge, modularity* and *networks*.

- *Identity*: An organization's purpose must reside in the heads and hearts of its members – a shared concept of what the organization fundamentally *is*.
- Knowledge: Information provides the medium through which an organization relates to its environment, but knowledge enables individuals within the organization to know how to react to external changes, and how to influence and shape the environment.
- *Modularity*: Structures based on loosely-coupled, semi-autonomous modules possess considerable adaptation advantages over more tightly integrated structures. Modular structures are particularly useful in reconciling the need for close collaboration at the small group level with the benefits of critical mass at divisional or organizational levels.
- *Networks*: Responsiveness to a wide range of external circumstances necessitates every individual to have a wide range of connections to other individuals, with the potential for unplanned connections. For `example, the use of intranets and extranets to link together the different parts of the organization and outside companies, as well as customers, has the effect of blurring the boundaries between internal units and external companies. The flexibility of these linkages enables the capabilities resident within inter-firm networks to be reconfigured in order to adapt quickly to external change.

Shifting the Conceptual Base of Strategic Management from an Ecosystems Model to a Socio-Cultural Model

From the above review of new strategic organizing structures, it is evident that the biological model of business ecosystems should be further expanded to a socio-cultural model. While ecosystems thinking is a useful analogy of business life as a natural organism (a biological model), it is limited to uni-minded systems thinking and not multi-minded systems thinking (a socio-cultural model)[12].

Table 3.2, below, indicates that a shift in the conceptual base (or mindset) of strategic management can occur in two categories: a change in the nature of perceived reality (organization perceived as a machine model, or living organism, or socio-cultural entity), or a change in the method of inquiry (analytical approach, or systems/holistic approach). We are now facing the challenge of a dual shift in the knowledge economy of the 21st century. Not only has there been a shift of paradigm in our understanding of the conception of an organization from *machine* to *organism* to *socio-cultural co-shaper*, but there has also been a profound shift in our assumptions regarding the means of knowing (or method of inquiry) from *analytical thinking*, i.e. the science of dealing with independent sets of variables, to *holistic thinking*, i.e. the art and science of handling interdependent sets of variables.

The resolution of the organizational paradoxes described previously requires a dual shift in the strategic management mindset. The first shift will result in the ability to see the organization as a multi-minded, socio-cultural system, consisting of a voluntary association of purposeful members who come together to serve themselves by serving a need in the environment. The second shift enables management to comprehend chaos and complexity, and to learn to deal with an interdependent set of variables. The nature of this dual shift is briefly reviewed:

Table 3.2 A Socio-Cultural Model as Conceptual Base of Strategic Management

Perception of Reality / Nature of Inquiry (Means of Knowing)	Machine Model *Mindless System*	Biological Model *Uni-minded System*	Socio-Cultural Model *Multi-minded System*
Analytical Approach	Division or Partition of Parts and Labour	Diversity & Growth	Participative Management
Independent Variables	Henry Ford's Mass Production System	Alfred Sloan's Divisional Structure	Participative Teams and Individuals
Systems Approach	Joint Optimization	Flexibility & Control	Interactive Management
Interdependent Variables	Operations Research	Cybernetics Model	Systemic Redesign Model

Source: Adapted from Gharajedaghi, J. (1999), *Systems Thinking: Managing Chaos and Complexity, Boston:* Butterworth-Heinemann.

- *The first paradigm shift: From a mechanistic view to a multi-minded socio-cultural view*

The *mechanistic view* maintains that the universe is a machine, and an organization consists of discrete parts, each performing only a simple task of horizontal, vertical and circular motions. The essence of the machine mode is that an organization is a mindless system – it has no purpose of its own. It is used by its owner/s as a tool to make profit, and is based on performance criteria of reliability and efficiency. The *biological view*, or living organism paradigm, is also simple and elegant: an organization is considered a uni-minded living system, just like a human being, with a purpose of its own. The purpose is survival, and to survive in unstable structures of open systems, it has to grow, with profit being the means to achieve this. In contrast to mechanistic views, in which profit is an end in itself, in the biological mode it is only a means to an end. Although uni-minded systems have a choice, their parts do not – the organization is seen as being under the control of an executive function, and its parts have no choice – if parts should display choice, conflict would arise and the organization as a system would experience major difficulties.

The *socio-cultural view* considers the organization as a voluntary association of purposeful members who manifest themselves as a choice of both ends and means. The critical variable is purpose – it is a purposeful system, and organizations are part of a larger purposeful whole, the society. Simultaneously, it has purposeful individuals and units as its own members. The fulfillment of a purposeful part's desires depends on fulfillment of the larger system's requirements, and vice versa. While the elements of mechanical systems are energy-bonded, those of biological systems are information and coordination bonded, and those of socio-cultural systems are knowledge and interaction bonded. The members of the socio-cultural organization are held together by coherence mechanisms, such as common objectives and sharing of values embedded in their culture. The culture is the "glue" that integrates the parts into a cohesive whole.

- *The second paradigm shift: From analytical thinking to systemic thinking*

Analytical thinking and systemic thinking are very distinct. Analysis is a three-step process of firstly taking apart, then observing and attempting to explain the behavior of the parts separately, and finally trying to understand the parts as an explanation of the whole. *Systemic thinking* uses a completely different process: it puts the system in the context of the larger environment of which it is part, and studies the role it plays (or should/could play) in the larger whole.

While the analytical approach has remained intact for the past four hundred years or more, systemic thinking has already progressed through three distinct generations of change, namely:

- First generation systems thinking: *operations research*
  (interdependency in the context of mechanistic systems)
- Second generation systems thinking: *cybernetics and open systems*
  (interdependency and self-organization in the context of living systems)

– Third generation systemic thinking: *systemic redesign*
(the triple challenge of interdependency, self-organization, and choice and design in socio-cultural systems).

Biological systems primarily self-organize through genetic codes, while socio-cultural systems primarily self-organize through cultural codes. In addition to being a living system, social organizations are also purposeful and capable of innovatively co-shaping (or co-designing) of their value propositions and other activities.

The DNA of social systems is their culture, and third generation systems thinking has to deal with both the existing cultural "prints" (or "memes", analogous to genes in biological metaphor), which are reproducing traditional value propositions, while also co-shaping innovative, new cultural "prints" necessary in a turbulent environment. Purposeful social systems are capable of recreating their future, and they do so by redesigning themselves – members of an organization, unlike the parts of a biological being, do not react passively to the information and knowledge they receive or engender.

In reality, a large part of organizational life in the world today is still caught in the analytical and mechanistic mindsets. Their analytical thinking cannot deal with the issues of trust, knowledge, belonging, care, nurturing, empowerment and co-shaping required in a world of increasing collaboration (e.g. strategic alliances), choice and personal fulfillment. Members increasingly behave knowledgeably and independently, and frustration associated with excessive levels of conflict, often reinforces the organizational inability to change. Shifting the conceptual base of strategic management to a socio-cultural model seems to be a prerequisite to handling the challenges of the networked knowledge economy of the 21st century.

Towards a synthesis: the new strategic management paradigm for the knowledge economy – systemic strategic management – and its underlying precepts

The new strategic management paradigm for the knowledge economy now becomes clear: **systemic strategic management**: *co-shaping viable value propositions through dynamic organizational capabilities in socio-cultural systems*. Co-designing, building and adapting socio-cultural value propositions require dynamic collaborative organizational capabilities of sense making, relating, choice and other processes, enabled by coherence mechanisms in open systems (including competitive systems).

The underlying precepts of this new strategic management paradigm are:

• The competitive orientation of the "outward-in" and "inward-out" approaches to strategic management is now replaced by a collaborative *and* competitive orientation.

• Departing from traditional views of structures being either external or internal to the organization, and relatively static, the new paradigm regards all structures as either fully external or partly external. For example, structures of "communities of practice", interactive teams, joint company-customer product development, "networked incubation" (see Chapter 5), and strategic alliances are all based on open systems thinking, with interactive external-internal linkages.

- Successful businesses today must be willing to "cannibalize" themselves to "save themselves" for future success. They must be willing to destroy the old practices and value propositions while they are still successful, if they wish to build the new before it is successful. If they do not destroy themselves, others will do so.

- Businesses that aim to grow rapidly must take advantage of technological disequilibriums, exploit developmental disequilibriums, or create socio-cultural disequilibriums. All other activities are likely to be imitative, defensive, slow-growth and eventually commodity-oriented in nature.

- There are no institutional or structural substitutes for individual entrepreneurial change agents. Any organization that values order above all else will not be creative, entrepreneurial and sustainable successful in the future.

- Recognizing, understanding and accepting the limits imposed by their genetic socio-cultural weaknesses are the beginning of organizational knowledge, wisdom and reinvention.

- One of the biggest challenges for strategic management is to provide the organization's members (including its human resources) with a knowledge-based, collaborative and "fulfilling" environment, rather than with careers in a system where no careers remain.

- Change from a "direction-and-control" mechanistic mindset to a "guidance and self-managing" mindset, i.e. enabling creative and adaptive organizational systems and self-managing processes, vested in empowered teams and individuals, guided by coherence mechanisms rooted in identity (e.g. purposes, values) and protocols (in knowledge creation and sharing, networking and modularity). Managing "at-the-edge-of-chaos" recognizes diversity and self-management, and coherence mechanisms prevent autonomy from dissolving into anarchy.

- Multiple structures and dichotomous strategic management are essential for "ambidextrous" organizations – some traditional parts of a business have to be managed by mechanistic approaches of efficiency, while other entrepreneurial, flexible parts have to be nurtured with a socio-cultural approach. Continuous waves of traditional business units being replaced by new ones are the order of the day in the knowledge economy.

- Change from a focus on strategy content and strategic commitment, to strategy processes and strategic flexibility. Organizational strategy now becomes an array of flexible strategic options with various capability potentials, instead of a fixed "plan" or fixed directional commitment. A range of robust strategy options enables development and rapid deployment of capabilities when it is advantageous to do so.

- Several key managerial challenges arise, as are evident from the above list. The nature, role and activities of the strategy "manager" or "leadership" now change significantly, and these are the theme of Chapter 6.

Conclusion

In conclusion, it is becoming evident that a new strategic management mindset (or paradigm) is necessary for creative, sustainable organizational success in the knowledge economy. The traditional mindset of competition-focused, "direct-and-control", and existing industry value chain optimization, simply cannot comprehensively deal with the increased fluidity and creativity engendered by the knowledge-networked economy of today. Having traced the nature and underlying elements of the *systemic strategic management* mindset, the next chapter (Chapter 4) focuses on frameworks (or models) to enable strategic organizational reinvention to take place either dually, i.e. alongside existing business models, or singly in separate organizations or organizational divisions.

Predators and Prey:
A New Ecology of Competition[*]

By James F. Moore

For most companies today, the only truly sustainable advantage comes from out-innovating the competition.

Successful businesses are those that evolve rapidly and effectively. Yet innovative businesses can't evolve in a vacuum. They must attract resources of all sorts, drawing in capital, partners, suppliers, and customers to create cooperative networks.

Much has been written about such networks, under the rubric of strategic alliances, virtual organizations, and the like. But these frameworks provide little systematic assistance for managers who seek to understand the underlying strategic logic of change. Even fewer of these theories help executives anticipate the managerial challenges of nurturing the complex business communities that bring innovations to market.

How is it that a company can create an entirely new business community – like IBM in personal computers – and then lose control and profitability in that same business? Is there a stable structure of community leadership that matches fast-changing conditions? And how can companies develop leadership that successfully adapts to continual waves of innovation and change? These questions remain unanswered because most managers still frame the problem in the old way: companies go head-to-head in an industry, battling for market share. But events of the last decade, particularly in high-technology businesses, amply illustrate the limits of that understanding.

In essence, executives must develop new ideas and tools for strategizing, tools for making tough choices when it comes to innovations, business alliances, and leadership of customers and suppliers. Anthropologist Gregory Bateson's definition of *co-evolution* in both natural and social systems provides a useful starting place. In his book *Mind and Nature,* Bateson describes co-evolution as a process in which interdependent species evolve in an endless reciprocal cycle – in which "changes in species A set the stage for the natural selection of changes in species B" – and vice versa. Consider predators and their prey, for instance, or flowering plants and their pollinators.

---

[*] Taken with permission from Harvard Business Review, May-June 1993, pp. 75-86

Another insight comes from biologist Stephen Jay Gould, who has observed that natural ecosystems sometimes collapse when environmental conditions change too radically. Dominant combinations of species may lose their leadership. New ecosystems then establish themselves, often with previously marginal plants and animals at the center. For current businesses dealing with the challenges of innovation, there are clear parallels and profound implications.

To extend a systematic approach to strategy, I suggest that a company be viewed not as a member of a single industry but as part of a *business ecosystem* that crosses a variety of industries. In a business ecosystem, companies co-evolve capabilities around a new innovation: they work cooperatively and competitively to support new products, satisfy customer needs, and eventually incorporate the next round of innovations.

For example, Apple Computer is the leader of an ecosystem that crosses at least four major industries: personal computers, consumer electronics, information, and communications. The Apple ecosystem encompasses an extended web of suppliers that includes Motorola and Sony and a large number of customers in various market segments.

Apple, IBM, Ford, Wal-Mart, and Merck have all been or still are the leaders of business ecosystems. While the center may shift over time, the role of the leader is valued by the rest of the community. Such leadership enables all ecosystem members to invest toward a shared future in which they anticipate profiting together.

Yet in any larger business environment, several ecosystems may vie for survival and dominance: the IBM and Apple ecosystems in personal computers, for example, or Wal-Mart and Kmart in discount retailing. In fact, it's competition among business ecosystems, not individual companies, that's largely fueling today's industrial transformation. Managers can't afford to ignore the birth of new ecosystems or the competition among those that already exist.

Whether that means investing in the right new technology, signing on suppliers to expand a growing business, developing crucial elements of value to maintain leadership, or incorporating new innovations to fend off obsolescence, executives must understand the stages that all business ecosystems pass through – and, more important, how to direct the changes.

The Birth of Business Ecosystems

Bet on a seed innovation that can lead to revolutionary products.
Discover the right customer value proposition.
Design a business that can serve the potential market.

A business ecosystem, like its biological counterpart, gradually moves from a random collection of elements to a more structured community. Think of a prairie grassland that is succeeded by stands of conifers, which in turn evolve into a more complex forest dominated by hardwoods. Business ecosystems condense out of the original swirl of capital, customer interest, and talent generated by a new innovation, just as successful species spring from the natural resources of sunlight, water, and soil nutrients.

Every business ecosystem develops in four distinct stages: birth, expansion, leadership, and self-renewal – or, if not self-renewal, death. In reality, of course, the evolutionary stages blur, and the managerial challenges of one stage often crop up in another. Yet I've observed the four stages in many companies over time, across businesses as diverse as retailing, entertainment, and pharmaceuticals. What remains the same from business to business is the process of co-evolution: the complex interplay between competitive and cooperative business strategies (see the table, "The Evolutionary Stages of a Business Ecosystem").

During Stage 1 of a business ecosystem, entrepreneurs focus on defining what customers want, that is, the value of a proposed new product or service and the best form for delivering it. Victory at the birth stage, in the short term, often goes to those who best define and implement this customer value proposition. Moreover, during Stage 1 of a business ecosystem, it often pays to cooperate. From the leader's standpoint, in particular, business partners help fill out the full package of value for customers. And by attracting important "follower" companies, leaders may stop them from helping other emerging ecosystems.

The rise of the personal computer is a revealing example of ecological business development. In the early 1970s, a new technology – the microprocessor – emerged with the potential to spawn vast new applications and dramatically reduce the cost of computing. Yet this innovation sat dormant for several years. By 1975, hobbyist machines like the Altair and IMSAI had penetrated a narrow market. But these computers were not products that could be used by the average person.

Starting in the late 1970s, Tandy Corporation, Apple, and others introduced early versions of what would eventually become the personal computer. The seed innovation they all chose was the microprocessor, but these first designers also recognized that other products and services had to be created to bring the whole package together. These ranged from hardware components to software to services like distribution and customer support.

Apple and Tandy each had a different strategy for creating a full, rich ecosystem. Apple worked with business partners and talked about "evangelizing" to encourage co-evolution. While the company tightly controlled its basic computer design and operating system software, it encouraged independent software developers to write programs for its machine. Apple also cooperated with independent magazines, computer stores, and training institutions – and even seeded a number of school districts with Apple IIs.

Tandy, on the other hand, took a more vertically integrated approach. It attempted to buy and then own its software, ranging from the operating system to programming languages and applications like word processors. The company controlled sales, service, support and training, and market development by selling exclusively through its Radio Shack stores. At the same time, it discouraged independent magazines devoted to its TRS-80 machines. Therefore, Tandy's simpler and more tightly controlled eco-

The Evolutionary Stages of a Business Ecosystem

	Cooperative Challenges	**Competitive Challenges**
Birth	Work with customers and suppliers to define the new value proposition around a seed innovation.	Protect your ideas from others who might be working toward defining similar offers. Tie up critical lead customers, key suppliers, and important channels.
Expansion	Bring the new offer to a large market by working with suppliers and partners to scale up supply to achieve maximum market coverage.	Defeat alternative implementations of similar ideas. Ensure that your approach is the market standard in its class through dominating key market segments.
Leadership	Provide a compelling vision for the future that encourages suppliers and customers to work together to continue improving the complete offer.	Maintain strong bargaining power in relation to other players in the ecosystem, including key customers and valued suppliers.
Self-Renewal	Work with innovators to bring new ideas to existing ecosystem.	Maintain high barriers to entry prevent innovators from building alternative ecosystems. Maintain high customers switching costs in order to buy time to incorporate new ideas into your own products and services.

system did not build the excitement, opportunities, and inner rivalries of Apple's, nor did it harness as much capital and talent through the participation of other companies.

Tandy's approach got the company out front fast; in 1979, it had sales of $95 million compared with Apple's $47.9 million. However, Tandy's tight control of its ecosystem ultimately led to slower growth at a time when establishing market share and a large user base was essential to success. By 1982, Apple's $583.1 million in sales had decisively passed Tandy's $466.4 million.

Meanwhile, a third business ecosystem emerged in the early days of personal computing. It never rivaled Apple's or Tandy's in size, but it did help IBM enter the fray. This third ecosystem centered around two software companies: Digital Research and Micropro. In 1977, Digital Research made its software operating system CP/M available independent of hardware. That separation allowed almost any small manufacturer to assemble components and put out a usable personal computer. Overnight, a variety of small companies entered the business, building on the same Zilog microprocessor used in the early Tandy machines.

In 1979, Micropro brought out a word processor that ran on CP/M-based machines. Wordstar was the first truly powerful word processor, and it took an important group of potential PC customers – writers and editors – by storm. Demand for CP/M machines soared, fueling the growth if not the fortunes of small companies like Morrow and Kaypro.

But during the first stage of any business ecosystem, co-evolving companies must do more than satisfy customers; a leader must also emerge to initiate a process of rapid, ongoing improvement that draws the entire community toward a grander future. In the Apple and Tandy ecosystems, the hardware companies provided such leadership by studying the market, defining new generations of functionality, and orchestrating suppliers and partners to bring improvements to market. In the CP/M ecosystem, however, the hardware companies were bedeviled by rivalry among themselves. Infighting kept down prices and profit margins, and none of the CP/M companies could afford heavy advertising programs.

In Stage 1, established companies like IBM are often better off waiting and watching carefully as a new market sorts itself out. The iterative process of trying out innovative ideas and discovering which solutions are attractive to customers is hard to accomplish in a traditional corporate culture. And the diverse experimentation that thrives in an entrepreneurial scene provides more "genetic diversity" from which the market can ultimately select the fittest offering.

Established companies can subsequently replicate successful ideas and broadcast them across a wider market. In other words, they can enter the market at Stage 2 by appropriating the developmental work of others. Meanwhile, original ecosystems that succeed, like Apple's, do so by consciously nurturing a full community of partners and suppliers right from the start.

Expansion: Capturing Territory

Compete against other ecosystems to control strategic markets.
Stimulate demand for your product or service offering.
Meet demand with adequate supply.

In Stage 2, business ecosystems expand to conquer broad new territories. Just as grasses and weeds rapidly cover the bare, scorched ground left after a forest fire, some business expansions meet little resistance. But in other cases, rival ecosystems may be closely matched and choose to attack the same territory. Direct battles for market share break out. Fighting can get ugly as each ecosystem tries to exert pressure on suppliers and customers to join up.

In the end, one business ecosystem may triumph, or rival ecosystems may reach semistable accommodations. Think of a hardwood forest that borders a grassland. The zone of conflict at the boundary may shift from year to year, but it never completely wipes out either ecosystem.

In general, two conditions are necessary for Stage 2 expansion: (1) a business concept that a large number of customers will value; and (2) the potential to scale up the concept to reach this broad market. During the expansion stage, established companies can exercise enormous power in marketing and sales, as well as in the management of large-scale production and distribution, literally crushing smaller ecosystems in the process.

IBM, for example, entered the personal computer business in 1981. In contrast to its own history and culture of vertical integration, IBM followed and extended the Apple model of building a community of supporters. IBM took on partners and opened its computer architecture to outside suppliers. Moreover, it adopted a microprocessor from Intel that incorporated all of the instructions available in the Zilog microprocessor in Tandy and CP/M machines. And IBM licensed MS-DOS, a software operating system from then tiny Microsoft, which was almost a near clone of CP/M. As a result, Wordstar and other popular application programs could easily be ported over to the IBM PC.

One of the most important managerial challenges in Stage 2 is to stimulate market demand without greatly exceeding your ability to meet it. IBM certainly stimulated demand for its new machine through a combination of heavy brand advertising, distribution through Sears and other channels, and building its own network of specialty stores. By anyone's measure, IBM's approach to expanding its PC ecosystem was a major success. Its personal computing business grew from $500 million in 1982 to $5.65 billion by 1986, and IBM's ecosystem rapidly dominated the market.

However, IBM also generated much more demand than it could meet. The company maintained high prices, which encouraged others to enter the market by setting a high price umbrella under which they could thrive. Compaq, for example, became the fastest company to join the *Fortune* "500" based on supplying machines to meet demand in the IBM ecosystem.

IBM did its best to keep up with demand. In the early 1980s, it invested directly in several key suppliers to help it grow fast enough to meet the market. Intel, for example, received $250 million from IBM in 1983. Concerned about its image as an insensitive behemoth, as well as possible antitrust objections, IBM managers carefully assured these suppliers that the help came without any strings attached.

IBM's relationships with suppliers were basically nonexclusive. Obviously, suppliers like Intel, Microsoft, and Lotus were happy to help the success of Compaq and others because it allowed them to diversify the risk of overdependence on IBM. For its part, IBM was flush with more demand and success than it knew what to do with. Top managers didn't focus on slowing the development of clone makers and nonexclusive suppliers – or keeping crucial elements of value like the microprocessor in-house. At first, IBM didn't attack new competitors within its ecosystem through the courts, through special promotions, or by lowering its own prices.

However clear the threat from the rest of the pack appears to us now, at the time, IBM and its business partners were pleased. By 1986, the combined revenues of companies in the IBM ecosystem were approximately $12 billion, dwarfing the Apple ecosystem's revenues of approximately $2 billion. IBM's leadership also forced Tandy and essentially every other non-Apple maker of personal computers to dump their proprietary designs and offer IBM PC compatibles.

In contrast with IBM, the story of Wal-Mart's retailing ecosystem shows how top management can take the right precautions when a business is expanding (see the insert "The Evolution of Wal-Mart: Savvy Expansion and Leadership"). In general, Stage 2 rewards fast expansion that squeezes competing ecosystems to the margin.

But managers must also prepare for future leadership and leverage in the next stage. To do so, companies need to maintain careful control of customer relationships and core centers of value and innovation. Moreover, they must develop relationships with their suppliers that constrain these followers from becoming leaders in Stage 3.

Leadership: The Fight for Control in an Ecosystem

Guide the ecosystem's investment directions and technical standards.
Make sure the ecosystem has a robust community of suppliers.
Maintain bargaining power by controlling key elements of value.

While the lion and antelope are both part of a healthy savanna ecosystem, they also struggle with each other to determine to what extent each species expands within it. Similarly, in business ecosystems, two conditions contribute to the onset of the leadership struggles that are the hallmark of Stage 3. First, the ecosystem must have strong enough growth and profitability to be considered worth fighting over. Second, the structure of the value-adding components and processes that are central to the business ecosystem must become reasonably stable.

This stability allows suppliers to target particular elements of value and to compete in contributing them. It encourages members of the ecosystem to consider expanding by taking over activities from those closest to them in the value chain. Most of all, it diminishes the dependence of the whole ecosystem on the original leader. It's in Stage 3 that companies become preoccupied with standards, interfaces, "the modular organization", and customer-supplier relations.

For example, by the mid-1980s, the IBM PC technical architecture defined the de facto business structure for the personal computer business as a whole. Virtually any company could figure out how to make components and services that would dovetail effectively with other elements of the PC ecosystem. Of course, this was a mixed blessing for IBM. The openness of its computer architecture encouraged third parties to support it, dramatically accelerating the ecosystem's growth. Yet this same openness decreased the dependence of suppliers on IBM's leadership, laying the foundations for Stage 3 "clone wars."

Lotus, Intel, Microsoft, and other suppliers started working together to determine common standards for hardware and software, with and without IBM's involvement. Other ecosystem members welcomed this new leadership since it seemed fairer to suppliers and more innovative than IBM's.

Belatedly, IBM sought to enforce its patents against clone makers, seeking licenses from major players – one of the many strategies that failed. A grim milestone of sorts was achieved in 1989 when clone shipments and product shipments from other smaller companies bypassed those of major personal computer manufacturers. Thus IBM was relegated to competing head-on with myriad "box makers." IBM still retained a large share of the market but only through offering extensive discounts to large volume purchasers.

Which brings us to the new structure of today's "Microsoft-Intel" ecosystem: Microsoft, with gross margins estimated at 80%; Intel, with gross margins of 40% and 50% on its new chips; and IBM's PC business with margins of about 30%, a far cry from the 70% to 90% margins in its mainframe business.

In Stage 3, bargaining power comes from having something the ecosystem needs and being the only practical source. Sometimes this sole-source status can be established contractually or through patent protection. But fundamentally, it depends on constant innovation – on creating value that is critical to the whole ecosystem's continued price/performance improvement. During expansion, IBM didn't find a way to keep innovating or even to achieve economies of scale. Power shifted to chips and software, areas in which IBM did not excel.

Now both Intel and Microsoft have bargaining power through control of a critical component. Each is a strong leader and plays the role of *central ecological contributor*. Central contributors maintain the much-coveted chokehold within a business ecosystem. In short, other members can't live without them. This central position enables them to bargain for a higher share of the total value produced by the ecosystem. For example, Intel and Microsoft have gross margins that are almost double the average for their whole ecosystem.

Central contributor status is maintained in part by the investments others have made in being followers. Hardware and software vendors have made heavy investments in Microsoft operating systems and in applications that work with Intel chips. Switching to other vendors would be risky and expensive; if possible, other co-evolving companies don't want the burden of learning how to work with a new leader.

In addition, central companies reinforce their roles by making important innovative contributions to the performance of the ecosystem as a whole. Intel, for instance, has enormous scale advantages in the fabrication of microprocessors. Its chip volumes allow it to work out fabrication-process advances sooner than other chip vendors. Ironically, IBM held a license to manufacture Intel-designed microprocessors. With its large volumes during the expansion stage, IBM could have been the one taking the fabrication and price/performance lead in chips – and it could have denied Intel the scale to keep up.

Finally, followers value a central contributor because of its grip on customers. End users are drawn to Microsoft operating systems and Intel chips because so many software applications are available for them. In turn, developers keep turning out such applications because they know Microsoft and Intel are customer gateways.

To some extent, these two companies achieved their current central position by being in the right place at the right time – that is, by serving IBM. Intel and Microsoft clearly appreciate what they have now and are working effectively to maintain their central contributions. Still, some companies like Wal-Mart have systematically gone about building a strong ecosystem, one that guarantees a leading role for themselves.

In any case, for dominant companies, the expansion and leadership stages of an ecosystem can make or break them. In Stage 3, lead producers must extend control by continuing to shape future directions and the investments of key customers and suppliers. And for healthy profits, any company in the ecosystem – leader or follower – must maintain bargaining power over other members.

Self-Renewal – or Death

Track new trends that may upend the ecosystem.
Build a management team that can, if necessary, start a new ecosystem.
Balance stability and change by incorporating new innovations

Stage 4 of a business ecosystem occurs when mature business communities are threatened by rising new ecosystems and innovations. Alternatively, a community might undergo the equivalent of an earthquake: sudden new environmental conditions that include changes in government regulations, customer buying patterns, or macroeconomic conditions. Moreover, these two factors reinforce each other. An altered environment is often more hospitable to new or formerly marginal business ecosystems.

In fact, how a dominant company deals with the threat of obsolescence is the ultimate challenge. Just because Microsoft and Intel are leaders now doesn't mean their current ecosystem is immortal. Nor does it mean that Microsoft NT ("New Technology" operating software) will form the basis for its successor. After all, Novell and UNIX Systems Laboratories have merged and will put forth a new generation of software, looking to strengthen a new ecosystem. Both Hewlett-Packard and Sun Microsystems remain strongly entrenched. And Motorola is now manufacturing a new generation microprocessor to be sold by both IBM and Apple, along with a jointly developed new software operating system.

Leading successive generations of innovation is clearly crucial to an ecosystem's long-term success and its ability to renew itself. Today's pharmaceutical companies provide some interesting insights into three general approaches to self-renewal, which can be used alone or in combination: (1) dominant companies can seek to slow the growth of a new ecosystem; (2) they can try to incorporate new innovations into their own ecosystems; or (3) they can fundamentally restructure themselves to try coping with a new reality.

During the past few decades, pharmaceutical companies have operated under a relatively consistent, if largely implicit, social compact with government regulators. In exchange for investing heavily in product and process innovation, drug companies have been allowed comparatively high margins and protection from competition through patent laws and lengthy approval processes. Traditional pharmaceutical ecosystems, therefore, have evolved around three major functions: R&D, testing and approval management, and marketing and sales. Each of these functions is expensive, hard to perfect, and thus presents a barrier to new competitors. In the past, these functions were carried out within large, vertically integrated companies that did not, until recently, consider themselves networked organizations.

In the 1980s, generic drug manufacturers that specialized in producing off-patent drugs posed a threat to the established pharmaceutical houses. The dominant companies responded by blocking these rival ecosystems in order to minimize their expansion. This included lobbying to slow generic-drug enabling legislation and to reinforce the natural conservatism of the U.S. Food and Drug Administration. Well-funded marketing and sales efforts convinced thousands of individual physicians to continue prescribing mostly branded drugs. While the generic drug manufacturers were able to establish alternative ecosystems, their penetration of the market has been held to about 30%, with little price cutting by the dominant companies.

Meanwhile, a variety of small biotechnology start-ups posed an even greater threat to the traditional pharmaceutical powerhouses. In general, biotech researchers concentrate on isolating complex substances that already exist in the human body and finding ways to manufacture them – for example, human insulin and human growth hormone. As many as one biotech try in ten may prove successful, which keeps the R&D cost down to between $100 million and $150 million per marketable product. Compare this with the traditional pharmaceutical average of 10,000 chemical tries to identify one marketable drug – and R&D costs of $250 million to $350 million per product.

Many of the founders of and investors in biotechnology start-ups believed that low R&D costs would provide the basis for creating whole newbusiness ecosystems that could compete with the established drug companies. For example, Genentech, one of the pioneering biotech companies, clearly intended to establish itself as a full competitor. By the mid-1980s, Genentech had five products in the market and was marketing three itself. It licensed its first two products: alpha-interferon to Hoffmann-La Roche and insulin to Eli Lilly. Using the cash from these licenses, Genentech sought to manufacture and market human growth hormone and tissue plasminogen activator on its own. Yet in 1990, 60% of Genentech was sold to Hoffmann-La Roche for $2.1 billion. A similar fate has befallen almost all of the original biotech companies.

In essence, these companies misjudged the difficulties of mastering the testing and approval process. The first biotech managers bet on the assumption that testing and approval would, like R&D, be less expensive and problematic than it was for their traditional competitors. Since biotech products were existing molecules already resident in the human body, these products would presumably require much less testing than synthetic chemical compounds. However, the FDA approval process in the United States, which grants access to the most important market worldwide, has not borne this out. From 1981 to 1991, only 12 biotech products were approved for general marketing.

Strapped for cash and unable to raise much more from their original investors, most biotech companies ended the 1980s in no position to lead their own business ecosystems. Biotech managers and investors were attracted to alliances with traditional companies and thus merged newbusiness ecosystems with powerful existing ones. In turn, dominant companies like Merck, Eli Lilly, and Bristol-Myers began to think like business ecosystem builders. In order to snap up licenses, patents, and talent to strengthen their own R&D, these companies affiliated themselves with the biotech companies rather than simply blocking their new rivals.

Of course, the leaders of a mature business ecosystem sometimes have no choice but to undertake profound structural and cultural changes. Pharmaceutical ecosystems now face new threats and a profoundly altered environment. The social compact to protect drug company profits in exchange for product and process innovation is breaking down. The public, government, and corporations all want health care costs reduced. Drug company leaders see lean times ahead as they confront the possibility of price and profit caps, as well as consolidated purchasing of drugs by HMOs and government agencies.

Responding to this environmental shift will force changes across all major functions. Companies will probably have to limit R&D spending and focus it carefully. Managers are likely to design a testing and approval process that highlights not only efficacy but also cost/benefit performance of new treatments. Finally, companies will probably market and sell less directly to individual physicians, focusing instead on negotiations with experts who represent third-party payers and government.

But despite the difficulties of such a complex business environment, managers can design longevity into an ecosystem. During the expansion and leadership stages, for instance, companies can work hard to micro-segment their markets, creating close, supportive ties with customers. These customers will then remain committed to a particular ecosystem long enough for its members to incorporate the benefits of new approaches.

And visionary executives like Merck's Roy Vagelos can sometimes lead an ecosystem so that it rapidly and effectively embraces anticipated developments – be they new technologies, regulatory openings, or consumer trends. Ultimately, there is no substitute for eternal vigilance. As Intel's Andy Grove noted recently, "Only the paranoid survive."

Clearly, pharmaceutical companies – and any other venture threatened by continual innovations – can no longer allow their particular ecosystems to evolve without direction. Using an ecological approach, executives can start making strategic changes by systematically questioning their company's current situation: Is the company linked with the very best suppliers and partners? Is the company betting its future on the most promising new ideas? Are suppliers leading the way in commercializing innovation? Over the long run, how will the company maintain sufficient bargaining power and autonomy to guarantee good financial returns?

Examining a company's key competitors from a business ecological point of view is also important: What hidden web of customer and supplier relationships have competitors worked to develop? Who do they depend on for ideas and supplier support? What are the nature and benefits of those relationships? How do these compare with what the company has?

And to prepare the ground for organizational breakthroughs, managers need to consider how the work of their company might be radically different: What seed innovations might make current businesses obsolete? What would it take to catalyze a cluster of ideas into a new and vital business ecosystem? What type of community would be required to bring these new ideas to the widest possible market?

Asking these questions, let alone acting on the answers, has become a difficult necessity for all companies. Superficially, competition among business ecosystems is a fight for market share. But below the surface, these new competitive struggles are fights over who will direct the future.

Yet it's precisely in the role of conscious direction that a strictly biological metaphor is no longer useful. Business communities, unlike biological communities of co-evolving organisms, are social systems. And social systems are made up of real people who make decisions; the larger patterns are maintained by a complex network of choices, which depend, at least in part, on what participants are aware of. As Gregory Bateson noted, if you change the ideas in a social system, you change the system itself.

I anticipate that as an ecological approach to management becomes more common-as an increasing number of executives become conscious of co-evolution and its consequences – the pace of business change itself will accelerate. Executives whose horizons are bounded by traditional industry perspectives will find themselves missing the real challenges and opportunities that face their companies. Shareholders and directors, sensing the new reality, will eventually remove them. Or, in light of the latest management shifts, they may have already done so.

Unfortunately for employees and investors, this often occurs only after the companies involved have been deeply damaged. Companies that once dominated their industries, as traditionally defined, have been blindsided by newcompetition. Whether such companies can find the appropriate leadership to renew the ecosystems on which their future depends remains an open question. If they cannot, they'll be supplanted by other companies, in other business ecosystems, that will expand and lead over the next few years.

For the individuals caught up in these ecosystem struggles, the stakes are high. As a society, we must find ways of helping members of dying ecosystems get into more vital ones while avoiding the temptation of propping up the failed ecosystems themselves. From an ecological perspective, it matters not which particular ecosystems stay alive; rather, it's only essential that competition among them is fierce and fair – and that the fittest survive.

Strategy at the edge of chaos[*]

By Eric D. Beinhocker

"Fishbowl" economics once provided the basis of corporate strategy, but no longer. New theories show that markets are "complex adaptive systems." Can managers be more than blind players in an evolutionary business game?

The economist Paul Krugman says that there are three types of economics: up-and-down economics ("stocks were up and unemployment was down today"), airport-bookstore economics *(Ten Easy Steps to Avoid Global Depression),* and Greek-letter economics. Greek-letter economics is the mathematical variety, practiced in universities and published in academic journals. And it is in serious trouble.

Historically, Greek-letter economics has rewarded mathematical pyrotechnics over fidelity to the real world. The core theories that Greek-letter economics has produced over the last few decades, such as "rational expectations" and "general equilibrium" theory, are mathematically elegant but lacking in empirical validation.

The dismal state of the dismal science matters to managers, chief operating officers, consultants, and business professors because much of modern management thinking has been built on a foundation of Greek-letter economics. The bad news is that this foundation is now in serious doubt. But take heart – the good news is that a radically new one is being put in place.

The roots of management thinking

Many of the most successful and widely used strategy tools today – the five-forces framework, cost curves, the structure-conduct-performance (SCP) model, and the concept of sustainable competitive advantage, to name a few – owe their origins to ideas developed in the 1950s in a field known as the theory of industrial organization. Industrial organization theory, which is concerned with industry structure and firm performance, is in turn based on microeconomic theory.

---

[*] Taken with permission from The McKinsey Quarterly, 1997, No.1, pp. 25-39

The ball rests at its lowest
energy state in equilibrium.

An exogenous shock
unsettles the system ...

... and reshapes the bowl,
creating a new equilibrium.

Exhibit 1: Equilibrium systems

Modern neoclassical microeconomics was founded by Leon Walras, William Stanley Jevons, and Carl Menger in the 1870s and synthesized into a coherent theory by Alfred Marshall at the turn of the last century. Seeking to make economics more scientific, Walras, Jevons, and Menger borrowed ideas and mathematical apparatus from the leading science of their day: energy physics. They copied the mathematics equation by equation, translating it metaphorically (and, according to many physicists, incorrectly) into economic concepts.[1]

In the mid-19th century, energy physicists developed a theory of closed equilibrium systems, which provides the core metaphor of Alfred Marshall's traditional economics and much of today's management thinking. Consider a ball at the bottom of a bowl. If no energy or mass enters or leaves the bowl – that is, if the system is closed – the ball will sit in equilibrium at its bottom forever. In economic terms, the sides of our bowl represent the structure of a market (for instance, producer costs and consumer preferences), and the gravity that pulls the ball to its lowest energy state represents profitseeking behavior, pulling a firm to its highest-profit state. If we know the economic forces at work, and if firms are rational, we can predict where the ball will come to rest in the bowl – in other words, the prices, quantities produced, and profitability of firms under equilibrium. If some exogenous shock hits the system (if, say, a technology shift alters producer costs), the sides of the bowl change shape, and the ball rolls to a new point of equilibrium (Exhibit 1).

In a typical modern strategic analysis, a company looks at its position in the current industry structure, considers the shocks and changes that are occurring or might occur, and then develops a point of view on how the industry is likely to change and what that means for its own strategy. Such an approach makes three important assumptions: that the industry structure is known, that diminishing returns apply, and that all firms are perfectly rational. But what happens if rapid technological or business system innovation makes producer costs and consumer preferences uncertain, as is increasingly the case in today's dynamic, high-tech, and service-dominated economy? What if we face not diminishing returns (where each additional acre of soybean planted is on poorer land and thus yields a lower return), but increasing returns (where each extra Netscape browser sold increases the value of the World Wide Web and thus yields a higher return)?[2] What if firms lack complete information, or different firms interpret the same information in different ways?

Should the fundamental assumptions underlying the equilibrium model be relaxed, the effect on the ball in the bowl will be dramatic. The sides of the bowl start to bend and flex, losing their smooth shape and becoming a landscape of hills and valleys; and the ball can no longer tell which way is up. Now it is impossible to predict where the ball will roll, and Alfred Marshall loses his equilibrium. And this is not merely a theoretical problem, since the ball-in-the-bowl equilibrium model is the basis for our ideas on strategy.

Complex adaptive systems

Anthills are marvelous things. With elaborate labyrinths of tunnels, layouts reflecting their occupants' social hierarchies, chambers dedicated to specific functions, and carefully sited entrances and exits, they are as thoughtfully constructed as any condominium complex. Yet who is the engineer? Where is the blueprint?

The answer, of course, is that none exists. The plan for the anthill does not reside in any individual ant. Rather, each ant is programmed by its DNA to obey a set of relatively simple rules, such as "stand between two other ants and pass

Individually, ants don't do much. But put them in an interactive group and an anthill emerges.

along anything that is handed to you." Ants communicate with each other via chemical signals known as pheromones, which provide inputs and outputs for the rules and switch them on and off. It is the dynamic interaction of the rules and signals that creates the anthill structure.

An ant community is an example of a complex adaptive system.[3] Such systems share the following three characteristics.

First, they are open, dynamic systems. The Marshall ball-in-a-bowl system is closed; no energy or mass enters or leaves, and the system can settle into an equilibrium state. By contrast, the energy and mass that constantly flow through a complex adaptive system keep it in dynamic disequilibrium. An anthill, for example, is a perpetual-motion machine in which patterns of behavior are constantly shifting; some patterns appear stable, others chaotic.

Second, these systems are made up of interacting agents, such as ants, people, molecules, or computer programs. What each agent does affects one or more of the other agents at least some of the time; this creates complexity and makes outcomes difficult to predict. The interactions of agents in a complex system are guided by rules: laws of physics, codes of conduct, or economic imperatives such as "cut prices if your competitor does." If the repertoire of rules is fixed, the result is a complex system. If the rules are evolving, as with genes encoded in DNA or the strategies pursued by players in a game, the result is a complex adaptive system.

Third, complex adaptive systems exhibit emergence and self-organization. As individuals, ants don't do much. But put them in a group where they can interact, and an anthill emerges. Because the anthill rises out of the bottom-up dynamic interactions of the ants and not from a top-down master plan, it is said to be self-organized. The emergent structure is independent of specific agents; while individual ants may come and go, the pattern of the anthill persists.

Other examples of complex adaptive systems include cities, forest ecosystems, the immune system, and the Internet. Over the past 20 years – aided by advances in mathematics, physics, chemistry, and biology and by the wide availability of cheap computing power – scientists have begun to find that complex adaptive systems are governed by deep common laws. Just as the laws of statistics can help us understand such ostensibly different systems as poker games and the spread of disease in populations, the laws of complexity may yield new insights into problems ranging from the origins of life to traffic jams in Los Angeles.

The new economics

To managers, this should be more than just interesting science. A number of economists are beginning to say that economies are complex adaptive systems. The case has yet to be proved, but there is circumstantial evidence as well as support from some eminent economists, among them Kenneth Arrow, a Nobel Prize winner and one of the prime architects of the modern neoclassical model, and Brian Arthur of the Santa Fe Institute. (Indeed, the new economics is sometimes referred to as the Santa Fe school of economics, after the interdisciplinary research center with which many economists working on ideas of complexity are affiliated.)

A new economics based on complex adaptive systems is still in its infancy, but enough work has been done to suggest what the key components might be.

Wisdom

First, the new economics will be based on a realistic model of cognitive behavior. Traditional economics assumes that people are alike in their thought processes (though their preferences may differ) and that they make choices as if they were solving complicated deductive equations that would enable them to make the best possible decisions. Economists have long realized that these assumptions are too simple, but such assumptions were needed to make the math work for the ball-in-the-bowl model. Computer simulation techniques and advances in cognitive science now allow economists

and others to make much more realistic assumptions about people's decision-making processes – assumptions based on skills such as the ability to recognize patterns and to develop inductive rules of thumb by learning from experience. Early work suggests that replacing perfect rationality with more realistic assumptions about inductive, nonoptimal decision making produces new insights and different strategic recommendations.

Webs

Second, the new economics will see agents interacting with one another in a dynamic web of relationships. It will not be enough to have a sound model of a firm's behavior; you must also know how people interact within the firm, how it interacts with other firms in its market, and how these interactions change over time.

Waves

Third, markets will be viewed as inherently dynamic rather than static systems, thus making possible an explanation of growth and innovation that traditional economics has never been able to provide. When adaptive agents interact in a web of relationships, evolutionary changes in one agent affect the evolution of others. This effect, known as coevolution, is frequently seen in nature and also occurs in economics when an innovation (such as the invention of the automobile) produces ripple effects throughout the whole economy (the development of the oil industry, motels, the growth of suburbs, and so on).[4]

Would-be worlds

Not only the substance but also the research techniques of economics will be transformed. Although the new economics will continue to make use of traditional mathematical proofs, it will increasingly turn to sophisticated computer simulations based on more realistic assumptions. In agent-based models, for example, a company can be modeled as an intelligent computer program capable of learning and adapting. You can put a set of these programs into a simulated competitive market, unleash the forces of evolution on them, and watch different futures unfold. Since complex systems can be difficult or impossible to forecast, such models will be of little help in forecasting the precise path an industry might take; however, they will be valuable in helping to determine how and why markets behave as they do.

Early thinking on management

The new economics has advanced far enough for us to begin to make preliminary hypotheses about its implications for strategy and organization. One characteristic of complex adaptive systems is punctuated equilibrium (Exhibit 2). This natural endogenous feature of the evolutionary process occurs when times of relative calm and stability are interrupted by stormy restructuring periods, or "punctuation points." Punctuated equilibrium makes it difficult for participants to survive for long periods, as their strategies and skills tend to get finely optimized for the stable periods and then suddenly become obsolete when the inevitable restructuring takes place. Similarly, companies have a hard time surviving the upheavals, shakeouts, and technology shifts that punctuate the evolution of markets. To prosper in the long run, a company must adapt as readily as its market, or more so. More specifically, it must be both a strong

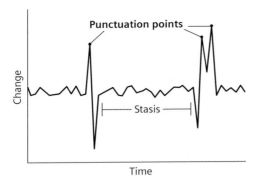

Exhibit 2:
Punctuated equilibrium

competitor in the current regime *and* a smart evolver, able to innovate ahead of the market or to adapt with it.

The equilibrium view of strategy has focused on how to be a good competitor; let us consider five critical aspects of being a good evolver.

Focused versus robust strategies

Traditional strategy tends to emphasize a single focused line of attack – a clear statement of where, how, and when to compete. In a complex adaptive system, a focused strategy to dominate a niche is necessary for day-to-day survival but not sufficient in the long run. Given an uncertain environment, strategies must also be robust – that is, capable of performing well in a variety of possible future environments.

Competitive advantage versus continuous adaptation

Evolutionary systems exhibit a phenomenon known as the Red Queen effect, after that character's remark in *Through the Looking Glass*: "It takes all the running you can do to keep in the same place."[4] In nature, the Red Queen effect is at work when a predator learns to run faster; its prey responds by acquiring better camouflage; the predator then develops a better sense of smell; the prey starts to climb trees; and so on. Evidence suggests that the business world resembles a Red Queen race.

A study of the performance of more than 400 companies over 30 years reveals that firms find it difficult to maintain higher performance levels than do their competitors for more than about five years at a time (Exhibit 3, on the next page). Longterm superior performance is achieved not through sustainable competitive advantage but by continuously developing and adapting new sources of temporary advantage and thus being the fastest runner in the race.

Conservative operator versus radical innovator

In a complex adaptive system, an agent that is resistant to change and not adaptable will have low fitness, and so, conversely, will an agent that is oversensitive to shifts in

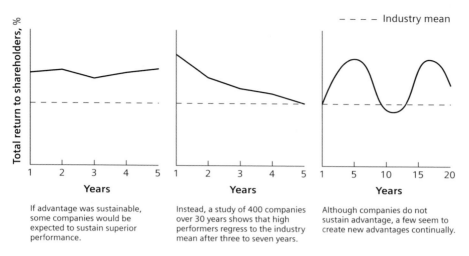

If advantage was sustainable, some companies would be expected to sustain superior performance.

Instead, a study of 400 companies over 30 years shows that high performers regress to the industry mean after three to seven years.

Although companies do not sustain advantage, a few seem to create new advantages continually.

Exhibit 3: The Red Queen effect

its environment and constantly making radical responses. But between these extremes of stasis and chaos lies a region – the edge of chaos – where fitness is maximized (Exhibit 4). Being at the edge of chaos means something more subtle than pursuing a moderate level of change. At the edge of chaos, one is simultaneously conservative and radical.

Evolution is adept at keeping things that work while at the same time making bold experiments. The morphology of the spinal cord is a robust adaptation that has survived eons of evolution and enormous environmental shifts. Yet nature has experimented wildly around this core idea, producing vertebrates that range from birds to whales to humans.

The Walt Disney Company is a firm that prospers at the edge of chaos. Its theme parks and other businesses are run in a deeply conservative fashion. A strong culture supports Disney's mission of providing family entertainment. In operations, no detail is

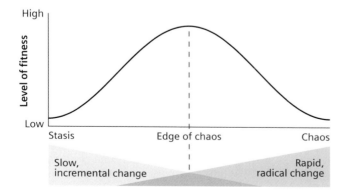

Exhibit 4:
The edge of chaos

163

too small, right down to the personal grooming of the parking-lot attendants. This culture is ingrained in the organization and constantly reinforced through management processes.

At many organizations, such a conservative culture and such tightly controlled operations would snuff out creativity. Yet Disney manages to be one of the most innovative companies in the world. It pioneered animated films and destination theme parks, built EPCOT, linked media and retail with its Disney Stores, and took an early lead in cable television. Disney manages the tension between conservatism and innovation by maintaining an almost cultlike attention to detail and discipline but at the same time forgiving honest mistakes made in the pursuit of innovation.

Routinized versus diverse strategies

Another requirement for success in evolutionary systems is a rich pool of possible strategies. This diversity represents the source of the innovations that keep a player ahead in the Red Queen race and can be drawn on to develop responses when the environment changes. But diversity also has its cost. Many mutations are harmful and selected against, limiting the diversity found in a species. Moreover, a certain level of standardization is beneficial: a relatively narrow range of mating behavior, for example, probably makes it easier for interested parties to find one another. Evolution strikes a balance, standardizing designs that work but seeding the population with enough variation to provide a basis for future innovation and adaptation.

Few companies are skilled at striking this balance. The result is firms that are either chaotic or vulnerable at punctuation points because they no longer have a well-stocked pool of ideas and experiences from which to draw.

Scale versus flexibility

In traditional strategic and organizational thinking, big is good. Benefits of scale are easy to identify in purchasing, operations, marketing, and so on. Why is it, then, that big companies can have such a hard time responding to attacks by smaller competitors? A complexity-based view can shed light on the downside of size.

A simple system with relatively few parts and interconnections isn't highly adaptable: the number of states it can manifest is small compared with the number of situations it might encounter. As the system grows bigger and more complex, the number of states it can manifest, and thus its repertoire of possible responses to changes in its environment, grows exponentially. However, beyond a certain level of scale and complexity, its adaptiveness drops off rapidly in what Stuart Kauffman calls a complexity catastrophe. This occurs when the epistasis, or interaction between the parts, builds to such an extent that any positive change in one part has ripple effects that cause negative changes elsewhere. The system thus becomes more conservative as it grows, and finding adaptations that don't have harmful side effects gets harder and harder.

When Dell Computer began to do well at selling inexpensive personal computers by mail, no doubt someone at IBM said, "Why don't we do that too?" But IBM couldn't follow suit without damaging its extensive distribution channels of dealers and direct salespeople. Its history and size created a trade-off that Dell didn't face and made it difficult for IBM to respond. Companies can mitigate the effect of complexity catastrophes through strategic and organizational changes. GM started Saturn in a greenfield organization precisely to free it from the constraints of corporate bureaucracy. AT&T split itself in three to create smaller organizations and reduce strategic conflict.

Becoming competitors *and* evolvers

As a complexity-based view of economics develops, new tools will be devised to help managers fashion better-evolving companies. Some of these tools will be analytical: options theory and evolutionary modeling to help develop robust strategies, for example. Others will be conceptual: new organizational forms that help avert complexity catastrophes, say, or practices that promote a rich fund of ideas.

Becoming a better evolver will be a major challenge for most companies; it is difficult enough just to be a successful competitor. And how do you motivate a thriving organization in a stable regime to take on the task of becoming more innovative and adaptive so as to meet challenges it can't even foresee? Equally, a company struggling through a major punctuation point finds it hard to worry about its long-term evolvability.

But for companies that do accept the challenge, the payoff promises to be considerable. Unlike creatures in nature, we are not blind, passive players in the evolutionary game. Through the sciences of complexity, we can come to understand how evolution works, the tricks it has up its sleeve, and the skills needed to survive in a complex world. If we do so, we may be able to harness one of the most powerful forces of all: evolution will then be the wave we ride to new levels of creativity and innovation rather than the tide that washes over us.

Holcim – A Faster Learning Group through Knowledge Management Tools

Holcim is a Swiss cement producing company, founded in 1912 in the Swiss village of Holderbank. It grew from humble beginnings to become a global network of companies and one of the world's largest producers of cement. At present the Holcim Group operates in more than 70 countries and has more than 48,000 employees. Its products include cement, clinker and related compounds. The company also offers consulting and engineering services for the entire cement production process.

The Holcim Group has a decentralized structure combined, however, with a clearly defined group strategy. This gives the individual companies high levels of autonomy and operational flexibility. Decisions are made by companies acting as local enterprises, therefore all actions have to satisfy both customer and market requirements.

Until May 2001 Holcim was known as Holderbank (from the village where it was founded) – a holding company with each local company throughout the world operating under its own name. These companies coordinated the production centers in their region and were run by local managers. Owing to the group's decentralized structure, the companies were largely monitored through their financial results; consequently, local management enjoyed a high level of autonomy.

The global nature of the company's activities results in an enormous variety: different markets, different company cultures, and different national cultures. This variety has always been regarded as an advantage since, in the words of one manager, it offers opportunities "to discern the specific predilection of each market and accumulate huge reserves of expertise in different environments".

At the start of the 21st century, globalization is a reality that cannot be overlooked: companies become actors on global markets and competition is therefore fiercer than ever. The importance of exchanging experiences amongst companies in the Holcim Group is escalating rapidly and these exchanges need to be implemented swiftly. The chairman of the group, Thomas Schmidheiny, posed himself the following questions: "What is the importance of knowledge? How strategic is knowledge sharing and multiplication in the cement industry? What role does knowledge, and therefore knowledge management, play in a company such as Holcim?"

The casual observer might imagine that such an industry does not rely on knowledge as much as on technology or equipment. This would be a misconception: in a variety of ways knowledge plays a surprisingly central role in a cement company's performance. First of all the variety of markets in which Holcim operates has to be taken into consideration. As previously noted, every market is different and requires an in-depth knowledge of its environment and function. Since cement consumption differs quite radically in keeping with local culture and habits, knowledge about these aspects is crucial for the company's performance. Such knowledge is, of course, not acquired overnight: the expertise emerges from long experience in the field and from direct contact with the different environments. This aspect also explains the Holcim's choice of a decentralized structure, which grants local management much autonomy.

On the other hand, the advantage of being a member of a global group is that constantly "reinventing the wheel" can be avoided and it is possible to profit from already available know-how. The following example shows how knowledge acquired through experience and shared within the company can become central to it:

In 1990, Alsen Breitenberg, a Holcim facility in Lägerdorf, Germany, needed to build production capacity in order to keep up with the market demand. The project management team budgeted in todays money €77 million for the expansion, but headquarters turned the project down as being too expensive. The project managers knew they needed to reduce the budget by approx. €13-15 million for it to be approved, so they turned to Holcim's Mexico operation where a new plant had been built according to a "stripped down" concept. In April 1993, the German project team visited the Mexican facility, learned this concept from the project managers there, and was convinced that by using the same high-quality/low-cost concept they could significantly reduce the cost of the German expansion to only €58 million. The project was approved and not only did the facility cost €17 million less than originally planned, it was also completed three months ahead of schedule.

This example clearly illustrates the impact knowledge transfer can have on a company's performance. Knowledge is acquired through experience and testing and it is of strategic importance that it is rapidly shared since, as we have seen, significant savings can be realized if information is passed on by companies in the Group. In contrast to the first type of knowledge discussed, we are presently not considering the aspects specific to one region or one market, but rather those aspects with which all companies in the group are confronted and which require optimal solutions that are applica-

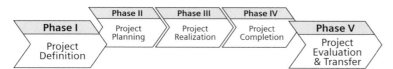

Phase includes:
1. Assessment of initial situation
2. Stakeholder analysis
3. Search for lessons learned
4. Definition of product or service
5. Milestone schedule
6. Outline project organization
7. Estimation of project costs
8. Risk identification and countermeasures
9. Agreement with the client

Phase V includes:
1. After Action Review
2. Learning summary
3. Knowledge Transfer

The five phases of the Holcim Project Management Approach

ble worldwide. The swift multiplication of knowledge is therefore of strategic importance to the entire Group of companies.

This is why Thomas Schmidheiny launched a program with the strategic intent of becoming an organization that learns faster. This meant tools and procedures had to be developed in order to prevent these successes from being a flash in the pan – which happens when documentation is not provided and knowledge sharing is not embedded in the corporate culture – and to promote the transfer of knowledge and best practices to all companies in the Group. Holcim consequently initiated several initiatives. First of all, the company developed a best-practice database: each local company was supposed to identify three successful practices and describe them. Yellow pages were also created to reflect the expertise available within the Group. Neither of these initiatives "really took off", in the words of Walter Baumgartner (Head of Training).

One of the lessons learned from these projects was that information technology is not a solution in itself. To overcome this problem, specific Communities of Practice were established. These Communities are organized around strategic topics and experiences such as maintenance, alternative fuel, or vertical mills. For successful Communities of Practice, the relevant participants needed to have a common interest, adequate incentives and a shared understanding, which included face-to-face knowledge transfer. To ensure that people with a common interest could meet and exchange experiences, learning events and transfers were systematically organized.

In the late nineties, a particular Project Management Approach (PMA) was developed by the internal Support and Consulting branch of Holcim to integrate learning aspects and activities new to this kind of process. This approach became a tool for transferring and optimizing the use of knowledge. In the first phase of a project (project definition), the lessons learned are integrated and in the last phase (Project evaluation and Transfer) the project participants proceed to an After Action Review in order to capture lessons learned for future projects and to integrate the output of knowledge gained into the learning summary.

The Holcim Management realized that the corporate culture needed to be receptive to the importance and sharing of knowledge. In a continual search for a "glue" that would hold the diversity together and promote knowledge sharing, Holcim created a large-scale training program covering all functions, countries and hierarchical levels.

The aims of this program are to improve employees' competencies and to create common working patterns to serve as a "common language". Participants exchange experiences during the training, and an international network of relationships is formed. What we are witnessing here is the will to create one company: the global branding (the gradual renaming of all companies within the Holcim Group started in May 2001) can also be seen as a further step to facilitate the transfer and sharing of knowledge. It is obviously easier to share knowledge internally when people feel they belong to the same company and even though a high level of autonomy is preserved, a common name contributes to a common "company feeling" that enhances knowledge-sharing practices.

The following represents an overview of tools used by Holcim in order to manage knowledge and become a "faster learning organization". It can be seen from this internal document that the company puts much effort into the "learning" aspect and considers it to be of high strategic importance.

Holcim, a Faster Learning Group

I. Why faster learning?

Holcim is a leading player in the cement industry, but being big and successful today is no guarantee of future success. To secure this position, we need to continually strengthen our performance. We therefore all constantly strive to improve operational efficiency, volumes and returns. This is where learning comes in. Holcim's Faster Learning approach systematically addresses the knowledge, skills, and processes necessary for performance improvement.

II. Holcim's core model

One of the most important aspects of Faster Learning is the two-fold focus on expertise and behavior. While improving our professional knowledge and skills, we must simultaneously address our attitudes. This includes communication, teamwork, taking responsibility, sharing knowledge, and striving for best practice – to mention just a few. Only the combination of both leads to performance improvement.

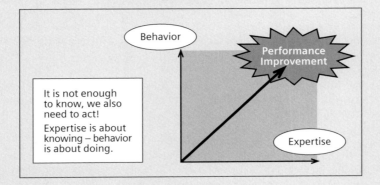

III. Practical tools for faster learning

Models need concrete tools and measures to facilitate their practical applicability. A system of practical and proven learning-related tools drives performance improvement. The core is the Training Master Plan and its three main instruments: Group Learning Events, Workforce Training, and Simulators. The Project Management Approach and Communities of Practice are direct, on-the-job performance drivers. Oscar & Gemini and e-learning are strong enablers of Group-wide knowledge transfer.

1. Training Master Plan (TMP)
   A TMP describes a needs-oriented training program focusing on individuals and teams. Many Group companies have such needs-driven plans, which in some cases also include vocational training. Based on their experiences, a standardized approach is being developed.

A case in point: Vocational training at Morning Star Cement, Vietnam

In May 1998, Morning Star's modern cement plant started operation in the remote area of Hon Chong. Approximately 375 employees work in the plant, producing 1.4 million tons of clinker per year. Young engineers and operators have been employed and trained according to the Training Master Plan in place. The plant estimates an annual need of 12 new cement technicians. In August 2001 a 3-year vocational training program – based on the Swiss apprenticeship system – was launched. Every year 12 participants (with an average starting age of 18) will become government-certified cement technicians. The system installed is integrated into the plant's workflow. It is therefore simple, low-cost, and efficient. Morning Star's investment of USD 30,000 per participant will provide the new technicians with excellent job opportunities within Morning Star or anywhere else in the Vietnamese industry.

2. *Group Learning Events*
   There is a coherent and consistent system of Group Learning Events for Holcim's management and functional specialists. The key objectives are direction setting, networking, and face-to-face knowledge transfer. The events aim at aligning participants to transform Group and business objectives into performance improvement.

3. *Workforce Training*
   Holcim's Training Master Plans are strongly focussed on its workforce. The workforce training is based on a simple, standardized, and focused modular system in which line managers transfer their knowledge by teaching.

4. *Simulators*
   Holcim has a long tradition of computer-based training. Their kiln-simulators are highly regarded in the cement industry throughout the world for the training of standard operating procedures as well as for experimentation with critical kiln conditions. The businesssimulation game ECOMAN provides everyone with commercial knowledge. It is also an excellent tool for communication of and alignment with business objectives.

5. *Project Management Approach*
   Many employees on all levels of the hierarchy are increasingly working in projects. Large investments in time and money are involved. Holcim's Project Management Approach encourages people to systematically and repeatedly use available knowledge in order to improve with every project. This approach provides a common structure and checklists, and explicitly integrates knowledge exchange.

6. *Communities of Practice*
   Although Holcim employees are scattered across the world, they often have similar tasks. Communities of Practice are platforms where people from different Group companies meet around a common topic of interest. They learn from one another, exchange knowledge, and develop new ideas.

7. *Holcim Innovation and Multiplication Awards "Oscar & Gemini"*
   Holcim's Oscar and Gemini award is a bi-annual, Group-wide competition for innovation and multiplication of best practices. Innovative ideas, which are transferable within the Group, have a chance of winning an Oscar. The take-over and local adaptation of an existing idea from another Group company is eligible for the Gemini award.

8. *e-Learning and Knowledge Structuring*
   All the tools above are supported by e-learning, ideally allowing training and knowledge sharing wherever and whenever required. A global e-learning platform is up and running and its content is continuously growing. Knowledge structuring means organizing knowledge in a way that allows it to be easily found and retrieved.

IV. How do we measure what we have learned?

Learning at Holcim focuses both on expertise and behavior. An increase in expertise and change of behavior are obviously difficult to measure. Nevertheless, change of behavior can be observed and assessed, and improvement in knowledge and skills can be verified. According to our core model, the combination of both leads to performance improvement, i.e. to directly measurable results.

Skilled and performance-oriented people are Holcim's sustainable edge. There is a system of practical and proven tools driving performance improvement. Use it to make people capable of achieving more ... more than they think they can!

Web sales and multiplication of best practices – a recent example

On 1 March 1999, Holcim obtained a stake in Siam City Cement in Thailand. Holcim had a clear vision: making a swift and radical change within the Asian company to transform it into a knowledge-based organization and installing clear procedures and system tools which would support the web sales of cement.

Sixty people were in charge of the *New Eagle Project* which was divided into two phases:

1) training Siam City employees to use software tools and SAP;

2) installing these IT tools so that information and knowledge could be shared efficiently within the company.

A web-based *Customer Support Center* would allow Siam City to help several clients simultaneously as well as knowing their needs.

The project was a great success. The first online cement order – the first in Asia – was placed on 15 September 2000. The knowledge that had been created and acquired during the project was codified and was consequently ready for re-use.

Holcim learned from its first experience in Thailand and is thus able to transfer its acquired knowledge on the multiplication of e-business solutions to other Asian cement markets based on a "copy-paste exactly" philosophy.

Holcim launched web sales in Vietnam on 1 November 2001, and in August 2002 launched them in Sri Lanka, using this "copy-paste exactly" method. In Indonesia, electronic cement sales are expected to start in 2003 and will be implemented according to the same procedures.

The "copy-paste exactly" solution to multiply e-business solutions seems to be appropriate to the Asian market. And it may well be a best practice to be multiplied in other parts of the group. Markus Akermann, Holcim's CEO, feels that it is important to extend the Faster Learning approach and since the beginning of 2002 has asked all top executive meetings for case presentations. People need to know about good practices, illustrations from within the group, the respective Oscar or Gemini Awards and unequivocal top management support.

Questions

1. Boundaries are a major tenet in the paradigm shifts from the machine model to the biological/socio-cultural model. Typically, these are transgressed, blurred, or simply abolished. Does this imply that boundaries are necessarily bad? Discuss strategic management approaches that explicitly use boundaries to stimulate strategic thinking.

2. Several new forms of organizing have emerged in the 1990s, including the metanational networked, and virtual forms. Do these co-exist with established, hierarchical forms of organizing? Discuss against the background of the Holcim case study.

3. Most examples for networked and virtual forms of organizing are drawn from high-technology industries such as software, electronics, electrical engineering, and bio-tech. In how far does the case study of Holcim, a cement manufacturer, reflect these forms of organizing? Can you think of other examples in mature, asset-intensive industries that illustrate such new forms of organizing?

4. Discuss Holcim's business environment through the looking glasses of the industrial and ecosystems perspective. What are the main differences in both perspectives? As the CEO of Holcim, which looking glass would you use for strategic planning in your company?

References

Chapter 3: A New Mindset: Systemic Strategic Management

[1] De Geus, A. (1993), *The Living Company*, London: Nicholas Brealey Publishing; Wheatley, M.J. (1992), *Leadership and the New Science*, San Francisco: Berrett-Koehler Publishers; Moore, J.F. (1993), "Predators and Prey: A New Ecology of Competition", *Harvard Business Review*, May-June, 75-86; Sherman, H. and Schulz, R. (1998), *Open Boundaries: Creating Business Innovation Through Complexity*, Reading, Massachusetts: Perseus Books; Clippinger, J.H. (1999), *The Biology of Business*, San Francisco: Jossey-Bass Publishers.

[2] Adapted from Lengnick-Hall, C.A. and Wolff, I.A. (1999): "The Similarities and Contradictions in the Core Logic of Three Strategy Research Streams", *Strategic Management Journal*, 20, 1109-1132.

[3] Brown, S.L. and Eisenhardt, K.M. (1998), *Competing on the Edge: Strategy as Structured Chaos*, Boston: Harvard Business School Press; Eisenhardt, K.M. and Sull, D. (2001), "Strategy as Simple Rules", *Harvard Business Review*, January-February, 107-116; Eisenhardt, K.M. and Galunic, D.C. (2000), "Co-evolving: At Last, a Way to Make Synergies Work", *Harvard Business Review*, January-February, 91-101; Eisenhardt, K.M. and Martin, J.A. (2000), "Dynamic Capabilities: What are They?", *Strategic Management Journal*, 21, 1105-21; Kelly, S. and Allison, M.A. (1999), *The Complexity Advantage*, New York: BusinessWeek Books.

[4] Eisenhardt K.M. and Sull, D. (2001), op.cit.

[5] Eisenhardt, K.M. and Galunic, D.C. (2000), op.cit.

[6] Teece, D.J., Pisano, G. and Shuen, A. (1997), "Dynamic Capabilities and Strategic Management", *Strategic Management Journal*, 18, 509-33.

[7] Adapted from Beinhocker, E.D. (1997), "Strategy at the Edge of Chaos", *McKinsey Quarterly*, Number 1, 34.

[8] Eisenhardt, K.M. and Martin, J.A. (2000), "Dynamic Capabilities: What are They?", *Strategic Management Journal*, 21, 1105-21.

[9] Grant, R.M. (2002), *Contemporary Strategy Analysis*, Fourth Edition, Oxford: Blackwell Publishers.

[10] Wenger, E.C. and Snyder, W.M. (2000), "Communities of Practice: The Organizational Frontiers", *Harvard Business Review*, January-February, 139-145.

[11] Tushman, M.L. and O'Reilly, C.A. (1996), "The Ambidextrous Organization: Managing Evolutionary and Revolutionary Change", *California Management Review*, 38(4), Summer, 8-30.

Strategy at the edge of chaos

[1] For an account of the interwoven history of economics and physics, see Philip Mirowski, *More Heat than Light: Economics as Social Physics, Physics as Nature's Economics,* Cambridge: Cambridge University Press, 1991.

[2] For a more detailed discussion of increasing returns, see W. Brian Arthur, *"Positive feedbacks in the economy", The McKinsey Quarterly,* 1994 Number 1, pp. 81-95; and "Increasing returns and the *new world of business", Harvard Business Review,* July-August 1996, pp. 100-9.

[3] For an excellent nontechnical introduction to the field of complex adaptive systems, see M. Mitchell Waldrop, Complexity, New York: Simon & Schuster, 1992; Stuart A. Kauffman, At Home in the Universe, New York: Oxford University Press, 1995; and John H. Holland, Hidden Order, Redwood City, CA: Addison-Wesley, 1995. For a more technical overview of complexity and economics, see Philip W. Anderson, Kenneth J. Arrow, and David Pines (eds.), The Economy as an Evolving, Complex System, Redwood City, CA: Addison-Wesley, 1988; and W. Brian Arthur, David Lane, Steven N. Durlauf (eds.), The Economy as an Evolving, Complex System II, Redwood City, CA: Addison-Wesley, 1997.

[4] See Stuart A. Kauffman, "Technology and evolution: Escaping the Red Queen effect", *The McKinsey Quarterly,* 1995 Number 1, pp. 118-29.

IV New Strategic Management Approaches and Processes

Chapter 4:
Frameworks for
Systemic Strategic Management

Understanding Systemic Strategic Management and its Role in Co-shaping an Organization's Business Model

In the previous chapter, the traditional view of organizations as mechanisms or organisms implied that they are constantly trying to get better (or "fitter") in order to surpass their competitors. However, the landscape in which they live keeps changing as evolution proceeds, so the struggle is continuous, and in a turbulent environment characterized by revolutionary shifts, it is obviously ineffective to only try and run harder and harder. Organizations should rather strive to run differently, i.e. strive to reinvent themselves with revolutionary value propositions for customers, enabled by new industry configurations, while appreciating that their existing business models may still have an evolutionary life and (some) should be co-maintained.

The challenge for strategic management is to develop frameworks to understand how new levels of order (innovative business models and new industries) emerge, and how one can enable them to emerge from complex, seemingly chaotic patterns of interaction in socio-cultural business systems. It is, furthermore, essential to understand the properties (or configurations) of these emergent business models in terms of their resilience to perturbation and their capacity for self-maintenance. According to Normann, continuous improvement of an existing business model often becomes a trap from which companies fail to see that the rules of the game are changing faster than the company, or that the game has changed altogether[1]. As stated in the previous chapter, the new strategic management paradigm now becomes *systemic strategic management: co-shaping of organizational value propositions through systemic organizational capabilities.*

The organization's role is now changing from being viewed as a value-providing entity in particular industry value-chains, just "fitting" reactively into value-chain configurations, to being a co-shaping organizer of value creation that may lead to new industry configurations. This is illustrated in Figure 4.1.

The question can be asked: why the emphasis on co-shaping of customer value propositions, and (re)configuration of value networks to create and provide these? The answer is that the knowledge economy has made it possible as well as being a driving force to unbundle traditional sets of industry activities and assets – often termed "deconstruction" or "disintermediation" of value chains and networks. Rapid cross-industry and global markets for assets, knowledge and competencies have been made possible, and it is now feasible to creatively and interactively rebundle (or reconfigure) activities, which have been unbundled or deconstructed, into new patterns.

This chapter focuses on strategic management frameworks to understand and co-shape the (re)configuration of customer value propositions and value networks. Such understanding often leads to reinvention of the organization's business model, i.e. its role or "way of doing business" in society. The chapter consists of several sections:

- Frameworks for *organizational sense making of socio-cultural business system dynamics*:
  - Understanding the *dynamics of socio-cultural business systems*.
  - Conceptions of *threats and new opportunities* in deconstructing/reconstructing value chains and networks in the knowledge economy.
  - New conceptions of *customers*, and creation of customer value propositions.
  - A framework of key lenses for systemic strategic management.
- Frameworks to understand the critical *systemic strategy-knowledge links* for co-shaping of customer value propositions and organizational capabilities.
- An integrated framework to co-shape the *development of new business models for an organization*.
- Guidelines to deal with *organizational inertia in business networks*.
- *Cautions* in shifting to a systemic strategic management approach.

The focus of the chapter is on frameworks to enable strategic management to co-shape business models for an organization in the knowledge economy. Such business models arise, or are adapted from managerial *sense making* of socio-cultural business system

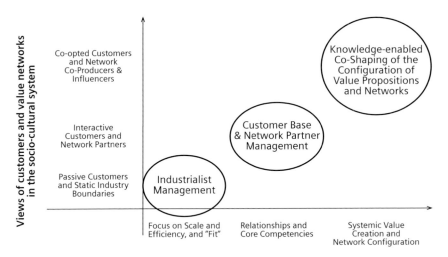

Views of the Organization's Strategic Role and Purpose

Figure 4.1 The Organization's Role as Co-Shaper of Value Creation

IV New Strategic Management Approaches and Processes

dynamics, and *understanding* the critical strategy-knowledge links underpinning the key systemic strategic management decisions.

Socio-Cultural Business System Dynamics

The knowledge economy points to a world that is increasingly interconnected and in which the pace of technological change has been accelerating, with new customer value propositions and business models rapidly arising, diffusing, declining, dying and often being renewed (or reinvented). Humans and other economic agents are boundedly rational creatures, and organizations are often viewed as devices for economizing on bounded rationality. They create routines for the purpose of reducing the volume of information and complexity, and these routines carry a strong cognitive component that reflects individual or collective sense making and understanding. Since the business environment is becoming increasingly complex, firms will need to shift from the complexity-reducing rules and strategies that secured their success in the 20th century, to place more emphasis on complexity-absorbing ones – a shift from bureaucracies to networked communities of interests, with organizational sense making of socio-cultural business system dynamics being an essential strategic capability. The structuring, creation and sharing of knowledge between agents lie at the center of organizational sense making as reviewed in the following sections.

Understanding the dynamics of socio-cultural business systems

In environments far from equilibrium, where multiple changes are constantly emerging and overlapping with one another, adaptation and co-shaping activities must be allowed to evolve, not to be planned. The task of strategic management is not to foresee the future or to implement organization-wide change programs; rather, such managers establish and modify the direction and boundaries within which effective, self-organized solutions can evolve. Non-linear social-cultural systems react to direction in ways that are difficult to predict and control. However, managers can guide the evolution of a self-organizing enterprise more effectively if they gain more knowledge of the dynamics of the organization's socio-cultural business system.

Social network analysis is a well-developed and fast-growing area of organizational sociology, and it provides a number of concepts and frameworks for understanding organizations as networks[2]. Unfortunately, there seems to be little empirical evidence on the dynamics of networks, i.e. how they evolve, and the types of configurations that produce an accepted theory of network evolution. Managers help guide the evolution of self-organizing systems by managing meaning, i.e. making sense and influencing the systems for improved co-evolution.

The dynamics of socio-cultural business systems can also be understood by looking at its components and their interactions, as depicted in Figure 4.2.

From the above figure it can be seen that a socio-cultural business system includes the ecosystem of which it forms part, and consists of an economic community of interact-

180

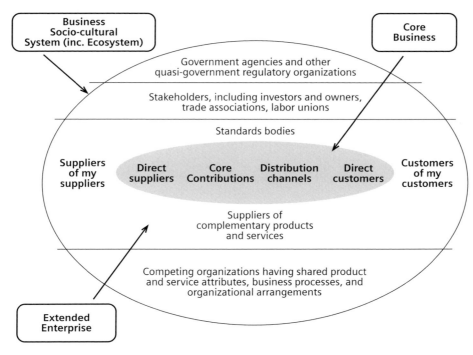

Figure 4.2
Components of a socio-cultural business system (*Source:* Adapted from Moore, J.F. (1996),
The Death of Competition, New York: HarperBusiness, 27)

ing, co-evolving organizations and individuals. This economic community produces
goods and services of value to customers, who are themselves members of the socio-
cultural business system. The members also include suppliers, lead producers, competitors, and other stakeholders. Over time, they co-evolve their capabilities and roles,
and tend to align themselves with the directions set by one or more leading companies. The companies holding leadership roles may change over time, but the function
of socio-cultural system leader is valued by the community, because it enables members to move towards shared visions to align their investments and actions, and to find
mutually supportive roles. Stakeholders include government agencies and regulators,
associations and standards bodies representing customers or suppliers, and also direct
competitors along with companies that might be able to compete with an organization,
or with any other important members making up the particular socio-cultural system.

The socio-cultural business system of interactions demands strategic management that
differs sharply from that in the past. Executives are dealing with co-evolving coali-
tions of diverse economic players that do not respect traditional industry boundaries –
they can thrive within conventional industry boundaries or straddle it, or reinvent new
industry configurations. Table 4.1 illustrates the changing dimensions of strategic
management to (systemically) enable the co-evolving of desired socio-cultural business systems, in contrast to the traditional focus on core products and services (posi-

Table 4.1

Changing dimensions of strategic management in the focus on co-evolving socio-cultural business systems

Dimensions of Strategic Managment	Core Products and Services	+ Extended Enterprise	+ Co-Evolving Socio-Cultural Business System
Concept of business relationships	A portfolio of transactional and long-term preferred customer and supplier relationships	Managed system of relationships	Co-evolving, symbiotic, self-reinforcing system of strategic contributions
Focus of continual improvement	Products and processes	Organizational interactions, extended processes	Investments in innovation by members of the community
Measure of improvement	Reduction in product defects; reduction in product deviations from standard	Rate of progress on improving products and processes	Rate of progress on creating end-to-end total experiences of dramatic value to customers
Most important contracts governing the relationship	Product specifications, process specifications, and TQM standards	Letters of agreement among key organizations	Community governance systems, quasi-democratic mechanisms
Alignment of the intentions of key parties	Alignment on the importance of consistency of customer/supplier satisfaction and performance on benchmarks	Alignment of the parties' strategic direction and investments	Alignment of the community around a shared vision of a desired future, and the road map and key contributions required

Source: Adapted from Moore, J.F. (1996), *The Death of Competition,* New York: HarperBusiness, 53

tioning and "fit") and the extended enterprise ("leveraging resources and core competencies in value chains").

Co-evolution occurs through both competition and collaboration. Moore provides a useful classification of tools to address the challenges of strategic leadership, collaboration and competition across four stages of business system development, and these are reviewed in Chapter 5.[3]

Conceptions of threats and new opportunities in deconstructing/reconstructing value chains and networks

In many ways, information and knowledge, and the mechanisms for delivering it, form and stabilize corporate and industry structures and underlie competitive and collaborative advantages. When knowledge is carried by (physical) elements and traditional communication media, it goes where the elements go and no further – it is constrained by the linear flow of the physical value chain. Once everyone is able to connect electronically, however, knowledge can travel by itself. The traditional link between the flow of product-related information and the flow of the product itself between the economics of information and the economics of elements, can be broken.[4] Where once a sales force, a branch network, a printing press, a chain of stores, or a delivery fleet served as formidable industry barriers to entry, because of the time and investment required to build these in the past, in the knowledge-networked economy they could suddenly become expensive liabilities, as was shown in the Encyclopaedia Britannica example.

The result is that the traditional integrated value chains of conventional industries are increasingly being deconstructed. All the functions, as well as some new ones will still be performed, but these will be in the form of new business models in new or adapted industries. The reason for this is that deconstruction of an integrated value chain does more than transform the structure of a business or an industry – it alters the sources of competitive advantage. It presents threats to established businesses, but also represents new sets of opportunities. Evans and Wurster summarize the strategic implications of the "changing economics of information" as follows[5]:

- Existing value chains will fragment into multiple businesses, each of which will have its own sources of competitive advantage.
- As value chains fragment and reconfigure, new opportunities will arise for purely physical businesses.
- Some new businesses will benefit from network economies of scale, which can give rise to monopolies.
- When a company focuses on different activities, the customer value proposition underlying its brand identity will change.
- New branding opportunities will emerge for third parties that neither produce a product nor deliver a primary service.
- Bargaining power will shift as a result of a radical reduction in the ability to monopolize the control of information and knowledge.
- Customer switching costs will drop, and companies will have to develop new ways of generating customer loyalty.
- Incumbents could easily become victims of their own obsolete physical infrastructures and their own psychology (compare the cautionary example of Encyclopaedia Britannica in Chapter 2).

The implications of the increasing deconstruction of traditional value chains are obvious: organizations have to improve their sense making of the dynamics of socio-cultural business systems, and acquire system strategy frameworks and tools to anticipate and counter threats, and utilize new opportunities, arising from the increasing deconstruction of traditional industry value chains. One such framework – of restructuring network possibilities – is provided by Jallat and Capek, as illustrated in Table 4.2.

Table 4.2 Restructured networks and intermediaries

	Maintaining Traditional Players	Spawning New Players
Same Network Organization	Traditional Intermediation	Substitution (e.g. amazon.com)
Different Network Organization	Reintermediation (e.g. Auto-by-Tel)	Disintermediation (e.g. Dell Computers)

Source: Adapted from Jallet, F. and Capek, M.J. (2001), *"Disintermediation in Question: New Economy, New Networks, New Middlemen"*, Business Horizons, March-April, 57.

New conceptions of customers and customer value propositions

Due to the knowledge economy, customers have become more informed, knowledge-able and competent in their awareness, utilization and influence of products and services. The competence that customers provide is a function of the knowledge and skills they possess, their willingness to learn and experiment, and their ability to engage in an active dialogue. That dialogue is no longer controlled by organizations; individual customers can address and learn about products and services through the collective knowledge of other customers, and they can initiate the dialogue with organizations.

A framework to understand the changing role of customers from passive audience to active participants is illustrated in Table 4.3.

With customers now becoming part of the enhanced socio-cultural network, the conception of customer value propositions (product and services configurations) changes drastically. The customer now has a joint role in developing value propositions, shaping expectations and co-creating market acceptance for products and services. Customer value propositions should not be seen only as customer satisfaction entities or potential income streams for the organization, but as contributors to customer success and socio-cultural systems enhancement.

A framework of key lenses for Systemic Strategic Management (SSM)

For sense making of socio-cultural business system dynamics, strategic managers have to adopt new lenses (or ways of looking) at the industry and market context, strategy purpose and relationships, and organizational capabilities.

Table 4.3 provides a framework of these new lenses, and how they differ from traditional ones.

From Table 4.4 it can be seen that strategic managers should adopt lenses that enable two principal levers to be at their disposal: first, they can shape the context within which strategy emerges; and second, they can influence the (re)configuration of the

Table 4.3 The Evolution and Transformation of Customers

	Customers as a Passive audience			Customers as Active Players
	Persuading predetermined groups of buyers	*Transacting with individual buyers*	*Lifetime bonds with individual customers*	*Customers as co-creators of value*
Time frame	1970s, early 1980s	Late 1980s and early 1990s	1990s	Beyond 2000
Nature of business exchange and role of customer	Customers are seen as passive buyers with a predetermined role of consumption.			Customers are part of the enhanced network; they co-create and extract business value. They are collaborators, co-developers, and competitors.
Managerial mind-set	The customer is an average statistic; groups of buyers are predetermined by the company.	The customer is an individual statistic in a transaction.	The customer is a person; cultivate trust and relationships.	The customer is not only an individual but also part of an emergent social and cultural fabric.
Company's interaction with customers, and development of products and services	Traditional market research and inquiries; products and services are created without much feedback.	Shift from selling to helping customers via help desks, call centers, and customer service programs; identify problems from customers, then redesign products and services based on that feedback.	Providing for customers through observation of users; identify solutions from lead users, and reconfigure products and services based on deep understanding of customers.	Customers are co-developers of personalized experiences. Companies and lead customers have joint roles in education, shaping expectations, and co-creating market acceptance for products and services.
Purpose and flow of communication	Gain access to and target predetermined groups of buyers. One-way communication.	Database marketing; two-way communication.	Relationship marketing; two-way communication and access.	Active dialogue with customers to shape expectations and create "buzz". Multilevel access and communication. Customer success marketing.

Source: Prahalad, C.K. & Ramaswamy, V. (2000), *"Co-opting Customer Competence",* Harvard Business Review, January-February, 80.

systemic and organizational architecture within which agents adapt. Rather than shaping the pattern that constitutes a strategy, managers can shape the context and architecture within which it emerges. This task requires an understanding of the critical links between strategy and knowledge, and its effective utilization, as reviewed in the next subsection.

Table 4.4 A Framework of Key Lenses for Systemic Strategic Management (SSM)

	Key SSM Lenses	Key Traditional Lenses
A: Industry & Market Context		
1. Industry & Market Conditions	SSM enacts a marketplace that results from cumulative and collective chains of activity and reactions. Market conditions reflect recurrent patterns in *unpredictable sequences*. Industry conditions can be shaped, and the focus is on *commonalities* in what customers value.	Traditional lenses enact a market setting that is *equilibrium-oriented*, with linear, dynamic relationships. Industry conditions are "given", and the focus is on the *differences* in what customers value.
2. Stakeholders	The dominant stakeholder for SSM is the socio-cultural business community. The primary focus is to ensure a healthy and well-nurtured business system, with improved success of *all stakeholders* within the system.	Traditional lenses emphasize the creation of value for *investors* by enhancing the firm's stock of assets and capabilities, and focus on extrinsic rewards, product attributes, and relative positions.
3. Competition	SSM views competitive advantage as defining a firm's potential relative to the overall processes and resources of the socio-cultural business network. Competitive advantage must be balanced against *collaboration*.	Traditional lenses reflect the rationale of attempting to achieve an *edge over rivals*.
4. Boundaries and Boundary Roles	SSM sees *boundaries as flexible* and permeable, and boundary roles as "ambassadors" and "bridge builders". Every organization member has important *boundary-spanning* responsibilities both inside and beyond an organization's borders.	Traditional lenses are based on *fixed boundaries*, focusing on protecting a firm's assets and competencies from imitation and preventing resource mobility, with organizational members acting as boundary "*protectors*", "guards" and transaction managers between the organization and external parties.
B: Strategic Purpose and Relationships		
1. Strategic Purpose[7]	The primary strategic purpose of SSM is to attain *organizational resilience*, resulting from a network of reciprocal, mutually beneficial relationships that does not require having an edge over other firms.	Traditional lenses contend that success is achieved when a firm is able to leverage its resources and competencies to achieve *sustainable competitive advantage*, i.e. a superior position in the marketplace.
2. Relationships and Influence	SSM focuses on building long-term, *collaborative relationships based on inter-dependence*. Key relationships are grounded in alliances formed by nested subsystems and interactive processes. This lens blurs traditional boundaries inside a firm and looks	In traditional lenses, relationships are ties created inside a firm and beyond a firm's boundaries, and are built around power derived from the control, protection and appropriability of resources and assets. Such relationships display a focus on

Table 4.4 (continued) A Framework of Key Lenses for Systemic Strategic Management (SSM)

	beyond an organization to define a variety of interacting communities of interest. Influence comes from developing relationships noted for reciprocity, stable patterns, and common interests. Power in SSM comes from understanding patterns, and intervening to change fundamental system attractors and processes.	*transactional exchanges, immediate benefits and transitory interests.*
3. Asset Imitability and Protection	SSM contends that successful organizations require *shared mental models*, mutual knowledge of important technologies, and networks for *sharing* tacit knowledge in business networks. Efforts to protect proprietary resources and knowledge are regarded as counterproductive and detrimental to system-wide achievements.	Traditional lenses are based on *preventing imitation* or appropriation of rare, valuable, and useful assets – it is considered highly desirable to *protect* key competitive assets and abilities.
4. Time Horizon	SSM thinks in terms of *strategic eras*, multiple life cycles, and discontinuities across a network of industries, products and technologies.	Traditional lenses have long-term and short-term *planning orientations*, typically using a calendar of market and product life cycles.
5. Product and Service Offerings	An SSM lens views in terms of the *total solution customers seek*, even if that involves the organization beyond its industry's traditional offerings.	An industry's traditional boundaries determine the discrete *products and services* a company offers. The goal is to maximize the value of those offerings.
C: Dynamic Capabilities[8]		
	SSM lenses view dynamic capabilities as specific organizational and strategic *processes* by which managers alter their resource base. Patterns depend on market dynamism, ranging from detailed routines to simple, experiential ones. Dynamic capabilities should enable organizational resilience, based on a range of robust adaptive strategies, i.e. various options and strategic path capabilities.	Traditional lenses view dynamic capabilities as detailed, analytic *routines* to learn procedures, with focus on predictable outcomes, unique paths and sustained competitive advantage.

187

Frameworks to Understand
Systemic Strategy-Knowledge Links

In the knowledge economy, successful strategic management is critically dependent on managing knowledge effectively in socio-cultural business systems. Knowledge is now recognized by business practitioners and academics as one of the most important sources of innovation and new customer value propositions, emanating from individual, organizational and communal knowledge creativity and utilization. While most extant knowledge management theory and application focus on the organization, and improving its competitive advantages, there is an increasing need to shift this focus to the socio-cultural business system, i.e. understanding and effectively enabling knowledge generation and utilization to enhance the dynamic capabilities of particular socio-cultural business systems.

The purpose of this section is to present three practical frameworks as a basis for understanding systemic strategy-knowledge links. The reader is encouraged to explore the various theories underlying systemic knowledge creation and utilization, e.g. complex adaptive systems theory and autopoiesis theory[9], and theories of how organizations can become "poised" in their knowledge landscapes by co-evolving with other stakeholders in their business system.[10] The three frameworks presented here are:

 – Identifying the systemic strategy-knowledge gap
 – Key dimensions of a systemic knowledge management system
 – A framework of the knowledge-creating process in a business system

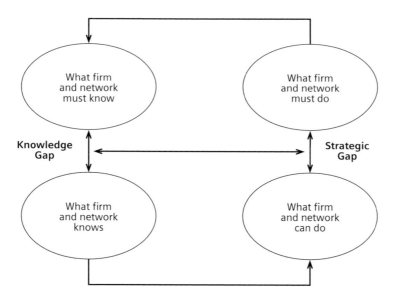

Figure 4.3
Identifying the systemic strategy-knowledge gap (*Source:* Adapted from Zack, M.H. (1999), "Developing a Knowledge Strategy", *California Management Review,* 41, 136)

- **Identifying the systemic strategy-knowledge gap**

  A logical symbiosis exists between strategy and knowledge: on the one hand, strategic gaps regularly arise for organizations or entire business systems due to realization that incongruencies between what they must do (adapt, change), and what they are currently capable of doing exist and this requires "new" knowledge for adapted dynamic capabilities. On the other hand, knowledge itself is so dynamic and pervasive inside and outside organizations, that it often creates the impetus for identifying strategic gaps and development of new strategic paths. This is illustrated in Figure 4.3.

  A gap between the current dynamic capabilities of a business system and what is required for future strategic resilience is indicative of a systemic strategy gap. Dynamic capabilities required for future strategic resilience indicate what knowledge (among other things) is required, and when compared with its existing knowledge base, it indicates the knowledge gap for the business system. Obviously, such gaps may be more acute in some parts of the business system, not necessarily equally in all of them. A tool for strategy-knowledge gap analysis is presented in Chapter 5.

- **Key Dimensions of a Systemic Knowledge Management System**

  Probst et al. propose key dimensions (or "building blocks") of a knowledge management system which can be utilized for understanding the systemic strategy-knowledge links (see Figure 4.4).[11]

  When looking at Figure 4.4 (below), a number of important points have to be emphasized:

  - Knowledge management in a particular business network has to be integrated into the system's overall strategy, as guided by the dominant organization(s) of the system (see Chapter 5 for SSM tools for leadership guidance in business networks).
  - Knowledge management is a system-wide task and must be rooted in systemic processes, structures and culture.
  - The framework illustrates an inner circle consisting of knowledge identification, acquisition, development, distribution, preservation and use of knowledge. An outer cycle consists of all these activities plus goal setting and measurements.
  - While there may not be a single "right" model of knowledge management, due to different requirements in various types of business networks, a simple criterion for evaluating any particular systemic knowledge management system is its effectiveness, i.e. enabling sustainable "fitness" and resilience of the network.

  The management system described by Probst et al. has been applied in many companies. The key dimensions include: On the one hand, the goal setting, transferring and measuring elements and, on the other hand, the creation of transparency, the generation and sharing of knowledge, as well as the preservation and use of the knowledge base.

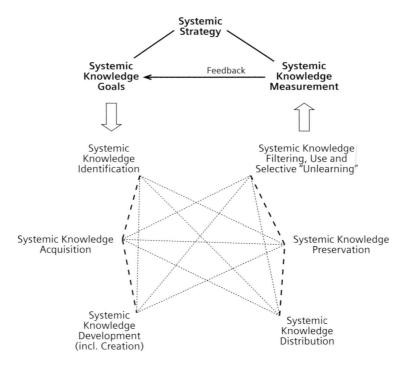

Figure 4.4

Key dimensions of a systemic knowledge management system (*Source:* Adapted from Probst et al. (1999) and Probst (1998), "Practical Knowledge Management: A Model That Works", *Prism,* Arthur D. Little, Second Quarter, 19)

The management system developed by Probst et al. comprises the following key dimensions:

Knowledge goals give direction to management activities. They determine which knowledge represents a strategic relevant resource and which abilities should be developed. These goals can be of a normative, strategic or operative nature.

Identifying knowledge is about retaining existing knowledge that is available both internally and externally. Often we discover that we do not at all know which knowledge is available. There is no clarity regarding the experts who are available and where they are, nor the skills which are available, or which experiences have already been gained and where. Restructuring, lean management and reengineering have often done nothing to increase transparency and knowledge has been unwittingly lost.

The *acquisition* of knowledge is frequently used to build future competencies quicker than it would be by means of internal potential and growth. Take-overs and integration of experienced colleagues or whole teams, often in a collaborative effort such as cooperative structures or through the complete integration of an organization or an institute, are all opportunities to acquire knowledge.

Central to *knowledge development* is the production of new capabilities, new products, better ideas and performance-enhancing processes. Knowledge development involves all kind of efforts in which management deliberately concerns itself with the production or the creation of both internal and external capabilities that do not as yet exist.

The *distribution and sharing of experiences* is the most important prerequisite for making isolated, available experience useful to the organization as a whole. The main questions are, who should or does know what to which extent? And, for whom can I facilitate the processes of knowledge distribution? Not everyone needs to know everything, but the economic principle of labor division demands a meaningful description and control of the extent of knowledge distribution and sharing.

The *use of knowledge*, in other words the productive exploitation of organizational knowledge for the institution's benefit, is knowledge management's goal and purpose. The successful identification and distribution of central knowledge does not mean that the use in everyday business has been guaranteed. In the end the willingness of a colleague to share his knowledge with others must be complemented by the willingness of other colleagues to actually use this knowledge. The use of "unfamiliar" knowledge is restricted by a spectrum of barriers. Many people find using "someone else's" experience or skills an "unnatural act", which they will avoid where possible. The preservation of "proven" routines forms a safety mechanism that safeguards the individual from domination and maintains his identity.

Skills, once gained, are not automatically available for future use. The intended *preservation* of experiences requires management efforts. In fact, today many organizations complain that, for instance, in the wake of reorganizations they have lost a part of their memories. This *organizational know-how risk* in the form of *collective amnesia* is frequently based on the thoughtless disruption of informal networks that control important, but infrequently studied, processes. Further losses of know-how capital can be traced to significant employees being made redundant or insufficient development activities.

The *measurement and evaluation* of organizational knowledge is one of most important challenges that knowledge management currently faces. In this regard, a decisive breakthrough has only been possible to a limited extent. Knowledge managers, in contrast to financial managers, cannot rely on a tried and trusted range of indicators and measuring procedures, but have to break new ground. Only if the measurement of the extent of key knowledge management processes could be simplified in future and if this is largely accepted, could the management circle be closed and would one be able to speak about true knowledge *management*.

• The Knowledge Creating Process in a Business System

The "raison d'être" of an organization and the socio-cultural business system of which it forms part is to continuously create knowledge and convert this knowledge into socio-cultural value. Knowledge and the capability to create and utilize such knowledge are the most important source of a business network's existence and its sustainability. Various authors, such as Nonaka, Teece, Drucker, Davenport, Probst,

Von Krogh and Stewart consider knowledge as the most important resource in today's economy.[12] Nonaka and Takeuchi propose a knowledge-creating model (the SECI model) for a firm that can also be applied to a business network.

In the above knowledge-creating system, knowledge is created through the SECI spiral (see Figure 4.5), that proceeds through four modes of conversion between tacit and explicit knowledge:

1) socialization (from tacit knowledge to tacit knowledge);

2) externalization (from tacit knowledge to explicit knowledge);

3) combination (from explicit knowledge to explicit knowledge); and

4) internalization (from explicit knowledge to tacit knowledge).

Knowledge is created through interactions among individuals in a business network with different types and contents of knowledge. Through this "social conversion" process, tacit and explicit knowledge expand in terms of both quality and quantity.

A Systemic Framework for the Development of New Business Models

The above-mentioned frameworks for understanding of the dynamics and lenses of systemic strategic management are relevant to the formation and change of organizational business models in socio-cultural business networks. Every organization has a business model, i.e. its "way of doing business" or its "business concept", and these are shaped and changed in symbiosis with market opportunities and other organizations in socio-cultural business systems. The knowledge economy has given rise to a plethora of new business models, as well as to changes in existing business models. In many instances, experimental business models are initiated alongside established business models, either inside organizations (e.g. various divisions) or outside organizations (e.g. separate firms). As indicated before, the challenge for strategic manage-

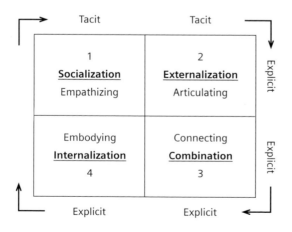

Figure 4.5
The SECI model of knowledge creation in a business system (*Source:* Adapted from Nonaka, I. and Takeuchi, H. (1995), *The Knowledge-Creating Company,* New York: Oxford University Press)

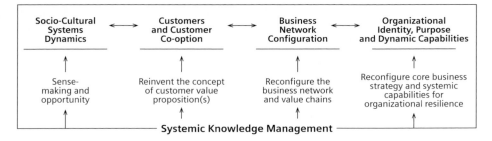

Figure 4.6 A systemic perspective of developing new business models

ment is to develop frameworks of how new business models and new industries emerge, and how one can enable their emergence. New business models, and reinvention of existing business models, rather than continuous improvement are required in the knowledge economy in which the "rules of the game" are changing rapidly for many industries and markets.

A number of authors, e.g. Beinhocker, Govindarajan and Gupta, Hamel, and Kim and Mauborgne, have suggested approaches for "changing the rules of the game".[13] Most of these approaches (or frameworks) consider business models from an individual organization perspective. A framework for co-shaping the development of new business models for an organization in systemic context is presented in Figure 4.6, which effectively encapsulates the previous frameworks discussed in this chapter.

Figure 4.6 indicates that a new business model arises not only from reconfiguring an organization's core business strategy and dynamic capabilities, but also from making sense of socio-cultural dynamics and gaps, reinventing of customer value proposition(s), and reconfiguring the business network and its value chains. A reconfigured core business strategy should be the *result* of systemic insight, foresight and sense making. Various strategic management tools to assist in the development of new business models are discussed in Chapter 5.

Guidelines to Deal with Organizational Inertia in Business Networks

Traditional strategic management approaches (see Chapter 2) could cause organizational inertia in business models and networks. It is human nature to prefer, to seek out, and even expect certainty. The knowledge economy with its paradoxes threatens that world view. So much time was spent on teaching organizations and managers to be systematized, analytical and orderly in the past that they often cannot respond to the fast-changing environment.

A crucial issue is how to identify the signals that point to a necessary shift in business model. A corollary issue is how to overcome organizational inertia and initiate advantageous changes, or how to to prevent disruptive "jolts" from occurring. Even in the face of overwhelming evidence for change, managers often fall into competence and path dependency traps. Shifting to a systemic strategic management paradigm means that many organizations should forcefully jettison many elements embedded in its traditional strategy mindset, and unlearn crucial assumptions and lenses that comprise traditional business models and strategies.

Firms attempting a shift to systemic strategic management face four types of inertia[14]:

- *Structural inertia* – established structural linkages of internal and external relationships, i.e. institutionalized patterns of culture, norms and ideologies, are often difficult to change.
- *Competitive inertia* – the focus on preserving an established competitive advantage, and on avoiding cannibalization of existing market shares and product lines, are powerful inertia factors.
- *Momentum inertia* – organizational momentum causes organization members to act in ways consistent with previous experience. Learning to act in ways that contradict experienced responses that have led to prior success are necessary to overcome this inertia.
- *Strategic architecture inertia* – inertia residing in different mental models (schemas) on which patterns of strategic responses are based, especially between various organizations in a business network.

These types of inertia cause particular managerial and leadership challenges, which are addressed in Chapter 6.

Cautions in Shifting to Systemic Strategic Management

Several cautions in adopting a systemic strategic management paradigm should be observed:

- Systemic strategic management does not mean an imminent or immediate discarding of an existing organizational business model – most often it means creating a "shadow organization", either internally or externally, to initiate, experiment with, and develop new business model(s), alongside the management of a traditional business model. It does require, however, a radical shift in strategic management mindset.
- Systemic strategic management promotes collaboration, connections and enduring ties – yet, the more tightly interwoven the various parts of a system become, the more difficult it is to initiate radical change, and the more vulnerable the entire system is to the weakness of an individual unit. This means that both competitive and collaborative orientations in strategic management are beneficial and should co-exist, although the collaborative orientation should predominate.
- Having a portfolio of business models, including traditional and experimenting/innovative ones, raises questions of managerial capabilities, organizational resources, spread of focus, commitment and culture, among others. Many arguments can be raised for focus on core competencies, strong existing brand devel-

opment, limited financial and other resources, high risk of radical innovation, disruption of drivers for efficiency and productivity gains etc. The simple response is that *"running harder and harder"* is not the route for enduring, resilient organizational survival in the knowledge economy, but *"running differently"* is – besides doing all of the efficiency improvement measures. This route requires new managerial capabilities, rooted in the paradoxical management that Charles Handy predicted some years ago.[15] These new managerial capabilities are reviewed in Chapter 6.

Conclusion

In this chapter various frameworks to understanding systemic strategic management were presented, and these were encapsulated in a framework of dimensions to develop new business models with a systemic socio-cultural perspective. The strategic management purpose is to co-shape systemic organizational capabilities for individual organizational and business network resilience in the fast-changing knowledge economy. Systemic knowledge creation and utilization are prerequisites for maintaining such business network resilience, providing the basis for continuous innovation, adaptation and enactment of environments through appropriate new (co-shaped) customer value propositions. Rather than seeking reduction of complexity and greater certainty, organizations should embrace and absorb complexity to avoid organizational and systemic inertia. The strategic management tools to effect such activities are presented in Chapter 5.

The Challenge Today:
Changing the Rules of the Game[*]

By Gary Hamel

*As the information age takes over from the industrial age and change accelerates, the key challenge for each company is to become the architect of revolution in its industry, leaving other companies to play catch-up. The author argues that the key competitive advantage for companies intent on winning in the new economy is non-linear innovation. Companies need to shift from a product-centric view of innovation to a systemic view of innovation: ie innovation of the **business** model itself. This article is derived from the last of the 1998 Stockton Lectures, delivered in April.*

Twenty or thirty years ago, Doctor Demming challenged companies on the issue of quality. Some listened, principally the Japanese. But most companies ignored the challenge, and went on to pay a heavy price for being caught behind the change curve. Only a few years ago, we thought the problem was globalisation. Europe worried about whether it could compete with the Germans and Japanese. Now these two economies are struggling to cope with many of the competitiveness issues that British companies started working on 15 or more years ago.

The challenge is no longer quality; nor is it globalisation. You've been there, done that, got the ISO 9001. This article is about the next great competitive challenge and building a capability to meet it. I believe that fewer than five per cent of companies are today explicitly addressing this new challenge. Certainly there is no book of best practices available from some consulting company, and there are no obvious exemplars.

What is this new challenge? I believe that the challenge today is to become the architect of industry revolution; to be the author of the kinds of fundamental change in business models that are transforming industries from telecoms to food retailing, from insurance to airlines, and from agriculture to education. Perhaps the revolutionary metaphor sounds like hyperbole. But it is not.

---

[*] Taken with permission from Business Strategy Review, 1998, Volume 9, Issue 2, pp. 19-26,
  Blackwell Publishing

I want to share with you my insights drawn from my experience in trying to teach companies how to be the architects of industry revolution, how to be deeply and truly entrepreneurial – in other words, how to lead and profit from the fundamental transition to a new economy that is now under way. It is almost tautological to say we are moving from the industrial age to the information age. Tautological though it may be, it is still true. The question is no longer: is it going to happen? The question is: what companies will create the new wealth in this transition? Let me put it more bluntly: on the road to the future, are you the windscreen or are you the bug?

I think many companies are only just beginning to perceive how fundamentally these changes will affect their businesses. Imagine that whenever you pick up your phone a piece of software immediately shops around and finds the world's lowest-cost routing for your call. You will no longer switch your longdistance provider every two or three years: you will switch it every time you make a call. Imagine deciding what you want for the week's groceries and then putting your shopping list out to auction – to find out who is going to deliver this list of items to you at the lowest price. These fundamental changes, and countless others, are literally just over the horizon.

Newcomers in the Driver's Seat

As we consider the recent past and near future, what we notice immediately is the number of newcomers who are in the driver's seat of industry revolution. As an individual consumer, you may well take a flight on Virgin, buy a computer from Dell, and buy insurance through Direct Line. There are dozens of things you buy today from vendors that didn't even exist a decade ago. Never has the world been a better place for industry revolutionaries; and never has it been a more dangerous place for complacent incumbents. Indeed, the dividing line between success and failure is today measured in months, not decades.

Some time ago, I heard Bill Gates say that he believes Microsoft is always two years away from failure (and he wasn't saying this for the benefit of lawyers at the US Justice Department). I think Mr. Gates really believes that Microsoft lives life on a precipice. Indeed, Microsoft came perilously close to missing the whole Internet wave. With a bit more foresight on the part of Microsoft, Netscape would never have existed. If Bill Gates feels that Microsoft is never more than two years away from failure, despite its dominance of the PC software business, how should the rest of us feel?

Every industry is ripe for revolution. Take financial services: how do banks and insurance companies make money today? In great measure their profits derive from two simple things – a locational monopoly (control over High Street locations), and customer ignorance. Very few people know whether their current account is the one with the highest interest rate. When buying insurance, most customers have no way of knowing the size of commission that went to the sale agent. Given the complexity and obfuscation that hangs like a shroud over every insurance product, most customers don't even know if they really bought the policy that best fills their needs. Until now financial institutions have always been able to trade on customer ignorance. The entrance to every bank should display a motto carved in stone: "Ignorance Welcomed Here!" But as in many other industries, that ignorance is disappearing fast. Customers will be able to make instant comparisons and find the cheapest, most suitable product. Economies of distribution – trying to shove a lot of product through a single High Street location-will give way to economies of search. I don't want to even go to the High Street. I want instant comparisons, of all relevant financial services products, accessible from my own home.

Today all businesses are living on the precipice. It's not just that product lifecycles are getting shorter; *strategy* lifecycles are getting shorter. Companies have to be able to ask themselves the fundamental questions – who are we and how do we compete, which customers do we serve, where are we going to – not once a decade, in the midst of a crisis when they trade out CEOs, but every two or three years.

What evidence supports these bold assertions? The telephone took almost 40 years to reach 10 million customers in the US (and that industry still seems to move at a glacial pace). Yet the Web browser reached 10 million customers in 18 months. Sun Microsystem's Java software platform was populated on 100 million computers in only 13 months.

In this topsy-turvy world, the fundamental competitive challenge is not achieving operating efficiency in capital-intensive industries. The challenge is unleashing innovation in imagination-intensive industries. And every industry out there is becoming an imagination-intensive industry, no matter how moribund it may look from outside. Take some more examples. America-Online competes as an online access company and worked for a nearly decade to sign up its first 10 million users. A newcomer, Hotmail, has built a base of more than 10 million users in the last 24 months by offering a free, advertising-supported e-mail service. Microsoft recently bought it for $400 million. At the time, Hotmail's annual revenues were $4m. But with Hotmail came access to 10 million pairs of eyes.

In a world where new business models rapidly supplant old business models, innovation must encompass more than product line extensions and incremental efficiency gains. Today the unit of analysis for innovation is the entire business system. And while the pace of change isn't always as rapid as it has been in the on-line world, it is nonetheless dramatic. For years the banks have been losing market share to mutual funds and other investment vehicles. Charles Schwab, a discount broker, has been one of the leaders of this transformation in the United States. Within the next year or two, mutual funds will probably supplant banks as the largest depositories of domestic savings.

I recently wrote an article in the *Financial Times* on the merger of Citibank and the Travellers Group. Though I used somewhat more prudent language, my basic point was that banking is the only place outside Jurassic Park where you can watch dinosaurs mate. The merger strategy may work for a few years. But it is not the future of financial services. Getting bigger is not a strategy. Getting better is not a strategy. Today, a company has to be willing to get different – profoundly different!

Innovation by Incumbents

In a recent survey sponsored by MCI, I asked 500 CEOs which companies within their industry had taken best advantage of change over the past ten years. The number one answer was "new competitors." The second question was: "if you look forward ten years, do you expect the competitors you face to be new competitors or traditional competitors?" Again, the number one answer was "new competitors". The third question was: "if you look at the most successful newcomers in your industry, how have they won – by executing better or by changing the rules of the game?" You wouldn't be surprised that "change the rules of the game" received an overwhelming majority of the votes.

If these CEOs have it right, and I believe they do, this raises profound questions for any incumbent. The questions are these:

- How do you build the spirit of an industry revolutionary inside the heart of a large successful company?
- How do you avoid anyone ever writing a turnaround story about your company?
- How do you go from success to success without ever dropping the ball?

There are two kinds of innovation that should interest us here. The first is innovation with respect to the firm's historic strategy. The second is innovation with respect to the firm's industry and its competitors. There are likewise two questions every organisation must address: "Can we change our own strategy?" And, "can we proactively reinvent our industry?" A lot of companies have done the former. Many have done the latter. But few have done both. For example, when IBM goes into the consulting business, that is innovation for IBM but not for the industry: EDS, Andersen Consulting and others are already well-established in the IT consulting business. Industry laggards often succeed in re-inventing their strategy, but they usually do this only under duress – only when their existing business model has been rendered more or less obsolete by unorthodox challengers.

Many start-ups are capable of changing the rules of the game but most of them never live to find a second strategy. Most of them run to the end of their founders' headlights and then crash and burn: Digital never got beyond Ken Olson's original vision. Indeed, Silicon Valley is littered with the bones of one-strategy companies. These bones are interesting to look at but they do not reveal much about how a company can again and again re-create the future of its industry.

So one-time visionaries hardly bear studying. And strategy transformation that is not driven by an agenda for industry transformation is equally uninteresting. Neither start-ups nor laggards deserve much study. But we can learn much from what I like to call the "grey-haired revolutionaries." Take Marks and Spencer for example – who would have bet they would be successful in food and financial services? Monsanto is in the midst of a mind-bending transformation from a sleepy chemical company to a hot biotech leader. So being successful at both kinds of innovation is not some impossible dream. But few companies are adept at this kind of metamorphosis.

I believe that to succeed in the new economy, companies are going to have to think about innovation in some very different ways, in particular:

- Companies will have to move beyond incrementalism to embrace non-linear innovation.
- Companies will have to understand innovation at the level of an entire business system as well as innovation at the level of an individual product or service.
- Companies will have to move beyond a view of innovation as the product of lone visionaries, and learn how to exploit the innovative ideas of activists throughout their organisations.
- Companies will have to develop approaches to innovation that combine diversity with coherence – a rich out-pouring of non-traditional ideas, with a tight, coherent point of view about the destiny of the entire enterprise.
- Companies will have to make innovation a systemic capability, in the same way that quality is a systemic capability. It's not enough to hope for serendipity.

Incrementalism is No Longer Enough

We live in a world where incrementalism is no longer enough. In a non-linear world, only non-linear strategies will create new wealth. In the car business, the margins of the largest companies are all coming down – and they're all clustered tightly around a rather low mean. What you see in that industry is what you see in nearly every industry today: companies whose strategies are converging and who are reaching the end of incrementalism. I recently asked the senior management of a large car company: "what kinds of idea would raise your margins from 2-3% up to 11-12%?. ... Well," they answered, "they'd be ideas that were entirely new to the industry." "They'd be ideas that wouldn't fit through our financial screens." "They'd be ideas that we couldn't evaluate using historical data. ... They'd be ideas that would provoke a lot of scepticism." And so on. "In fact," I summarised, "they'd be exactly the kinds of ideas that you, as senior managers, are trained to kill ... oh no, there's another crazy idea ... Kablammm!"

In our survey, we asked CEOs whether the strategies of their largest competitors had been getting more alike or more dissimilar over the last decade. Not surprisingly, they answered that the strategies of the largest incumbents had been getting more and more alike. Strategy convergence is not a good thing. And it has been aided and abetted by consulting companies. Hawking their surveys of "best practices", consulting companies carry orthodoxies, like a deadly virus, across companies. Here's a simple way of testing whether strategies are converging in your industry: go to ordinary employees and ask them if they feel that they are working harder and harder to achieve less and less in terms of competitive differentiation and real wealth creation.

Executives must understand that "non-linear" does not mean "high risk." The proof of this is the fact that most industry revolutionaries began poor: they did not start out with resource advantages. The market capitalisation of Dell recently passed that of

General Motors. But Dell did not start out that way. A decade ago, I remember being asked for career advice by an MBA student thinking of going to work at Dell. I told him to give it a try. He's a multimillionaire now.

When I challenge executives to get to the future first, and to go non-linear, there is usually much sucking of teeth and pulling of forelocks. The implicit assumption is that you have to bet big, and risk much to be an industry revolutionary. But think about this: which number is bigger in most companies – the amount that has been written off over the past decade for hanging on to the past for too long, or the amount that has been written off because the company experimented with the future too soon? Being incremental may be the biggest risk of all.

One thing that makes the future appear to be very risky is that senior management is often not living close enough to the voice of the customer and the voice of the future. A few months ago, I spoke to a gathering of top executives from large US groceries companies. I asked these executives whether they really believed that people would one day order their groceries on-line. The immediate consensus was that on-line grocery sales would never amount to much. "You'd have to pay $10 to get the groceries delivered – no way! ... Our customers are incredibly price sensitive and it's just not going to happen in our industry," they reasoned. Yet when these folks were faced with a computer and told to order their own products on-line, right then and there, a new perspective emerged. What was the response of executives after going down the aisles of the virtual supermarket? One executive found his market-leading product at the bottom of a black and white listing of 40 competing products. His product was at the bottom because the list was arranged by price per gram and fat content per serving, and his product was both expensive and unhealthy. He had to ask himself, what will be the value of all my delivery vans and shelf-merchandising efforts in this brave new world?

The lesson from this little story is that if you want people in a company to understand the future, the learning they need is not just analytical. That group could have been shown all the trends about Internet usage and at-home shopping. To see the future, people need experiential learning. You don't commit to the future because it is intellectually the right thing to do. You commit to the future because your viscera tells you that it is inevitable. You have to do more than see the future, you must feel the future. This can only happen if top management is willing to embark on an odyssey of deep, experiential learning. Here's a question to put to your senior management group: are you learning as fast as the world around you is changing? And is your learning experiential? If the answer to these two questions is "no", then your company won't embrace the future, and top management will become the bottleneck on innovation.

Innovation of the Business Model

We need to shift from a product-centric view of innovation to a systemic view of innovation. 3M's Post-It-Notes was product innovation. First Direct is systemic innovation. The VCR was product innovation. Amazon.com is systemic innovation.

Trade 500 shares of IBM through a full service broker and it will cost you nearly $500.00 The same transaction through an on-line broker can be accomplished for as little as $7. That difference is not the product of re-engineering; its the product of a fundamentally different business model. Dell turns its inventory over 50 times a quarter and Compaq manages just 10-12 times per quarter. That, too, is not a re-engineering outcome; it is a different business model. Recently, Starbucks bought Seattle Coffee in the UK. But where has Nestle been these last few years? Nestle is the number one coffee company in the world and Nescafe is the number one brand. Was anyone sitting around at Nestle wondering how to get a construction worker or a bus driver to line up and pay $3 for a latte coffee?

This example also illustrates very clearly why we need to think in a new way about how to measure corporate success. Market share is no longer enough. Does it really matter that Nestle claws back a bit of market share from Procter & Gamble in the aisles of the supermarket, if a revolutionary is creating most of the new wealth in the coffee business with a very different business model? Does it matter if Peugeot gets a little bit of market share from Fiat if most of the new wealth in the car business is being created by companies reinventing distribution and car-buying? This sort of change is happening in every industry. Take an almost absurd example, lettuce – a simple, mature market if ever there was one. The market for pre-washed and pre-packaged lettuce has gone from zero to about $1bn in the last seven years in the US. If you can do this with a head of lettuce there is no excuse for failing to innovate in any business.

We have only just begun to think about innovation at the level of the business model. There are very few people in companies today that can think holistically about entirely new business models as opposed to seeing innovation as a technology or product issue.

Activists not Visionaries

Yet another way we need to rethink innovation is by moving from innovation as the product of visionaries to innovation as the product of activists. There is a very subtle distinction there. When we look at where new strategies come from, we typically point to a visionary – be it Bill Gates, Anita Roddick or Rupert Murdoch. But the sad reality is that most companies are not run by visionaries: they are run by managers and administrators. We also know that today's visionary is tomorrow's intellectual straight-jacket, and that sooner or later he or she will imperil the success they spawned. How can we set about unleashing the activists in our organisations? I believe there are revolutionaries in every company. Silicon valley is a refugee camp for revolutionaries who didn't get a hearing somewhere else. As part of a recent consultancy programme, I asked individuals throughout a large global company to identify the company's "renegades." An e-mail was sent out asking people to identify those who thought differently, those who were always asking interesting questions, those who were frustrated by the status quo. This question was the first step in building a world-wide network of renegades in this company – renegades who now have attention of top management.

It is ironic that people often say that change must start at the top. This is patent nonsense. How often does the revolution start with a monarchy? Not often, I contend.

Some frustrated middle manager in one of the big telecommunications companies recently sent me a little chart that her company was using as part of its umpteenth cultural change programme. Top management had sent this chart to everyone in the organisation. One side of the chart listed all the new behaviours that employees were expected to adopt. The other side of the matrix portrayed the hierarchical levels in the company: "executives", "managers", "individual contributors" and so on. One of the desired behaviours was "thinking strategically." Yet the chart indicated that only executives had this responsibility. In one stroke this company had disenfranchised 99.9% of the organisation from any responsibility for the future. No wonder Dilbert resonates with people.

And before you're too quick to say, "this would never happen in my company," ask yourself the question: what percentage of the employees in your organisation wake up every morning with the belief that they have a personal responsibility for innovation and new wealth creation? Most companies today have largely disenfranchised their employees from being a part of a conversation about the future. So I don't think change starts at the top. In the state where I live, California, it is quite possible for an ordinary citizen to place a proposal on a state-wide ballot. Through this kind of activist-driven democracy California has led the country in adopting all kinds of social and political reforms. Can an ordinary employee put anything on the strategy "ballot" in your company?

If you look through history you will find that it is the activists who change things. In a typical organisational pyramid, where do you find the least genetic diversity? At the top. Where do you find people who have most of their emotional equity invested in the past? At the top. In other words, the typical organisational pyramid is a hierarchy of experience, and strategy is the product of experience. This is happening at the very time that experience is being devalued as never before. What is needed to create the future is not a hierarchy of experience, but a hierarchy of imagination.

In practice that means involving three kinds of constituencies that typically do not have a large share of voice in conversations about the future: young people, those on the geographic periphery of the organisation and newcomers.

Young people live close to the future. Recently, when my teenage son started to drive, I asked him to phone our insurance agent and find out what it would cost to add him to our vehicles' insurance policy. He looked at me with that look reserved for hopelessly out-of-date parents and said: "if it's not on-line, I don't have time." So on-line he went and shopped around until he had found the best insurance value out there. Why is it that the people who are living closest to the future are usually disenfranchised from the strategy process? How often do CEOs or board members have a 23-year-old make a presentation to the top management committee? How often do CEOs and board members talk to a 14-year-old on how their perceptions of the world are different?

The geographic periphery is often left out of conversations about the future. Corporate imagination rises for every kilometre you go from head office. This is not because the people at head office are stupid, but because those at the edges have fewer resources and have to be more creative. Those at the edges are far enough from the centre to be able to try new things without getting stomped on right away.

Newcomers are particularly useful if you can find people with experience in other industries. And they are especially valuable if they have somehow managed to thus far escape all the corporate training, which is designed, after all, to socialise individuals into a common way of thinking.

Structured Anarchy

We've all heard a lot about skunk works and "intrapreneurship." But innovation is more than letting a thousand flowers bloom – letting everyone have an idea. In most industries scale still counts, cumulative learning is important, and resources are limited. Hence, unfettered innovation is a recipe for fragmentation and sub-optimisation. Typically, when we talk about innovation, we emphasise diversity; but coherence in strategy is equally important. At the extreme, fragmentation results in anarchy – there is no structure that unites individuals in common causes. At the other extreme, coherence becomes authoritarianism or group-think-uniformity kills a company's ability to experiment and adapt.

Think of experimentation and optimisation as two axes at right angles. Over the past decade or two most companies have focused almost exclusively on optimisation – wringing out every little bit of efficiency from existing business models. Few companies have a rich set of experiments under way that help them to discover and exploit the boundaries of new markets, new customer groups, and new business models. If you don't believe that this imbalance exists in most companies, go to a middle level manager in your own organisation and ask the following question: "What are the four or five experiments under way in your business that you believe offer the greatest potential for opening up fundamentally new competitive space? You'll probably get a blank stare.

How do you open up a deep conversation within your company, get the young people involved and take off the blinders – but at the end of the process also achieve a coherent point of view of what you are becoming as a company? GE Capital has been one of the most innovative companies in financial services over the last decade or two. If you ask people at GE Capital to identify the core of their innovative success, you get an extraordinarily consistent answer: "we are riding the wave of decapitalisation around the world". When British Airways or some other airline wants to take capital off its balance sheet, it turns to GE Capital. GE Capital is also extraordinarily good at pricing risk and laying it off onto others. One fundamental dimension of innovation for the company has been inventing new ways of handling risk. GE Capital has also been very creative in finding ways of adding new, value-added services to commodity service offerings. Decapitalisation, risk management, service enhancement – these are the broad vectors of innovation that have given coherence to GE Capital's seemingly boundless imagination.

I sometimes think of this innovation process in the following way. Imagine a simple diamond-shaped diagram. Starting at the top of the diamond, the lines describing its shape diverge; but at some point, they began to converge again, reaching another point at the bottom of the diagram. A diverse, yet coherent strategy conversation can be thought of in an analogous way. First expand the boundaries of strategic thought – by challenging orthodoxies, bringing new voices into the conversation, reconceiving the company in terms of competencies, and so on. The goal is to develop a rich menu of nontraditional strategic options. But at some point you need to re-converge. The challenge is to look across all those ideas and options and search for themes and threads: if this set of options is pursued we become this kind of a company, whereas if we pursue this other set of options we become another kind of company. The goal is to provoke convergence around a few simple but powerful themes that serve to broadly bound the scope of innovation in the firm.

The Internet provides another useful analogy. Some see the Internet as an essentially chaotic, unstructured phenomenon. But the explosion of innovation on the Web has been possible because there is a deep set of rules – a strategic architecture, as I might call it – that sets the boundaries on innovation. One of those rules is that the Web is an "open system." The Web is platform-independent, it is not based on the proprietary technology of one company. The Web is robust – a fault in one part of the Web doesn't destroy the whole. There are protocols which ensure that the movement of data, images and voice is relatively seamless, and so on. If any of these boundary conditions were missing, innovation would quickly grind to a halt. And someone had to set these boundaries, they were not the product of some spontaneous, self-organising impulse.

Likewise, the essential role of senior management is to set the strategic boundaries, or the innovation vectors as I prefer to call them, that will give coherence, consistency and cumulativeness to innovation. But these vectors must grow out of a broadly engaging, deeply creative process of strategic enquiry. They are not invented by a few superannuated divisional directors attending a two-day strategy "retreat."

New Lenses Reveal New Possibilities

To see new opportunities, individuals must look through new lenses. There are three fundamental lenses that help people find the unconventional. The first lens is the lens of orthodoxy. When you can look at your industry and separate dogma from gravity-what is simply the product of unquestioned precedence and what is an irrevocable fact of life-you can discover new and unanticipated ways of challenging industry rules. Industry revolutionaries always challenge the orthodoxies of the incumbents. The starting point of any strategic conversation must be a systematic deconstruction of existing industry orthodoxies. Without this, one doesn't create the degrees of intellectual freedom that are needed in order to discover the new.

The second lens is the ability to peer deeply into trends that have the potential to generate gamechanging discontinuities. This is not about forecasting, or scenario planning, or gazing into some crystal ball. Instead it is about understanding what is already changing – what is the revolutionary portent in things that are right now in the process of changing. There is no such thing as *the* future. There are millions of possible futures waiting to be invented. The future is not something that happens to you. The future is something you create.

The simple question to be answered is this: what are the fundamental discontinuities that could be leveraged to create new benefits for customers and wrong-foot competitors?

The BBC may be the finest news-gathering organisation in the world, but it was CNN that created global news. This was not because CNN did a lot of scenario planning and forecasting. Instead, Ted Turner and his colleagues saw things that were already changing, but had been missed by other broadcasters: changes in lifestyle and technology and in the regulatory environment. The challenge is not prediction, but to deeply understand the discontinuities which, if harnessed, could form the foundation of new opportunities.

There is a third lens that I believe is central to being able to perceive non-traditional opportunities. Most companies define themselves by what they *do:* we are a bank, we are an airline, we are a car company, etc. You see new opportunities when you can escape a product- or service-centric definition of a company, and see it in terms of what it *knows* – its core competencies. If Disney had defined itself as a company that makes animated feature films and runs theme parks – that would have been the end of its growth. I don't think Disney is really eager to have another experience like Euro-Disney right away again. Yet when Disney was able to reconceive its identity in terms of competencies like story-telling and creating sets, it found an array of new, logically related, opportunities. Given Disney's core competencies, it should be no surprise that Disney has succeeded in producing some of Broadway's most successful shows over the past few years. Marks and Spencer has leveraged its competencies and assets into new in equally imaginative ways.

Getting Lucky Twice

Innovation is often viewed as the product of serendipity. But if corporate vitality depends as never before on discontinuous innovation, we had better learn how to make innovation a capability. This may seem like an impossible goal, a goal that is based on an unresolvable contradiction. But think about this analogy. If you had asked someone thirty years ago where quality comes from, they would have thought for a minute, mentioned Tiffany's or Rolls Royce or Burberry's and replied that quality comes from the artisan, from the craftsman. Then a few early quality gurus came along and said: "maybe we can institutionalise quality." The result was the quality movement: statistical process control, quality circles, group problem-solving, and so on. Is it any more of a stretch to imagine that innovation can be made a corporate-wide capability than to imagine, twenty years ago, that a Toyota could be made to be as reliable as a Rolls Royce or Mercedes Benz?

I believe non-linear innovation is *the* competitive advantage for companies intent on winning in the new economy. It will be as important over the next twenty to thirty years as quality has been over the last few decades. If innovation is the goal, strategy cannot be formulated by an elite, and then implemented by the masses. Strategy must leverage every ounce of imagination across the company. The strategy process I have been describing is one that can best be characterised as discovery, synthesis and experimentation. Discovery comes as you find the revolutionaries in your own company, help them look at the world through new lenses, and instil in them a passion for creating the future. Synthesis is the work of top management; searching for patterns in an array of unconventional ideas. Once a broad direction has been set, experimentation serves to elaborate that direction in ways that could never have been anticipated by a small senior executive group. If the goal is to create new wealth-generating strategies, year after year, companies will have to master this process in the same way they had to master the disciplines of quality management if they hoped to produce superior products year after year.

Strategic Innovation:
A Conceptual Road Map*

By Vijay Govindarajan and Anil K. Gupta

Competitive advantage is not just a function of how well a company plays by the existing rules of the game. More important, it depends on the firm's ability to radically change those rules. This is as true of a newcomer like eBay as it is of an established player like Ford Motor Company or General Electric.

Transforming the game, no doubt, is fundamentally a creative undertaking; it cannot result from a purely deliberate and purposeful process. Neither is strategic innovation a function of luck, accident, or opportunism. In fact, it is possible to use an explicit and systematic framework to guide that creative process. Here we shall provide such a framework, illustrating it through detailed case examples.

There are several reasons why every company must cultivate a bias for changing the rules within its industry:

Major Discontinuities in the External Environment. The external environment of a firm is constantly changing – sometimes incrementally, sometimes in a quantum and discontinuous fashion. Such changes almost always require inventing at least some new rules of the game. From the perspective of a financial service firm such as Merrill Lynch, the aging of the population represents an ongoing, incremental change, whereas the emergence of Internet trading represents a radical, discontinuous change.

Proactive Reshaping of the Industry Structure. Changes in the external environment do not always originate from external forces. Large and small firms alike can often reshape that environment. In late 1999, Sun Microsystems announced that it would offer application software, including word-processing programs, over the Internet. Unlike the historical approach to application software, the programs did not need to be purchased for installation on the personal computer; instead, they could be rented from Web servers on an as-needed basis. Sun's move was aimed squarely at undercutting the power of Microsoft's core product, its Windows operating system. Despite its market dominance, Microsoft was forced to follow suit and announced that it too would embrace the renting of application programs over Web servers.

The quest for changing the rules of the game is never-ending. The question of who takes the initiative in doing so is up to you.

---

* Taken with permission from Business Horizons, July-August 2001, pp. 3-12

Elements of a Business Model

Need to Break Out of the Competitive Pack. In the absence of collusion, it is a given that competitors will inevitably find themselves knocking heads with each other for diminishing gains. At various times in the PC industry, at least three of the major players – Compaq, Dell, and Hewlett-Packard – have declared their intention to be the market share leader in the industry. In a situation such as this, continuing to play by the old rules leaves a firm highly vulnerable to preemption by the more innovative competitors.

Three Arenas for Attack

The business model shown in Figure 1 results from answering three questions:

1. Who are my target customers?
2. What value do I want to deliver to them?
3. How will I create it?

The answers to these questions operate as a *system* – the individual answers must be self-reinforcing and internally consistent. Take the case of Procter & Gamble's Ivory soap. Consumer households, the target customer segment for this product, place a value on hygiene. So P&G has assembled a value chain (R&D, sourcing, manufacturing, marketing, distribution, and so on) that can deliver a low-cost, basic soap that is gentle to the skin but still has the necessary cleaning ability.

If a business model involves the three areas of customer definition, customer value identification, and value creation process design, it follows that there are three arenas in which the rules of the game can be changed into winning rules from the customer's viewpoint, as illustrated in Figure 2:

1. dramatic redesign of the end-to-end value chain architecture ("How can we make the value chain much more efficient?");
2. dramatic reinvention of the concept of customer value ("How can we transform the value customers receive?"); and
3. dramatic redefinition of the customer base ("How do we expand market size?").

These three arenas are highly interconnected. Changes in any one of them will almost always have implications for the other two. Dramatic redesign of the value chain could fundamentally alter the concept of customer value. Similarly, redefining the customer base would require a radically different system of creating value. *When one internally consistent business model is converted into another internally consistent business model, the rules of the game are changed.*

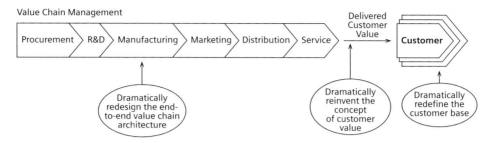

Three Arenas for Changing the Rules of the Game

Redesigning the End-To-End Value Chain

A value chain is the linked set of value-creating activities all the way through from basic raw material sources for component suppliers to the ultimate end-use product delivered into the final customer's hands. A superior value chain architecture is one that, from the customer's point of view, has slashed costs and/or greatly enhanced the value. Examples of companies that have designed far superior value chain architectures include Nucor, the world's most efficient steel manufacturer; Ikea, the world's largest furniture retailer; Wal-Mart, the world's largest retailer; Amazon.com, the world's largest virtual bookstore; and our specific example here, Dell, the world's largest "direct sales" personal computer company.

Dell Computer: Background

As of 1999, Dell Computer Corporation boasted 16,000 employees in 33 countries and millions of customers in 170 countries. Headquartered in Round Rock, Texas, near Austin, the company was founded in 1984 when Michael Dell pioneered the process of selling custom-built computers directly to customers. Within its short life of 17 years, Dell has become the number one retailer of PCs, outselling IBM, Hewlett-Packard, and Compaq. Businesses of all sizes, government agencies, educational institutions, and individual customers have ordered Dell's desktop and notebook computers, workstations, and network servers by phone or via the Net.

In 1996, Dell embraced the Web. By late 1999, more than 40 percent of its sales emanated from this channel. On the Internet, customers are in "control." They can use the Web 24 hours a day, 7 days a week, at their own convenience, to configure, price, and order computer systems, get current information on order status and delivery, and access technical reference materials on hardware and software. Dell computer systems are assembled one at a time, as ordered, at factories in Austin; Limerick, Ireland; and Penang, Malaysia. Dell outsources delivery to other firms with far superior core competencies in logistics to ensure that custom orders are delivered within a few days. It also provides an extensive range of value-added services, including system installation and management, after-sales service, and technology-transition planning and execution. Its own on-site system engineers and consultants as well as employees of strategic service partners give Dell an army of more than 10,000 service providers around the world.

Dell has outpaced its competitors in both growth and profitability. Its market capitalization was about $700 million at its June 1988 IPO. By 1999, that had grown to well over $100 billion-an increase of more than 140 times over an 11-year period, dramatically above that of Standard & Poor's 500. At age 34, Michael Dell had become the richest man in the world under 40. His company had created enormous value for customers and shareholders by adopting a radically different value chain architecture in the PC industry.

How Dell Redesigned the Value Chain

The traditional value chain in the personal computer industry could be characterized as "build-to-stock." PC manufacturers designed and built their products with preconfigured options based on market forecasts. The products were first stored in company warehouses and later dispatched to resellers, retailers, and other intermediaries, who typically added a 20 to 30 percent markup before selling to their customers. Manufacturers controlled the upstream part of the value chain, leaving the downstream part for middlemen. Retailers justified their margins by providing several benefits to customers: easily accessed locations; selection across multiple brands; the opportunity to see and test products before purchasing; and knowledgeable salespeople who could educate customers regarding their choices.

Two trends in the 1980s allowed Michael Dell to radically reengineer the value chain. First, corporate customers were becoming more and more sophisticated and no longer required intense personal selling by salespeople. By the end of the decade, even individuals – especially those buying their second or third PCs – had become savvy and experienced technology users. Second, the different components of a PC (monitor, keyboard, memory, disk drive, software, and so on) became standard modules, permitting mass customization in system configuration.

When Dell developed its "direct" model, it dramatically transformed the value chain architecture by departing from the industry's historical rules on several fronts:

1. It outsourced all components, but performed assembly.
2. It eliminated retailers and shipped directly from its factories to end customers.
3. It took customized orders for hardware and software over the phone or via the Internet.
4. It designed an integrated supply chain linking its suppliers closely to its assembly factories and the order-intake system.

Three major benefits ensued from this new architecture: technology advantage; cost advantage; and customer knowledge advantage.

Technology Advantage. Dell custom-built its machines after receiving an order, instead of making them for inventory in anticipation of orders. Thus, it had very low levels of components as well as of finished goods inventory; on average, inventory turnover for

Dell was 7 to 11 days, compared to 70 to 100 days for other PC manufacturers and their resellers. Low inventory translated into a huge technology advantage.

Microprocessors and other component technologies kept advancing at a relentless pace. Because Dell essentially had no finished goods inventory in the pipeline, it enjoyed a first-mover advantage in bringing leading-edge component technology to the marketplace. Its components were 60 to 80 days newer than those in IBM or Compaq PCs, so it could introduce new products faster than its competitors.

Cost Advantage. Dell derived cost advantage in three areas: component purchasing; inventory, and working capital; and selling and administration. First, because the cost of computer components kept declining, and because Dell purchased its components on a just-in-time basis, it enjoyed a component cost nearly 6 percent lower than that of its competitors.

Second, radical reductions in inventory helped Dell save on the interest of financing the inventory as well as warehousing and storage costs. With its direct channel to customers, Dell eliminated the need to mark down inventory not sold by retailers, thereby minimizing the cost of product obsolescence. And its direct dealings with individual customers ensured immediate payment by credit card, which meant a lower investment in accounts receivable and insignificant bad debt risks. Moreover, Dell enjoyed normal credit terms from its component suppliers. As a consequence, it operated with *negative working capital:* in 1998 it had 36 days in accounts receivable and seven days in inventory, but 51 days in accounts payable – for a *negative* 18 days of sales in working capital!

Third, bypassing the retailer and establishing a direct interface with customers via phone and/ or the Net eliminated the typical markup and extra sales force of the middleman, as well as the need for physical space at distributors' showrooms. And the Net helped reduce sales costs further by cutting down on telephone personnel salaries, toll-free call charges, and the bricks and mortar for the telephone service center.

Customer Knowledge Advantage. Direct contact with customers helped Dell gain a superior understanding of specific customer needs. Each of its several market segments multinational corporations (MNCs), medium-sized businesses, small firms, individuals, the federal government, state and local governments, and educational institutions – had unique computing needs and different buying processes. Global service capabilities were critical for MNCs; mid-sized companies placed a high value on presale, product repair, and help-desk support; and so on. By organizing its marketing and sales functions around distinct customer groups, Dell was able to address varying customer needs with greater precision and speed.

Proprietary information about customers' purchasing patterns also gave Dell a superior ability to forecast demand, which in turn helped it maintain minimum inventory without suffering the problem of "stock-outs." Those purchasing patterns helped Dell forge lifelong customer relationships. For instance, it understood better than its competitors which customers would benefit most when newer versions of hardware and software were available, so it could actively market them to the right customer segments. By owning these relationships with customers, Dell not only avoided getting "filtered" information from third-party retailers but also insulated itself from poor service and a lack of product knowledge on the part of retailers.

Dell's "Virtuous" Cycle

As depicted in Figure 3, Dell created a "virtuous" cycle (the opposite of a vicious cycle) by rewriting the rules of the PC industry, custom-configuring PCs through direct dealings with end users. Customer intimacy gave Dell superior forecasting ability, which allowed it to pursue JIT manufacturing with very low levels of finished goods and components inventory and little risk of stock-outs. Radical reductions in inventory not only lowered costs but also enabled Dell to be first to market with the latest products. The net result was that Dell had the dominant share of the PC market, which in turn led to more customer contacts-thereby starting the cycle all over again.

The new value chain architecture also enabled Dell to globalize faster and more profitably than its competitors for two reasons. First, Dell's direct model yielded the same benefits in non-U.S. markets as it did at home. Second, because of its direct channel, Dell – in contrast to IBM and Compaq – did not require access to local distribution channels and so faced lower entry barriers into foreign markets. Whereas many MNCs found it difficult to make money in China, Dell had achieved profitability within a year of entering the country in August 1998.

IBM, Compaq, and Hewlett-Packard probably found it difficult to imitate and neutralize Dell's direct model for fear of alienating their dealers. The bulk of these companies' sales came through third-party dealers. If they set up direct channels, their distributors, retailers, and resellers would be upset at the loss of market share, and the companies could not run the risk of angering their critical constituency. As Michael Dell put it, "Our competitors are prisoners of their history. They're stuck with their dealers" (Pitta 1999).

Key Ideas for Value Chain Redesign

As the case of Dell Computer illustrates, there are three principles that should guide the redesign of the end-to-end value chain architecture. First, its two central attributes must be redesigned: (1) the set of activities that will constitute the new value chain, and (2) the interfaces across the activities. In eliminating the role of middlemen altogether, Dell redesigned the set of activities comprising the chain. However, the company did not stop there. It built deep relationships at both ends – with suppliers as well as customers. Such virtual integration without vertical integration represents a redesign of the interface across activities on Dell's part.

Second, the new value chain must create dramatic gains in one or more of three areas: cost structure, asset investment, and speed of responsiveness to external changes. Compared to traditional competitors, Dell's direct model had the following unique combination of features: significantly lower costs, negative working capital investment, custom-built machines, first-mover advantage in offering leading-edge component technologies, high quality and reliability, an efficient and convenient purchasing process, speed of delivery, and excellent after-sales service.

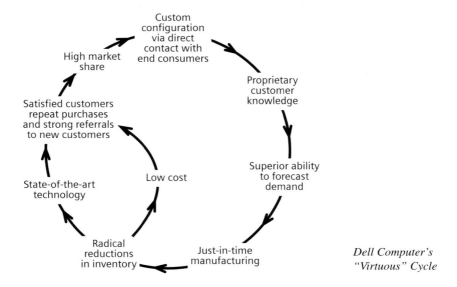

Custom
configuration
via direct
contact with
end consumers

High market
share

Proprietary
customer
knowledge

Satisfied customers
repeat purchases
and strong referrals
to new customers

State-of-the-art
technology

Low cost

Superior ability
to forecast
demand

Radical
reductions
in inventory

Just-in-time
manufacturing

Dell Computer's
"Virtuous" Cycle

Third, the new value chain must enable the company to scale up its business model to ensure rapid growth in market share, high-velocity globalization, and expansion into related products and services. On the upstream side, Dell relied totally on third-party component suppliers; on the downstream side, it completely eliminated reliance on local distributor channels; and the Net-based Dell Online channel allowed it to sell a large variety of PC-related peripheral products, such as printers and cameras. As a result, Dell's business model has perhaps been the most rapidly scalable within the PC industry.

Reinventing the Concept of Customer Value

The typical approach of dramatically reinventing the concept of customer value is to shift from selling discrete products to supplying total systems and solutions. Consider several examples:

- from selling hardware and software to supplying total business solutions;
- from a country-by-country advertising campaign to coordinated global advertising;
- from selling insurance, banking, mortgages, and mutual funds as discrete products to providing financial security and freedom through an integrated system of products and services;
- from selling automotive paint to providing a complete paint shop;
- from selling packaging materials to supplying total packaging systems.

Here is how Tetra Pak changed the rules of the game in the global liquid packaging industry by reinventing the concept of customer value.

Tetra Pak: Background

Tetra Pak, a Swedish multinational corporation, is dedicated to the development, manufacture, and sale of systems for processing, packaging, and distributing liquid food products. It is the only company of its kind capable of supplying customers with comprehensive systems that integrate processing lines with packaging and distribution. A division of Tetra Laval, it accounts for 70 percent of the sales of that group. Two brothers, Hans and Gad Rausing, have transformed the company from a small Swedish milk carton firm into a global liquid-packaging powerhouse.

- Tetra Pak was a niche player focused on only one product category: packaging for liquid food items. It did not make cartons for shampoos, detergents, or other nonfoods, nor did it diversify outside the packaging sector. So its growth had to come from global expansion in its product category. Financial data on this privately owned company are not published. However, several indicators point to its phenomenal growth and financial success:

- Tetra Pak was a small presence in the paper carton business 25 years ago when other companies, such as Enso (Finland) and International Paper (U.S.), dominated the segment. Yet by 1999, Tetra Pak was producing packaging materials at 57 plants and selling 90 billion containers a year in more than 165 countries. Moreover, it had captured a 40 percent share of the European liquid-packaging market.

- In 1991, Tetra Pak paid £1.4 billion in cash to acquire Alfa-Laval, a Swedish firm that made and sold systems for separation, heat transfer, and fluid handling for the food industry.

- In 1993, the Rausing brothers, who lived in England, surpassed the queen as the richest individuals in the U.K.

- In 1998, Gad Rausing paid $7 billion to acquire his brother's 50 percent share in the company, thereby placing its value at $14 billion.

Tetra Pak's success can be attributed to the way it changed the concept of customer value in the global liquid-pakkaging industry.

From Traditional to Reinvented Value

There are many options for packaging materials, including steel, aluminum, glass, plastic, paper, and fiber-foil (metal and paper composite). Traditionally, it was typical for package manufacturers to make these containers and then ship them to processors of milk, juice, and other liquids. The processors filled the containers and transported them to supermarkets for sale to consumers.

Tetra Pak altered this model by offering customers a total system: filling equipment, packaging materials, and distribution equipment such as conveyors, tray packers, and film wrappers. Customer value was transformed from the traditional model – pouring liquids into containers – to Tetra Pak's model: containers made at the point where beverages are ready to be packed.

The Tetra Pak system has two unique features. First, the firm installs its filling equipment on the beverage producers' premises. Inside each machine is a continuous roll of paper with four layers of plastic coating and an additional layer of aluminum coating. When liquid is poured, the roll of paper curls into a tube which is then heat-sealed and cut into a carton. There is essentially *zero* time lag between making and using the container. Second, air and light inside cartons tend to cause much faster decay in liquids. With Tetra Pak's process, the fact that cartons are formed *after* the liquid is poured enables Tetra Pak to use a special vacuum-falling technology that keeps air out of the liquids during the filling process. Then, once the package is sealed, the plastic and aluminum coatings continue to keep air out of the carton while creating a secure barrier against light. With such an "aseptic" property, Tetra Pak cartons do not require refrigeration to preserve liquids. Milk has a shelf life of six months, juices 12 months.

Producers also enjoy the benefit of one-stop shopping for complete systems, with matching equipment at every stage.

Tetra Pak's business model has altered the concept of value at every stage of the traditional industry value chain:

For Container Manufacturers. Completely eliminating this stage of the chain has yielded several benefits. First are the obvious savings in factory space as well as the labor and overhead costs involved in making the containers. Second, Tetra Pak saves the cost of "transporting air" from container manufacturers to beverage producers. Not only is transportation expensive, but some containers, such as glass bottles, are breakable in transit. Third, the company avoids handling costs at two points: loading the empty containers onto the truck at one end and unloading and storing them at the other.

For Beverage Processors. In addition to eliminating the cost of inbound handling of empty containers for beverage processors, several additional benefits have accrued at this stage. Cartons are made only when needed, thereby ensuring "zero" inventories of empty cartons in the pipeline and saving financing costs and storage space. Once filled and sealed, the beverages do not require refrigerated trucks for transport to supermarkets, even on long hauls. Whereas glass bottles, plastic jugs, and "gable top" paper cartons cannot be stacked on top of each other, the box-shaped Tetra Briks can be stacked up easily. Traditional containers require crating; in the case of glass bottles, partitions are even needed between each bottle to prevent breakage. Moreover, the narrow necks of bottles and jugs and the gabled tops of paper cartons waste space. But the rectangular, flat structure of Tetra Briks ensures efficient use of space.

Producers also enjoy the benefit of one-stop shopping for complete systems, with matching equipment at every stage. This means customers have a single point of accountability, ensuring uninterrupted production. Tetra Pak in turn has assembled an experienced and well-trained service force that assures customers fast, efficient repairs and equipment maintenance.

Tetra Pak's close relationships with beverage companies have prompted it to dedicate more than 1,000 R&D engineers worldwide to focus on customer needs, develop new packaging designs, and continuously improve processing and distribution systems. As a result, the company has up-to-date technology in its filling and sealing systems, which have been rated the best in the industry. By leasing its filling machines, Tetra Pak offers customers two attractive features: low rental outflow and protection from technological obsolescence. Having locked up beverage companies on long-term machine leases, Tetra Pak enters into contracts with customers to supply them with packaging materials at attractive margins. The materials have been custom designed for Tetra Pak machines, effectively giving the company a virtual monopoly in providing raw materials to the filling machines. Once familiar with Tetra Pak machines, and having trained employees to operate them, beverage companies have little incentive to switch to other suppliers.

For Supermarkets. A significant added value for supermarkets has been the savings in handling – a major cost element. Because Tetra Briks can be stacked up, beverage producers usually load them onto trucks on a wheeled cart. At the supermarket, the drivers wheel the cart inside the store and set it up on the display space. In contrast, glass bottles, plastic jugs, and paper cartons still cannot be stacked up and require unloading and handling by supermarket personnel. Further, unlike Tetra Pak cartons, other types of packages require refrigerated sections inside the supermarket to preserve the shelf life of the liquids – another major cost item.

For End-Use Customers. A major value for end-use customers is the convenience of the Tetra Pak cartons. Glass bottles are heavy, bulky, and breakable. Plastic jugs and paper cartons require refrigeration and are not as convenient in school lunches and on picnics. Tetra Pak cartons, on the other hand, are compact in size, convenient to use, appealing in appearance, and competitive in price. And in emerging economies like India, China, and Brazil, where sizable populations live in places with minimal or no refrigeration facilities, the Tetra Pak system is especially well suited. Without Tetra Pak cartons, these markets would be woefully underserved.

Key Ideas for Reinventing Customer Value

When a company redefines its value proposition from selling discrete products to selling an integrated system of products and services, as the Tetra Pak example illustrates, customers' dependence on the company significantly increases. But customers typically do not like relying on a single source because the provider has the ability to exploit the resulting bargaining power. So from the customer's standpoint, offering total solutions will be a winning value proposition *only* if the following three conditions hold:

1. The firm is best-in-class in every product offered under the "one stop shopping" umbrella. If not, customer value is reduced because customers can obtain that product from another, superior source.

2. The integrated solution is genuinely superior to the alternative of customers buying discrete products and services and bundling them on their own. Such superiority can result from one or more of several sources: system design, system assembly, and customization of user needs.

3. The firm offers the bundle at a price lower than what customers would pay to assemble the individual products from separate providers. That is, the firm should

not only demonstrate that the bundle is superior but also be willing to share its gains with customers.

As this case illustrates, Tetra Pak's success has been the result of paying careful attention to meeting all three of these conditions.

Redefining the Customer Base

By "redefining the customer base", we mean uncovering a hidden customer segment so large as to result in a dramatic expansion of the industry's total customer base. Apple began to offer personal computers to every man, woman, and child at a time when computers were used primarily by corporations, scientific establishments, educational institutions, and governments. Schwab found it could sell financial products to do-it-yourself, knowledgeable individual investors with small trading volumes at a time when such products were sold mainly to investment institutions and the wealthy.

As for Canon, it discovered a need for personal copiers among individuals and small businesses at a time when copiers were aimed at large corporations. Canon changed the rules of the game in the global photocopier industry by redefining the target customer base.

Canon: Background

Chester Carlson invented the electrostatic process that led to the birth of the copier industry. In 1956, he sold his patents to Haloid Corporation, which changed its name to Xerox in 1961. The introduction of the 914 machine in 1959 – named because of its ability to copy documents 9" x 14" in size – signaled the emergence of Xerox as the dominant force in the copier industry. The first of its kind to make both multiple copies and the fastest number of copies per minute, the 914 opened up the era of mass copying. Xerox seized the initiative by assembling a business model targeted at large corporations requiring high-volume copying.

The results were spectacular. By 1961, a mere two years after the introduction of the 914, Xerox became a *Fortune* 500 company. *Business Week* displayed the 914 on its cover. Fortune went a step further, declaring the 914 to be "the most successful product ever marketed in America." Even the Smithsonian displays a 914 original. By 1970, Xerox had reached the *Fortune* 60 status. It crossed the $1 billion sales mark in 1968 – the fastest company to reach that landmark at that time. Xerox wasted no time in globalizing its business. It created a joint venture with the Rank Organization of the U.K. to form Rank Xerox, which dominated the European market. In addition, Rank Xerox and Fuji Photo Films in Japan created

"In fact, in 1978 Fuji Xerox was willing to sell low-end copiers to Xerox to counterattack Canon in the United States. But Xerox refused the offer, and Canon prevailed."

another joint venture, Fuji Xerox, which came to dominate the Asian market. By 1970, Xerox held a 95 percent market share in the global copier industry.

Then Canon, a Japanese multinational and an industry upstart in the mid-1970s, created entirely new market segments for copiers not served by Xerox in the United States – small firms and individuals. In the late 1970s, Canon designed a value delivery system offering a $1,000 personal copier to target these segments. For almost a decade, Xerox largely ignored these new low-end markets Canon had created. In fact, in 1978 Fuji Xerox was willing to sell low-end copiers to Xerox to counterattack Canon in the United States. But Xerox refused the offer, and Canon prevailed. Canon's leadership in low-end copiers illustrates the power of changing the rules of the game by radically redefining the customer base.

Xerox's Big Copier Business Model

Xerox's decision to serve large corporate customers allowed it to build a business model with huge entry barriers. Xerox had more than 500 patents that protected its plain paper copying (PPC) technology. The alternative technology at that time was coated-paper copying (CPC), which was inferior to PPC for two reasons: coated paper was more expensive than plain paper; and CPC machines produced one copy at a time, whereas PPC machines could handle high-volume, multiple copies. With their massive duplicating needs, corporate customers preferred scale-efficient big machines. PPC patenting effectively ruled out new entrants.

The choice of corporate customers also allowed Xerox to build a direct sales force, since there was a limited number of customers to serve. By 1970 Xerox had created an enviable sales force capability: tremendous technical expertise, long-term customer relationships, and deep product knowledge. Any new entrant that wanted to imitate its business model would have to replicate such a sales network – a high fixed-cost activity and thus a major entry barrier.

Xerox's customers, primarily *Fortune* 500 companies, did not care as much about price as they did about the need for 100 percent up-time on their machines. Because central copy centers typically had one large machine, the entire center came to a standstill when the machine broke down. So it was not enough for Xerox to offer excellent service; it had to guarantee outstanding service 24 hours a day. As soon as a machine went down, Xerox sent service staff to fix it. By 1970, Xerox had built a world-class, round-the-clock servicing capability – another formidable entry barrier.

Instead of selling machines outright, Xerox leased them. Lease financing of a complex product in the context of rapidly evolving technology is always a high-risk activity. But Xerox understood and controlled the pace of technological evolution much better than any other photocopier company, so its level of risk in lease financing was much lower than that of its competitors.

Finally, through a decade of expenditures on marketing and advertising, Xerox established a powerful brand name in the industry. In fact, copying and "xeroxing" became virtually synonymous. Any new entrant to the market had to contend with Xerox's strong brand image.

All of these combined entry barriers – PPC patents, direct sales force, 24-hour service, leasing, and brand name – were simply overwhelming for a start-up firm. They posed significant problems even for an established office equipment supplier like IBM. Certainly, IBM faced an insurmountable barrier in the form of technology patents over PPC. And it sold mainframes to corporate customers through a sales force and serviced them through an extensive servicing network in the 1960s. Even so, its sales and service staff at the time were not easily transferable to the copier market without additional large investments in technology and product-specific training. It is not surprising, therefore, that Xerox enjoyed a virtual monopoly in the big copier industry.

Canon's Distributed Copier Business Model

Canon dedicated its research efforts during the 1960s to develop an alternative to Xerox's PPC technology. In 1968, it invented the "New Process" (NP) technology, which used plain paper to photocopy but did not violate Xerox's patents. Canon deployed two of its existing competency bases – microelectronics (from its calculator business) and optics and imaging (from its camera business) – in developing the NP technology. Further, it benefited from a 1975 FTC ruling that forced Xerox to license its dry-toner PPC technology freely to competitors.

In the late 1970s, Canon successfully designed personal copiers at a price point significantly below Xerox's big copiers to appeal to small businesses and individuals. Its personal copiers, which made 8 to 10 copies per minute, ranged in price from $700 to $1,200. In contrast, Xerox's high-speed machines, which made 90 to 120 copies per minute, had a price range of $80,000 to $129,000. Canon's effect on the copier industry was similar to its earlier effect on the camera industry when it introduced AE-1, the first mass-market, 35-mm, single-lens reflex camera with microprocessor control that could produce close to professional quality photographs but sold for significantly less than Leica and Nikon.

Because Canon's target segments involved millions of customers, it could not use the direct sales force approach. Instead, it chose to distribute its personal copiers through traditional third-party distributors: office product dealers, computer stores, and mass merchandisers like Sears. This distribution approach not only eliminated Canon's need for a huge cash outlay but allowed it rapid market entry.

Canon overcame Xerox's formidable advantage in 24-hour servicing capability by several means. First, because of the obvious inverse relationship between product reliability and the need for service, it designed its machines for reliability. Its copier had just eight units that could be assembled on an automated line by robots without any human help. Second, it made replacement parts modular so that end-use customers could replace them when they wore out. Copier drum, charging device, toner assembly, and cleaner were combined into a single disposable cartridge the customer could remove and replace after 2,000 copies. Third, Canon's design was so simple that traditional office product dealers could be trained to repair the machines. Fourth, with distributed copying, people could use other departments' machines when their own were down. Unlike central copying, 24-hour service was not required.

Canon's low-cost personal copiers were sold outright for cash, so leasing was not an issue. And its strong brand name for high quality and low cost in the camera business was leveraged successfully when it launched personal copiers.

Thus, Canon achieved leadership in low-end copiers by radically redefining the customer base (see Figure 4). There might be several reasons why Xerox did not respond soon enough to Canon's attack with its own version of distributed copying. It might not have perceived Canon as a serious threat because Canon did not initially go head-to-head against Xerox. Perhaps Xerox simply did not expect low-end copiers to become a huge market segment. In fact, during the 1970s Xerox was more worried about IBM and Kodak, which entered the copier industry at the high end by playing by Xerox's rules. Big machines had a high profit margin per unit, whereas personal copiers had a low one. Xerox might have feared potentially cannibalizing its high-margin business for low-margin copiers. It had invested heavily in a sales force, which probably would not have welcomed the use of third-party dealers to sell personal copiers that would compete with big ones. Similarly, Xerox's service network, which operated as a profit center, had little incentive to support programs to produce quantum improvements in product reliability. Moreover, under the leasing policy Xerox had not fully recovered its investment on its installed base, so it likely did not want to risk making that base prematurely obsolete by offering personal copiers. Finally, Xerox's customers – heads of copy centers in large corporations – were critical to Xerox's success and so might have had an important influence in its internal decisions.

	XEROX	**CANON**
Target Customer Segments	Large corporation	Small offices; individuals
Concept of Customer Value	Central controlled photocopying	Individual controlled decentralized copying
Value Chain Elements		
R&D	Focus on product technology	Focus on product and process technology
Design	Complex; many parts; customized components; minimum acceptable quality[*]	Simple; fewer parts; standard components; high reliability
Manufacture	Discrete; high cost; acceptable quality[*]	Mass production; low cost; high quality
Product attributes	High price; high speed	Low price; low speed
Marketing		
Financing	Own sales force	Third-party dealers
Servicing	Leasing	Outfight sale
	Own service	Third-party dealers; self-service

[*] *Backed up by outstanding after-sales field service*

Exhibit 1: How Canon Radically Redefined the Customer Base

They would naturally resist the introduction of distributed copying for fear of losing their power base.

Key Ideas for Redefining the Customer Base

The Canon case is an example of a firm that discovered a hidden mega-segment and built the capabilities to serve it. Such an approach can alter the rules of the global game in three ways:

1. The new segment changes the value potential of the industry. Its discovery dramatically increases the size and growth rate of the overall marketplace. And the higher growth rate of the new segment begins to draw resources away from the established segment.

2. Solutions designed for the new segment begin to substitute for the historical solutions of the original segment. As the distributed copying concept pioneered by Canon penetrated the large corporate market, personal copiers began to chip away at least partly at Xerox's sales of medium and high-end copiers. Such partial substitution can also be observed in many other industries, such as PCs versus mainframes and the discount brokerage model of Charles Schwab versus the full-service model of Merrill Lynch.

3. Technological, financial, and organizational capabilities accumulated in the process of discovering and dominating the new segment can be leveraged to launch a direct attack on the incumbent players. This is what happened in the global photocopier industry. Canon used its stronghold in the low end of the industry to build technological capabilities, market understanding, and financial muscle, then leveraged these strengths in the mid- to late 1990s to move upscale and attack Xerox head on in high-speed copiers.

Every company should cultivate a bias for changing the rules of the game. The external environment constantly shifts along a host of dimensions – technology (the growth of e-commerce), global landscape (China's entry into the WTO), demography (population aging in the U.S., Europe, and Japan), and so on. In addition to exogenous changes, firms often have the power to actively reshape the boundaries, structure, and dynamics of their industry's environment (MCI in the U.S. telecommunications industry over the last three decades). Being a first mover in responding to impending environmental change, or being a pioneer in actively initiating change in one's environment, can give a firm a major competitive advantage.

When exploring the opportunities for changing the rules, three potential arenas for analysis and radical transformation exist: the boundaries of the targeted customer base, redefined concepts of the value to be delivered to customers, and design of the end-to-end value chain architecture.

In terms of redefining the customer base, the opportunity lies primarily in discovering and serving a previously hidden but potentially very large customer segment. As with Canon, such redefinition not only provides the innovator with a large, profitable, and undefended marketspace, it can also serve as the platform from which to challenge the incumbent in its own arena.

For reinventing the customer value proposition, the typical opportunity lies in turning from selling discrete products and services to providing a comprehensive customer solution and offering an integrated bundle of products and services to address a generic underlying need. Such a move not only deepens the firm's relationships with its customers but is also likely to be seen by customers as potentially increasing the supplier's market power. To guard against any negative responses by the customer, the firm must ensure that the comprehensive solution approach is not only genuinely superior (in terms of effectiveness and efficiency) but also that the resulting benefits are shared between the firm and its customers.

Redesigning the end-to-end value chain architecture entails transforming not only the set of activities comprising the chain but also the interfaces across the activities. The firm should ask the following questions: Will the new architecture allow us to market, sell, and deliver the intended products and services to the target customers much more effectively and efficiently? And will it give us the flexibility to scale up, expand the product and service bundle, and, ff needed, switch to a superior architecture in the future?

The quest for changing the rules of the game should be a never-ending process. As competitors wake up to the reality of a new and superior business model, every innovation will eventually be imitated. However, before your current competitive advantages are totally neutralized, you must already have moved ahead – by exploiting new developments in your external environment and/or changing industry dynamics. The relevant question for most firms is not *whether* the rules of the game will change; rather, it is who will take the initiative to do so – you, your competitors, or a new entrant.

Developing and Implementing a New Business Model in the Global Wine Industry – the BRL Hardy Experience[*]

BRL Hardy is an Australian wine company that has made inroads into the global wine market in the past decade. From a 1991 base of US$31 million in export sales – much of it bulk for private labels and the rest an assortment of bottled products sold through distributors – Hardy has built its foreign sales to US$178 million in 1998, almost all of it directly marketed as branded products. Managing director Steve Millar describes the insight that triggered this turnaround: "We began to realize that for a lot of historical reasons, the wine business – unlike the soft-drinks or packaged-foods industries – had very few true multinational companies and therefore very few true global brands. Wine consumers were getting more discerning and knowledgeable in the early 1990s, and, to our reasoning, a great opportunity existed for a company to build a well-known international wine brand of quality and reliability".

Industry Production Fragmentation and Strategic Gap Identification

BRL Hardy noticed the inflexibility of the European practice of labeling wines by region, subregion, and even village – the French *appellation* or the Italian *dominazione* systems are classic examples. A vineyard could be further categorized according to its historical quality classification such as the French premier grand cru, the grand cru, and so on. The resulting complexity not only confuses consumers, but also fragments producers whose small scale prevents them from building brand strength or distribution capability. This created an opportunity for major retailers, such as Sainsbury and Tesco in the United Kingdom, to overcome consumers' confusion – and capture more value themselves – by buying in bulk and selling under their stores' own label.

The most striking aspect about wine shelves of the average supermarket in developing countries is the sheer range and profusion of wines on offer. A large supermarket store sells hundreds of different wines made by a huge variety of producers. This proliferation reflects the highly fragmented nature of the world's wine production industry.

---

[*] Adapted from: Bartlett, C.A. and Ghoshal, S. (2000), Going Global: Lessons from Late Movers", *Harvard Business Review*, March-April, 139-140.

Even the world's largest wine company in terms of volume (although not revenue), California's E&J Gallo, represents just over 1% of world production. The fragmentation is most evident in the "old world" wine industries of Western Europe: Bordeaux in France, for example, has over 12,000 producers; Italy has over a million separate wine-growing units in private ownership; Germany and Austria have similar characteristics of small, family-owned wine production units. In the "new world" wine industries, such as in Australia, the USA, South Africa, Chile and Argentina, the situation is markedly different. In Australia, just four companies dominate 80% of the local wine industry, of which BLR Hardy is one. In world terms, however, Australia produces only 2% of the world's total wine production.

Industry Demand Situation and Customer Value Propositions

Since 1982 the global demand for wine, in overall volume terms, has declined by 25%, causing some observers to remark that the world has a "wine lake" of enormous proportions. This "wine lake" is only evident in the lower quality, lower-priced wine categories, as the demand for quality wines, noble varietal wines, new style red wines, and wines from "new world" producers has not been affected by the overall decline in demand. In the 1980s and early 1990s, BRL Hardy's international business was caught in the "trap" of providing bulk wines of lower quality. It distributed its Hardy label wines to international retailers through local agents, and sold bulk wine for private labels directly.

Millar's insights gave the company a way out, if it was willing to change the "rules of the game" on both the demand and supply sides. First, new staff was appointed and new resources allocated to upgrade the overseas sales offices. Instead of simply supporting the sales activities of distributing agents, they took direct control of the full sales, distribution, and marketing. Their primary objective was to establish Hardy as a viable global brand, with more direct linkages to customers. A key issue was the realization that the major knowledgeable wine customer need, or customer value proposition, was made up of three elements: well-known global brands; consistency of quality and availability; and value for money, including affordability and competitive pricing.

Reconfiguring the Hardy Value System and Value Chain

The company's supply-side decisions were even more significant than those on the demand side. In order to exploit the growing marketing expertise of its overseas units, Hardy encouraged them to supplement their Australian product line by sourcing wine from around the world. Not only did Hardy offset the vintage uncertainties and currency risks of sourcing from a single country, it also gained clout in its dealings with retailers. By breaking the tradition of selling only its own wine, Hardy was able to build the scale necessary for creating strong brands and negotiating with retail stores. The company's new strategy and capabilities are visible in its recent introduction of a branded wine from Sicily called D'istinto. Under a supply agreement and marketing program initiated by BRL Hardy Europe, this product has in its first year sold 200,000 cases in the United Kingdom alone – an exceptional performance. By 2003, when the brand has been introduced to the rest of Europe, North America and Australia, Hardy expects sales to top a million cases.

The advantages of the gap identification to Hardy have been clear and powerful: The company's range of wines – from Australia as well as France, Italy, and Chile – responds to supermarket companies' need to deal with only a few broad line suppliers. Simultaneously, the scale of operation has supported the brand development so vital to transforming products from the commodity range. Results have been outstanding. In Europe, the volume of Hardy's brands has increased 12-fold in seven years, making it the leading Australian wine brand in the huge UK market, and number two overall to Gallo in the United Kingdom. Branded products from other countries have grown to represent about a quarter of Hardy's European volume. Hardy has evolved from an Australian wine exporter to a truly global wine company, utilizing global scope and scale economies and drawing on knowledge and skills from many parts of the world.

Internal Consolidation and Cultural Change

In 1991, Christopher Carson, and experienced international wine marketer, was appointed managing director of the company's UK operations. Over the next 18 months, he pruned three-quarters of the items in the fragmented product line, replaced half his management team, and began building a culture around creativity and disci-plined execution. Within three years, sales of Hardy brands not only quadrupled, but one of its imported wines from Chile was also transformed into the best-selling Chilean brand in the United Kingdom. Hardy's revenues and profits have amply rewarded its investment, and the organization has developed a worldwide pool of knowledge and expertise that benefits the entire company. Carson, for example, has become the company's acknowledged expert in structuring and sourcing partnerships, and marketing outsourced wine brands.

Cautions and Lessons

In theory, companies can sidestep the disadvantages of alliancing by buying the neces-sary capabilities, thereby owning them. But this can create problems of its own. Initially, when Hardy made its commitment to international expansion, the company's management had snapped up two established London wine merchants, a large French winery and estate, and a historic Italian vineyard. Hardy believed the acquisitions would provide an asset base and knowledge pool with which to broaden its product sources and increase its marketing clout. But the challenge of simultaneously develop-ing expertise in Italian and French wine-making as well as English marketing proved overwhelming and soon placed huge financial and management strains on the com-pany.

After this false start, Hardy realized that in international business new capabilities can not simply be installed; they have to be developed and embedded through purposeful internalizing. This is the reason why, despite acute financial pressures, the company rejected a tempting opportunity to rapidly expand its UK market volume by supplying wine for a leading supermarket chain's private label. Instead, it opted for the more difficult and time-consuming task of building Hardy's own brand image and the marketing and distribution capabilities to support it. This task has required considerable investment in new personnel and training, as well as a major reorientation of the internal culture.

A radical corporate strategy, as in the case of BRL Hardy, is to introduce new business models that challenge an industry's established rules of competition, or "ways of doing business". Though risky, this approach can be very effective in industries in which tradition is deeply embedded or which are comfortably divided among an established oligopoly. Potential risks can be minimized by innovatively optimizing an industry value system and organizational value chains through integrated processes, with a strong focus on the key customer value proposition(s).

Strategic Elements for Kuoni Business Travel International

The Company and its Structure

The Kuoni Group is a multinational travel organization and among the top four in Europe. The Group was founded in 1906 by Alfred Kuoni and has systematically built and expanded its market position. Currently the Group owns operating subsidiaries in more than 20 countries worldwide, with a staff of approximately 7,000 employees.

The Group is divided into 5 Strategic Business Units (SBUs) in order to better adjust to local or specialized markets. While 4 of these SBUs dealing with leisure travel are determined solely by geographical issues, the fifth is a specialized unit for Central Europe that deals with business travel.

In the 1990s, providers of business travel specialized rapidly: trips were often international, requiring arrangements and bookings that could be made in different ways. Internal employees who were having to arrange a company's business travel were under increased pressure to deliver optimal organization and often felt overwhelmed at the prospect of having to do this alone. Companies therefore sought support from travel agencies and expected them to deal efficiently with all of their travel needs.

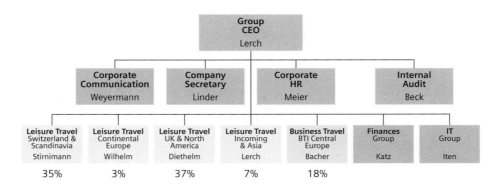

BTI and Kuoni

BTI (Business Travel International) is a joint venture for travel management founded in 1990 with the purpose of offering corporate travelers a comprehensive, worldwide

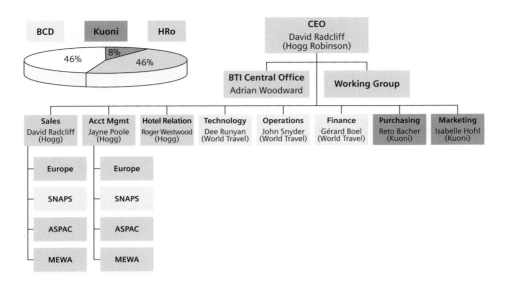

network for their travel needs. A partner of Kuoni Travel Holding Ltd., BTI operates in 80 countries with more than 3,000 offices and 33,000 employees. In 1998, the Kuoni Executive Board decided to create a clear separation between its divisional activities and all of Kuoni's business travel units adopted the BTI brand. The result was that all other business fields (leisure travel) were clearly separated from the business travel segment.

Business Travel

The growth in companies' travel expenditures (after salaries and IT, travel is often the third largest expense category), meant that the nature of competencies and services had to change. The globalization of markets requires all participants to muster a maximum of flexibility and mobility. As mentioned above, this increases the pressure on those employees having to organize travels for their company and leads them to seek support from travel agencies.

The competencies of travel agencies specializing in business travel have also changed during the past decade. The tasks required are no longer simply making reservations and buying tickets. Companies are looking for ways of reducing their travel costs and expect their travel agency to provide them with a true "consulting" service, advice and recommendations, to help them optimize their costs.

How can a travel agency provide such services? What are the tools necessary for providing companies with customized solutions?

Kuoni's success in the business travel segment lies in a knowledge-enriched service. Its computerized customer files contain all data relevant to business travel in the companies it serves. It can store the relevant information on class of travel, car rental

BTI's competencies

Upon our people and their skills we are building and developing our competencies for the future.

Travel Demand Management

Fulfillment of all travel requirements with individual drawup of achievements and goal directed service quality.

Travel Change Management

Professional dealing with different achievements and wishes, e.g. cancellations, returns and changes.

Optimized run of services and IT supported control. Influence on cost factors for reduction of client expenses.

Travel Investment Management

A Member of the Kuoni Group

BTI's Kuoni's optimization tools

To help our customers improve all business travel related processes BTI has developed a wide range of optimization tools.

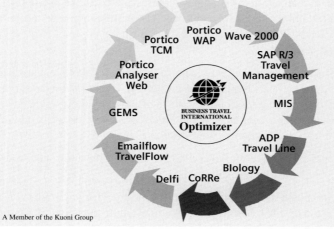

A Member of the Kuoni Group

category and personal preferences regarding seating or food for each employee of a company. At the heart of Kuoni's knowledge-oriented approach to customer support lies a software system for analyzing the costs of journeys. The KNOWS (Kuoni Nationally Offered Worldwide Statistics) system enables the company to collect and process all data regarding a Kuoni customer's previous travel details. The data package can be evaluated and presented in response to customer requirements and affords maximum transparency of travel costs. The costs of flights, hotels and car rental can be broken down by destination, class of travel, provider and period.

The information is presented in a convenient format which makes it easy to answer questions such as which airline has attracted the greatest share of bookings, or which destination is the most expensive. Business travel can therefore be monitored more efficiently and helps Kuoni to retain a customer's business in the long term. It is by relating and interpretation and by making sense of the information that knowledge is created and shared.

The Role of Knowledge in Business Travel

But the importance of knowledge in the travel business segment does not lie only with the client information that can be stored and systematically used by travel agents. As we will see in the following example, knowledge has become a necessary tool for retaining business not only on a customer-level but also on the staff-level.

Strategic knowledge lies in customer relationship, trustworthy relations, experiences, teamwork, know-how about the market situation and development etc. Consequently, you cannot simply build an IT solution, nor can you enter a new market by building a business and starting new travel offices. This would cost too much time, effort and money, since knowledge is not built over night. Kuoni has to buy its knowledge or, even better, a company to meet the challenge of growth.

Buying Knowledge

This is in fact what happened in Germany in 1996/97: the German company Kuoni Reisen GmbH was too small to cover much of the Federal Republic of Germany. It lacked volume to be a very profitable business with knowledge of customers, culture, and politics. As established, the key element for success in the travel sector is knowledge, which can't be acquired rapidly through organic growth alone. The chances to win bigger accounts were limited to certain regions and only the acquisition of established business travel providers would enable Kuoni to attain a dominant market position in the foreseeable future. This initiated a search for a takeover candidate through which Kuoni could acquire the necessary competencies and contacts to cover the German market efficiently.

At the end of 1997, Euro Lloyd Reisebüro GmbH was found to be a suitable candidate for this takeover. Euro Lloyd was a chain of travel agencies three times as large as

Kuoni's German subsidiary. After a due diligence inquiry, the acquisition was finalized. The two companies merged and formed BTI Euro Lloyd Reisebüro GmbH & Co. KG with headquarters in Cologne.

The acquisition had been faultlessly investigated and audited from an operational, financial and legal point of view. A risk analysis had been performed in respect to customers (possible losses due to existing compensation deals between the principal partners), commission income (giving due regard to Lufthansa's commission capping), operational systems, the introduction of the Euro as well as the potential year 2000 IT problems. The productivity of the different profit centers as well as the administration, management structures and possible synergies had also been analyzed.

The results of this process had been considered positive and the Board of Directors approved the acquisition, which was finalized on 24 February 1998 when the contracts were signed.

Merging Companies and Knowledge

The merger was meticulously planned and had several targets it wished to realize. These were: a rapid integration of the two companies into one enterprise with clearly defined management and operational organizations; minimization of the loss of customers and important staff members by means of a clean information policy outlining the advantages of the merger and, finally, avoiding duplications and using the resultant savings and cost-cutting potentials as quickly as possible. The new top management consisted of members of the Senior Management of both Euro Lloyd and Kuoni. Mixed project teams were used to implement the individual measures and perform the integration tasks.

The situation seemed to be a winning one and it was hard to imagine that something could go drastically wrong. In reality, the merger and integration of the two German companies took a different course from that originally planned. It turned out that the two companies were characterized by very different corporate cultures. In contrast to Kuoni, Euro Lloyd was led in a very patriarchal manner. There was no decentralized decision-making authority and the company was heavily regimented, organized along strictly centralized lines and managed in an authoritarian style. This meant that Kuoni managers simply had no chance in these encrusted structures.

The reality of what was happening only became clear after a wave of resignations perturbed the company. The resignations were mostly limited to locations where the two companies' offices had been combined and here the number of resignations was extremely high. Barely two months after the acquisition, more than 40 employees, mainly former Kuoni employees, had resigned. The personnel turnover rate continued to rise in the following months, reaching more than 30%. The reasons given for leaving the organization were mainly the loss of the Kuoni corporate and management culture.

The result of this wave of departures was felt quite keenly in such a knowledge-intensive environment. The new company lost customers on a massive scale: after a couple of months, customer losses already amounted to as much as €100 million in travel volume. This must be added to the losses in the small- and medium-sized companies customer segments, which could not be precisely quantified.

Looking ahead

As pointed out earlier, the strategic knowledge of the travel sector lies in customer relationships, trustworthy relations, experience, teamwork and know-how about the market. All these key elements are mostly retained by experienced staff members who have been able to establish long term relationships with customers and have developed a know-how in the sector. By underestimating the importance of the human factor early on in the due diligence process, and by only focusing on the operational analysis, the potential loss of staff and, therefore, the loss of privileged relationships with customers were miscalculated.

This case perfectly illustrates the strategic importance of knowledge for the company: it is not the operational structure, but the web of know-how, customer relationships

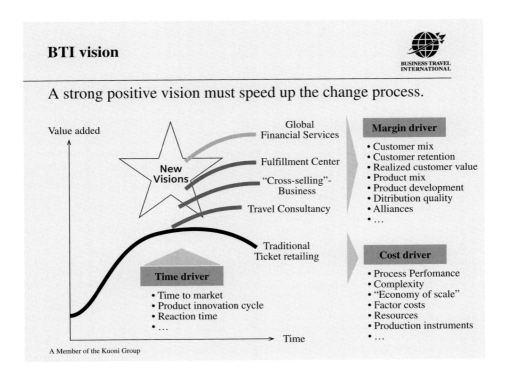

and experience that determines success. With the loss of this capital, the company lost customers who had developed trust in the services of competent staff. Reto Bacher, the company's CEO, therefore not only concentrates on strategy which is based on volume, consulting and operations with the intent of enhancing profit, cost and time levers, but also strongly supports the vision of a knowledge-based company by integrating knowledge management in the BTI Culture.

Bacher wondered if the employee-turnover rate could be brought down. All the measures taken led to a culture that aimed at a highly consultative, knowledge- and technology-based application and operations know-how and the feeling that the company was on the verge of a new beginning and steady improvement. The employees regained faith in the enterprise and did their best. The customers realized that a new wind was blowing and that the service quality had improved. The loss of customers came to an end and new business was acquired at an increased rate. The restoration of trust and confidence formed the foundation for the upswing at BTI Euro Lloyd.

To maintain the feeling and further develop a positive corporate atmosphere, various instruments were implemented. Reto Bacher introduced a direct hot line to him for staff members with comments, questions or concerns. Both office visits and road shows to promote the company image internally became common place. Corporate newsletters were circulated as well as special edition newsletters, and employee surveys became the norm. Last, but not least, there was an overall increase in the creation and retention of knowledge. A conscious and well-structured customer-based knowledge management became the rule.

Questions

1. Review and discuss the various approaches to the development of new business models, including their key dimensions. What are the commonalities and differences in these approaches?

2. Is the development of new business models applicable to all types of industries and organizations? Trace and compare new business models in at least three different industries, and relate these to traditional business models in those industries.

3. Knowledge management (KM) and intellectual capital management (ICM) have received much attention in the past few years. Discuss the relationships between KM and ICM, both in organizational and systemic network contexts.

4. Reinventing the concept of customer value proposition, and reconfiguring business networks require particular sense-making capabilities. Review these and illustrate how they can be practically applied in a particular industry network.

5. What does "organizational resilience" and "systemic organizational capabilities" mean? Discuss these concepts by way of practical business examples.

6. Discuss the managerial requirements for the development of Hardy's new business model. What are the strategic management lessons to be learned?

7. Critically discuss the elements in Kuoni BTI's business model based on the framework of Systemic Strategic Management. What additional strategic management elements should Kuoni BTI consider for a possible new business model?

References

Chapter 4: Frameworks for Systemic Strategic Management

[1] Normann, R. (2001), *Reframing Business*, Chichester. Wiley.

[2] Anderson P. (1999), "Seven Levers for Creating the Evolutionary Enterprise", in Clippinger, J.H. (Ed) (1999), *The Biology of Business*, San Francisco: Jossey-Bass Publishers, 113-152.

[3] Moore, J.F. (1993), "Predators and Prey: A New Ecology of Competition", *Harvard Business Review*, May-June, 75-86.

[4] Evans, P.B. and Wurster, T.S. (1997), "Strategy and the New Economics of Information", *Harvard Business Review*, September-October, 71.

[5] Evans, P.B. and Wurster, T.S. (2000), *Blown to Bits*, Boston: Harvard Business School Press.

[6] Prahalad, C.K. and Ramaswamy, V. (2000), "Co-opting Customer Competence", *Harvard Business Review*, January-February, 79-87.

[7] Lengnick-Hall, C.A. and Wolff, J.A. (1999), "Similarities and Contradictions in the Core Logic of Three Strategy Research Streams", *Strategic Management Journal*, 20, 1118.

[8] Eisenhardt, K.M. and Martin, J.A. (2000), "Dynamic Capabilities: What Are They?", *Strategic Management Journal*, 21, 1111.

[9] Oliver, D. and Roos, J. (2000), *Striking a Balance: Complexity and Knowledge Landscapes*, New York: McGraw-Hill Publishing Company.

[10] Lissack, M. and Roos, J. (1999), *The Next Common Sense*, London: Nicholas Brealey Publishing.

[11] Probst, G.J.B. (1998), "Practical Knowledge Management: A Model That Works", *Prism*, Arthur D. Little, Second Quarter, 17-29.; Probst, G.J.B., Raub, S. and Romhardt, K. (1999), *Managing Knowledge: Building Blocks for Success*, Chichester: Wiley.

[12] Nonaka, I. (1991), "The Knowledge Creating Company", *Harvard Business Review*, November-December, 96-104; Teece, D.J. (2000), "Strategies for Managing Knowledge Assets: The Role of Firm Structure and Industrial Context", *Long Range Planning*, 33, 35-54; Drucker P. (1993), *Post-Capitalist Society*, Butterworth-Heinemann: London; Davenport, T.H. and Probst, G.J.B. (2002), *Knowledge Management Case Book*, Erlangen: Publicis/Wiley; Davenport, T.H. and Prusak, L. (1998), *Working Knowledge*, Boston: Harvard Business School Press; Von Krogh, G. (1998), "Care in Knowledge Creation", *California Management Review*, 40, 133-153; Stewart, T.A. (1997), *Intellectual Capital*, London: Nicholas Brealey Publishing.

[13] Beinhocker, E.D. (1999), "Robust Adaptive Strategies", *Sloan Management Review*, Spring, 95-106; Govindarajan, V. and Gupta, A. (2001), "Strategic Innovation: A Conceptual Road Map", *Business Horizons*, July-August, 3-12; Hamel, G. (2000), *Leading the Revolution*,

Boston: Harvard Business School Press; Kim, C. and Mauborgne, R. (1999), "Strategy, Value Innovation and the Knowledge Economy", *Sloan Management Review*, Spring, 41-54.

[14] Adapted from Lengnick-Hall, C.A. and Wolff, J.A. (1999), *op.cit.*, 1126-1127.

[15] Handy, C. (1994), *The Age of Paradox*, Boston: Harvard Business School Press.

Strategic Innovation: A Conceptual Road Map

"Conquest of the Carton", *Marketing,* November 26, 1987, p. 40.

Dell Computer: additional case data obtained from www.dell.com, Annual Reports, and 10-Ks.

"Dell Tops Compaq in U.S. Sales", *Wall Street Journal,* October 28, 1999, p. E6.

"Dell's China Sales in Black After One Year", *Wall Street Journal,* September 29, 1999, p. 22

J. Dessauer, *My Years with Xerox: The Billions Nobody Wanted* (Garden City, NY: Doubleday, 1971).

P. Furhman, "Boxed In", *Forbes,* October 29, 1990, pp. 102-103.

V. Govindarajan and J.K. Shank, "Value Chain Analysis: A Field Study", *Journal of Management Accounting Research,* Fall 1991, pp. 47-65.

G. Jacobson and J. Hillkirk, *Xerox: American Samurai* (New York: Collier Books, 1986).

H.G. Jones, "Tetra Pak – A Model for Successful Innovation", *Long Range Planning,* 15, 6 (1982): 31-37.

L. Kehoe, "Online Sales Drive Deli Up 41%", *Financial Times,* November 12, 1999, p. 15.

"Leader of the Pak", *Marketing Week,* July 8, 1994, pp. 36-37.

J. Magretta, "The Power of Virtual Integration: An Interview with Dell Computer's Michael Dell", *Harvard Business Review,* March-April 1998, pp. 72-83.

K. McQuade and B. Gomes-Casseres, "Xerox and Fuji Xerox", HBS Case No. 9-391-156 (1992).

G. McWilliams, "Whirlwind on the Web", *Business Week,* April 7, 1997, pp. 132+.

J. Pitta, "Computers", *Forbes,* January 11, 1999, pp. 148, 150.

Tetra Pak: additional case data obtained from www.tetralaval.com, www.tetrapak.com, and "Tetra-Laval", company brochure, 1999.

"Tetra Pak: The Inside Story", *Financial Times,* December 16, 1998, p. 28.

V   A New Strategic Management Toolbox

Chapter 5:
Strategic Management Tools for the Knowledge Economy

Introduction

The knowledge-networked economy of the 21st century requires different strategic management tools than the familiar ones of the industrialist era. In Chapter 4, the new frameworks for understanding of business systems and knowledge-driven socio-cultural business networks were reviewed, and approaches to the development of new business models discussed. These frameworks and approaches provide conceptual clarity of the more complex task of systemic strategic management in the knowledge economy. The next question concerns the relevant tools, or methodologies, that could be devised and applied for this purpose. The traditional analytical tools of strategic management (see Table 2.1) include the well-known "5-forces" model of industry analysis, value chain analysis, resource-based VIEW (RBV), business process reengineering (BPR), and business portfolio techniques. As currently conceived, these tools have major deficiencies in coping with the demands of systemic strategic management in the knowledge economy, and have to be complemented with additional and new tools.

This chapter proposes new strategic management tools and methodologies, all of which are systemically interlinked. The chapter consists of the following sections:

- Strategic management tools to develop new business models
  - Four dimensions of business model reinvention
  - Six dimensions of new market space creation
- Strategic management tools to guide knowledge management and innovation in business networks
  - Customer knowledge management (CKM)
  - Communities of practice (COP)
  - Networked incubators
  - Organizational knowledge audit
  - SECI model of knowledge creation
  - "Serious Play" for strategy innovation
- Tools to enhance and measure the "fitness" of a socio-cultural business system
  - Checklists in managing phases of business system development

- The Systemic Scorecard (SSC) as expansion of the Balanced Scorecard (BSC)
- Tools to co-shape organizational strategy poise in knowledge-networked landscapes

Strategic Management Tools to Develop New Business Models

In Chapter 4 a framework of major components of a business model and its reinvention were reviewed. The question of how to make sense of the environment, how to reinvent customer value propositions, how to reconfigure business value networks, and how to reinvent organizational strategy are now addressed in the following subsections.

- **Four dimensions of business model reinvention**

  Figure 5.1 illustrates a 4-dimensional tool of business reinvention, making sense of environmental changes and the relevance of a possible new business model by way of four dimensions of customer sensing (including new customer value propositions), technology sensing, business infrastructure sensing (organizational and business network infrastructure), and economics/profitability sensing.

  In Figure 5.1, *customers* refer to the relative ease of acceptance of a new value proposition, e.g. if it is likely to be fast or slow. *Technology* indicates the relative strength, direction and impact of technology on customer value and the business network, i.e. the impact on new customer value and the efficiencies of network role-players. *Business system infrastructure* refers to the relative responsiveness of the traditional business network to reconfiguration, or relative ease of configuring a new business network. *Economics/profitability* indicates the relative economic feasibility and profitability of the proposed model, i.e. where it scores on a scale from poor to favorable. The closer the results are to the outer limits of the figure, the more likely business model reinvention becomes. Whenever new technologies emerge, new

Reinventing the used car business model[1]

Carmax, a subsidiary of Circuit City, is using multimedia and networking technology to radically change the way Americans shop for used cars. The basic concept is to replace the difficult-to-access used car market with an efficient, information-intensive market. Carmax buys used cars at wholesale auctions, and then uses multimedia technology to provide customers with complete and reliable information. The vehicles are resold at accessible Carmax locations. The keys to the success of this new business model are the availability and reliability of its information, the large selection of cars, the convenient locations, the customer-friendly buying process, the effective new business network infrastructure with direct links to wholesalers, and the mutual economic and profitability benefits for Carmax, wholesalers, banks and other systemic role-players.

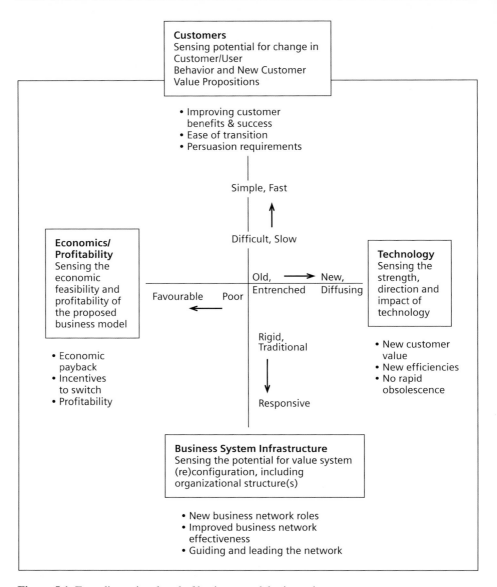

Figure 5.1 Four-dimensional tool of business model reinvention

businesses are likely to be created, and some distinct advantages could accrue to effective early movers.

- **Six dimensions of new market space creation**

Another tool that can assist in developing new business models is a six-dimensional "new market space" creation instrument, as illustrated and discussed in the article (included in this book) by Kim and Mauborgne[2]. This tool enables strategic managers to look outside the traditional boundaries that define how they compete by systematically looking across them – across substitute industries, across strategic groups within their industry, across buyer groups, across complementary product and service offerings, across the functional-emotional orientation of an industry, and across time by participating in the shaping of external trends.

Strategic Tools to Guide Knowledge Management and Innovation in Business Networks

As shown in Figure 4.5 in the previous chapter, systemic knowledge is the underlying force in enabling the development of new business models in the knowledge economy. While the knowledge management (KM) frameworks presented the "what" of respectively knowledge gap identification, a KM system, and knowledge creation (SECI-model), the "how" of knowledge management can be illustrated by the tools presented in this section.

- **Customer Knowledge Management (CKM)**

    Customer knowledge management (CKM) refers to the management of knowledge *from* customers, i.e. the knowledge that is resident in customers. By managing the knowledge of their customers, an organization is more likely to sense emerging market opportunities before its competitors, to constructively challenge the traditional ways of doing business, and to more rapidly create new value for the organization, its stakeholders, the business network, and especially for its customers.

    Five methods (or "styles") of CKM have been identified, viz. prosumerism, team-based co-learning, mutual innovation, communities of creation, and joint intellectual property (IP) ownership, as described in the article (included in this book) by Gibbert, Leibold and Probst.[3]

- **Communities of Practice (COPs)**

    Communities of practice (COP's) are groups of people informally linked across traditional boundaries by shared expertise, interests and mutual enterprise passions, either physically (e.g. face-to-face meetings) or virtually (e.g. by email networks).[4] COPs complement existing organizational and network structures, and radically galvanize knowledge sharing, learning and change across organizational and other boundaries.

    COPs differ from other forms of organization in several ways, as illustrated in Table 5.1.

    From the table it can be seen that COPs are informal. They organize themselves, meaning they set their own agendas and establish their own leadership, with membership being self-selected by individual sensing of contributions and benefits. Although COPs are fundamentally informal and self-organizing, they benefit from

Table 5.1 Communities of practice contrasted with other forms of organization

	What is the purpose?	Who belongs?	What holds it together	How long does it last?
Community of practice	To develop members' capabilities; to build and exchange knowledge	Members who select themselves	Passion, commitment, and identification with the group's expertise	As long as there is interest in maintaining the group
Formal work group	To deliver a product or service	Everyone who reports to the group's manager	Job requirements and common goals	Until the next reorganization
Project team	To accomplish a specified task	Employees assigned by senior management	The project's milestones and goals	Until the project has been completed
Informal network	To collect and pass on business information	Friends and business acquaintances	Mutual needs	As long as people have a reason to connect

Source: Wenger, E.C. and Snyder, W.M. (2000), "Communities of Practice: The Organizational Frontier", *Harvard Business Review,* January-February, 142.

cultivation. To initiate COPs and cultivate them for on-going effectiveness, managers should implement three related activities:

- Identify potential COP's that will enhance the organization and its business network's strategic capabilities, e.g.
  - Find commonalities of challenges and problems.
  - Define a community's domain, i.e. area of expertise and forms of interest.
- Provide the infrastructure that will support such communities, e.g.
  - Designate official sponsors and support teams.
  - Invest time and money in support of COP's.
  - Cultivate incentives for motivation and reward.
- Use non-traditional methods to measure value, e.g.
  - Review members' experience and success through interviews.
  - Encourage conversations and mutual agreement on value created.

For example, at both the World Bank and American Management Systems (AMS), senior management boards identify and sponsor COPs. Support teams help with COP development and coordinate regular community conferences, knowledge fairs, library services and technical support.[5] A corporate university is also a method to initiate and coordinate COPs within a larger KM system for an organization or business network.

• **Networked incubators**

The key distinguishing feature of a networked incubator is that it has mechanisms to foster partnerships among start-up teams and other business entities, thus facilitating the flow of knowledge and talent across companies and forging relationships among them.[6] Incubators exploit networking by providing fledgling companies with preferential access to potential partners and advisers. The two critical characteristics are that a) networking is institutionalized, and b) networking leads to preferential access, but not preferential treatment. This is illustrated in the case of Ford's ConsumerConnect networked incubator.

Ford's ConsumerConnect networked incubator in 2001

Business incubators are not just for venture capitalists and Silicon Valley-style entrepreneurs. Ford recently established an incubator to speed the process of creating and developing Internet businesses. Called ConsumerConnect, the group provides new e-business ventures with basic services, operational and strategic advice, and networking connections with existing Ford businesses. The main purpose of ConsumerConnect is to find new ways to leverage Ford's assets in the new economy, including the company's vast customer base and huge purchasing power.

For example, consider the new venture Covisint, an on-line B2B exchange for the auto industry that was formed as a joint venture among Ford, General Motors, DaimlerChrysler, and Renault/Nissan. By connecting Ford's US$80 billion purchasing volume with Covisint, ConsumerConnect instantly made the start-up a large and viable business.

When setting up ConsumerConnect, Ford executives followed two organizational design principles to ensure that the incubator would work effectively with existing business while promoting entrepreneurial drive. First, they established the group as an independent but powerful entity – ConsumerConnect CEO Brian Kelley has direct access to Ford CEO Jacques Nasser. Second, the incubator was staffed with people from both inside and outside Ford. This mixture combined intimate knowledge of Ford's businesses with a fresh entrepreneurial drive, thus encouraging the creative leveraging of existing assets in new e-business ventures.

Adapted from Hansen, M.T., et al. (2000), "Networked Incubators. Hothouses of the New Economy", Harvard Business Review, September-October, 78-79.

Networked incubators combine the benefits of two diverse worlds – the scale and scope of large established organizations and the entrepreneurial drive of small venture-capital firms, as illustrated in Table 5.2. However, there are also pitfalls: networking may become a slogan rather than a reality, and the incubator may impede the entrepreneurial drive of start-ups by taking too much equity and imposing stringent rules. Entrepreneurs who prefer doing everything themselves might easily become frustrated in an organization that expects networking.

Two organizational practices help executives to avoid the pitfalls of networked incubators, namely portfolio strategy and network design.

Table 5.2
Benefits of networked incubators in comparison to established companies
and venture capitalists

	Established Companies	**Venture Capitalists**	**Networked Incubators**
Scale and Scope *leveraging size and reach in order to lower costs by pooling resources and spreading them across units*	*High* Historically the key advantage of large global companies.	*Low* VC-backed start-ups are left alone to obtain services and buy supplies.	*Medium* Common services and pooling of resources ensure some benefits, especially time savings.
Entrepreneurial Drive *stimulating individuals to pursue risky and disruptive innovations*	*Low* Red tape hinders new ventures; entrepreneurs are not rewarded	*High* Entrepreneurs are free to pursue ventures and own large equity stakes	*High* Entrepreneurs are free of red tape and own equity in ventures
Network Access *forging partnerships, obtaining advice, and recruiting people*	*Medium* Many established companies have some, but not extensive, contacts with Internet companies	*Low* A VC partner may have an excellent personal network, but it doesn't go beyond the individual partner	*High* Organized and active networking among portfolio companies and strategic partners

Source: Hansen, M.T., et al. (2000), "Networked Incubators: Hothouses of the New Economy", *Harvard Business Review,* September-October, 80.

- *Portfolio strategy*: A high-performing networked incubator creates a portfolio of related companies and advisors that incubatees can leverage. When enlisting a set of related strategic partners, the difficulties of traditional conglomerates with highly diversified portfolios are avoided.
- *Network design*: To institutionalize networking, the goal is to establish connections and relationships that are anchored to the incubator rather than to particular individuals. This can be done by the creation of formal links to external experts, bringing outside experts on site, scheduling regular meetings, implementing economic incentives, and hiring specialized deal brokers.

- **Organizational knowledge audit**

Zack proposes the tool of a "knowledge audit" for systemic strategy-knowledge gap analysis, which is essentially a checklist of 14 steps. These are indicated in Table 5.3.[7]

The major limitation of the knowledge audit tool proposed by Zack is that it assumes (from step 1 onwards) that one can articulate a desired or intended strategy, which then forms the basis for progressing towards a knowledge strategy. In self-organizing business systems, the strategy is often the *result* of strategic purpose emanating from business model reinvention, based on new knowledge, and not vice versa. Nevertheless, the knowledge audit presents a logical sequence of steps by periodically reviewing a business system's knowledge strategy, bearing its major limitation in mind.

Table 5.3 Knowledge audit for determining systemic strategy-knowledge gap analysis

Step	Key Question	Action
1	How do you want to play the game?	Articulate desired or intended strategy
2	What do you need to know?	Articulate strategy -> knowledge link
3	What do you know?	Create internal knowledge map
4	What's your internal knowledge gap?	Compare what you need to know to what you do know
5	What do your competitors know?	Create external (competition/industry) knowledge map
6	What's your external knowledge gap?	Compare what you know to what your competitors know
7	What is your learning cycle?	Assess your dynamic learning capabilities as intentions
8	What are your competitors' and industry learning cycles and capabilities	Assess your industry's and competitors' dynamic learning capabilities and intentions
9	What is your learning gap?	Compare your dynamic learning capabilities those of your competitors and your industry
10	What's your internal strategic gap?	Assess how your internal knowledge gap affects your current strategy
11	What's your external strategic gap?	Assess how your external knowledge gap affects your current strategy
12	What's your industry cycle strategic gap?	Assess how your dynamic learning gap affect your future strategy
13	What's your new current and future strategy?	Determine if and how your knowledge and learning gaps require a revision in strategy
14	What's your knowledge strategy?	Determine how aggressive you will be to close your knowledge gaps • regarding exploration vs. exploitation • regarding internal vs. external sources

Source: Zack, M.H. (2000), "Developing a Knowledge Strategy", *California Management Review,* 41(3), 143.

- **The SECI model of knowledge creation**

  The SECI (Socialization-Externalization-Combination-Internalization) model can
  be applied as a tool for knowledge creation. An organization or business system
  creates knowledge through the interactions between explicit and tacit knowledge,
  which is called knowledge conversion. Understanding and influencing this reciprocal relationship is the key to understand the knowledge-creating process. As stated
  previously, a firm creates knowledge through the knowledge spiral of the SECI
  process. Whether the SECI process brings about extension or reduction of knowledge depends on the interaction's propensity to knowledge conversion.

  The factors (or toolkit) that determine the knowledge conversion rate of an organization have been identified as:[8] knowledge vision, organizational form, incentive
  systems, corporate culture and organizational routines, and leadership.

  – *Knowledge vision*
    The knowledge vision determines the mission and domain of the firm, and defines
    the value system that evaluates, justifies and determines the types and quality of
    knowledge that are to be aimed at, created and retained. It is important for an
    organization to have a knowledge vision that transcends the boundaries of existing
    products, divisions, markets, organizations and industries, and yet enables the
    organization to focus on a certain domain.

  – *Organizational form*
    How the organization and business system are configured and structured can
    promote or hinder functional interactions of the SECI process. For example, it has
    been demonstrated that internalization and socialization contribute high perfor-
    mance in functional departments, while externalization and combination contrib-
    ute high performance in project teams.

  – *Incentive systems*
    Since sharing of tacit knowledge could lessen the value of the original owner of
    the knowledge, it is possible that such an individual might not co-operate in
    externalizing his/her tacit knowledge. In such a case, it is important to develop
    various incentive systems that motivate individuals to share their knowledge.
    Monetary compensations is not the only incentive for an individual. The self-
    satisfaction of being able to create something can be a great incentive. Peer
    recognition and the sense of belonging are also important incentives for an indi-
    vidual to contribute to the organization to which s/he belongs.

  – *Corporate culture and organizational routines*
    A firm's comparative efficiency arises through the formation of "firm-specific
    language and routines", which both enhance the performance of a knowledge
    activity itself and aid in ensuring its efficient governance. How organization mem-
    bers view the approach to knowledge and the knowledge-creating process, and
    how they interact with one another, greatly affect the knowledge conversion rate.
    For example, love, care, trust and commitment among organizational members are
    important as they form the foundation of knowledge creation (von Krogh, 1998).[9]
    However, an organization is simultaneously subject to inertia and it is difficult for
    an organization to diverge from the course set by its previous experiences. There-

fore, current capabilities may both impel and constrain future learning and actions taken by a firm and core capabilities can turn into "core rigidities" (Leonard-Barton, 1992).[10]

– *Leadership*

Leadership gives an organization will and direction that cannot be found in market forces. Leaders affect the knowledge conversion rate by creating the knowledge vision, configuring knowledge architectures, and fostering the organizational and business network culture. Crucial to this process is the role of managers who are at the intersections of vertical and horizontal knowledge flows within and across organizations. "Distributed leadership", where every member can be a leader depending on the context, is the key.[11]

• **"Serious play" as a tool to enhance knowledge sharing and innovation**

Roos and Victor propose the "serious play" tool to enhance knowledge sharing and strategy innovation.[12] This is illustrated in Figure 5.2.

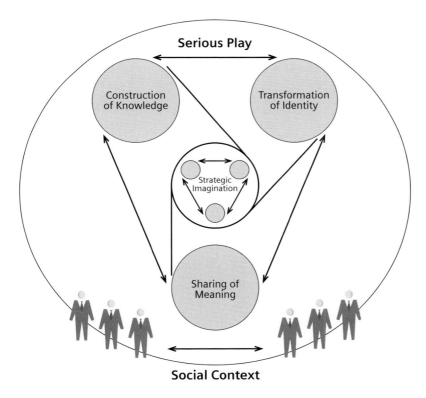

Figure 5.2
Serious play as a basis for strategy making (*Source:* Roos, J. and Victor, B. (1999), "Towards a New Model of Strategy-Making as Serious Play", *European Management Journal,* 17(4), 353).

Serious play ("as-if", "make believe") refers to the purposeful social dynamics among organizational and business network members from which original strategy emerges. Its major feature is the complex interplay among three types of strategic imagination, namely descriptive, creative and challenging imaginations, that result in three critical strategy-making elements: a) the construction of knowledge gathered from analysis and experience; b) the sharing of meaning emerging from that knowledge; and c) the transformation of identity assimilating the new knowledge. The human imagination is employed to generate ideas and construct mutual knowledge, a conversation about "what-if" or "make-believe" is created to communication and share meaning, and socialization is engaged to develop new identity and commitment. The meaning of ideas is shared through e.g. storytelling and satirical examples, which are especially relevant to imaginative strategy and new business model formation in socio-cultural business systems.

Tools to Enhance and Measure the Fitness of a Socio-Cultural Business System

While the previous sections of this chapter focused on systemic strategic management tools to develop new business models, and to improve knowledge management and innovation in organization and business networks, the questions of how an entire socio-cultural business network can be strategically reviewed, enhanced and measured are addressed in this section.

- **A checklist toolkit for managing phases of a business system**

  In the article "Predators and Prey" by Moore (included in Part 3 of this book), a checklist (or toolkit) for managing four phases of evolution of a business system is provided. These are summarized in Table 5.4.

  The critical issue for strategic leadership is to identify a particular business system's phase of evolution, to realize the managerial focus required in a particular phase, and to be aware of the cooperative and competitive activity challenges in a particular phase.

- **The System Strategy Scorecard (SSC)**

  The well-known balanced scorecard (BSC) of Kaplan and Norton focuses predominantly on the individual organization's, i.e. as a concept to manage an organization strategy and measure its performance on various interlinked organizational dimensions.[13] This concept can be expanded into a systemic strategy scorecard (SSC), as illustrated in Table 5.5.

  For each of the four systemic dimensions of the SSC a range of practical management (including measurement) tools can be proposed. These include specific *objectives, targets, initiatives* and *measures*. Some of these have already been indicated in the previous sections of this chapter.

Table 5.4 Managing phases in a business system

Stage of Evolution of the Business System	Overall Managerial Focus	Managerial Challenges	
		Cooperative Challenges	**Competitive Challenges**
Pioneering (birth of business system)	Value proposition and designing business model	Work with customers and suppliers to develop the seed innovation and define the new value proposition (dramatically more effective than what is available).	Protect your ideas from others who might be working toward defining similar offers. Commit critical lead customers, key suppliers and distribution channels.
Expansion	Critical mass	Bring the new offer to a large market by working with suppliers and partners to increase supply, and to achieve maximum market coverage and critical mass.	Defeat alternative business system implementations of similar ideas; ensure that the new approach is the market standard in its class by dominating key market segments.
Leadership	Lead Co-evolution	Provide a compelling vision for the future that encourages suppliers and customers to work together to continue to improve the value proposition and business system. Ensure the business system has a robust community of suppliers.	Maintain strong bargaining power in relation to other players in the business system by controlling key elements of value.
Renewal	Continuous performance improvement	Work with innovators to bring new ideas to the existing business system. Track new trends that may transform the business system.	Maintain high barriers to entry to prevent innovators from building alternative business systems. Maintain high customer switching costs in order to buy time to incorporate new ideas into your own products and services. Ensure robustness of management and other system members.

Source: Adapted from Moore, J.F. (1996), *The Death of Competition*, New York: HarperBusiness, 83.

• Tools to co-shape organizational poise in knowledge-networked landcapes

Roos proposes the concept of the "poised organization", i.e. a firm that continuously and successfully adapts in its knowledge landscape – a particular arena of activity in the fast-changing knowledge-networked environment of today.[14] The concept of

Table 5.5 The Systemic Strategy Scorecard

Dimension	Balanced Scorecard Focus	Systemic Strategy Scorecard Focus
Financial	Improve organizational shareholder value	Improve network stakeholder value
Customer	Improve customer satisfaction and relations	Improve customer success and customer partnerships
Business processes	Optimize particular internal business processes	Robustness and resilience of business network processes, both competitive and collaborative
Learning and growth	Continuous organizational learning and growth	Systemic knowledge management

"organizational poise" refers to a balancing between simultaneous survival and advancement (including reinvention) activities on different scales in time and space.

Knowledge landscapes share several similarities with the concept of fitness landscapes, relevant to evolutionary (Darwinian) science. Species on fitness landscapes take "adaptive walks", thus climbing peaks to improve their chances of survival. Organizations on knowledge landscapes take "knowledge development expeditions", intentionally exploring for and developing new, potential knowledge. Firms, like species, co-evolve with their business system members, including competitors, in a seemingly endless "knowledge race". To achieve and maintain "poise" in a knowledge landscape, four characteristics have to be developed and sustained:[15]

- *Identity characteristics*
  Organizational identity is a reflection of the organization's nature in its knowledge landscape, e.g. its mission in a particular industry. Identity can be seen as a purposeful attractor, i.e. a defined range of possible states in which a firm can act in its pursuit of knowledge.

- *Exploration characteristics*
  Poised firms climb and explore the dynamics of their landscapes, e.g. through experimentation, socialization and structural coupling. They are aware of the risk of focusing too much on "climbing", which can lock into path dependency of single or a few peaks. Poised organizations are able to recognize new patterns and distinguish between large and small avalanches of change.

- *Co-Evolution characteristics*
  Engaging in external relationships, such as strategic alliances, enables an organization to explore different peaks on its knowledge landscapes, and, perhaps, even to discover entirely foreign, but relevant, knowledge landscapes. A poised organization is able to simultaneously explore distant parts of its fitness landscape, while continuing to climb its local peak by allowing itself to reconfigure its network of relationships.

– *Internal coherence characteristics*

The degree of internal coupling of organizational units must be recognized, i.e. the degree of interconnectedness between sub-units of the organization, and between these units and their environments. A high degree of interconnectedness could rigidify an organization's knowledge landscape, while a low degree of coupling could lead to idiosyncratic or selfish behavior, with each unit climbing its own peak. A poised organization resolves this issue of coherence by balancing the degree of coupling as may be necessary.

How Skandia aims at organizational poise

One firm that exhibits many of these poise-development characteristics, prioritizing pattern recognition and knowledge development, is the Swedish insurance company Skandia. In 1996 it launched a new process called "Skandia Future Centers" with the intention of "adapting, hedging, and shaping the future". It accomplished this task by inquiring about the future, focusing on what was coming next and what the company could do to climb developing knowledge peaks, but also to shift the landscape in its favor by actively shaping the future. This process began through the creation of a "three generation future team", comprised of 25 members chosen from several hundred organization members across the various operating units and countries of the organization, who were given some initial discussion topics. The group communicates regularly using communication technology, and meets occasionally at a specially designed "energy spot" in Vaxholm, Sweden.

One of the main tasks of the future teams is relationship building, both within and outside the company. In this way, the teams allow the firm to identify and develop new knowledge sources and climb existing peaks on its landscape. More importantly it allows Skandia to monitor the height and dynamics of surrounding peaks, and to explore its landscape further afield than would otherwise be possible. Knowledge developed within the Skandia Future Centers can potentially lead to "hopping" actions or ways to develop useful strategic alliances that shift Skandia's knowledge landscape.

Source: Adapted from Roos, J. and Oliver, D. (1999),
"The Poised Organization: Navigating Effectively on Knowledge Landscapes",
http://www.ind.ch/fac/roos/paper_po.html, November 2.

Conclusion

The knowledge economy, with its manifestation of greater systemic networking capabilities across traditional industry and organizational boundaries, requires new strategic management tools. The traditional strategic management tools are deficient when dealing with fast-changing industries and business model reinvention. Systemic strategic management tools enable appropriate new business models, as well as new organizational knowledge landscapes and industries to emerge. Such tools, and their utilization, are based on a sound understanding of the dimensions and methodologies of business model reinvention, knowledge management in organizations and business networks, identification of and differentiated management in the various phases of business system evolution, and systemic scorecard(s) and organizational poise characteristics. Leadership and managerial qualities are particularly necessary for handling such tools successfully, and for overall systemic strategic management, as indicated in Chapter 6.

Creating New Market Space[*]

By W. Chan Kim and Renée Mauborgne

A systematic approach to value innovation can help companies break free from the competitive pack.

Competing head-to-head can be cutthroat, especially when markets are flat or growing slowly. Managers caught in this kind of competition almost universally say they dislike it and wish they could find a better alternative. They often know instinctively that innovation is the only way they can break free from the pack. But they simply don't know where to begin. Admonitions to develop more creative strategies or to think outside the box are rarely accompanied by practical advice.

For almost a decade, we have researched companies that have created such fundamentally new and superior value. We have looked for patterns in the way companies create new markets and re-create existing ones, and we have found six basic approaches. All come from looking at familiar data from a new perspective; none requires any special vision or foresight about the future.

Most companies focus on matching and beating their rivals, and as a result their strategies tend to converge along the same basic dimensions of competition. Such companies share an implicit set of beliefs about "how we compete in our industry or in our strategic group." They share a conventional wisdom about who their customers are and what they value, and about the scope of products and services their industry should be offering. The more that companies share this conventional wisdom about how they compete, the greater the competitive convergence. As rivals try to outdo one another, they end up competing solely on the basis of incremental improvements in cost or quality or both.

Creating new market space requires a different pattern of strategic thinking. Instead of looking within the accepted boundaries that define how we compete, managers can look systematically across them. By doing so, they can find unoccupied territory that represents a real breakthrough in value. This article will describe how companies can systematically pursue value innovation by looking across the conventionally defined boundaries of competition – across substitute industries, across strategic groups, across buyer groups, across complementary product and service offerings, across the functional-emotional orientation of an industry, and even across time.

---

[*] Taken with permission from Harvard Business Review, January 1999, pp. 83-93

Looking Across Substitute Industries

In the broadest sense, a company competes not only with the companies in its own industry but also with companies in those other industries that produce substitute products or services. In making every purchase decision, buyers implicitly weigh substitutes, often unconsciously. Going into town for dinner and a show? At some level, you've probably decided whether to drive, take the train, or call a taxi. The thought process is intuitive for individual consumers and industrial buyers alike.

For some reason, however, we often abandon this intuitive thinking when we become sellers. Rarely do sellers think consciously about how their customers make trade-offs across substitute industries. A shift in price, a change in model, even a new ad campaign can elicit a tremendous response from rivals within an industry, but the same actions in a substitute industry usually go unnoticed. Trade journals, trade

Creating a New Value Curve

The value curve – a graphic depiction of the way a company or an industry configures its offering to customers – is a powerfull tool for creating new market space. It is drawn by plotting the perfomance of the offering relative to other alternatives along the success factors that define competition in the industry or category.

To identify those alternatives, Intuit, for example, looked within its own industry – software to manage personal finances – and it also looked across substitute products to understand why customers chose one over the other. The dominant substitute for software was the lowly pencil. The value curves for these two alternatives map out the existing competitive space.

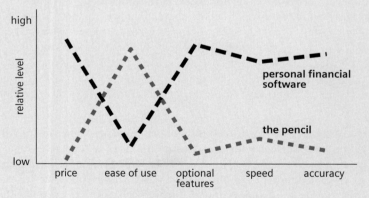

The Value Curves in Personal Finance Before Quicken

The software offered relatively high levels of speed and accuracy. But customers often chose the pencil because of its advantages in price and ease of use, and most customers never used the software's optional features, which added cost and complexity to the product.

shows, and consumer rating reports reinforce the vertical walls that stand between one industry and another. Often, however, the space between substitute industries provides opportunities for value innovation.

Consider Home Depot, the company that has revolutionized the do-it-yourself market in North America. In 20 years, Home Depot has become a $24 billion business, creating over 130,000 new jobs in more than 660 stores. By the end of the year 2000, the company expects to have over 1,100 stores in the Americas. Home Depot did not achieve that level of growth simply by taking market share away from other hardware stores; rather, it has created a new market of do-it-yourselfers out of ordinary home owners.

There are many explanations for Home Depot's success: its warehouse format, its relatively low-cost store locations, its knowledgeable service, its combination of large stores and low prices generating high volumes and economies of scale. But such explanations miss the more fundamental question: Where did Home Depot get its original insight into how to revolutionize and expand its market?

Home Depot looked at the existing industries serving home improvement needs. It saw that people had two choices: they could hire contractors, or they could buy tools and materials from a hardware store and do the work themselves. The key to Home Depot's original insight was understanding why buyers would choose one substitute over another. (It is essential here to keep the analysis at the industry, and not the company, level.)

Why do people hire a contractor? Surely not because they value having a stranger in their house who will charge them top dollar. Surely not because they enjoy taking time off from work to wait for the contractor to show up. In fact, professional contractors have only one decisive advantage: they have specialized know-how that the home owner lacks.

So executives at Home Depot have made it their mission to bolster the competence and confidence of customers whose expertise in home repair is limited. They recruit sales assistants with significant trade experience, often former carpenters or painters. These assistants are trained to walk customers through any project-installing kitchen cabinets, for example, or building a deck. In addition, Home Depot sponsors in-store clinics that teach customers such skills as electrical wiring, carpentry, and plumbing.

To understand the rest of the Home Depot formula, now consider the flip side: Why do people choose hardware stores over professional contractors? The most common answer would be to save money. Most people can do without the features that add cost to the typical hardware store. They don't need the city locations, the neighborly service, or the nice display shelves. So Home Depot has eliminated those costly features, employing a self-service warehouse format that lowers overhead and mainte-nance costs, generates economies of scale in purchasing, and minimizes stock-outs.

Essentially, Home Depot offers the expertise of professional home contractors at markedly lower prices than hardware stores. By delivering the decisive advantages of both substitute industries-and eliminating or reducing everything else-Home Depot has transformed enormous latent demand for home improvement into real demand.

257

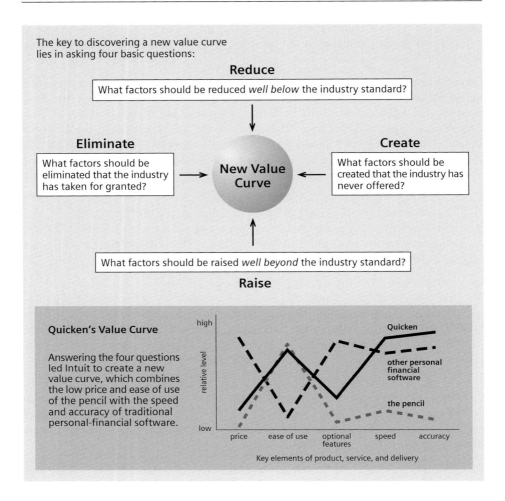

The key to discovering a new value curve lies in asking four basic questions:

Reduce

What factors should be reduced *well below* the industry standard?

Eliminate

What factors should be eliminated that the industry has taken for granted?

New Value Curve

Create

What factors should be created that the industry has never offered?

What factors should be raised *well beyond* the industry standard?

Raise

Quicken's Value Curve

Answering the four questions led Intuit to create a new value curve, which combines the low price and ease of use of the pencil with the speed and accuracy of traditional personal-financial software.

Quicken

other personal financial software

the pencil

relative level — high / low

price   ease of use   optional features   speed   accuracy

Key elements of product, service, and delivery

Intuit, the company that changed the way individuals and small businesses manage their finances, also got its insight into value innovation by thinking about how customers make trade-offs across substitutes. Its Quicken software allows individuals to organize, understand, and manage their personal finances. Every household goes through the monthly drudgery of paying bills. Hence, in principle, personal financial software should be a big and broad market. Yet before Quicken, few people used software to automate this tedious and repetitive task. At the time of Quicken's release in 1984, the 42 existing software packages for personal finance had yet to crack the market.

Why? As Intuit founder Scott Cook recalls, "The greatest competitor we saw was not in the industry. It was the pencil. The pencil is a really tough and resilient substitute. Yet the entire industry had overlooked it."

Asking why buyers trade across substitutes led Intuit to an important insight: the pencil had two decisive advantages over computerized solutions amazingly low cost and extreme simplicity of use. At prices of around $300, existing software packages were too expensive. They were also hard to use, presenting intimidating interfaces full of accounting terminology.

Intuit focused on bringing out both the decisive advantages that the computer has over the pencil speed and accuracy-and the decisive advantages that the pencil has over computers-simplicity of use and low price-and eliminated or reduced everything else. With its user-friendly interface that resembles the familiar checkbook, Quicken is far faster and more accurate than the pencil, yet almost as simple to use. Intuit eliminated the accounting jargon and all the sophisticated features that were part of the industry's conventional wisdom about "how we compete." It offered instead only the few basic functions that most customers use. Simplifying the software cut costs. Quicken retailed at about $90, a 70% price drop. Neither the pencil nor other software packages could compete with Quicken's divergent value curve. Quicken created breakthrough value and re-created the industry, and has expanded the market some too-fold. (See the exhibit "Creating a New Value Curve.")

There is a further lesson to be drawn from the way Intuit thought about and looked across substitutes. In looking for other products or services that could perform the same function as its own, Intuit could have focused on private accounting firms that handle finances for individuals. But when there is more than one substitute, it is smart to explore the ones with the greatest volumes in usage as well as in dollar value. Framed that way, more Americans use pencils than accountants to manage their personal finances.

Many of the well-known success stories of the past decade have followed this path of looking across substitutes to create new markets. Consider Federal Express and United Parcel Service, which deliver mail at close to the speed of the telephone, and Southwest Airlines, which combines the speed of flying with the convenience of frequent departures and the low cost of driving. Note that Southwest Airlines concentrated on driving as the relevant substitute, not other surface transportation such as buses, because only a minority of Americans travels long distances by bus.

Looking Across Strategic Groups Within Industries

Just as new market space often can be found by looking across substitute industries, so can it be found by looking across *strategic groups*. The term refers to a group of companies within an industry that pursue a similar strategy. In most industries, all the fundamental strategic differences among industry players are captured by a small number of strategic groups.

Strategic groups can generally be ranked in a rough hierarchical order built on two dimensions, price and performance. Each jump in price tends to bring a corresponding jump in some dimension of performance. Most companies focus on improving their competitive position *within* a strategic group. The key to creating new market space across existing strategic groups is to understand what factors determine buyers' decisions to trade up or down from one group to another.

Consider Polo Ralph Lauren, which created an entirely new and paradoxical market in clothing: high fashion with no fashion. With worldwide retail sales exceeding $5 billion, Ralph Lauren is the first American design house to successfully take its brand worldwide.

At Polo Ralph Lauren's inception more than 30 years ago, fashion industry experts of almost every stripe criticized the company. Where, they asked, was the fashion? Lacking creativity in design, how could Ralph Lauren charge such high prices? Yet the same people who criticized the company bought its clothes, as did affluent people everywhere. Lauren's lack of fashion was its greatest strength. Ralph Lauren built on the decisive advantages of the two strategic groups that dominated the high-end clothing market – designer haute couture and the higher-volume, but lower-priced, classical lines of Burberry's, Brooks Brothers, Aquascutum, and the like.

What makes people trade either up or down between haute couture and the classic lines? Most customers don't trade up to haute couture to get frivolous fashions that are rapidly outdated. Nor do they enjoy paying ridiculous prices that can reach $500 for a T-shirt. They buy haute couture for the emotional value of wearing an exclusive designer's name, a name that says, "I am different; I appreciate the finer things in life." They also value the wonderfully luxurious feel of the materials and the fine craftsmanship of the garments.

The trendy designs the fashion houses work so hard to create are, ironically, the major drawback of haute couture for most high-end customers, few of whom have the sophistication or the bodies to wear such original clothing. Conversely, customers who trade down for classic lines over haute couture want to buy garments of lasting quality that justifies high prices.

Ralph Lauren has built its brand in the space between these two strategic groups, but it didn't do so by taking the average of the groups' differences. Instead, Lauren captured the advantages of trading both up and down. Its designer name, the elegance of its stores, and the luxury of its materials capture what most customers value in haute couture; its updated classical look and price capture the best of the classical lines. By combining the most attractive factors of both groups, and eliminating or reducing everything else, Polo Ralph Lauren not only captured share from both segments but also drew many new customers into the market.

Many companies have found new market space by looking across strategic groups. In the luxury car market, Toyota's Lexus carved out a new space by offering the quality of the high-end Mercedes, BMW, and Jaguar at a price closer to the lower-end Cadillac and Lincoln. And think of the Sony Walkman. By combining the acoustics and the "cool" image of boom boxes with the low price and the convenient size and weight of transistor radios, Sony created the personal portable-stereo market in the late 1970s. The Walkman took share from these two strategic groups. In addition, its quantum leap in value drew into the market new customers like joggers and commuters.

Michigan-based Champion Enterprises found a similar opportunity by looking across two strategic groups in the housing industry: makers of prefabricated housing and on-site developers. Prefabricated houses are cheap and quick to build, but they are also dismally standardized and project an image of low quality. Houses built by developers on-site offer variety and an image of high quality but are dramatically more expensive and take longer to build.

Champion created new market space by offering the decisive advantages of both strategic groups. Its prefabricated houses are quick to build and benefit from tremendous economies of scale and lower costs, but Champion also allows buyers to choose such high-end options as fireplaces, skylights, and even vaulted ceilings. In essence, Champion has changed the definition of prefabricated housing. As a result, far more lower-to-middle-income consumers have become interested in purchasing prefabricated housing rather than renting or buying an apartment, and even some affluent people are being drawn into the market.

Looking Across the Chain of Buyers

In most industries, competitors converge around a common definition of who the target customer is when in reality there is a chain of "customers" who are directly or indirectly involved in the buying decision. The *purchasers* who pay for the product or service may differ from the actual users, and in some cases there are important *influencers,* as well. While these three groups may overlap, they often differ.

When they do, they frequently hold different definitions of value. A corporate purchasing agent, for example, may be more concerned with costs than the corporate user, who is likely to be far more concerned with ease of use. Likewise, a retailer may value a manufacturer's just-in-time stock-replenishment and innovative financing. But consumer purchasers, although strongly influenced by the channel, do not value these things.

Individual companies in an industry often target different customer segments-large versus small customers, for example. But an industry typically converges on a single buyer group. The pharmaceutical industry, for example, focuses overridingly on influencers-the doctors. The office equipment industry focuses heavily on purchasers-corporate purchasing departments. And the clothing industry sells predominantly to users. Sometimes there is a strong economic rationale for this focus. But often it is the result of industry practices that have never been questioned.

Challenging an industry's conventional wisdom about which buyer group to target can lead to the discovery of new market space. By looking across buyer groups, companies can gain new insights into how to redesign their value curves to focus on a previously overlooked set of customers.

Consider Bloomberg. In little over a decade, Bloomberg has become one of the largest and most profitable business-information providers in the world. Until Bloomberg's debut in the early 1980s, Reuters and Telerate dominated the on-line financial-information industry, providing news and prices in real time to the brokerage and investment community. The industry focused on purchasers the IT managers-who valued standardized systems, which made their lives easier.

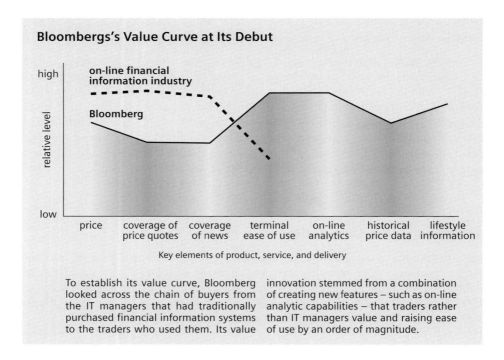

Bloombergs's Value Curve at Its Debut

To establish its value curve, Bloomberg looked across the chain of buyers from the IT managers that had traditionally purchased financial information systems to the traders who used them. Its value innovation stemmed from a combination of creating new features – such as on-line analytic capabilities – that traders rather than IT managers value and raising ease of use by an order of magnitude.

This made no sense to Bloomberg. Traders and analysts, not IT managers, make or lose millions of dollars for their employers each day. Profit opportunities come from disparities in information. When markets are active, traders and analysts must make rapid decisions. Every second counts.

So Bloomberg designed a system specifically to offer traders better value, one with easy-to-use terminals and keyboards labeled with familiar financial terms. The systems also have two flat-panel monitors, so traders can see all the information they need at once without having to open and close numerous windows. Since traders have to analyze information before they act, Bloomberg added a built-in analytic capability that works with the press of a button. Before, traders and analysts had to download data and use a pencil and calculator to perform important financial calculations. Now users can quickly run "what if" scenarios to compute returns on alternative investments, and they can perform longitudinal analyses of historical data.

By focusing on users, Bloomberg was also able to see the paradox of traders' and analysts' personal lives. They have tremendous income but work such long hours that they have little time to spend it. Realizing that markets have slow times during the day when little trading takes place, Bloomberg decided to add information and purchasing services aimed at enhancing traders' personal lives. Traders can buy items like flowers, clothing, and jewelry; make travel arrangements; get information about wines; or search through real estate listings.

By shifting its focus upstream from purchasers to users, Bloomberg created a value curve that was radically different from anything the industry had ever seen. The traders and analysts wielded their power within their firms to force IT managers to purchase Bloomberg terminals. Bloomberg did not simply win customers away from competitors-it grew the market. "We are in a business that need not be either-or," explains founder Mike Bloomberg. "Our customers can afford to have two products. Many of them take other financial news services and us because we offer uncommon value." (See the graph "Bloomberg's Value Curve at Its Debut.")

Philips Lighting Company, the North American division of the Dutch company Philips Electronics, re-created its industrial lighting business by shifting downstream from purchasers to influencers. Traditionally, the industry focused on corporate purchasing managers who bought on the basis of how much the lightbulbs cost and how long they lasted. Everyone in the industry competed head-to-head along those two dimensions.

By focusing on influencers, including CFOs and public relations people, Philips came to understand that the price and life of bulbs did not account for the full cost of lighting. Because lamps contained environmentally toxic mercury, companies faced high disposal costs at the end of a lamp's life. The purchasing department never saw those costs, but CFOs did. So in 1995, Philips introduced the Alto, an environmentally friendly bulb that it promotes to CFOs and to public relations people, using those influencers to drive sales. The Alto reduced customers' overall costs and garnered companies positive press for promoting environmental concerns. The new market Alto created has superior margins and is growing rapidly; the product has already replaced more than 25% of traditional T-12 fluorescent lamps used in stores, schools, and office buildings in the United States.

Many industries afford similar opportunities to create new market space. By questioning conventional definitions of who can and should be the target customer, companies can often see fundamentally new ways to create value.

Looking Across Complementary Product and Service Offerings

Few products and services are used in a vacuum; in most cases, other products and services affect their value. But in most industries, rivals converge within the bounds of their industry's product and service offerings. Take movie theaters as an example. The ease and cost of getting a babysitter and parking the car affect the perceived value of going to the movies, although these complementary services are beyond the bounds of the movie theater industry as it has been traditionally defined. Few cinema operators worry about how hard or costly it is for people to get babysitters. But they should, because it affects demand for their business.

Untapped value is often hidden in complementary products and services. The key is to define the total solution buyers seek when they choose a product or service. A simple way to do so is to think about what happens before, during, and after your product is used. Babysitting and parking the car are needed before going to the movies. Operating and application software are used along with computer hardware. In the airline

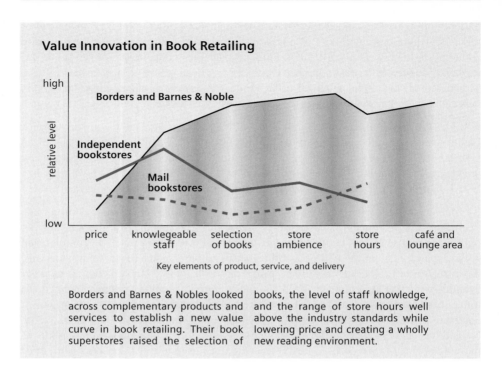

Value Innovation in Book Retailing

Borders and Barnes & Nobles looked across complementary products and services to establish a new value curve in book retailing. Their book superstores raised the selection of books, the level of staff knowledge, and the range of store hours well above the industry standards while lowering price and creating a wholly new reading environment.

industry, ground transportation is used after the flight but is clearly part of what the customer needs to travel from one place to another.

Companies can create new market space by zeroing in on the complements that detract from the value of their own product or service. Look at Borders Books & Music and Barnes & Noble in the United States. By the late 1980s, the U.S. retail book industry appeared to be in decline. Americans were reading less and less. The large chains of mall bookstores were engaged in intense competition, and the small, independent bookstore appeared to be an endangered species.

Against this backdrop, Borders and B&N created a new format-book superstores-and woke up an entire industry. When either company enters a market, the overall consumption of books often increases by more than 50%.

The traditional business of a bookstore had been narrowly defined as selling books. People came, they bought, they left. Borders and B&N, however, thought more broadly about the total experience people seek when they buy books-and what they focused on was the joy of lifelong learning and discovery. Yes, that involves the physical purchase of books. But it also includes related activities: searching and hunting, evaluating potential purchases, and actually sampling books.

Traditional retail-book chains imposed tremendous inefficiencies and inconveniences on consumers. Their staffs were generally trained as cashiers and stock clerks; few could help customers find the right book. In small stores, selection was limited, frustrating the search for an exciting title. People who hadn't read a good book review recently or picked up a recommendation from a friend would be unlikely to patronize these bookstores. As a rule, the stores discouraged browsing, forcing customers to assume a large part of the risk in buying a book, since people would not know until after they bought it whether they would like it. As for consumption, that activity was supposed to occur at home. But as people's lives have become increasingly harried, home has become less likely to be a peaceful oasis where a person can enjoy a wonderful book.

Borders and B&N saw value trapped in these complementary activities. They hired staff with extensive knowledge of books to help customers make selections. Many staff members have college or even advanced degrees, and all are passionate book lovers. Furthermore, they're given a monthly book allowance, and they're actually encouraged to read whenever business is slow.

The superstores stock more than 150,000 titles, whereas the average bookstore contains around 20,000. The superstores are furnished with armchairs, reading tables, and sofas to encourage people not just to dip into a book or two but to read them through. Their coffee bars, classical music, and wide aisles invite people to linger comfortably. They stay open until 11 at night, offering a relaxing destination for an evening of quiet reading, not a quick shopping stop. (See the graph "Value Innovation in Book Retailing.")

Book superstores redefined the scope of the service they offer. They transformed the product from the book itself into the pleasure of reading and intellectual exploration. In less than six years, Borders and B&N have emerged as the two largest bookstore chains in the United States, with a total of more than 650 superstores between them.

We could cite many other examples of companies that have followed this path to creating new market space. Virgin Entertainment's stores combine CDs, videos, computer games, and stereo and audio equipment to satisfy buyers' complete entertainment needs. Dyson designs its vacuum cleaners to obliterate the costly and annoying activities of buying and changing vacuum cleaner bags. Zeneca's Salick cancer centers combine all the cancer treatments their patients might need under one roof so they don't have to go from one specialized center to another, making separate appointments for each service they require.

Looking Across Functional or Emotional Appeal to Buyers

Competition in an industry tends to converge not only around an accepted notion of the scope of its products and services but also around one of two possible bases of appeal. Some industries compete principally on price and function based largely on calculations of utility; their appeal is rational. Other industries compete largely on feelings; their appeal is emotional.

Yet the appeal of most products or services is rarely intrinsically one or the other. The phenomenon is a result of the way companies have competed in the past, which has unconsciously educated consumers on what to expect. Companies' behavior affects customers' expectations in a reinforcing cycle. Over time, functionally oriented industries become more functionally oriented; emotionally oriented industries become more emotionally oriented. No wonder market research rarely reveals new insights into what customers really want. Industries have trained customers in what to expect. When surveyed, they echo back: more of the same for less.

Companies often find new market space when they are willing to challenge the functional-emotional orientation of their industry. We have observed two common patterns. Emotionally oriented industries offer many extras that add price without enhancing functionality. Stripping those extras away may create a fundamentally simpler, lower-priced, lower-cost business model that customers would welcome. Conversely, functionally oriented industries can often infuse commodity products with new life by adding a dose of emotion – and in so doing, can stimulate new demand.

Look at how Starbucks transformed a functional product into an emotional one. In the late 1980s, General Foods, Nestle, and Procter & Gamble dominated the U.S. coffee market. Consumers drank coffee as part of a daily routine. Coffee was considered a commodity industry, marked by heavy price-cutting and an ongoing battle for market share. The industry had taught customers to shop based on price, discount coupons, and brand names that are expensive for companies to build. The result was paper-thin profit margins and low growth.

Instead of viewing coffee as a functional product, Starbucks set out to make coffee an emotional experience, what customers often refer to as a "caffeine-induced oasis." The big three sold a commodity-coffee by the can; Starbucks sold a retailing concept – the coffee bar. The coffee bars offered a chic gathering place, status, relaxation, conversation, and creative coffee drinks. Starbucks turned coffee into an emotional experience and ordinary people into coffee connoisseurs for whom the steep $3-per-cup price seemed reasonable. With almost no advertising, Starbucks became a national brand with margins roughly five times the industry average.

What Starbucks did for coffee, Swatch did for budget watches. Long considered a functional item, budget watches were bought merely to keep track of time. Citizen and Seiko, the leaders in the industry, competed through advances in functionality by using quartz technology to improve accuracy, for example, or by making digital displays that were easier to read. Swatch turned budget watches into fashion accessories.

SMH, the Swiss parent company, created a design lab in Italy to turn its watches into a fashion statement, combining powerful technology with fantasy. "You wear a watch on your wrist, right against your skin," explains chairman Nicholas Hayek. "It can be an important part of your image. I believed that if we could add genuine emotion to the product and a strong message, we could succeed in dominating the industry and creating a powerful market." Before Swatch, people usually purchased only one watch. Swatch made repeat purchases the standard. In Italy, the average person owns six Swatches to fit their different moods and looks.

The Body Shop created new market space by shifting in the opposite direction, from an emotional appeal to a functional one. Few industries are more emotionally oriented than cosmetics. The industry sells glamour and beauty, hopes and dreams as much as

Is the Body Shop a Cosmetics Company?

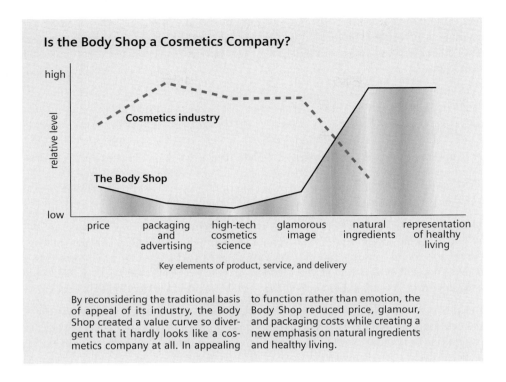

By reconsidering the traditional basis of appeal of its industry, the Body Shop created a value curve so divergent that it hardly looks like a cosmetics company at all. In appealing to function rather than emotion, the Body Shop reduced price, glamour, and packaging costs while creating a new emphasis on natural ingredients and healthy living.

it sells products. On average, packaging and advertising constitute 85% of cosmetics companies' costs.

By stripping away the emotional appeal, the Body Shop realized tremendous cost savings. Since customers get no practical value from the money the industry spends on packaging, the Body Shop uses simple refillable plastic bottles. The Body Shop spends little on advertising, again because its customers get no functional value from it. In short, the Body Shop hardly looks like a cosmetics company at all. The company's approach-and its emphasis on natural ingredients and healthy living-was so refreshingly simple that it won consumers over through common sense and created new market space in an industry accustomed to competing on a tried-and-true formula. (See the graph "Is the Body Shop a Cosmetics Company?").

A burst of new market creation is under way in a number of service industries that are following this pattern. Relationship businesses like insurance, banking, and investing have relied heavily on the emotional bond between broker and client. They are ripe for change. Direct Line Insurance in Britain, for example, has done away with traditional brokers. It reasoned that customers would not need the hand-holding and emotional comfort that brokers traditionally provide if the company did a better job of, for example, paying claims rapidly and eliminating complicated paperwork. So instead of using brokers and regional branch offices, Direct Line substitutes information technology to improve claims handling, and it passes on some of the cost savings to customers in the form of lower insurance premiums. In the United States, Vanguard Group in index funds and Charles Schwab in brokerage services are doing the same in the investment industry, creating new market space by transforming emotionally oriented businesses based on personal relationships into high-performance, low-cost functional businesses.

Looking Across Time

All industries are subject to external trends that affect their businesses over time. Think of the rapid rise of the Internet or the global movement toward protecting the environment. Looking at these trends with the right perspective can unlock innovation that creates new market space.

Most companies adapt incrementally and somewhat passively as events unfold. Whether it's the emergence of new technologies or major regulatory changes, managers tend to focus on projecting the trend itself. That is, they ask in which direction a technology will evolve, how it will be adopted, whether it will become scalable. They pace their own actions to keep up with the development of the trends they're tracking.

But key insights into new market spaces rarely come from projecting the trend itself. Instead they arise from business insights into how the trend will change value to customers. By looking across time-from the value a market delivers today to the value it might deliver tomorrow-managers can actively shape their future and lay claim to new market space. Looking across time is perhaps more difficult than the previous approaches we've discussed, but it can be made subject to the same disciplined approach. We're not talking about predicting the future, which is inherently impossible. We're talking about finding insight in trends that are observable today. (See the diagram "Shifting the Focus of Strategy.")

Three principles are critical to assessing trends across time. To form the basis of a new value curve, these trends must be decisive to your business, they must be irreversible, and they must have a clear trajectory. Many trends can be observed at any one time-a discontinuity in technology, the rise of a new lifestyle, or a change in regulatory or social environments, for example. But usually only one or two will have a decisive impact on any particular business. And it may be possible to see a trend or major event without being able to predict its direction. In 1998, for example, the mounting Asian crisis was an important trend certain to have a big impact on financial services. But the direction that trend would take was impossible to predict and therefore envisioning a new value curve that might result from it would have been a risky enterprise. In contrast, the euro is evolving along a constant trajectory as it replaces Europe's multiple currencies. This is a decisive, irreversible, and clearly developing trend upon which new market space might be created in financial services.

Having identified a trend of this nature, managers can then look across time and ask themselves what the market would look like if the trend were taken to its logical conclusion. Working back from that vision of a new value curve, they can then identify what must be changed today to unlock superior value for buyers.

From Head-to-Head Competition to Creating New Market Space

The Conventional Boundaries of Competition	Head-To-Head Competition		Creating New Market Space
Industry	focuses on rivals within its industry	→	looks across substitute industries
Strategic group	focuses on competitive position within strategic group	→	looks across strategic groups within its industry
Buyer group	focuses on better serving the buyer group	→	redefines the buyer group of the industry
Scope of product and service offerings	focuses on maximizing the value of product and service offerings within the bounds of its industry	→	looks across to complementary product and service offerings that go beyond the bounds of its industry
Functional-emotional orientation of an industry	focuses on improving price-performance in line with the functional-emotional orientation of its industry	→	rethinks the functional-emotional orientation of its industry
Time	focuses on adapting to external trends as they occur	→	participates in shaping external trends over time

Exhibit 1: Shifting the Focus of Strategy

Consider Enron, an energy company based in Houston, Texas. In the 1980s, Enron's business centered on gas pipelines. Deregulation of the gas industry was on the horizon. Such an event would certainly be decisive for Enron. The U.S. government had just deregulated the telecom and transportation industries, so a reversal in its intent to deregulate the gas industry was highly unlikely. Not only was the trend irreversible, its logical conclusion was also predictable-the end of price controls and the breakup of local gas monopolies. By assessing the gap between the market as it stood and the market as it was to be, Enron gained insight into how to create new market space.

When local gas monopolies were broken up, gas could be purchased from anywhere in the nation. At the time, the cost of gas varied dramatically from region to region. Gas was much more expensive, for example, in New York and Chicago than it was in Oregon and Idaho. Enron saw that deregulation would make possible a national market in which gas could be bought where it was cheap and sold where it was expensive. By examining how the gas market could operate with deregulation, Enron saw a way to unlock tremendous trapped value on a national scale.

Accordingly, Enron worked with government agencies to push for deregulation. It purchased regional gas-pipeline companies across the nation, tied them together, and created a national market for gas. That allowed Enron to buy the lowest cost gas from numerous sources across North America and to operate with the best spreads in the industry. Enron became the largest transporter of natural gas in North America, and its customers benefited from more reliable delivery and a drop in costs of as much as 40%.

Cisco Systems created a new market space in a similar way. It started with a decisive and irreversible trend that had a clear trajectory: the growing demand for high-speed data exchange. Cisco looked at the world as it was-and that world was hampered by slow data rates and incompatible computer networks. Demand was exploding as, among other factors, the number of Internet users doubled roughly every 100 days. So Cisco could clearly see that the problem would inevitably worsen. Cisco's routers, switches, and other networking devices were designed to create breakthrough value for customers, offering fast data exchanges in a seamless networking environment. Thus Cisco's insight is as much about value innovation as it is about technology. Today more than 80% of all traffic on the Internet flows through Cisco's products, and its margins in this new market space are in the 60% range.

Regenerating Large Companies

Creating new market space is critical not just for start-ups but also for the prosperity and survival of even the world's largest companies. Take Toyota as an example. Within three years of its launch in 1989, the Lexus accounted for nearly one-third of Toyota's operating profit while representing only 2% of its unit volume. Moreover, the Lexus boosted Toyota's brand image across its entire range of cars. Or think of Sony. The greatest contribution to Sony's profitable growth and its reputation in the last 20 years was the Walkman. Since its introduction in 1979, the Walkman has dominated the personal portable-stereo market, generating a huge positive spillover effect on Sony's other lines of business throughout the world.

Likewise, think of SMH. Its collection of watch companies ranges from Blancpain, whose watches retail for over $200,000, to Omega, the watch of astronauts, to midrange classics like Hamilton and Tissot to the sporty, chic watches of Longines and Rado. Yet it was the creation of the Swatch and the market of fun, fashionable watches that revitalized the entire Swiss watch industry and made SMH the darling of investors and customers the world over.

It is no wonder that corporate leaders throughout the world see market creation as a central strategic challenge to their organizations in the upcoming decade. They understand that in an overcrowded and demand-starved economy, profitable growth is not sustainable without creating, and re-creating, markets. That is what allows small companies to become big and what allows big companies to regenerate themselves.

Five styles of Customer Knowledge Management, and how smart companies use them to create value[*]

By Michael Gibbert, Marius Leibold and Gilbert Probst

*Corporations begin to realize that the proverbial "if we only knew what we know" also includes "if we only knew what our customers know." The authors discuss the concept of Customer Knowledge Management (CKM), which refers to the management of knowledge **from** customers, i.e. knowledge resident in customers. CKM is contrasted with knowledge **about** customers, e.g. customer characteristics and preferences prevalent in previous work on knowledge management and customer relationship management. Five styles of CKM are proposed and practically illustrated by way of corporate examples. Implications are discussed for knowledge management, the resource based view, and strategy process research.*

Introduction

In the emphasis on knowledge as a key competitive factor in the global economy, corporations may be overlooking a major element – customer knowledge. For example: Old Mutual, the largest insurance company in South Africa (and an internationally expanding FTSE 100 quoted company on the London Stock Exchange) has been incorporating the knowledge of patients concerning their own health condition and treatment directly by way of electronic means, instead of relying only on medical doctors to provide this. Customer knowledge is being used by Old Mutual both to screen applicants for medical insurance and more importantly to develop new medical insurance products.

What is the reason for the increasing success of Old Mutual in South Africa and internationally? Partly due to a process called Customer Knowledge Management (CKM). It works like this: where patients' health evaluation forms were previously completed manually by their doctors, it has been replaced by electronic forms that can

[*] Taken with permission from European Management Journal, October 2002 Vol. 20

be filled in mainly by patients themselves, from the convenience of their homes. Patients still require medical examination by their doctors, but the advantage to all parties are speed, greater accuracy (doctors are notorious for poor handwriting), more information, and especially additional knowledge input from patients themselves. The issues of ethics and professionalism (e.g. security of information, patient-doctor relationship) of course have to be carefully managed, but the advantages of customer knowledge input of their condition, treatment, effects of particular drugs, perception of medical insurance companies and their products are substantial and valuable to pharmaceutical companies, insurance companies, doctors and other stakeholders in the health management industry.

Does CKM only happen in the pharmaceutical/insurance industries? We think not. Over the last six years, we have studied more than two-dozen companies, and found that smart companies are prolific customer knowledge managers (see insert Box 1: "Our research"). Indeed, most companies today consider themselves as market driven, or customer-oriented. Yet only a few companies are actually managing well their perhaps most precious resource: the knowledge *of*, i.e. *residing in* their customers, as opposed to knowledge *about* their customers.

Our research shows that by managing the knowledge of their customers, corporations are more likely to sense emerging market opportunities before their competitors, to constructively challenge the established wisdom of "doing things around here", and to more rapidly create economic value for the corporation, its shareholders, and last, but not least, its customers. CKM is the strategic process by which cutting edge companies emancipate their customers from passive recipients of products and services, to empowerment as knowledge partners. CKM is about gaining, sharing, and expanding the knowledge residing in customers, to both customer and corporate benefit. It can take the form of prosumerism, mutual innovation, team-based co-learning, communities of practice, and joint intellectual property (IP) management. We have identified these as five styles of CKM, which are distinctively different practices, but not mutually exclusive.

Expanding on Customer Relationship Management and Knowledge Management

At first glance, CKM may seem just another name for Customer Relationship Management (CRM), or Knowledge Management (KM). But customer knowledge managers require a different mindset along a number of key variables (see Table 1). Customer knowledge managers first and foremost focus on knowledge *from* the customer (i.e. knowledge residing in customers), rather than focusing on knowledge *about* the customer, as characteristic of customer relationship management. In other words, smart companies realize that corporate customers are more knowledgeable than one might think, and consequently seek knowledge through direct interaction with customers, in addition to seeking knowledge about customers from their sales representatives. Similarly, conventional knowledge managers typically focus on trying to convert employees from knowledge hoarders into knowledge sharers. This is typically done by intra-net based knowledge sharing platforms, Yellow Page initiatives, and so-called "ShareNets", i.e. platforms and tools that have often sophisticated functions such as urgent requests, or incentive systems that reward both the giver and taker of knowledge using a "miles and more approach" (e.g. Davenport and Probst, 2002). Clearly, traditional KM fulfills a vitally important role to the extent that knowledge becomes the key value-added resource in companies. However, this knowledge is typically

Our research approach

Over the past six years, we have studied more than two dozen companies, using a joint case writing approach (Davenport and Probst, 2002; Leibold, Probst, Gibbert, 2002). The objective of our research has been to discover what can be achieved if managers write their own accounts of change projects in which they have taken part or which they have researched personally. Such reports contain the managers' own reflections on the project and its results, including the lessons they learned, the difficulties they encountered, how they coped with them, what mistakes they made, and what they would do differently next time. All those who took part in the project are questioned not only about what happened, but also about how it happened:

1. The group of case writers contains a group of managers from the "case company", i.e. the company where the change project took place (the "insiders"), and other involved people, i.e. research assistants, consultants, business partners, and coaches (the "outsiders"). This adds an important dimension because the outsiders may play devil's advocate, questioning and challenging the inside view of the project.

2. Since the outsiders did not participate in the project, they are expected to research the details and to try to understand how things work in the "foreign" company. This obliges the insiders to give careful explanations of details that they would otherwise take for granted. The outsiders in turn contribute an additional perspective because they come to the group with their own mental models of how things work in their own company.

3. When the "outsiders" are exposed to the different approaches existing in the case company, they often become aware of tacit assumptions, rules and behavioral codes which are prevalent in their own organizations, and which might otherwise never be questioned. Differences that are not otherwise obvious are thus revealed between the "case" company and the outside company. Discussion of these differences may also create a new awareness of certain rules, habits and behaviors in the case organization itself that are usually hidden below the surface.

The accounts produced in this fashion have been written jointly by a group of managers from insiders of the "case company", i.e. the company where the change project took place, and outsiders. The inclusion of both "insiders" and "outsiders" as well as the inclusion of archival data as well as participant and direct observation allowed for extensive *data, researcher, and method triangulation*, adding richness to the evaluation and interpretation of the cases, thereby enhancing *internal and construct validity* of the conclusions drawn (Stake, 1995; Yin, 1994). In this fashion, an extensive case database and numerous case protocols were produced over the last six years, ensuring the *reliability* of the findings. Finally, concerns for *external validity* (particularly statistical generalizability) were traded off against the opportunity to gain in-depth insights, but cross case analyses were used to ensure at least analytical generalizability due to the wide range of industries studied (Yin, 1994; Eisenhardt, 1989).

shared, expanded and leveraged among employees (e.g. Davenport and Prusak, 1998), or between companies (e.g. Badaracco, 1991), with little systematic attention accorded to what could be the company's most important partner in the value creation process, namely the customer.

In contrast to KM's very appropriate focus on fostering productive and collaborative relationships along the lines of "if only we knew what we know", CKM proposes an additional dimension, namely "if only we also knew what our customers know." The logic of CKM seems counter-intuitive: the challenges of getting employees to share

Table 5.6 CKM versus Knowledge Management & Customer Relationship Management

	KM	**CRM**	**CKM**
Knowledge sought in	Employee, team, company, network of companies.	Customer Database.	Customer experience, creativity, and (dis)satisfaction with products/ services.
Axioms	"If only we knew what we know."	"Retention is cheaper than acquisition."	"If only we knew what our customers know."
Rationale	Unlock and integrate employees' knowledge about customers, sales processes, and R&D.	Mining knowledge about the customer in company's databases.	Gaining knowledge directly from the customer, as well as sharing and expanding this knowledge.
Objectives	Efficiency gains, cost saving, and avoidance of re-inventing the wheel.	Customer base nurturing, maintaining company's customer base.	Collaboration with customers for joint value creation.
Metrics	Performance against budget.	Performance in terms of customer satisfaction and loyalty.	Performance against competitors in innovation and growth, contribution to customer success.
Benefits	Customer satisfaction.	Customer retention.	Customer success, innovation, organizational learning.
Recipient of Incentives	Employee.	Customer.	Customer.
Role of customer	Passive, recipient of product.	Captive, tied to product/ service by loyalty schemes.	Active, partner in value-creation process.
Corporate role	Encourage employees to share their knowledge with their colleagues.	Build lasting relationships with customers	Emancipate customers from passive recipients of products to active co-creators of value.

their knowledge with one another are daunting enough. In our discussions with more than a dozen Chief Knowledge Officers, the key problems expressed were "How do we get our employees to accept, build on, and enrich the knowledge of their colleagues?" "How can we get rid of "not invented here" when we want to feed in sales process knowledge from local companies at our corporate headquarters?" Given these challenges associated with KM, why would customers, of all people, want to share their knowledge to create value for the company and then pay for their own knowledge once it is deployed in the company's products and services? This is further exacerbated because customers, like employees, are often not able to make knowledge, i.e. their experiences with the company's products, their skills, and reflections explicit, and thereby easily transferable and shareable. The concern here is the cost of establishing CKM approaches – are existing KM approaches scalable, or do they need to be revamped completely? The answer to these two challenges (motivational and cognitive barriers to knowledge sharing) are twofold. First, the customer knowledge manager need to put himself in the shoes of corporate customers, kindling their intrinsic, rather than extrinsic motivation to share their knowledge for the benefit of the company. Second, the costs of establishing CKM need to be evaluated.

Consider Amazon.com: The Internet retailer manages customer knowledge successfully through providing book reviews, the customer's own order histories, order history of other customers, and customized suggestions based on prior orders. Effectively, Amazon.com, a commercial enterprise, developed into a platform of book enthusiasts that are keen to exchange knowledge about their favorite topics (intrinsic motivation). Motivating customers to share their knowledge the Amazon way is a remarkable achievement, particularly if contrasted with the often vain efforts to evangelize employees from egoistic knowledge hoarders to altruistic knowledge sharers by way of rewards systems that are mostly extrinsic. While some (tentative) approaches exist that tie employee promotion and demotion to their propensity to share knowledge (e.g. Davenport and Probst, 2002), human resources is still struggling with the legal implications associated with the establishment of the employee's knowledge sharing record as a basis for instilling an intrinsic motivation in employees to share their knowledge. What seems to prevail in KM so far are extrinsic motivation systems allowing, for example, prolific knowledge sharers to spend weekends in attractive locations.

An issue related to motivational factors are the knowledge sharing and relationship maintaining costs involved in CKM. To enable joint value creation, CKM Websites for Internet companies need to go beyond what Angehrn calls a "non-committal brochure approach" (Angehrn, 1998: 291). Logically, to afford joint value creation between customer and company, Websites need to cater for interactivity. Interactivity is a matter of degree and can be seen as contingent on the nature of the company's product or service. Using interactive multimedia technology can significantly enhance the degree of interactivity. Consider banks. Most banks are now offering cost-effective interactive sites aim to create highly personalized services to the consumer, including the virtual counter, and the real impact of the economic slow-down on the investment portfolio of the customer, thereby the increasing motivation of customers to participate as well as reducing the cost. Such interactivity, using, for example, emerging approaches such as intelligent agent technology, can be costly to build from scratch,

How the international cement manufacturer Holcim manages customer knowledge

Holcim's companies in North America recently were conducting analysis how to deliver e-commerce solutions to their customers. But Holcim's aspiration was much more ambitious than simply doing e-commerce. The idea was to create a knowledge sharing platform, where any member of the community of cement and aggregates consumers (concrete producers, distributors, but also engineers, architects) would be able not only to transact business (place orders, pay online), but also share and exchange knowledge (e.g. share cement order forecast, share good and bad experience with specific applications, etc.).

In order to test and further develop this aspiration, Holcim's customer knowledge managers conducted meetings with selected customers in the US. It was ensured that their different customer segments were adequately represented: The customer mix was intentionally varied, comprising selected large multinationals, medium domestic and small family owned companies. The objective of the meeting was to discuss current and emerging trends in the cement industry and the potential impact of these developments on Holcim's customers, thereby jointly ascertaining how Holcim could create value for their customers.

The discussion was open and free flowing – although Holcim had developed a set of value added services that were thought appropriate, Holcim did not implement these until after the customers had given their views, thereby adding value to the company's services. As one customer knowledge manager at the cement manufacturer has it: "As part of the focus group discussions, Holcim's customers were impressed the company was talking to them – no other supplier had chosen to do this – all they were seeing were press releases. This made customers feel ownership in our project."

In the meantime, Holcim has built and implemented the knowledge sharing platform in North America and Western Europe. What's more, during the entire "build" phase, the company kept close contact with the customers and permanently validated with them – which was much-appreciated by Holcim's customers. A representative of a large multinational mentioned: "I like your knowledge sharing platform, because you were listening to what I told you during the first visit and really took my comments very serious."[1]

but often existing KM systems and databases are scalable to allow them to be opened up to the customer.

Clearly, Internet companies are at a competitive advantage when it comes to engaging in CKM, due to the Internet being a particularly cost-effective locus for such knowledge sharing. But CKM is not limited to successful Internet companies. Brick and mortar companies do it, too. Indeed, Holcim, an international cement company that produces the very stuff brick and mortars are made of, is a keen customer knowledge manager (see Insert: How Holcim manages customer knowledge).

---

[1] Alois Zwinggi and Lucas Epple provided this example.

A shift in mindset towards looking at the customer as a knowledgeable entity has far-reaching implications. Most importantly, the customer is emancipated from being a passive recipient of products and services as in traditional knowledge management. Likewise, the customer is liberated from the ball and chain of customer loyalty schemes prevalent in CRM. CKM is also different from traditional KM in the objective pursued. Whereas traditional KM is about efficiency gains (avoidance of "re-inventing the wheel"), CKM is about innovation and growth. Customer knowledge

Table 5.7 Holcim's CKM approach

Key area	General description	Benefits
Trouble-shooting	Online solutions to customer-related inquiries (i.e., cement- and concrete-related problems, strengths).	Reduced time to solve problems savings in labor and materials if rework is prevented, increased satisfaction of concrete manufacturer's customer, enhanced reputation of cement manufacturer.
Quality Control & Product optimization	Collection of test data, document submittal and approvals, mix design.	Reduction in usage of cement, optimization of setting times, optimization of raw material resources (co-development of products), reduction of cement customer claims.
Inventory/supply management	Automatization of the inventory and supply processes.	Elimination of costly plant shutdowns for lack of cement.
Purchasing	Enable customer to access HBK purchasing platform	Price reductions in raw materials, trucks, and equipment.
Technical library	Comprehensive data warehouse on HBK core products.	Easy access to rich sources of information of the cement manufacturer's knowledge base.
Engineering consulting	Provide business services and expertise.	Educating concrete manufacturers in business management will improve their efficiency.
Promotions/ testimonials	Access to tools and information to "grow the pie."	Educating specifiers in concrete lifecycle costs will increase the adoption of concrete vs. other materials.
Market information	Consolidation of micro and macro analysis of market information.	Exposure of the concrete manufacturer to business opportunities and market tracking information.

managers seek opportunities for partnering with their customers as equal co-creators of organizational value. This is also in stark contrast to the desire to maintain and nurture an existing customer base. The well-known CRM adage "retention is cheaper than acquisition" comes to mind. Unfortunately, retention becomes increasingly difficult in an age where competitors' product offerings are often close imitations and only three mouse-clicks away. Therefore, customer knowledge managers are much less concerned with customer retention figures. Instead, they focus on how to generate growth for the corporation through acquiring new customers and through engaging in an active and value-creating dialogue with them.

How do customer knowledge managers create innovation and growth? Again consider Amazon.com. The book retailer's customers not only provide their insights, tips and tricks in terms of book reviews, they also provide useful pointers for further reading on a given subject, giving a custom-tailored, non-intimidating impetus for other customers to investigate – and possibly buy – these sources. What is more, this customer knowledge can be shared with the authors of new books, giving them ideas for further publications and their market potential. This process bears all the hallmarks of KM: it provides useful information that is used in actions, creates sense, asks for interpretation, and leads to new combinations. Only, the knowledge is not that of the employee, but that of the customer, leading to value creation through innovation and growth, rather than to cost savings as in traditional KM. Returning to Holcim, the concrete manufacturer provides an example of how a brick and mortar company reaps the benefits of CKM.

CKM in Theory and Practice

Customer-driven companies need to harness their capabilities to manage the knowledge of those who buy their products (Baker, 2000; Davenport and Klahr, 1998). The question is, why do many customer-driven companies not access the knowledge of their customers directly? The problem is that the existing mindset, as evidenced by the literature, provides very little assistance to these companies.

Traditionally, market research was used to shed more light on what the customer knew and thought about the product, and how this differed from what the company had to afford the customer, resulting in enormous CRM databases (Galbreath and Rogers, 1999; Wilkestrom, 1996; Woodruff, 1997). More recently, firms thought they had found a new approach to access customer knowledge. Drawing on best practices from service companies, such as the big consulting businesses, most large organizations have instituted KM systems. These systems, however, are based in an indirect understanding of what customers want. KM systems are typically geared towards disseminating what their sales force or intermediary has understood from listening to the customers who bought – or didn't buy – the company's products.

It's ironic: the conceptual predecessor of KM has surpassed its own offspring. Ten years ago, proponents of the resource based view to strategy have proclaimed that a company be best conceptualized as a bundle of unique resources, or competencies, rather than as a bundle of product market positions (Barney, 1991). More recent contributions to the resource-based view question this one-sided thinking about the locus of competence (Prahalad and Ramaswamy, 2000; Inkpen, 1996). It has now been claimed that such competence actually moved beyond corporate boundaries, and that it is therefore worthwhile to also look for competence in the heads of customers, rather than only in the heads of employees.

Similarly, CRM has been traditionally popular as a means to tie customers to the company through various loyalty schemes, but left perhaps the greatest source of value under-leveraged: the knowledge residing in customers. While both KM and CRM focused on gaining knowledge *about* the customer, managing customer knowledge is geared towards gaining knowledge directly *from* the customer.

Whilst the literature provides little guidance for aspiring customer knowledge managers, we have found in our research of two dozen companies (including the medical, financial services, measurement, agricultural chemicals, telecommunications, and beverages industries) a wide variety of different approaches to managing customer knowledge. Indeed, the very chasm between the wealth of practical examples of (intuitive) CKM and the dearth of (explicit) literature and guidance for managers seems remarkable. While we detected a wide variety of different approaches used by companies who manage customer knowledge, what was even more intriguing were the similarities among the individual approaches. We have crystallized these similarities in five styles of CKM, as displayed in Table 3.

Five Styles of CKM and their Application

Section discusses our research findings in terms of the five styles of CKM by elaborating on Table 5.8.

Prosumerism

Alvin Toffler (1980) first used the expression "prosumer" to denote that the customer could fill the dual roles of producer and consumer. Such co-production is not new, e.g. Bosch develops engine management systems in co-production with Mercedes-Benz, who conceives and assembles the automobile. What is new is the way that knowledge co-production with the customer expresses itself in role patterns and codes of interactivity. For example, Quicken enables the customer to learn more about the available resources in financial services, thus creating options and a predisposition within the customer to rapidly tailor-make an offering in the future, also based on creatively suggesting new ideas and benefits.

The way IKEA, the living environment furniture retailer, presents itself to customers is all about co-production, about how benefits and activities have been reallocated between producer and customer. The CKM process in IKEA transforms the customer into a co-value creator, endowing him/her with new competencies and benefaction opportunities. It liberates the customer from the platform of only past, accumulated

Table 5.8 Five styles of CKM

Style/ Characteristic	Prosumerism	Team-based Co-learning	Mutual Innovation	Communities of Creation	Joint Intellectual Property/ownership
Focus	Developing tangible assets and benefits	Creating corporate social capital	Creating new products & processes	Mission-specific. Professional expertise	Tangible Customer IP sharing
Objective	Improved products & resulting benefits	Facilitate team learning for dealing with systemic change	Create max. return from new ideas	Obtain & explicate professional expertise	Max. returns on IP (jointly)
Processes	Pre, -Concurrent- & post production integration	Teamwork, empowerment, case development, quality programs	Idea Fairs; Brainstorming; Customer Incubation	Best Practices CoP's, expert Networks	Apprenticeships Formal training programs On job training
Systems	Planning, control and decision supply systems	Knowledge sharing systems, Digital "nervous" systems, customer visits in teams	Idea generation support systems	Expert Systems, shared E-workspaces, group support Systems	Group IP support systems
Performance Measures	Effectiveness & efficiency, customer satisfaction & success	Systems Productivity, quality, customer satisfaction & success	ROI from new products & processes, Customer success	K-sharing behavior, timeliness of decisions, Rate of hyperlinked results	Value of New IP, incremental ROI on new revenue streams
Case Examples	Quicken; IKEA	Amazon.com: Xerox, Holcim, Mettler Toledo	Silicon Graphics, Ryder	Microsoft; Sony; eBay, Holcim	Skandia
Intensity of interaction	Relatively low	Low to high	Relatively low	Relatively high	Relatively high
Type of knowledge	More explicit	Explicit and tacit	More tacit	More tacit	More explicit

knowledge by stimulating him with a pattern of open-ended value-creating ideas, thereby effecting co-production and mutual new value evidenced in new IKEA furniture products and services.

Team-based Co-Learning

The way that Amazon.com has manifested itself structurally has created a whole new set of team-based value chain (or systemic) learning relationships utilizing the knowledge of its customers. For example, the inter-linkages with the customer base and their interactive joint learning performance have made the company an attractive channel also for many other companies – we may now conceive Amazon.com no longer as a bookstore but a generalized access channel (or "portal") for a wide range of products and services, many offered by separate but systemic-linked companies. Through the customer-systemic knowledge and co-learning interactions Amazon.com's original identity has been transformed, which in turn implies new value chain systems relationships.

The change process in Xerox Corporation, from being a "copying machine company" to becoming the "document company" is similarly based on organizational learning resulting from CKM. Customer knowledge was the key to reconfigure the entire system of document management and its infrastructure, spanning resources and processes much broader than its own traditional realm of activities. Whereas the Prosumerism CKM style focuses more on co-production of products and services, team-based co-learning focuses on reconfiguring entire organizations and systems of value.

Mutual Innovation

In the 1970's, Eric von Hippel found that most product innovations come not from within the company that produces the product but from end-users of the product (Von Hippel, 1977). More recently, Thomke and Von Hippel (2002) suggested ways in which customers can become co-innovators and co-developers of custom products, and illustrating examples of GE and General Mills. For Silicon Graphics, lead customers from the movie industry have become an important source of new ideas and innovation. Silicon Graphics sends its best R&D people to Hollywood to learn first-hand what the most creative users of its products might want in the future. In addition, Silicon Graphics nurtures relationships with lead users from other industries that require massive computation and high-end graphics – such as for drug design and aerospace landing gear. Simply asking users about their future needs is unlikely to result in new products (although it can lead to continuous product improvement); the major breakthroughs come from mutual and closely integrated innovation practices.

Ryder Systems in the trucking industry is another example of utilizing customer knowledge through mutual innovation. In close collaboration with customers Ryder developed complex and extensive logistics solutions for its customers, probing deeply into the operations and even manufacturing and supply chain strategies of customers. Jointly they developed special knowledge of truck driver requirements, thereby reconfiguring truck personnel management activities. Ryder in effect has become, via mutual customer innovation, a logistics systems solutions expert, transcending its identity as a trucking company.

Communities of Creation

Communities of creation as a CKM style is reflected by the process of putting together customer groups of expert knowledge that interact not only with the company, but importantly also with each other (Sawhney and Prandelli, 2000; Wikstrom, 1996). Similar to communities of practice, communities of creation are groups of people who first work together over a longer period of time, second they have an interest in a common topic and third, want to jointly create and share knowledge. Unlike the traditional communities of practice, however, communities of creation span organizational, rather than functional boundaries to create common knowledge and value. In the traditional computer software development process, Netscape and Microsoft make use of free "beta" versions of its products for use, testing, comments and reporting not only to the company, but also among the user community themselves. They enlist thousands of willing, devoted testers, some just interested in using the free "beta" product and others intent on looking for "bugs" to show off and perhaps even collect a prize. Customers appreciate product newsgroups and "chat rooms", where they can also learn how the companies are acting on their feedback – resulting in loyalty and even a sense of ownership.

Sony and Panasonic in the consumer electronics market have set up "antenna shops" at locations such as shopping centers and airports, where demanding customers frequent and prototype products are featured. Customers can experiment, test, and converse with each other, and development engineers and product managers are available to talk to and watch customers, getting first-hand knowledge of customers reactions and what they would really want. Another example of a company effectively utilizing a community of creation style of CKM is the Weight Watchers. This company brings groups of customers together in order for customers to exchange knowledge and experience, and for weight watchers to obtain insights for CKM. The important point is that this does not happen in itself – it has to be carefully managed even if participation is voluntary and intrinsic as tends to be the case with Weight Watchers.

Joint Intellectual Property

This style of CRM is probably the most intense involvement between customer and corporation – the notion of the corporation being "owned" by its customers. The Swedish companies Skandia Insurance and Kooperativa Förbundet (KF) increasingly think of themselves as businesses owned by customers, i.e. being in business for and because of its customers. Thus, intellectual property does not reside in the company, but is "owned" partly by the customers. This formula enabled KF to make remarkable achievements over a long period of time, becoming a pioneer in customer education and the consumer movement through joint knowledge ownership and its continuous development. Instead of just co-producing products and services together, customers and company co-create future business together. For example, the broker, banking and other retail customers of Skandia combine with the company's key strategy decision-makers to review the scope of joint business, possible joint new strategic initiatives, and joint knowledge expansion of e.g. emerging markets. Customer success in fact becomes corporate success, and vice versa.

Discussion and Implications:
Common Stumbling Blocks for CKM

CKM can provide a significant competitive advantage to companies, but its possible stumbling blocks have to be appreciated. We have identified two major stumbling blocks, first the cultural challenge (in terms of re-thinking the role of the customer and the far-reaching implications this has for the mindset of employees within the organization), and second the competency challenge (in terms of the skills and processes needed to take full advantage of participative techniques).

In our discussions with managers, the *cultural challenge* was most fundamental. Companies affected by this challenge typically perceived customers as a source of revenue, rather than as a source of knowledge. We encountered three reactions. The first could be called "corporate narcissism" and was characterized by statements such as "we know our own business better than our customers do." This was compounded by well-known business aphorisms such as Sony's proclaiming that "no customer ever asked us to develop the Walkman." The second reaction was the exact opposite of corporate narcissism, namely, lack of a critical perspective when it comes to customer knowledge. For example, Harley Davidson's chairman and CEO Jeffrey L. Bleustein said at the Fortune Leadership Conference in Chicago in April 2002 that Harley customers asked the company to produce cigarettes with the Harley Davidson Brand, a venture that was soon discontinued, even though market research showed that 80% of the company's customers are smokers. The third reaction, which might be dubbed "corporate shyness" was colorfully illustrated by a senior manager at Siemens' headquarters in Munich, who succinctly summarized the increase in transparency of internal processes and the sharpened scrutiny from the side of the customer as "walking around naked on a crowded Marienplatz at noon." With regard to the first two reactions, companies interested in CKM need to appreciate that customer knowledge should be taken with a grain of salt. Customer knowledge constitutes an important ingredient in innovation processes, but it is not a panacea, and certainly does not replace the R&D department. With regard to the third reaction, just as CKM does not mean accepting all customer knowledge at face value, companies need to realize that CKM does not mean disclosing all knowledge of the company to all customers. This calls for appropriate network security processes ("Chinese Walls"), as well as trust-building processes that enable companies to purposefully encourage the flow of knowledge in certain areas, while controlling or limiting it in others.

The second challenge, the *competency challenge*, was inextricably related with the cultural challenge discussed above. Companies faced with the competency challenge realize that their existing KM or CRM systems were developed with a specific purpose in mind – typically as an intra-company knowledge sharing platform for sales and marketing knowledge. Companies interested in opening up these systems to their customers find that platforms designed for internal usage are scalable only to a limited extend and certainly do not allow the kind of interactivity and convenience of single-point of entry access that customers expect. To be seamless, the CKM system should embrace a suite of technologies, including intelligent agent software which, if properly integrated, provides a single user interface for access to knowledge resources and business processes. The purpose of a model for CKM is to provide customers with access to all relevant knowledge resources – in essence, to act as a universal integration mechanism. Content needs to be available through both pull – finding a document or a person – and through push – publishing and alerts originating from elsewhere.

While user-friendliness is a necessary condition, it is not a sufficient one. Customers need to be afforded a tangible benefit from the interaction with the company, besides mere user-friendliness. CKM means realizing value not only for the company, but also for customers. To the extent that the locus of competence shifts from within the corporate boundary to the customer, CKM not only requires re-thinking the locus of competence, it also requires re-thinking the primary beneficiary of corporate value creation. Value appropriation in customer networks (Prahalad and Ramaswamy, 2000; Sawhney and Prandelli, 2000) and in the open source community (e.g. Lakhani and von Hippel, 2000) has been attracting some debate recently. For CKM to be sustainable, companies may need to feed back some of the value to its co-creator, the customer. These forms of value-sharing would include obvious approaches such as "greater customer satisfaction" and personalized products and services, but might also mean actually monetary compensation for the customer for his/her services, e.g. in the form of special offers, preferential financing agreements, or even outright payments.

Overall, if you are a CEO or a senior manager who is planning to or has already initiated a CKM project, we would like to suggest that you consider the following two key questions:

- How do we perceive the customer today, does the mindset in our corporation allow for treating the customer as a potential source of value, and are we ready to share this value?

- What are our current skills and competencies when it comes to designing and implementing collaborative knowledge exchange processes that cross our corporate boundary?

Conclusion

Customer knowledge management (CKM) creates new knowledge sharing platforms and processes between companies and their customers. We suggest that the five styles of CKM can be prosumerism, group learning, mutual innovation, communities of creativity, and joint intellectual capital. Any company, depending on the nature of its various customers, can apply several of these five styles of CKM simultaneously. Certain cautions have to be observed when applying CKM, and if these are well incorporated, the competitive advantages of sound CKM applications in the expanding digital economy seem significant.

CKM constitutes a continuous strategic process by which companies enable their customers to move from passive information sources and recipients of products and services to empowered knowledge partners. Available case-study evidence points to CKM as a potentially powerful competitive tool, contributing to improved success of both companies and their customers. It incorporates principles of KM and customer relationship management, but moves decisively beyond both to a higher level of mutual value creation and performance. More specifically, the notion of CKM as presented here contributes to the KM literature by providing an expanded view of "organizational epistemology" (von Krogh and Roos, 1995; von Krogh, Ichijo and Nonaka, 2000), i.e. one that includes the customer as a knowledgeable agent in the knowledge creation process. More generally, we contribute to the resource-based view of corporate strategy by offering a perspective of how KM, as an outgrowth of the resource based view (Grant, 1996, Spender, 1996), incorporates customer knowledge as an important organizational resource residing outside the corporate boundary (e.g. Prahalad and Ramaswamy, 2000). Finally, we endeavor to add value to the strategy process literature by suggesting that customers, in addition to managers, can induce strategy-making processes in the firm (e.g. Mintzberg and Lampel, 1999; Burgelman, 2002).

It will remain for future research to refine, expand, and operationalize this list of styles. At this point, however, some general implications of these styles are apparent.

First, it is important to note that, on the whole, the interrelationship between the five styles with different industries could be tested. While our comparative within and between case analysis involving a variety of industries seems to ensure the external validity of our findings (Eisenhardt, 1989: 547), clearly further research could investigate whether and how one or more of the five styles is brought into sharper focus than the other in different industries.

Second, we suggest that joint value creation also implies joint value appropriation. We also suggest that the five styles differ in the intensity of value creation and value sharing mechanisms. If the five styles were to be made more relevant for managerial practice, research could investigate the contractual mechanisms that need to be in place to ensure that the partnership company/customer proceeds in ways compatible with its original rationale. We propose that these investigations probe deeper in the extent to which contractual agreements are necessary for each of the five styles.

Finally, the conclusions reinforce assertions of knowledge being "socially constructed" (e.g. Spender, 1996), in our case through the interaction of the customer with members of the organization. This observations goes beyond the traditional realm within which such construction occurs, namely the intra-organizational space (von Krogh and Roos, 1995), and suggests that it should be interesting to investigate if, and to what extent the customers' views differ from the "way we do things around here" in the firm. This could help shed new light on the question why some core competencies turn into core rigidities (Leonard, 1995).

Knowledge as a Strategic Resource at Novartis

The Background

Novartis was created in December 1996 by the merger of Ciba and Sandoz, two Swiss-based chemical and pharmaceutical companies with almost three hundred years of tradition, both located in Basel in Switzerland. At the time this was the largest corporate merger in business history.

The company operated 275 affiliates in 142 countries world-wide. With over 70,000 employees (71,116 at the end of 2001) and total sales of 32,038 billion Sfr, it is among the world's major players in the field of life sciences. Novartis has a very decentralised structure. The Group is composed of three main divisions (Pharmaceuticals, Generics and Consumer Health) which are further divided into ten operationally independent and legally autonomous sectors. Research and development expenditures exceeded 4 billion Sfr (4,189 billion Sfr in 2001).

Novartis aims to be a "high performance organisation" and considers knowledge as a crucial factor.

"Our success in building a high performance organisation will be substantially based on the capability of sharing and exploiting our professional knowledge better and faster than our competitors."

This quote by Dan Vasella, the first Chairman and CEO of the company, demonstrates that knowledge was considered to be of great strategic importance and central to the company's priorities.

The following example furthermore illustrates the benefits that can be derived from knowledge sharing across sectors, departments and borders.

Early in 1998, Frank Lasarasina of Novartis Pharmaceuticals in New Jersey wished to implement a Balanced Scorecard[1]. In order to obtain advice, he accessed the Novartis Virtual Forum to see if anyone could help. Bernard Wasen, from Seeds in the Netherlands, also showed interest. David Chu, of Consumer Health in Nyon, Switzerland, joined the debate and, within a few days, came up with a tool to implement this methodology.

---

[1] Methodology invented by Kaplan and Norton of the Harvard Business School.

Increasingly, companies are becoming aware of the fact that a great reservoir of information and knowledge is available internally and become conscious of the strategic importance of exploiting this potential. To enable this objective, a number of tools are required to facilitate the sharing of the internally available knowledge.

Facilitating the Sharing of Knowledge

Novartis is a relatively young company that combines the knowledge and know-how of the two original companies, Sandoz and Ciba. Since research and development are two very important factors in this industry, the use of such knowledge and know-how is vital. Within Novartis it is, however, not easy to spread information and knowledge. In fact, the company is geographically very widespread and expertise is often kept within the autonomous sectors because of its organizational structure. Therefore, since people cannot automatically meet for such exchanges, the development of tools for a systematic management of internal knowledge becomes all the more essential.

This is why, following the merger, a knowledge management program was introduced at Novartis. It aimed at facilitating the use of Novartis knowledge and know-how across the boundaries formed by the various company cultures and structures. Discussions on this subject had already been held prior to the merger. It was clear that one objective of sharing knowledge was to avoid re-inventing the wheel and to re-use previously gained knowledge in order to reduce time to market. It takes an average of 11,3 years to get a product to the market at a total cost of US\$500 million. Every missed day on the market is equivalent to about US\$1 million in lost sales – a vital reason for Novartis to exploit knowledge sharing and systematize it with concrete tools.

On an informal level knowledge sharing happens automatically: informal gatherings around a cup of coffee or a beer while people talk about work and exchange information are called "Champion Communities" by Novartis management. In general, scientists are enthusiastic to share knowledge when they are together. However, in a multinational company it is not always possible to bring people together: Novartis therefore decided to create virtual links in order to be able to best leverage this sharing.

Three interlinked tools make up the Marketplace[2]: the *Yellow Pages* (a directory of internal experts), the *Blue Pages* (a directory of outside experts) and the *Virtual Forum* (a newsgroup type discussion forum).

The Knowledge MarketPlace

In an article Dr J. Staeheli, Norvartis' first Officer of the Science Boards – who was also responsible for the Knowledge MarketPlace – explained the reason for focusing

---

[2] the Novartis Intranet platform for Knowledge Management

on knowledge-sharing tools by pointing out the required and critical factors when implementing a knowledge management process, "finally, the process of knowledge building and knowledge retention must be supported by functional databases and appropriate infrastructure"[3].

At Novartis, this infrastructure, designed by Arthur Andersen, is known as the Knowledge MarketPlace. It can either be accessed through the company's Intranet or via Lotus Notes. Paul Sartori, another manager, defined the Knowledge MarketPlace as "a means for people to contribute, participate, influence and shape their future. Sharing knowledge is part of one's job. The real assets of Novartis are the intellectual capabilities of its people. How we tap into that, and how we nurture that development is the basis of our differentiation from other companies".

The Yellow Pages

As in most large companies, Novartis also routinely struggles to find people with the right knowledge and expertise needed to handle ad hoc assignments or to collaborate on a project. Traditional ways of identifying such expertise included internal phone directories, card files or personal networks, emergency faxes/emails sent to offices around the world, memos etc., but the Yellow Pages as a tool is all of these and more.

The Yellow Pages can be described as an internal Novartis directory. Individual members of the directory are listed according to name or expertise, similar to listings in the telephone directory. Every employee at Novartis is invited to enter his personal profile in a structured electronic sheet which, as with other Knowledge MarketPlace applications, is accessible either through Lotus Notes or the Intranet.

The Yellow Pages is therefore a vital source of information for a number of actors within and outside the company such as management, employees, human resources, partners, clients etc. The Yellow Pages are designed to search through any criteria set, enabling the company to form teams, assign projects or locate experts quickly and efficiently. It can help to identify talents, languages spoken, industry expertise, trade affiliation and employee contact details. Novartis makes this information available and accessible regardless of where people are located geographically, or the kind of system they happen to be using, by taking advantage of Intranet or Lotus Notes technology.

Novartis applies the auto-responsibility principle in the way it manages people since, as Dr Staeheli stated, "there is a lot of willingness to transfer knowledge among scientists as soon as they are together". This implies that every employee decides if he or she wants to register in the Yellow Pages and what information he or she wants to make available to others. These principles resolve the problem of personal data protection, since everyone is responsible for the information that is included in the system.

---

[3] *Management Bilanz*, July 1998, pp.26-29

The greatest difference between the Yellow Pages and the corporate directory is that it is created and updated by every Novartis employee personally and not by a centralized organism.

The Blue Pages

The Blue Pages can be regarded as a directory of outside experts who have provided outstanding service to Novartis and are therefore recommended for additional projects. The external sources are contributed by the Knowledge MarketPlace members.

In the words of Dr Joerg Staeheli:

"First we look inside for knowledge that is available within the organization. If we do not find it inside, we contact universities and other research institutions that are specialists in the domain we are looking for. Depending on the requirements of the project they might meet once a year or once a month. If we do not have any other choice, we contract the work out."

The Virtual Forum

The Virtual Forum is where group discussions on specific themes are held. One person opens the discussion while others check in periodically to monitor new subjects as well as to contribute to ongoing debates. The building of such a forum creates an international library of information on the subject. To follow up, members also email or telephone colleagues directly to pursue or develop the subject. A Novartis executive commented: "The enormous potential of the forum is clear. There will be a paradigm shift in the way information is exchanged and knowledge is shared throughout Novartis […] The Virtual Forum exchange provided us with expertise earlier than would otherwise have been possible. We posted our results on the Virtual Forum for others who have the same problem"[4].

This tool allows everybody in the company looking for a special topic or area of expertise to perform an automatic search by keywords or sentences. Once the proper interlocutor has been identified the initial contact and sharing of knowledge with this person can take place with all the advantages that this sharing brings, as we have already pointed out.

If it had not been for the Virtual Forum a satisfactory answer to the vexing problem experienced by Frank Lasarasina in America, Bernard Wasen in the Netherlands and David Chu in Switzerland in 1998, may not have been obtained as efficiently and swiftly as through their combined expertise and knowledge.

---

[4] in : "If Novartis Knew what Novartis Knows" published by the Science Boards of Novartis, January 1998

People! – A strategic Risk Management Approach at Deutsche Bank

Deutsche Bank was founded in 1870 by Adelbert Delbruck whom the Prussian government granted a banking license that same year. The name Deutsche Bank was chosen by the founder with "the purpose of providing banking transactions of all types, in particular the promotion and facilitation of trade relations between Germany, the other European countries and overseas markets". At the end of 1999, as the largest bank, Deutsche Bank dominated the Euro zone with share capital of €1,572 million and a market capitalization of €51.4 billion.

In 2000, Deutsche Bank was run as a holding company by the board of managing directors. The board formulated overall strategy and defined group targets. Senior management development, the allocation of capital, the determining of risk policy and the coordination of the business policy of the group divisions were its main responsibilities. Each one of the group divisions had an independent profit responsibility and, together, they serviced over 9 million customers. To insure a certain degree of uniformity of policies group-wide, the Corporate Center provided guidance to each of the divisions in the virtual holding company. Heinz Fischer was the Global Head of Human Resources. He was in charge of strategic human resource leadership, client focus (reflecting the different divisions) and operational excellence.

Deutsche Bank pursued a global expansion strategy and tried to enhance its international investment banking business. For some time Deutsche Bank attempted to "grow" in the United States and to build its staff in the sector by hiring well-known bankers and traders. Not only did this strategy prove very expensive, it also was unsuccessful. In fact, a newspaper reported that in 1998 Deutsche Bank suffered a "brain drain" as many of their dealmakers had gone over to the bank's rivals. Most of these defections occurred in the United States, and included the departure of Carter McClelland, who ran the bank's Wall Street operations, and a mass exodus of 130 Silicon Valley dealmakers in July".[1]

It became clear to the company that the best way of rapidly expanding its business and acquiring the necessary know-how and expertise to enter Wall Street, was to take over a company already well established in the specific market it wanted to enter. The declines in the American stock markets at that particular time had ravaged the stocks of several big banks and brokerage firms, making them cheaper potential acquisi-

---

[1] *International Herald Tribune*, October 21, 1998.

[2] *New York Times*, October 21, 1998.

Table 5.9

Cost of Losing an Investment Banking Employee (approximate calculation based on average annual salary)

Out-of-pocket expenses	
Search costs (head hunters, consulting firms, advertising)	90,000
Hiring costs (interviews, pre-selection, administration) & training	6,000
Reduction in productivity	
No output during vacancy period	60,000
Increased costs to superior during vacancy period and training	30,000
Increased costs to other employees during vacancy period	30,000
Reduced productivity during introductory period for new employee	
Phase 1: 80% reduced productivity	240,000
Phase 2: 40% reduced productivity	120,000
Phase 3: 20% reduced productivity	60,000
Total cost of losing an investment banking employee[*]	**636,000**

[*] without accounting for the costs of climate and customer relations
DM 1 = €0.51 = $0.46 (April 9, 2001)

tions.[2] Deutsche Bank decided to buy Bankers Trust, considering it a good vehicle for creating an investment-banking presence in the United States. The merger was to give Deutsche Bank a strong presence as a securities guardian and provide it with more than $500 billion in assets under management.

The merger was completed in May 2000, sealing the bank's position as the world's largest. Rolf Breuer, the chief executive officer of Deutsche Bank, had previously said: "… the entire wealth of experience of Bankers Trust and additional economies of scale are now available".[3]

But there was a surprise ahead.

"The Asset Management Group of Deutsche Bank lost its biggest customer, New York City Retirement System, in the US. The pension fund of the city of New York is changing partners by moving capital of $44 billion from Deutsche Bank to Barclays Global Investors and Merill Lynch & Co. With this move, Deutsche Bank Asset Management lost $60 billion, approximately a third of the Index Investments that Deutsche Bank gained when acquiring Bankers Trust last year. New York City Fund managers cited the move of key fund managers from Deutsche Bank to Merill Lynch as the reason for this change."[4]

---

[3] *Financial Times*, December 1, 1998.

[4] *Süddeutsche Zeitung*, No. 87, March 9, 2000:87 (translation)

Basic Data	DM
Annual salary of investment banking employee	300,000
Annual salary of investment banking employee's superior	350,000
Notification time	3 months

Source: Company information

After this alarming, high-impact event, Deutsche Bank needed to determine what the financial repercussions of losing key personnel were. In March 2001, it was calculated that the cost of losing an investment banker exceeded € 325,000 (DM 636,000, see Table 1. This sum includes loss of productivity due to the vacancy, and expenses incurred during recruiting and training of new people.

There is, however, one aspect that might impact even more on the company: investment bankers possess a great deal of information about their customers, since they also manage customer relationships. It is not only knowledge and expertise that are lost when a key employee leaves, but the important client that goes with him/her. Indeed, the bank's management had always considered losing an investment banker as a looming danger:

"The prospect of losing key people is daunting. We need to discover the reasons and work on turnover before it actually occurs."
   Heinz Fischer, Global Head Human Resources

Losing key people was clearly regarded as a risk and this is why Heinz Fischer decided that the issue needed to be actively managed. Since it had become clear that a company's knowledge, skills and competencies, and therefore success, are related to its employees, this type of risk had to be included in the bank's overall risk management initiative. The loss of key personnel, and, consequently, the loss of available strategic resources, means a loss of market share as clearly illustrated by Deutsche Bank's experience.

Deutsche Bank believed that one of the success factors of a global financial institution was its ability to comprehensively measure, monitor and control risks. In the context of human resources, it was clear to Heinz Fischer that losing key people was the most serious and costly risk exposure, and he decided that the bank needed an early-warning system that would increase managers' human resource risk awareness. Human capital is far too important to be neglected, since it contains expertise and experience.

As early as 1998, Fischer initiated a preliminary study within the Global Corporates & Institutions (GCI) Division (now CIB) whose goal was to evaluate the risk involved in losing key people in this important division, which was composed of five businesses primarily focusing on investment banking.[5] It was vital to understand the factors that might lead to people leaving the bank in order to implement preventive action.

---

[5] This study was conducted by Birgit Knaese-Witte (Probst, G., Knaese, B. (1998). Risikofaktor Wissen. Wiesbaden: Gabler)

In the first phase of the study a thorough review of the existing literature and documents, and approximately 60 interviews with the investment bankers of several banks were used to identify the reasons why employees left Deutsche Bank. The following risk factors (reasons for leaving) were uncovered and linked to staff satisfaction and commitment:

1. Lack of recognition
2. Unfulfilling work content
3. Unstructured organizational processes
4. High work volume
5. Lack of developmental opportunities
6. Lack of leadership
7. Insufficient opportunities to work on global business issues
8. Unattractive customer base
9. Insufficient training and networking possibilities
10. Narrow product choice
11. Unclear strategy and vision
12. Not member of a team
13. Lack of responsibility
14. Lack of innovative compensation packages

It was expected that improvements in these areas would bring about increased satisfaction and commitment among Deutsche Bank personnel. In phase two of the study

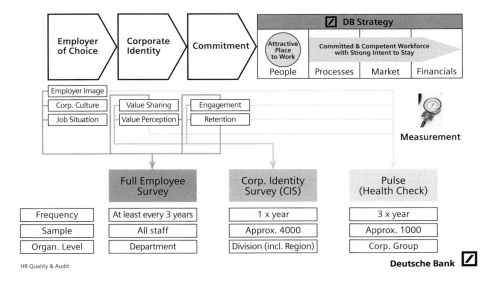

Figure 5.3 The employee surveying model

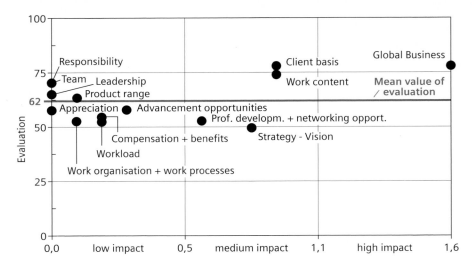

Figure 5.4 The risk factors and turnover intention

the 14 risk factors were tested through a survey developed to measure employee satisfaction and commitment. All investment banking employees in Germany completed the questionnaire and investment banking division heads were asked to identify their key people (or top 10%) so that the study could isolate the answers of this group.

The results of the survey showed four key risk factors: the ability to work globally, access to a large customer base, understanding the strategy and vision and access to developmental opportunities. Of these four, only the first two were of high importance to key employees. It therefore became clear that to avoid the loss of strategically

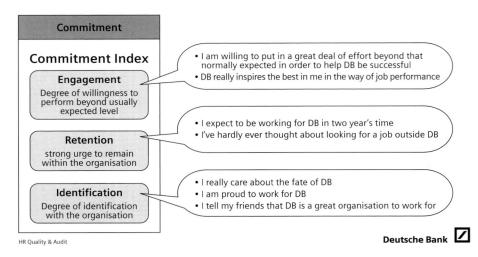

Figure 5.5 Corporate Identity Survey: Example of survey statements

important personnel, managers had to provide them with the possibility to work globally and to have access to a wide customer base. In Figure 2 the 14 risk factors are classified in terms of 2 dimensions, the assessment of the risk factor by the employee and the impact of each factor on commitment. The results were forwarded to business area managers for them to discuss with their people.

Heinz Fischer knew now that by using the questionnaire to track commitment, managers could anticipate dissatisfaction and manage retention. He was convinced that to support Deutsche Bank's strategy, the company needed a committed and competent workforce with a firm intention to stay. In order to track commitment, Fischer used several surveys, all intended to measure the three components of commitment: engagement, degree of willingness to perform beyond usually expected levels and intention to stay with Deutsche Bank. All this was done in order to avoiding the defection of key personnel – people who possess the know-how on which the bank builds its success.

Questions

1. Choose a particular industry and illustrate how you would practically apply the 4-dimensional tool of business model reinvention.

2. Are you part of a "Community of Practice" (COP)? Describe this COP and your role in it, and if you are not part of a COP, explain why and how you would join a particular COP.

3. The "networked incubators" tool is more generally known in the IT/high technology field. Research and contrast three networked incubators in various non-IT fields, and highlight their benefits and limitations.

4. Draw a map of your organization's (or your own choice of) knowledge management system. Explain how you would use a knowledge audit to identify the knowledge gaps and knowledge strategy of the organization.

5. Illustrate the use of the SECI model of knowledge conversion in an organization of your choice.

6. Provide a map of the Systemic Strategy Scorecard (SSC) for a particular business network in the wine industry, and describe the particular objectives, targets, initiatives and measures that could be implemented in its utilization.

7. You are the newly-hired assistant to the Head of Deutsche Bank HR. Deutsche Bank is in the process of downsizing, with the resulting staff redundancies. Your first task is to sift through a list of candidates from various departments. What decision criteria do you use when deciding whom to make redundant?

References

Chapter 5: Strategic Management Tools for the Knowledge Economy

[1] Adapted from Bradley, S.P., "Capturing Value in the Network Era", in Bradley, S.P. and Nolan, R.L. (1998), *Sense and Respond*, Boston: Harvard Business School Press.

[2] Kim, W.C. and Mauborgne, R. (1999), "Creating New Market Space", *Harvard Business Review*, January-February, 83-93.

[3] Gibbert, M., Leibold, M. and Probst, G.J.B. (2002), "Five Styles of Customer Knowledge Management, and How Smart Companies use them to Create Value", *European Management Journal*, October, Volume 20.

[4] Wenger, E.C. and Snyder, W.M. (2000), "Communities of Practice: The Organizational Frontier", *Harvard Business Review*, January-February, 139.

[5] Wenger, E.C. and Snyder, W.M. (2000), *op. cit.*, 145.

[6] Hansen, M.T., Chesbrough, H.W., Nohria, N. and Sull, D.N. (2000), "Networked Incubators: Hothouses of the New Economy", *Harvard Business Review*, September-October, 76.

[7] Zack, M.H. (2000), "Developing a Knowledge Strategy", *California Management Review*, 41(3), 125-145.

[8] Nonaka, I., Toyama, R. and Nagata, A. (2000), "A Firm as a Knowledge-Creating Entity: A New Perspective on the Theory of the Firm", *Industrial and Corporate Change*, 9(1), 1-20.

[9] Von Krogh, G. (1998), "Care in Knowledge Creation", *California Management Review*, 40, 133-153.

[10] Leonard-Barton, D. (1992), "Core Capabilities and Core Rigidities: A Paradox in Managing Product Development", *Strategic Management Journal*, 13, 363-380.

[11] Nonaka, I., et al., *op. cit.*, 14.

[12] Roos, J. and Victor, B. (1999), "Towards a New Model of Strategy-Making as Serious Play", *European Management Journal*, 17(4), 348-355.

[13] Kaplan, R.S. and Norton, D.P. (1996), *The Balanced Scorecard*, Boston: Harvard Business School Press; Kaplan, R.S. and Norton, D. P. (2000), "Having Trouble With Your Strategy? Then Map it", *Harvard Business Review*, September-October, 167-176.

[14] Roos, J. and Oliver, D. (1999), "The Poised Organization: Navigating Effectively on Knowledge Landscapes", *http://www.imd.ch./fac/roos/paper_po.html*, November 2, 1-21.

[15] Roos, J. and Oliver, D. (1999), *op. cit.*, 14-17.

Five styles of Customer Knowledge Management

Angehrn, A.A. (1998). Towards the high tech, high touch Website. *Financial Times,* November 9, 1998: pp. 287-291.

Baker, M. (2000) Creating an alliance between employees and customers. *Knowledge Management Review* **3,5**, pp. 10-11.

Bardaracco, J. (1991). *The knowledge link: How firms compete through strategic alliances.* Boston, MA.: Harvard Business School Press.

Barney, J.B. (1991). Firm resources and sustained competitive advantage. *Journal of Management,* 17(1), pp. 99-120.

Burgelman, R.A. (2002). *Strategy as destiny.* Cambridge, MA.: Harvard Business School Press.

Davenport, T.H. & Klahr, P. (1998) Managing customer knowledge. *California Management Review* 40(3), pp. 195-208.

Davenport, T.H. & Probst, G.J.B. (2002). *Knowledge Management Case Book.* Wiley: Weinheim.

Davenport, T.H. & Prusak, L. (1998) *Working Knowledge.* Harvard Business School Press, Boston.

Eisenhardt, K.M. (1989). Building theories from case study research. *Academy of Management Review,* 14(4), pp. 532-550.

Galbreath, J. and Rogers, T. (1999) Customer relationship leadership: a leadership and motivation model for the twenty-first century business. *The TQM Magazine* 11(3), pp. 161-171.

Grant, R. (1996). Toward a knowledge based theory of the firm. *Strategic Management Journal,* 17, pp. 109-123.

Inkpen, A.C. (1996) Creating knowledge through collaboration. *California Management Review* 39(1), pp. 123-139.

Lakhani, K. & von Hippel, E. (2000). How open source software works. *MIT working paper* # 4117.

Leonard-Barton, D. (1995). *Wellsprings of knowledge.* Boston, MA.: Harvard Business School Press.

Mintzberg, H. & Lampel, J. (1999). Reflecting on the strategy process. *Sloan Management Review,* 40(3), pp. 21-30.

Prahalad, C. and Ramaswamy, V. (2000) Co-opting customer competence. *Harvard Business Review,* Jan-Feb, pp. 79-87.

Sawhney, M. & Prandelli, E. (2000). Communities of creation: managing distributed knowledge in turbulent markets. *California Management Review,* 42(4), pp. 24-54.

Spender, J. (1996). Making knowledge the basis of a dynamic theory of the firm. *Strategic Management Journal,* 17, pp. 45-62.

Stake, R.E. (1995). *The art of case study research.* London: Sage.

Thomke, S. & Von Hippel, E. (2002). Customers as Innovators. *Harvard Business Review,* April, pp. 5-11.

Toffler, A. (1980). *The third wave.* New York, NY.: Morrow.

von Hippel, E.A. (1977). Has a customer already developed your next product? *Sloan Management Review*, 18(2), pp. 63-74.

von Krogh, G. & Roos, J. (1995). *Organizational epistemology.* London: MacMillan.

von Krogh, G., Ichijo, K., & Nonaka, I. (2000). *Enabling knowledge creation.* Oxford: New Oxford University Press.

Wikestrom, S. (1996). The customer as co-producer. *European Journal of Marketing,* 30(4), pp. 6-19.

Woodruff, R.B. (1997) Customer value: the next source for competitive advantage. *Journal of the Academy of Marketing Science,* 25(2), pp. 139-153.

Yin, R.K. (1994). Case study research: Design and methods. London: Sage.

VI Strategic Management – The Challenging Road Ahead

Chapter 6:
Managing the New Strategic Leadership Challenges

Introduction

The impacts of the knowledge-networked economy of the 21st century pose particular challenges to traditional organizational leadership and strategic management practices. Systemic strategic management requires very different managerial mentalities and characteristics than the traditional requirements of strategic management in more stable conditions. The questions have been asked if the traditional styles and tools of strategic management are "dead", and if, in fact, the subject field of strategic management is "teachable" at all.

The answer to these questions is a qualified "no", as it has been shown that traditional strategic management approaches and tools still have a relevancy in some environments. However, the nature of systemic strategic management in the knowledge economy does require fundamentally new managerial mentalities, characteristics and abilities. From the previous chapters it is evident that the activities of enabling, guiding, cohering and co-shaping of business models and industry configurations for renewal and collaborative success are fundamentally different from the traditional managerial qualities of visioning, directing, ordering, coordinating and controlling individual organizations for purpose of competitive effectiveness.

This chapter reviews the leadership and managerial challenges for systemic strategic management in the following sections:

- Major strategic leadership qualities in socio-cultural business networks:
  - Providing context and clarifying domain
  - Destabilizing, energizing and guiding the business system
  - Configuring and cultivating business networks and business models
  - Managing paradox and building resilience
- Strategic managerial qualities to "manage at the edge of chaos", i.e. to facilitate self-organization and self-discipline
  - Mechanisms for managing the self-organizing enterprise
  - Simultaneously managing order and disorder
  - Developing and implementing coherence mechanisms

- Developing robust adaptive strategies
  - Developing strategy for various uncertainty levels
  - Developing and sustaining a family of robust strategies

Major Strategic Leadership Qualities in Socio-Cultural Business Networks

Four major leadership qualities are required for resilient socio-cultural business networks.[1]

Providing context and clarifying domain

Leadership in socio-cultural business networks is contingent on having a clear identity – a context for action and landscape domains. Identity in networks and organizations is established through shared vision, culture and beliefs, mutual understanding, and member alignment.

- *Clarifying shared vision*
  The leaders bring into focus the shared vision of the network and its organizations. They provide the initial impetus of the shared vision, which is co-shaped by the members of the network, and then they act as the main agent for its clarification and focus.

- *Enriching the culture and beliefs*
  Members are able to operate with the guidance of only a few rules and still create self-directed, productive, purposeful results through the organizing power of a strong culture. The culture is the network's collective mindset – its intentions, memories and beliefs. The leaders actively nurture and expand the network's culture, which involve changing traditional mindsets and overcoming inertia.

- *Mutual understanding*
  The leaders assist the network in understanding and interpreting information and events, clarifying contradictory "noise", and gaining mutual meaning and a sense of why the network arose, exists and benefits from collaboration and competition.

- *Member alignment*
  A highly aligned network of members and activities is focused and purposeful, yet made up of independent, self-organizing organizations. The leaders use their overall perspective of socio-cultural systems and align the network around a shared vision, purpose and core beliefs.

Destabilizing, energizing and guiding the business system

Leaders need to create an environment that elicits, supports and nurtures creativity by deliberately upsetting the status quo, escalating some changes while dampening others, and seeking states of disequilibrium. Such instability can be created by compel-

ling goals and slogans, enabling supportive information flows to members, promoting
diversity of opinion, and maintaining a state of tension.

- *Compelling goals and slogans*
  Large, audacious and contentious (even alarming) goals and slogans can destabilize and energize a business network and individuals. Jack Welch's slogan of
  "managing yourself out of a job within a year", and Motorola's "six-sigma quality
  goals" are good examples. Such goals have the features of being a) inspiring, b)
  audacious, and c) unifying in common – they inflame the imagination, stretch
  credibility, and lead to collaboration among members.

- *Enabling supportive information flows*
  Leaders are essential in enabling members to obtain relevant and accurate information and feedback from the socio-cultural business network. Leaders especially
  help members to see important information that is being ignored, denied or distorted.

- *Promoting diversity of opinion*
  Systems thrive on diversity, which leads to change and growth. The issue is to
  develop networks and members that value different viewpoints, instead of fearing
  them. Conflict, a natural outcome of diversity, is an opportunity for catalyzing
  novel ideas and approaches.

- *Maintaining a state of tension*
  Change and disturbance create anxiety in people, and the leadership challenge is to
  maintain this anxiety and still function positively – as energizing "sparks" for
  creative action – without exceeding people's ability to handle the stress engendered. Another way is to seek disconfirmation of beliefs by e.g. using humor and
  satire to hold conventional thinking up to ridicule and self-deprecation, thus testing
  ideas and rewarding tough questions and contrary views.

Configuring and cultivating business networks and business models

Leadership plays a critical role in configuring and cultivating business networks and
business models by way of promoting self-organization mechanisms, enabling ownership, shaping business models and systems, while nurturing relationships and nourishing learning and the human spirit:

- *Promoting self-organizing mechanisms*
  Leadership should initiate and promote self-organizing mechanisms such as communities of practice and networked incubators, and also incentivize specifically
  identified agents to consider membership of a network.

- *Enabling ownership*
  Leadership enables members to experience ownership of their work, their organization and the business network. They communicate the importance of commitment and self-reliance, and of belonging to a co-owned and co-beneficial group of
  dynamic, value-creating entities.

- *Shaping the business model and system, and nurturing relationships*
  Leaders reinforce the vital importance of the long-term health of relationships,

actively promoting collaboration, cooperation and mutual enrichment. In the web-like structures of socio-cultural business networks, strong relationships are essential for individual and group effectiveness. They have to adapt to or shape each phase of the business socio-cultural system, e.g. the pioneering, growth, leadership and renewal phases (see Chapter 5).

- *Nourishing learning and the human spirit*
  People need inspiration, hope, meaning and satisfaction in achievements. Given the right environment and atmosphere by leaders, people will self-organize to create a dynamic, thriving, vital organization through their commitment and positive energy. Instead of repressing emotions, leaders should seek to channel them into positive and productive directions by nourishing these emotions. Learning is a process of expanding people's self-awareness and broadening their worldview, and leaders diffuse learning and knowledge in the business network for further knowledge creation, personal meaning and satisfaction. The learning process includes tolerance of failures and mistakes as an essential part of learning through trial and error.

Managing paradox and building resilience

The self-organizing principles of co-shaping business networks might lead one to conclude that leaders and managers are superfluous. On the contrary, they have a critical role in providing the balance between the need for order and the imperative to change. This paradox, which is really a constellation of paradoxes consisting of stability and instability, simplicity and complexity, predictability and unpredictability, and effectiveness and innovation, calls for tremendous agility. This can be achieved through separate teams, shadow organizations, self-reinforcing groups, and resilience techniques:

- *Separate teams*
  Separate teams, e.g. a present business team (focused on today) and a future business team (focused on tomorrow), can be guided by leadership and cohered on overall network levels.
- *Shadow organizations*
  Besides the "normal", traditional business organization and network, leadership can initiate a "shadow" organization and network – a form of experimentation and self-development which falls outside the normal structures and activities.
- *Self-reinforcing groups*
  Leadership could avoid the potential difficulties of organizational politics and dissensions arising from separate teams and shadow organizations by integrating order and disorder into the same group of people or business entities. Such groups are self-reinforcing, i.e. they reinforce each other by enriching both efficiency and innovation objectives. A strong, shared vision and culture particularly contribute to the success of such a practice.
- *Building resilience*
  People, organizations and networks become resilient if they are able to adapt to and to enact in a responsive and appropriate manner to environmental turbulence.

Destabilizing the Equilibrium at Shell[2]

In 1996, Shell found itself captive to its hundred-year-old history. The numbing effects of tradition – a staggering US$130 billion in annual revenues, 105,000 predominantly long-tenured employees, and global operations – left Shell vulnerable.

Steve Miller was appointed group managing director of Shell's worldwide oil products business (known as "Downstream"), which accounts for $40 billion of revenues within the Shell group, in 1996. During the previous two years the company had been engaged in a program to "transform" the organization. Yet the regimen of massive reorganization, traumatic downsizing, and senior management workshops accomplished little. Shell's earnings, while solid, were disappointing to financial analysts who expected more from the industry's largest competitor. There were widespread resignation and cynicism among employees.

For Steve Miller, Shell's impenetrable culture was worrisome. The Downstream business accounted for 37 percent of Shell's assets. Of the businesses in the Shell Group's portfolio, Downstream faced the gravest competitive threats. New competitors, global customers, and shrewder national oil companies were demanding a radically different approach to the marketplace. In addition to Downstream's 61,000 full-time employees, Shell's 47,000 filling stations employed hundreds of thousands of, mostly part-time, attendants and catered to more than 10 million customers every day. In the language of complexity, Miller believed it necessary to tap the emergent properties of Shell's enormous distribution system and to shift the locus of strategic initiative to the front lines. The alternative wasn't centralization – it was a radical change in the responsiveness of the Downstream business to the dynamics of the market place. This change had to occur from top to bottom, so that people could come together in appropriate groups, solve problems, and operate in a manner which transcended the old headquarters versus field schism. What initially seemed like a huge conflict has gradually melted away, because leadership stopped treating the Downstream business like a machine to be driven and began to regard it as a living system that needed to evolve.

Miller's solution was to cut through the organization's layers and barriers, put senior management in direct contact with the people at the grassroots level, foster strategic initiatives, create a new sense of urgency, and overwhelm the old order. The first wave of initiatives spawned other initiatives. In Malaysia, for example, Miller's pilot efforts with four initiative teams (called "action labs") have proliferated to forty. "It worked," he states, "because the people at the coal face usually know what's going on. They see the competitive threats and our inadequate response every day. Once you give them the context, they can do a better job of spotting opportunities and stepping up to decisions. In less than two years, we've seen astonishing progress in our retail business in some twenty-five countries. This represents around 85 percent or our retail sales volume, and we have now begun to use this approach in our service organizations and lubricant business". Results? Overall, Shell gained in brand-share preference throughout Europe and ranked first in share among other major oil companies. By the close of 1998, approximately 10,000 Downstream employees had been involved in this effort with audited results (directly attributed to the program), exceeding a $300 million contribution to Shell's bottom line.

Leaders should always have either a number of shadow organizations, separate teams, or self-reinforcing groups simultaneously active to enable resilient responses to environmental impacts of whatever magnitude. This requires various strategic options for distinct levels of uncertainty, as subsequently described.

Requirements to Facilitate Self-organization, Self-discipline and Resilience

Qualities to manage the self-organizing enterprise

Anderson proposes seven qualities (or "levers") for guiding the self-organizing enterprise. These are environment selection, performance definition, managing meaning, choosing people, reconfiguring the network, developing indirect selection systems, and energizing the system.[3] To understand what managers do in self-organizing enterprises, it is useful to ask why management exists at all. Self-organization does not mean "no management necessary", but rather "no central controller necessary". Managers provide context influence and governance, not control.

- *Environment selection*
  Self-organizing systems structure themselves to fit their environment. Managers decide what environments (or landscapes) to occupy, and this provides the external "scaffolding" that allow members to focus on a few controllable parameters. The managerial quality is to define the environments to occupy, thereby channeling the rate and direction of evolution.

- *Defining performance*
  Business systems adapt by changing their behavior to move upwards on particular peaks in a knowledge landscape. Given particular performance indicators, they move towards higher fitness levels without a central controller. Managers must be able to provide the relevant performance indicators, in both financial and non-financial terms (see the systemic strategy scorecard (SSC) in Chapter 5).

- *Managing meaning*
  Managers help guide the evolution of a self-organizing system by managing meaning, which is accomplished more through the managing of symbols (e.g. "stretching" goals and slogans) than by the managing of things. They have to propagate mores, values and culture through tools such as stories, myths and play-making rituals. In a sense, management consists in part of asking agents "what do you think you are doing?", i.e. tagging and retagging flows through the network to increase the general understanding.

- *Choosing people*
  Managers have to select the members of a network. Attracting the most capable agents is only one part of the task. The requirements of sufficient diversity, to avoid constraining homogeneity, and positive connective behavior and association have to be adhered to.

- *Reconfiguring the network*
  In business networks, managers alter the node structure when they add or delete roles. When managers establish strategic alliances, create programs to attract value-added resellers and complementary asset providers, build user communities, or join R&D associations, they create new sources of variation that can alter the network's evolutionary path. Managers may also reshape network flows by making or breaking connections between nodes, e.g. by linking internal communities of practice with external communities of customers through the Internet, or by placing people together in temporary, cross-functional teams, thereby altering interaction patterns.

- *Develop indirect selection systems*
  Managers should be able to develop and implement indirect selection systems for choosing among various options, e.g. various business models. Such indirect (or "vicarious") selection systems predict outcomes and detect possible failures of various strategic options. Managers should be careful that indirect selection systems do not become institutionalized and prone to manipulation.

- *Energizing the system*
  Managers should have the ability to provide inspiration and challenges to network members. By setting aggressive goals, managers create a perceived mismatch between present performance and required performance. Often a business network becomes "stuck" on a local peak in a fitness landscape, and managers have to drive its behaviour beyond the normal comfort zone.

Simultaneously managing order and disorder

In complex, adaptive business networks, between the extremes of stasis and chaos, lies a region where fitness is maximized – the "edge of chaos". At the edge of chaos, one is simultaneously conservative and radical. Evolution is adept at keeping existing things work well, while at the same time making bold experiments.

Developing and implementing coherence mechanisms

A poised organization and business network that are being managed at the edge of chaos, are provided with just enough structure and discipline to allow them to capture the best opportunities. Besides strong vision, values and culture that act as coherence mechanisms for diverse actions, they also make use of simple rules to focus on key processes and routines – i.e., disciplined flexibility. Examples of simple rules are provided by Eisenhardt and Sull, as summarized in Table 6.1.[4]

Managers should encourage improvisation among business network members, but also ensure that they know how to do it according to embedded simple rules. Poised organizations have three traits in common, as illustrated in Figure 6.1: Adaptive culture, semi-structures and real-time communication.[5]

Self-Organization at Shell[6]

Building on the principles of self-organization and utilizing "action labs", Steve Miller and his colleagues at Shell channeled the potential of co-evolving networks. He says: "Shell has always been a wholesaler. Yet the forecourt of every service station is an artery for commerce that any retailer would envy. Our task was to tap the potential of that real estate, and we needed both the insight and the initiatives of our front-line troops to pull it off. For a company as large as Shell, leadership can't drive these answers down from the top. We needed to tap into ideas that were out there in the ranks – latent but ready to bear fruit if given encouragement."

Miller began bringing six- to eight-person teams from six operating companies from around the world into "retailing boot camps". The first five-day workshop introduced tools for identifying and exploiting market opportunities. The participants returned home ready to apply the tools to achieve breakthroughs, such as doubling the net income of filling stations on the major north-south highways of Malaysia, or tripling the market share of bottled gas in South Africa. They were then replaced by six other teams.

During the next sixty days, the first group of teams used the analytical tools to sample customers, identify segments, and develop a value proposition. The group would then return to the workshop for a "peer challenge" – tough give-and-take exchanges with other teams. Thereafter it would return home for another sixty days to perfect a business plan. At the close of the third workshop, each action lab spent three hours in the "fishbowl" with Miller and several of his direct reportees, reviewing business plans, while the other teams observed the proceedings. At the close of each session, plans were approved, rejected, amended. Financial commitments were made in exchange for promised results. Then the teams went back to the field for another sixty days to put their ideas into action and returned for a follow-up session for a total of four workshops.

"Week after week, team after team," says Miller, "my six direct reportees and I and our internal coaches reached out and worked directly with a diverse cross-section of customers, dealers, shop stewards, and young and mid-level professionals. And it worked. Operating company CEOs, historically leery of any "help" from headquarters, saw their people return energized and armed with solid plans to beat the competition. The grassroots employees who participated in the program got to touch and feel the new Shell – a far more informal, give-and-take culture. The conversation down in the ranks of the organization began to change. "Guerrilla" leaders, historically resigned to Shell's conventional way of doing things, stepped forward to champion ingenious marketplace innovations (such as the Coca-Cola Challenge in Malaysia – a free Coke to any service-station customer who is not offered the full menu of forecourt services. It sounds trivial, but it increased volume by 15 percent). Many, if not most, of the ideas came from the lower ranks of our company who are in direct contact with the customer. Best of all, we learned together. I can't overstate how infectious the optimism and energy of these committed employees was for the many managers above them".

Miller pioneered a very different model from that which had always prevailed at Shell. His "design for emergence" generated hundreds of informal connections between headquarters and the field, resembling the parallel networks of the nervous system to the brain. It contrasted with the historical model of mechanical linkages analogous to those that transfer the energy from the engine in a car through a drive train to the tires that perform the "work."

The Walt Disney Company: Managing at the Edge of Chaos[7]

The Walt Disney Company is a firm that prospers at the edge of chaos. Its theme parks and other businesses are run in a deeply conservative fashion. A strong culture supports Disney's mission of providing family entertainment. In operations, no detail is too small, right down to the personal grooming of the parking-lot attendants. This culture is ingrained in the organization and constantly reinforced through management processes.

In many organizations such a conservative culture and such tightly controlled operations would snuff out creativity. Yet Disney manages to be one of the most innovative companies in the world. It pioneered animated films and destination theme parks, built EPCOT, linked media and retail with its Disney Stores, and took an early lead in cable television. Disney manages the tension between conservatism and innovation by maintaining an almost cult-like attention to detail and discipline, while simultaneously forgiving honest mistakes made in the pursuit of innovation.

Disney's core value of wholesome family entertainment, its dedication to putting smiles on customers' faces, and its strict operating discipline are the spinal cord around which it has innovated. Simultaneously conservative and radical, it has forged its success at the edge of chaos, becoming a poised organization.

Developing robust adaptive strategies

When coping with more complex internal and external environments in the knowledge economy, managers should be able to develop robust adaptive strategies, i.e. strategies that provide general direction and guidance but without confirming activities and behavior. Qualities required for this are awareness and interpretation of various environmental uncertainty levels, and the ability to develop and sustain a family (or range) of robust strategies.[8]

Interpretation of and strategic responses to various environmental uncertainty levels

Courtney specifies that strategic managers should develop awareness, interpretation and appropriate responses to at least four levels of uncertainty. These responses serve as the filter for responding appropriately to the paradoxical questions of shape or adapt, focus or diversify, acting now or later, and using traditional tools or new systemic tools.[9] The four levels of uncertainty are:

Level 1: *Clear enough future*: Single view of the future.

Level 2: *Alternative future*: Limited set of possible future outcomes, one of which will occur.

Level 3: *Range of futures:* Range of possible future outcomes.

Level 4: *True ambiguity*: No range of possible future outcomes.

Table 6.1 Simple rules

Type	Purpose	Example
How-to rules	They spell out key features of how a process is executed – "What makes our process unique?"	Akamai's *rules for the customer service process:* staff must consist of technical gurus, every question must be answered on the first call or email, and R&D staff must rotate through customer service.
Boundary rules	They focus managers on the opportunities that can be pursued and help to determine those that are not feasible.	Cisco's *early acquisitions rule:* companies to be acquired must have no more than 75 employees, 75% of whom are engineers.
Priority rules	They help managers rank the accepted opportunities.	Intel's rule for *allocating manufacturing capacity:* allocation is based on *a product's gross margin.*
Timing rules	They synchronize managers with the pace of emerging opportunities and other parts of the company.	Nortel's rules for product development: project teams must know when a product has to be delivered to the leading customer to win, and *product development time* must be less than 18 months.
Exit rules	They help managers decide when to pull out of yesterday's opportunities.	Oticon's *rule for pulling the plug on projects in development:* if a key team member – manger or not – chooses to leave the project for another within the company, the project is killed.

Source: Eisenhardt, K.M. and Sull, D.N. (2001), "Strategy as Simple Rules", *Harvard Business Review,* January, 111.

As a rule of thumb, *shaping* strategies makes the most sense when uncertainty is high, since it can be influenced by an organization's actions. When confronting a future that seems clear enough to predict, strategists have traditionally favored *adapting* strategies geared to the existing industry. Yet even the most stable business environments are susceptible to periodic bouts of upheaval. Shaping strategies at the lowest level of uncertainty, intentionally seeks to create chaos out of order – for example, Federal Express reshaped the sleepy mail-and-package delivery industry. Shaping strategies in more uncertain environments attempts to lower the level of uncertainty, thereby creating new order out of chaos.

As executives face their shape-or-adapt choices, they must weigh factors beyond the level of residual uncertainty – factors such as the external market environment and the company's capabilities and aspirations. Shaping strategies, for example, makes most sense in markets that offer strong first-mover advantages. One market that they may find challenging is Internet-based commerce, which, by its very nature, invites comparison shopping, thus perhaps undermining one of the most important potential first-mover advantages: brand and customer loyalty. As a result, it isn't yet clear whether e-

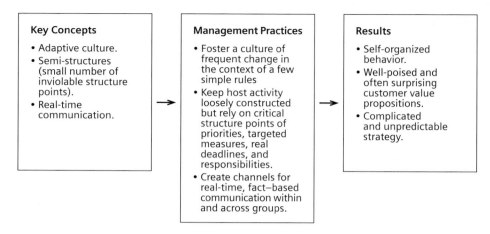

Figure 6.1
Adaptive culture, semi structures, and real-time communication: Navigating at the edge of chaos (*Source:* Eisenhardt, K.M. and Brown, S.L. (1998), Competing on the Edge: Strategy as Structured Chaos, Boston: *Harvard Business School Press,* 47)

commerce shapers, such as Amazon.com and eBay, have established any sustainable first-mover advantages. Being an e-commerce adapter – replicating good ideas and avoiding bad ones – may offer returns similar to those won by pioneering shapers, but without the risk.

Even excellent strategists are not cut out to be shapers in all situations. Successful shaping usually requires a clear vision of an industry's future evolutionary direction (such as Bill Gates had of PCs); deep pockets; a strong reputation; a leadership position in a related business; world-class technology, innovation skills, or both; and operational excellence. Not all strategists have these qualities.

Successful shapers share a formidable list of attributes. Managers might be tempted to regard adapting as the easy or fallback strategy alternative. This idea would be mistaken on two fronts. *First*, it leads managers to assume that adapting, unlike shaping, doesn't require proactive strategic commitments. Nothing could be further from the truth. Following a potential shaper's lead, hedging against possible future outcomes, experimenting continually, and even building a flexible organization require real upfront commitments – financial and human.

Second, the mistaken idea that adapting is the easy alternative, leads managers to assume that passive – not active – management is required to see it through. Yet adapters in highly uncertain environments must be skilled at spotting new opportunities and threats, and at responding quickly to reorient their companies when necessary. This is hardly passive and, for many companies, hardly easy. For a company that has difficulty dealing with ambiguity, a bold, shaping strategy may be the only way to avoid the dangerous "do nothing" trap. Strategists who develop a thorough understanding of the level and nature of the residual uncertainty their company faces, can develop a richer set of feasible alternatives and make better-informed choices to shape or adapt.

Ability to develop and sustain a family of robust strategies

Beinhocker contends that strategic managers should develop and sustain a family (or population) of strategies that cover a range of uncertainties and options.[10] He states that the "best strategy" for searching a fitness landscape and building sustainable strategies is a mixture of an adaptive walk (adaptation) and the occasional medium and long (reinvention) "jumps".

Thus, in creating a population of strategies, it is essential that the population contains a balanced mixture of initiatives, ranging from short-jump incremental extensions of the current business, to long-jump initiatives, which have longer time frames, are higher in risk and farther afield, but have the potential to build capability and create opportunity.

In general, successful strategists would manage a portfolio of strategic initiatives across three horizons:

Horizon 1 initiatives are efforts to extend and defend existing businesses (adaptive walks).

Horizon 2 initiatives seek to build on existing capabilities to create new businesses (medium jumps).

Horizon 3 initiatives plant the seeds for future businesses that do not as yet exist (long jumps).

For example, Bombardier, the Canadian aerospace, transportation, and recreational vehicles company, has achieved more than 20 percent annual revenue and earnings growth for ten years by constantly creating and harvesting strategic initiatives that cover all three horizons. Current initiatives include a new class of ultra long-range business jets (Horizon 1), military aircraft maintenance services (Horizon 2), and electric vehicles for neighborhood transportation (Horizon 3).

Shifting managers to a mindset of robust strategies is not easy. Often the organizational processes, measurement metrics, and incentives are geared toward a linear view of strategy and this must change to support a new mindset. Beinhocker proposes six actions that can reinforce the robust adaptive mindset, namely investing in a diversity of people, valuing potential strategies as real options, mapping "jumps" on the landscape, testing the population of strategies (e.g. systems dynamics modeling, and game theory), bringing financiers such as venture capitalists on board at an early stage, and using differential performance metrics for each type of strategy initiative.[11]

Conclusion

Organizational leadership and strategic managers require particular qualities and capabilities in the knowledge economy. Leadership should have the ability to provide context and meaning to the organization and its networks, to destabilize (or "disturb") and guide the system and its evolvement, and to configure appropriate new business models and networks. Strategic managers should be able to "manage at the edge of chaos" by developing and implementing appropriate coherence mechanisms, and handling the challenges of paradox by developing robust adaptive strategies.

These invaluable agents of future change seek neither stability nor predictability, developing a comfort level that tolerates disequilibrium. They know that "messiness" and ambiguity are part of the process of self-organization and self-emergence and that, rather than attempting to manage it through command-and-control, their role is to support it by the enabling of resources and the design of an appropriate culture. They recognize the futility of attempting to draw a map of the future in advance, appreciating the fact that when the waters are uncharted, their destination can only be discovered through the actual process in real time; that the map can only get drawn as they go along. Being a successful manager in the 21st century knowledge economy calls for a new mental model – a manager suited to a world of turbulence and seeming chaos.

Understanding Organizational Sense Making: A Diagnostic Tool for Strategic Leadership in Conditions of Complexity[*]

By Johann Kinghorn

Sense making is a universal and continuous human activity. Although theorists, particularly philosophers and linguists, have reflected on the phenomenon for almost a century, interest within the ambit of organizational life has begun to emerge only over the last decade or two. This was a direct reaction to the unprecedented changes in the environment in which organizations have to navigate and the shortcomings of conventional strategies and models of leadership.

The first part of this contribution briefly characterizes the *conceptual roots* of the growing interest in organizational sense making. This is followed by an overview of the *basic tenets* of sense-making theory. We conclude with pointers to *implications* for and possible applications of sense making in organizations.

To distinguish *general* from *organizational* sense making, the latter will be referred to as OSM throughout. Since sense-making theory is very complex, it will be dealt with in a highly cursorily manner. This contribution can do no more than invite further reflection, in particular to the contribution that a sound understanding of our topic can make to a new vision of strategic leadership in conditions of complexity.

Complex Adaptive Systems – The Emergence of a New World View

Let us, for the moment, define sense making as that human activity in which we convert the flow of meanings that we continuously encounter into coherent pictures of the world, thus creating mind maps, which we use to steer our individual and collective lives.

The conversion is mostly done sub- or unconsciously. It is only triggered into consciousness when our pictures fail to make the world around us comprehensible and

[*] Johann Kinghorn is Director of the Programme in Value and Policy Studies, and Director of the Centre for Knowledge Dynamics and Decision-making at the University of Stellenbosch, South Africa.

navigable. This is the moment the world appears to be "not what it used to be". This is when things "no longer make sense" and paralysis sets in, feeding on feelings of confusion, ambiguity, and lack of direction.

Since the late eighties, this has become the default experience of much of the world. The default reaction is to devote even more time and energy to strategic planning and process engineering. But as experience has shown, more planning very often produces more paralysis. Perhaps then, the problem is not "out there", but in the mind maps we create of the world "out there". If so, we need a new view of the world with which to inform our strategic leadership efforts.

Chronicling the sweeping socio-economic changes of the last two decades, which have contributed to this situation, in the space of a chapter is not feasible, save to point out that no dimension of life is exempt from this. Most people probably register them most acutely in the areas of global politics[*], the international financial systems, natural sciences and personal and group values. But these are merely symptoms of a comprehensive change in the way the world is being interpreted and experienced.

Embedded in and driving the socio-economic transformations is (what is best described as) the *revolution of networked virtuality*, popularized and vaguely embodied in the form of electronic communication technologies, systems and symbols over the last two decades. As we are really only at the beginning of the digital (and perhaps the quantum?)[1] age, it is difficult to gauge the extent of its impact. But it cannot be denied that the foundations of our world are being reshaped in the wake of this revolution, not least through the exponential intensification of information flows and the pressures consequently exerted on knowledge capabilities, human relations and the global economy.

Virtuality is a notion that does not fit well with the knowledge systems and human experiences on which the world's socio-economic achievements of the past 50 years were built. The knowledge requirements and human skills of a world, which increasingly has the means for human interactions and artefacts to evolve undeterred by the limitations of sequence and location, are very different from those on which the industrial era was built. Never before have we had to think about our world as a placeless place and about our existence in terms of timeless time. Yet that is exactly what the revolution of networked virtuality[2] is forcing us to do. The extent of the impact on the functioning of organizations and in particular on strategic leadership is a topic urgently in need of attention.

If it is possible to capture the essence of the world of networked virtuality in one concept, this will be the notion of *complexity*. Previously the world was *complicated*[3], now it has become *complex*. The difference is enormous.

---

[*] The dramatic and substantial shifting of foundations and rearrangement of global relations and options were nowhere better epitomized than in the fall of the Berlin wall. The latter is an abbreviation for a torrent of change which started in Latin America in the mid-eighties (the fall of the military regimes) and China (the advent of Deng Ziao Peng and the Communist market economy). It continued into the nineties via Perestroika in the erstwhile USSR, the emergence of Japan as a world economic power and the subsequent Southern Asian boom, liberalization in India, the emergence of islands of democracy in Africa, the unification of Europe, and the coalescing of anti-modernizing forces (predominantly under the umbrella of Muslim fundamentalism).

A complicated worldview is based on the assumption of our ability to identify definitively – and then manage – all the constituent elements of any given phenomenon, including their interrelationships. There may be a vast number of such elements and they may be difficult to track and comprehend, but it is assumed that with the sound application of mechanical rationality, a problem-solving methodology and dedication, this can be achieved. In philosophical terms, this conviction is rooted in a *teleological view on agency* and the assumptions of *linearity* and *sequentiality* as the basic systemic properties of the universe.

> *A complicated worldview is based on the assumption of our ability to identify definitively all the constituent elements of any given phenomenon, including their interrelationships.*

A complex world, on the other hand, is one in which we come to see things as fluid moments in continuously adapting organic processes. The basic systemic characteristic of the universe is, therefore, its *indeterminate emergent*[4] nature. Rather than through identifying "properties", we get to know the universe through the recognition of flows and patterns – of which we are as much part as we are observers. Rather than bounded rationality, we need to observe bounded chaos in managing ourselves and our organizations, for the principles of bounded chaos – *autopoiesis*[5], *indeterminate circularity* and *simultaneity* within the context of N-dimensionality – provide a far more plausible understanding of the systemic nature of our existence.

Complexity and chaos theory is not new in the biophysical and philosophic sciences. What is new – and exciting – is the convergence of these, together with social and management sciences, around the notions of complex adaptive systems. This is the wellspring from which sense-making theory emerges.

Sense and Sense making

Sense-making theory shares the assumptions of complex adaptive systems and applies them to the individual and systemic *cognitive* processes. In particular, sense making sharpens our understanding of cognitive dissonance in conditions of extreme complexity.

> *Sense-making theory starts out from the proposition that there is a fundamental difference between meaning and sense.*

Sense-making theory starts out from the proposition that there is a fundamental difference between *meaning* and *sense*. We derive meaning from interpreting what we see, hear and feel. Sense, on the other hand, is a *holistic construction* of our own making as we weld different meanings into a coherent understanding of their purpose and base our actions upon this understanding.

For example, the meanings of the numbers 90, 180, 270 and 360 are clear. But they can be used for different purposes. For a pilot of an aircraft they make sense as compass headings. For a person reading a book the sense lies in the fact that they are page numbers – unless, of course, it is a book about piloting, in which case they may *also* make sense as compass headings. Or it could be a book on trigonometry – in which case they are angles. Then again, they may be lottery ticket numbers.

This example shows three fundamental aspects of what sense is or is not. Firstly, sense is not inherent in meaning. Sense is always the *imputed* value of a set of meanings. Meanings are inferred, but sense is *made*. Secondly, it is entirely possible for one person to make multiple "senses" of any given set of meanings, or no sense at all. There is no one universal true sense. Thirdly, sense is always related to some form of purpose. In this respect, sense is a synonym for direction and movement. There may be mountains of meaning, but if no sense can be made, the effect is paralysis.

The latter aspect is of the utmost importance for the issue of strategic leadership, as we shall see. But first we need to form a mind picture of sense and sense making.

Karl E. Weick[6], considered the doyen of OSM theory, has crafted a very useful metaphor to describe sense making. To him sense making is the act whereby human beings construct mental *frames* and use them as filters and references to interpret the cues they pick up from events and objects. If we succeed in matching *cues* with a frame, we have a mental picture that enables action.

Perhaps the concept of framing is best explained with reference to light particles. Although there is a continuous flow of particles "out there", they need to collide with material objects from which they are momentarily reflected in order to be made visible to the human eye. Only a very small proportion is made visible in this way. Our mental frames likewise reflect only a small proportion of the ongoing flow of reality to render it, momentarily, interpretable.

Another aspect of framing can be explained if we also regard it as a metaphor drawn from the world of cinema. Reality "out there" is an endless and comprehensive stream. By using a lens, the cinematographer captures only selected moments and confined cuts of this flow. The flow of events is thus suspended and the moments frozen. But precisely by doing this, the cinematographer creates a new reality by rearranging the moments into a new sequence. In fact, the rearranged product eventually becomes the only surviving reality.

In very much the same way, human beings select and freeze the cuts they make of the flow of reality. This filtering process starts with the individual construction of the frames to be used – how wide or how confined a view one wants to take. The filtering proceeds in the selection of moments to be preserved and converted into mind pictures of the world "out there". And, finally, the filtering consists of the rearrangement of the individual frames into a comprehensive mind picture.

A few characteristics of this process are significant. Firstly, the sense made is always selective. Secondly, sense making is always interactive. Thirdly, *sense* (as opposed to anticipation, hope, or wishful thinking) can only be made from past moments. For this reason debates will always be about interpretations of (snippets of) the past in times of conflict and consensus seeking.

It follows that sense making is a highly subjective activity. But that does not mean that it is arbitrary or solipsistic. The reason why we perform the act of sense making mostly unconsciously, is because we mostly draw on previously accumulated frames of shared understanding which we have stored in our reservoir of tacit understandings of the world. Unconscious sense making is thus an indication of shared assumptions and shared sense. Thus conventions, cultures, systems and structures can be seen as sets of collective frames that provide us with shared tacit tools of sensing. When we perform an act of unconscious sense making, it is as much a personal act as it is a way of tacit acknowledgement of our integration into some collective mind picture.

It could thus be said that in the process of framing, identities are constructed. These are the identities of the "self" and the "world". But this statement is open to serious misconception, for the notion of "identity" in popular parlance carries the connotation of fixed, singular and immutable. This is precisely not the case. Sense-making theory teaches that identity construction is a never completed task, and the "world" and the "self" thus constructed are constantly in a process of reconstruction. Identity construction must thus be understood as a continuous activity whereby we look for ways and targets "out there" with which to identify.

In fact, the activity of identity construction includes a perpetual reconstruction of the frames themselves. At any given moment we all have a vast number of frames in our individual reservoirs. Part of the process of construction is to select an appropriate frame from this, or – if none is deemed satisfactory – to create a new one.

This is probably the most difficult part of sense making, for, particularly in new situations, we have to negotiate with ourselves to determine which one of the selves that we are, we would want to employ[*] – if at all. In reality this is the moment where people experience the debilitating effect of equivocality. The ensuing paralysis can be extremely harmful and painful.

Now we must turn to sense making in organizations. If we are all sensemakers, what is different about sense making in an organization?

Sense making in organizations

As a field of inquiry, OSM came into being over a decade ago at the point of confluence of three main intellectual pursuits of the 20th century. These are hermeneutics (philosophy), complexity and chaos theories (mainly developed in the disciplines of physics and biology) and cognitive dissonance studies (psychology). These now converge on the turf of organization theory and, as a consequence, the picture of organizations changes rather dramatically.

To understand the uniqueness of sense making in organizations, the following characteristics of organization have to be borne in mind:

---

[*] Identities are constituted out of the process of interaction. To shift among interactions is to shift among definitions of self. Thus the sensemaker is himself or herself an ongoing puzzle undergoing continual redefinition, coincident with presenting some self to others and trying to decide which self is appropriate … Whenever I define self, I define "it", but to define it is also to define self. (Weick 1995, 20)

The first observation is about human relations in organizational contexts. Not only are they dense, they are also impersonal and unnatural. Organizations are never constituted on the basis of friendship, kinship or shared interests. (These are, at best, by-products). Organizations exist for a purpose extrinsic to the relationships of the members. This purpose is the sole force that keeps the organization intact and provides coherence to the functional relationships of the members. The consequence of this fact is that the foundation on which sense making is predicated in conventional human relationships, can not readily serve as a template for sense making in organizational contexts. If "trust" is not seen as an emotional act only, but also – perhaps primarily – as a cognitive activity, it could be said that organizations are characterized by extremely and endemically low levels of systemic trust. The need for conscious sense making, therefore, increases exponentially within organizational contexts. So does the probability for conflict and paralysis.

Secondly, an organization is a site of intense information competition. Despite many of the idealistic pictures of organizations as unifocal bodies of dedicated goals and aligned strategies, organizations are messy arenas where various types of conflicting bits of information vie for attention and open up 360° strategy directions. The fact that this is seldom acknowledged, can partially be ascribed to the misguided belief that the use of standardized technologies and programs and a neat-looking organizational chart produces homogenized knowledge and shared sense. Knowledge of sense making eradicates this idea.

Thirdly, there is the factor of N-dimensionality. There are two sides to this – the personal and the institutional. Regarding the personal, every member of an organization has to make sense – selectively as we have seen – of N number of meanings created in the organization through personal interpretations by co-workers and the environment. This is intensified by the need for continuous adaptation as new meanings keep superseding previous ones. On top of this, the various meanings are at different stages of coherence and levels of maturity and they move in N directions (as we have seen in the previous point). A very low level of collective tacit sense is probably the most significant consequence thereof (a condition normally papered over by ever-increasing regulatory measures and rigid operational procedures, or – worse – organizational dictatorship, improperly called "strong leadership"). Another consequence is that individuals quickly learn to adapt the survival mechanism of severe selectivity and reductionism – they create their own one-dimensionality by only clinging to that of which they are absolutely certain. In a context in which the shared sense is already low, this can be very little indeed.

This is exacerbated by the fact that the individual, singly or in concert, is not the only site of sense making in an organization. Perpendicular to the horizontal processes of sense making is the sense-making need of the institution itself. The – assumed – unifocal institutional purpose of the organization poses a frame that superimposes an implied sense of its own on the already complex processes of sense making. It is the sense-making version of Henry Ford's reputed statement that any color was possible as long as it was black. But since meaning, unlike color, is not visible, there is no guarantee that the sense being made by individuals or divisions correlates to the institutional requirement.

What are the implications? Given the three aspects noted above, contemporary organization, particularly highly knowledge intensive ones, turn out to be extremely unnatural vehicles for sense-making activities. There is no intrinsic guarantee that horizontal relations of mutually supportive sense-making exist. In fact, the opposite is the default situation. Yet it is the capacity to make collectively coherent sense that defines the contemporary knowledge intensive organization and lays the foundation for innovation.

Thus, when organizations are interpreted from a sense-making perspective, the picture that emerges is one of sites of contestation of sense cluttered with loads of meanings, leading to an institutional inertia which is overcome only with a great deal of energy. It also becomes clear that unless organizational sense making is cultivated (it can never be ordained or managed in conventional terms), the very nature of organization (as an "artificial" gathering of people) will forever preclude a condition of shared sense. No wonder organizations are perpetual arenas of flux. As vessels of human interaction they are extremely vulnerable.

The organizational clash of sense making can be described in somewhat more abstract terms. In organizational contexts, sense making takes place at three levels[7]. They are the *inter-subjective* (where the nature of the relationships are such that named individuals can be attached to them), the *generic subjective* (no concrete human beings are present, merely functional structures and roles) and the *extra-subjective* levels (where pure abstracts such as culture or strategy and scenario building are the concern).

Whereas individuals normally make sense at the inter-subjective, and sometimes at the extra-subjective levels, their participation in organizational life requires first and foremost that they make sense at the generic subjective level. This is not a natural sense-making activity. Generic sense is required only in the unique context of organizations. This necessitates the continuous bridging of levels – both by and in the individual and by and in the organization.

Thus, the art of organizing – in sense-making terms – is the act of bridging. At the generic level the focus is on order, pattern and substitutability, yet creativity is a function of the inter-subjective level. In principle there is a tension. In reality the successful organization is the one that finds the optimal balance and turns the tension into innovation. This balance is never the product of concerted motivational strategies (like group retreats for instance), or authoritative decrees from the top. Sense-making theory makes it clear that it is the result of shared sense[*] cultivated in the context of an organizational structure, which is correlated with human sense-making processes.

In reality the successful organization is the one that finds the optimal balance and turns the tension into innovation.

---

[*] Quoting Smircich and Stubbart, Weick (1995, 73) sums it up as follows: "Organization is a set of people who share many beliefs, values, and assumptions that encourage them to make mutually-reinforcing interpretations of their own acts and the acts of others and that encourage them to act in ways that have mutual relevance."

Applications and implications

It should now be clear that knowledge of sense making, in particular OSM, will have a huge impact on the working of any organization. It obviously also has many implications for strategic leadership. Just a few pointers in this respect will have to suffice.

It may sound simple, but the primary application of sense making is to realize that organizations today not only function in complex and adaptive environments, but that they themselves are complex adaptive systems. However, this realization requires a paradigm shift for managers who have been brought up on management and organizational theories rooted in assumptions of linearity and mechanical rationality.

When this is realized, it is important to understand that OSM will never become a management system in itself. Following the very useful taxonomy of "intelligence density"[8], OSM falls in the upper ranges of organizational intelligence work, characterized by abstract notions and sophisticated linguistic expressions. This means that OSM does not lend itself to quantifiable and geometric expressions, nor is it open to computation methodologies as symbolized by hard or software applications.

Consequently the primary thrust of OSM lies in the diagnostic capabilities it delivers to those who understand sense making and organizational life in conditions of complexity. These diagnostic capabilities apply equally to both strategic leadership and strategic leaders. In fact, they have the potential to redefine strategy altogether.

Let us conclude the chapter by briefly outlining six diagnostic applications of OSM.

- *Firstly,*
  OSM shows why motivational strategies and information technologies – on their own – consistently deliver less than they promise. Very often there is nothing wrong with levels of motivation or with personal information skills or the digital networks. However, *none of these provide sufficient conditions to make the transformation of meaning into sense possible.* Sense making is essentially a cognitive action – without which the best motivational practices and the sleekest wiring will serve merely to increase meaning overload and thus to intensify confusion. Thus OSM theory lets us see the priority of collective *cognition* over conditioned behavior.

- *Secondly,*
  once this becomes clear, OSM triggers a rethink of organizational structuring itself. This is a daunting task and one not yet adequately explored. But this time the restructuring on the radar screen is not another version of TQM, or BPR, or any such notions. What is at stake is the challenge to fashion organizational flows and processes to create a systemic habitat for organizational sense making. As was pointed out above, this centers on the challenge of bridging the two implicitly contradicting levels of sense making.

- *Thirdly,*
  understanding OSM can contribute to alleviating serious implosions that are characteristic of organizational relations. The high density of human interactions systemically creates opportunities to obstruct productive workflows. This leads to high levels of frustration and quickly degenerates into systemic infighting.

Instead of viewing this as an embarrassing exception, or unhappy lapses of loyalty, OSM helps us to see this as the result of conflicting and mutually canceling meanings – a clash of pictures. The ensuing paralysis can be seen as the result of the destruction of mental frames. Rather than replacing staff (as most companies do), the answer to the problem is to find ways in which frames can be merged, increased and enlarged. Achieving this requires an alternative way of organizational governance in which design thinking is the core organizational value, and it requires both internal and external strategic *leadership*.

- *Fourthly,*
OSM provides us with a new starting point in that – as yet – elusive quest to grasp the core element of organizational leadership. For in its sense-making essence, organizational leadership is the act of enlarging existing and constructing credible new frames. In other words, it is the act of broadening the organization's horizons by broadening the sense-making horizons of every member.

Enlarging and creating frames mean the creation of space. Space means less tension, more room in the organization for innovation and a mental release, which registers in an above average level of action.

But space also means that the organization becomes empowered to look ahead – further and with more clarity. If leadership is defined as the creation of frames, it is tantamount to the activity of enlarging and prolonging the organization's horizons. Leadership becomes the art of long-term sensing and the imparting of a sense of long-term direction.

Fostering the creation of new frames and enlarging the existing ones is, however, not a mechanistic exercise. Least of all can it be cascaded down the ranks of the organization. This requires a redefinition of leadership and a relocation to *all levels* of the organization. And it requires a foundational value system that is conducive to "big picture" thinking. Management has little control over this, except in setting the general direction. It requires the sacrifice of assumptions of predictable sequentiality embedded in a stable macrocosm.

- *Fifthly,*
the verdict is still out on which methodology – once this process is embarked upon – is the best. More and more, however, the evidence points to a creative use of human narrativity[*]. After all, sense is made retrospectively, and for this reason we all crave opportunities where we can "tell it as it happened". At present exciting research is being done in this respect, notably by IBM's Cynefin Centre on the role

---

[*] A particularly intricate but convincing argument is put forward by Ralph D Stacey, 2001 (139) in this respect. He argues that "throughout life, the interactive communication between people forms narrative-like sequences and it seems that there are biological correlates for this. It is not just that people tell each other stories but that their very experience together is organized in story-like patterns that emerge in their turn-taking going on together. Experience is narrative-like in its formation and patterning in the living present and afterwards that experience may also be recounted in the form of the narrative "told", but only ever partially and such "narratives told" feature prominently, as a tool, in the ongoing process of communicative negotiation between people in the living present."

of narrativity in organizations. Narrativity is, however, too intricate to explore further here.

- *Sixthly,*
  OSM sheds light on organizational communication, information, learning and knowledge management strategies. What is touted as organizational communication and learning often turns out to be little more than organizational training. It also makes clear why the overflow of information is a major productivity impediment.

Finally, sense making in itself is not an optional skill to be acquired or not. Since we all always make sense, it can only be improved. Knowledge and application of OSM, on the other hand, is a form of strategic leadership that can be adopted and integrated into the organizational mindset. It is, however, not an entertainment exercise – the stuff for a weekend team-building effort. People do not want to make sense, they are forced to do so in the light of ambiguity and confusion. It takes a brave leader to acknowledge that any organization is a site of precisely that – no matter whether it is managed well. But those who do, and adapt their strategies and planning accordingly, will reap the benefit of increased productivity, and sometimes a dash of innovation, based on sense created from within the entire organization.

Leadership at the Edge of Chaos:
From Control to Creativity*

By Mark D. Youngblood

"A new breed of companies is emerging that seems to thrive on chaos. These companies – which I call "Quantum Organizations" – operate on an organic model that closely mirrors the functioning of natural systems."

There are fewer than a thousand days remaining until we usher in a new millennium. Most of us, however, have already entered a new age, one that is fundamentally different from the world in which we developed our business skills and experience. Ours is a *quantum* world – fast paced, complex, and chaotic – with unique challenges that require unique approaches.

The desperate call-to-arms, "Change or die", which can be heard echoing down the corridors of businesses everywhere, is ample evidence that leaders have recognized the need to change. Executives know that companies must be fast, flexible, responsive, resilient, and creative to survive. Most of them also know that our Industrial Era mind-sets, techniques, and tools are ineffective for creating such an organization. Yet the vast majority of companies are reluctant to give up these most sacred of sacred cows, and so continue to languish even as forward-thinking competitors are passing them by.

Quantum Organizations

A new breed of companies is emerging that seems to thrive on chaos. These companies – which I call "Quantum Organizations" – operate on an organic model that closely mirrors the functioning of natural systems. Although most are emerging in the high-tech arena, they can be found in almost any industry. Microsoft, Cisco Systems, Intel, Marshall Industries, Whole Foods Markets, Starbucks, Wainwright Industries, and HarleyDavidson are all examples of Quantum Organizations. The success of these nimble giants is nothing short of astonishing. Each is breaking the traditional rules of management and organizational design, and cumulatively they are defining new paths to success.

---

* Taken with permission from Strategy & Leadership, September-October 1997, pp. 8-14

The notion that organizations are machines for producing profit – a principle first formulated over 100 years ago – is no longer effective. The machine model emphasizes control, predictability, and efficiency techniques that do not work as they once did. Quantum Organizations have found that the organic model, with its emphasis on responsiveness and creativity, is much better suited for this quantum world.

One basic difference between machines and organic (living) systems is in their openness to the environment. Machines are closed systems, that is, they have no way of renewing themselves and so wind down and stop (the law of entropy). Living systems, however, are open to their environment. Although they expend a great deal of energy and resources, they also take in an equivalent amount. Living systems *creatively evolve – machines break down.* Exhibit 1 illustrates the difference between open and closed systems. In the diagram, the degree of openness increases from left to right. The left side of the diagram, where the lines come together at a point, represents a completely closed system. This is equilibrium – complete stasis – where there is no change, just stillness. In a totally closed system, stasis is the equivalent of death. On the right side of the diagram, where the lines are furthest apart is complete chaos. In a totally open system, there is so much change that it cannot sustain itself and it slips into chaos, which is also the equivalent of death to the system.

Systems that are either too open or too closed will perish. The vertical lines on the diagram represent the limits at which systems can continue to function. The line labeled "Control" is on the edge of equilibrium. This is where companies that base their functioning on the machine model attempt to operate. Following a central tenet of the traditional management model, they work to minimize disturbances, variations, and change.

The line labeled "Creativity" is on the edge of chaos. Scientists who have studied the functioning of organic systems tell us that it is at the edge of chaos that living systems are most flexible and have the greatest potential for novelty and creativity. When organic systems reach critical levels of stability – that is when they operate far from equilibrium but have not slipped over into chaos – they creatively self-organize into higher levels of order that are both more complex and more stable.

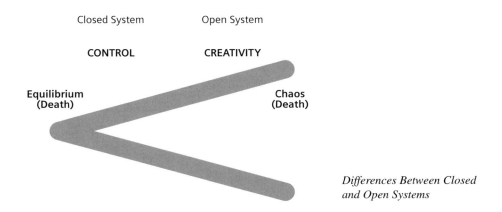

Differences Between Closed and Open Systems

Traditional organizations operate at the edge of equilibrium, while Quantum Organizations, in direct contrast, operate at the edge of chaos. The control orientation was suited for much of the 20th century, but beginning in the early 1970s, its effectiveness began to erode. As George Washington University professor Peter Vaill explains, today's environment is comparable to "white-water rafting." The techniques that worked in calm water simply do not work in white water. In order to survive in the 21st century, companies will be forced by the ever-evolving marketplace to shift to a creativity orientation. They must transform themselves to operate at the edge of chaos.

This need for transformation poses a significant challenge for many leaders. Most people in positions of leadership today gained their success through their mastery of traditional management techniques and approaches. The transformation of their companies to Quantum Organizations will carry with it profound changes in how they will lead.

The New Leader

In the mechanistic, command-and-control architecture, hierarchy and clear lines of authority are the "load-bearing structures" that keep the company intact. As a result, the fate of the organization rests on the shoulders of a few key leaders. These leaders are expected to select a winning strategy, develop detailed operating plans, direct the activities of subordinates, be smarter than anyone else, know more than anyone else, and leap tall buildings in a single bound. Not only is it impossible for companies to succeed this way, these expectations are an impossible burden for leaders to carry. In Quantum Organizations, the load-bearing structure is the system's ability to self-organize. The role of leaders, then, shifts to activities that promote the richest possible environment for this self-organization to occur.

There are three broad categories of activities for which the "new leader" is chiefly responsible. These are: (1) establishing context, (2) disturbing the system, and (3) cultivating the organization.

Establishing Context

Creativity and self-organization in living systems are contingent on having a clear identity – a context for taking action. In organizations, identity is established through purpose, principles, strategy, and culture, all of which come together in a "shared vision."

By now, many companies have defined their shared vision. They will have committed time, resources, and money to carefully crafting every word in their *One basic difference between machines and organic (living) systems is in their openness to the environment ... living systems creatively evolve – machines break down.*

vision statements. It will have been printed, framed, and hung in offices and hallways throughout the organization. Miniature versions will lie tucked away in wallets and desk drawers. But ask any employee what the company's vision is, and how it affects his or her everyday job, and 99 out of 100 won't be able to tell you – and this includes the executives! This must change.

A strong, well-understood, core ideology is *vital* to a Quantum Organization. It is through shared beliefs and intentions that people are able to act autonomously and remain in accord with the whole – thus drastically reducing the need for external controls. This is an area that bureaucratic organizations typically ignore.

Bureaucracies establish order through external controls and rigid structures, so they perceive little need for and have little interest in the organizing power of shared purpose and principles. Quantum Organizations, however, rely heavily on core ideology and shared vision for creating order and make little use of external controls. The new leaders have several responsibilities in this regard:

Clarifying shared vision. The new leaders bring into focus the shared vision that the organization is trying to manifest and connect the people in the organization to it through active participation and extensive dialogue. Employees are encouraged to develop and maintain "20/20 vision"; that is, a focus on both the long-term and short-term organizational goals.

Enriching the culture. Organic systems rely on the self-directed actions of its agents in support of the whole. One way that employees are able to operate with few rules and still create productive, purposeful results is through the organizing power of a strong culture. A culture is an organization's collective mind-set – its beliefs, intentions, and memories. The new leaders actively nurture and expand the organization's culture, becoming living examples of the desired behaviors.

Developing alignment. Even the best-intentioned employees cannot create organizational performance if all of the elements of the organization are not aligned. A highly aligned organization has the focus and power of a laser beam. Lasers are little more than normal light in which the light rays are aligned in the same direction. In organizations, coherence occurs when people and organizational design align around a universally shared purpose, strategy, and guiding principles. The new leaders use their global perspective to create this alignment around the achievement of the shared vision.

Promoting understanding. The new leaders assist the organization in understanding and interpreting information and events in the context of the organization's shared vision. People are inundated with data that are often ambiguous, contradictory, and confusing – the new leaders clarify this "noise" and transform it into meaningful information. People in organizations work in many different contexts, and leaders need to find the language that speaks to people where they are, both physically and psychologically. The message to engineers cannot be delivered in the same manner as the message to manufacturing plant workers. Their realities, cares, and concerns are totally different.

Disturbing the System

Seen through the lens of classical management, the messiness that comes with changes and variations in the work environment has been an indication that things were going wrong – that the organizational machine was breaking down. One of the most surprising conclusions to come out of the new science is that living systems have the most vitality and creativity when they are experiencing a *great deal of disturbance.*

This turns one of the basic tenets of management on its head: instead of creating stability, the new leader does the opposite – ensures that the organization is sufffciently *de*-stabilized. Some of the actions that new leaders take are:

Creating compelling goals. In their book *Built to Last,* Collins and Porras described what they called "Big Hairy Audacious Goals" (BHAGs). In change management terminology, these are called "super-ordinate goals." BHAGs are important for stimulating progress in organizations and can be powerful motivators during times of organizational transformation. Examples of BHAGs are NASA's 1962 goal to "put a man on the moon and return him home safely by the end of the decade", Motorola's goal of six sigma quality, and Microsoft's vision of a computer on every desk and all of them running Microsoft software. Effective BHAGs have three characteristics. They are: () audacious – they stretch the limits of credibility; () inspiring – they enflame the imagination and inspire the human spirit; and () unifying – they cannot be achieved without the collaboration and cooperation of the entire organization.

Ensuring the rich flow of information. The new leaders are essential in helping the organization obtain accurate and useful information and: feedback from the ecosystem in which they are operating. They reflect the performance of the organization so individuals and groups can self-correct to bring their efforts into accord with the company's goals. In particular, the new leaders help the organization see important information that is being ignored, denied, or distorted.

Promoting diversity of opinion. Diversity is essential for change and growth. Interactions that are homogenous in content and outlook are the equivalent of "empty calories" – lots of sugar and no nutritional value. Systems thrive on diversity. Consider, for instance, the importance of the exchange of diverse DNA materials to the health of a species. In-breeding ideas has the same potential for "genetic" deformity as does in-breeding physical species. Although many organizations have initiated diversity programs, these programs are generally oriented toward cultivating social tolerances between different ethnic and gender groups. This is an essen#a/first step, bur the issue for the new leader is to develop organizations that truly value rather than fear different viewpoints. Conflict, which is a natural outcome of diversity, should be seen as an opportunity for enriching the understanding of an issue. Leaders need to promote the understanding that the crossfertilization of opinion is the catalyst for generating novel ideas and approaches – the wellspring of creativity.

Holding anxiety. Change and disturbance evoke anxiety in people. Being able to hold this anxiety and still function effectively is the mark of both mature people and mature organizations. Leaders in Quantum Organizations help people to hold and use this anxiety by putting it into its proper perspective as the energizing spark for creative action.

Cultivating the Organization

Creativity and self-organization in living systems is contingent on having a clear identity (shared vision), a high degree of autonomy among the systems agents (personal leadership), and openness (the free flow of information, interactions between agents, and diverse viewpoints). The new leaders understand that the organization does not need to be controlled, that it will generate its own order and respond creatively to the environment once these conditions are met. The new leader's responsibility is to assist the organization in creating these conditions.

Promoting ownership. The new leaders are constantly promoting employees' ownership of the company's success, as well as employees' self-reliance in doing whatever is necessary to achieve the goals. They communicate the importance of commitment and self-reliance and strive to create the conditions where people can feel ownership for both their work and the company.

Nurturing relationships. In the web-like structure of the Quantum Organization, strong relationships are essential to individual and group effectiveness. The new leaders look for opportunities to help people and groups connect with each other. This includes relationships with key external stakeholders as well as those among the constituents of the organization. Leaders reinforce the vital importance of the long-term health of relationships, actively promoting collaboration, cooperation, and mutual enrichment.

> *At the same time leaders are helping to unleash the creative potential of their organizations, they are unleashing their own potential.*

Encouraging learning. The new leaders promote the diffusion of learning within the company. They seek out innovations throughout the firm and introduce them to others who might benefit. They advise the organization on skills and competencies that may need to be added to its repertoire. The new leaders recognize that learning is a process of trial and error, and promote risktaking and tolerance for failures and mistakes. Learning is also a process of expanding people's awareness, of broadening their worldview. The new leaders encourage diverse ideas and viewpoints.

Nourishing the human spirit. Organizations are about *people.* They are the gardens in which the collective hopes, aspirations, and beliefs of the people within them are planted, grown, and harvested. People breathe life into organizations through their commitment and positive energy. Given the right environment, people will selforganize to create a dynamic, thriving, successful organization, and they will do so in good times and bad. However, this sort of vitality requires conditions that are deliberately avoided in the traditional, mechanistic organization.

People are inspired by participating in something important, something from which they can derive personal meaning and satisfaction. People need personal meaning in their work – not to be some faceless cog in the corporate machine. They also need to bring their whole selves to work: body, mind, and spirit. The impoverished caricature of employees as unemotional androids must give way to the reality that humans are emotional creatures. Emotions carry power, vitality, creativity. The new leaders know this and, instead of repressing emotions, seek to channel them into positive and productive directions.

Personal Leadership

In Quantum Organizations, leadership is not a position, it is a process. It isn't limited to a few people; it is something in which everyone participates. This is a dramatic turnabout for the classical management model. In bureaucratic, command-and-control organizations, 100 percent of the power is resident in the chief executive officer. The board of directors grants this power on behalf of the stockholders, but short of extreme malfeasance by the chief officer, the board is often essentially impotent regarding corporate policy. The chief executive then delegates his or her power to the next level, and they to the next level, and so on down the line. Eventually, authority to perform certain tasks is delegated to some front-line worker. The key point is that no one in this kind of an organization owns (has power over) his or her work. The CEO has the power, but doesn't do any of the work.

What we have, in their essence, are *powerless* organizations. The CEO – who has all of the authority – cannot do the work; the people – who do the work – have no power over what that work is or how it is done. Powerless people struggle relentlessly to regain control of their lives and circumstances, usually by taking it from someone else through psychological or physical abuse, domination, and repression, or manipulation and exploitation. People also gain power by hoarding information, knowledge, and access to people or other resources. These behaviors – which are inherently counter-productive and destructive – can be seen throughout bureaucratic organizations. Regretfully, they do not remain there. Due to the indivisible connectedness of systems, these abuses are carried over and passed on to other people throughout the social system, creating an epidemic of fear, powerlessness, and abuse.

In Quantum Organizations, the goal is to restore power to individual employees. Being "powerful" means that people are *full of power* – isn't that the kind of person that every organization needs? Who really thinks an organization can survive for long with fearful, powerless people who are more intent on keeping the boss happy than in doing what is right for the customer and the company's greater interest?

Living systems thrive when their agents are powerful, when they are able to operate independently and creatively. In organizations, this means that decision-making authority and power must be held at the closest possible point to where the work is being done. This is not the same thing as *delegating* authority. Delegation is an artifact of the traditional management model where authority is on loan to someone "lower" in the organization. The main product of this approach is the blurring of accountability and the stifling of creativity and initiative.

The healthy functioning of Quantum Organizations requires the *transfer* of both authority and accountability to the person or group who accepts responsibility for producing results. With such power comes responsibility and accountability for its use and an end to the traditional caretaking activity of managers and leaders. People learn to stand on their own – to accept the risk of personal accountability and to become a whole person. Personal power and responsibility are, in fact, the essential elements of personal leadership.

The Evolution of Leadership

My study of the functioning of organic systems has left me with an indelible realization: nature will evolve relentlessly toward ever-higher levels of complexity and order, with or without humanity's permission. What, then, would be a higher order of organization of leadership? More extreme methods of control and manipulation, abuse and exploitation? Of course not. Classical managers are justified in feeling threatened by the emerging model of the new leader – these modern-day dinosaurs face the same choice as did their ancient predecessors: evolve or face extinction.

However, for any classical manager willing to take the time to truly understand the changes I have described, the news is certainly not all bad. Leadership in a traditional organization – with all its power and glory – is no picnic. Witness the early retirements of executives in top positions who "want a life", like Jeffrey Stiegler who resigned as president of American Express in 1995.

The role of the new leader is not only more productive for the organization, it is liberating for the leader as well. At the same time leaders are helping to unleash the creative potential of their organizations, they are unleashing their own potential. For many leaders who go through this transformation there is an astonishing realization: the chains that were used to restrict and control the organization had – the entire time – been wrapped just as tightly about themselves. Liberation, they have learned, is exhilarating!

Unisys Switzerland –
A Change for a Knowledge-based Culture

In June 2001, Dominique Freymond, Unisys' manager for Switzerland, had reason to feel reassured. For the first time since November 1999 he had received a clear signal from his employees that the Momentum 2000 change had finally been successfully integrated into the culture of the company. This had been symbolized during a Unisys "corner" – a company gathering dedicated to account managers and their teams – when all the employees in charge of the UBS account presented their project while tied by a rope to the account manager and client. This gesture thus symbolically expressed the new values of the company. At that moment Freymond knew he could count on teams – teams both in word and deed – who would focus on the customer's needs, on transparency, communication and cooperation as well as on the company's growth.

He recalled that he had not always felt as optimistic – quite the opposite, actually. After the Unisys headquarters had first introduced structural reorganization (Momentum 2000) in November 1999, he experienced the worst semester of his professional life with the loss of 35% of his staff, mainly talented people, and a drop of 30% in revenue for the first quarter in the fiscal year 2000. By then, 50% of his top managers had left Unisys Switzerland, new recruits were difficult to find and his attempts to create a pilot team were unsuccessful.

Although the bad results weren't directly caused by the reorganization, they acted as a wake-up call to all employees. Freymond and his team had to find a way to reverse the disastrous financial tendency by taking their future into their own hands, rather than leaving it to the company headquarters.

About Unisys

Unisys is an electronic business solutions company whose 35,000 employees help customers in 100 countries apply information technology to seize opportunities and overcome the challenges of the Internet economy. Unisys people integrate and deliver solutions, services, platforms, and network infrastructure required by business and government to transform these organizations for success in a new era.

The primary vertical markets Unisys serves worldwide include financial services, transportation, communications, publishing and commercial sectors, as well as the public sector, which includes USA federal government agencies. Unisys is headquartered in Blue Bell, Pennsylvania, in the Greater Philadelphia area.

In 1999, Unisys had a total revenue of $7.54 billion, employed 35,800 employees and declared a total profit of $500 million.

Unisys (Switzerland) AG

Unisys Switzerland is the result of the 1986 merger of Burroughs (Switzerland) AG and Sperry AG following the worldwide merger of Burroughs and Sperry.

In 1999, Unisys Switzerland had a total revenue of CHF 325 million and employed 510 co-workers (Unisys Switzerland did not declare the total profit for that year).

Unisys: A History of Excellence

Unisys is the end result of a long process of innovations by various companies during the 20th century. It is also a history of mergers among these companies.

Its history starts in 1873 when E. Remington & Sons introduced the first commercially viable typewriter. Thirteen years later, in 1886, William Seward Burroughs invented the first commercially viable adding and listing machine and founded American Arithmometer Co., which would be renamed Burroughs Adding Machine Co. in 1905. The third actor forming the foundation of Unisys is the Sperry Gyroscope Co. founded in 1910 to manufacture and sell navigational equipment. This company would become the Sperry Corp. in 1933.

After producing various versions of its typewriters, notably America's first electric typewriter in 1925, Remington Typewriter Co. and Rand Kardex Co. merge to form Remington Rand.

The year 1946 marks a change in technology that would affect the three companies underlying Unisys. In effect, ENIAC, the world's first large-scale, general-purpose, digital computer developed at the University of Pennsylvania by J. Presper Eckert and John Mauchly, started the "computer era". In 1949, following on this new technology, Remington Rand produced the 409 – the world's first business computer – which was later sold as the Univac 60 and 120. This was the first computer used by the American Internal Revenue Service and the first computer installed in Japan.

In 1955, Sperry Corp. and Remington Rand merged to form Sperry Rand. During the following thirty one years, Sperry Rand and Burroughs competed on the field of computer technology innovations, each of them adding its milestone to the path of computer science development.

Finally, in 1986, Sperry and Burroughs merged to form Unisys Corporation that, eight years later, would focus on services and solutions. In 1994 this became the company's single largest business.

Lawrence A. Weinbach – named chairman, president, and CEO of the Unisys Corporation in 1997 – launched a new business strategy in order to focus on quality and better service to customers. For Weinbach it was vital "to change the way Unisys goes to market".

He remarked that, "We talked to our customers, and they told us they're not just interested in discrete products, but in how we can help them solve their business problems." He then launched the "go to market" task force in 1999, which was formed by 14 top managers, and a few consultants and was headed by Joseph W. McGrath. As a result, Unisys unveiled a comprehensive strategy and an integrated portfolio of services, solutions and technologies to help its clients succeed in e-business. Unisys e-@ction Solutions enable organizations to take advantage of the operational efficiencies and growth opportunities of the Internet economy.

How Unisys Had to Change

There had to be a single point of accountability for each customer per domain of expertise, which means that certain employees, primarily sales people, had to fulfil this role. In this capacity they are called "Client Relationship Executives" (CREs). This setup differs from the old Unisys where different sales people would approach a client independently, and only be accountable for the product/service each was offering. Furthermore, only portions of the sales force were previously aligned through their vertical industry expertise.

Unisys had to offer solution sets that were built around key customer business issues and would increase the company's market penetration by maximizing the cross selling of Unisys products. Previously the sales force had just sold isolated technologies/services and had not provided the full value that is only realized by all the portfolio components working together.

Finally, to produce an important shift in the staff's behavior, it was necessary to concentrate all resources and efforts on solving the customer's business problems and to ensure a "zero tolerance for internal competition".

The Swiss Structure and Products after Momentum 2000

After the launching of the new structure "Go to market" in November 1999 by the CEO, Lawrence A. Weinbach, the management at Unisys Switzerland was not yet home and dry. The largest challenge was to discover how to apply the new organization strategy at the national level. After many discussions and meetings, the management approved a plan that took into account the specificities of the Swiss market.

"The purpose of our plan is sell our entire portfolio to our large, existing clients in order to provide our activities with a broader base," said Dominique Freymond, Unisys' manager for Switzerland.

In effect, Unisys Switzerland is focused on financial entities (banks, insurance companies etc.), public services (for both the Swiss Confederation and its states), telecommunications, transport services, publishing, commerce and industry. In these sectors,
management positions, called "Customer Relationship Executives (CRE)", were created to take charge of client relations. The CRE help their clients world-wide to use
the whole range of Unisys' products in an efficient and cost effective way. CREs
furthermore synchronize the numerous internal and external reports and in doing so
sometimes have to manage global account teams. The following accounts are managed by CREs:

- UBS Group (banking)
- Credit Suisse Group (banking)
- Real Time Center AG (computer outsourcing services) and
  RBA services (banking)
- Zurich Financial Services and other insurance companies
- Swisscom (telecommunications)
- La Poste (Postal services)
- Confederation (Swiss government)
- SAir Group, Danzas and Panalpina (transport services)
- Migros, Denner and Waro (retailing)

The CREs are not specialized in all details of the Unisys servers such as Enterprise or
Managed Services. To manage the technical aspects of the job, the CREs are helped
by "Portfolio Sales Executives (PSE)" who know all the technical details and are
dispersed across four departments:

1. Systems & Technology
2. Global Industries Group, Sector Finance
3. Global Industries Group, Sector Non-Finance
4. Global Network Services

Since the only two sectors that had a critical mass of co-workers in Switzerland at the
time were Finance and Cross Industry and in order to efficiently distribute the staff
internationally, the top management decided to use international teams for the Telecommunications, Transportation and Publishing sectors.

Implementing the Change in Unisys Switzerland

Although the change had been eagerly awaited at national level, these changes were
difficult to implement in Switzerland, due in part to Weinbach's vision that focused
mainly on the big picture and large teams and not on a national level.

When he was informed of the new corporate strategy in November 1999, Freymond
started to think of how to implement Momentum 2000 in his country. The new
structure gave him more responsibility as a national manager, which was satisfying for

him, but the new strategy matrix was rather complicated and wasn't going to please the sales force then in place. The CRE would have a far more visible position than the PSE, which could be perceived as a loss of power. Freymond anticipated much resistance and relied on his communication skills to introduce the change successfully.

The CEO Weinbach put much effort into turning Unisys into a people-oriented company with a focus on customer needs rather than on results only. In doing so, he surrounded himself with national managers who fit into that environment where communication, trust and cooperation were essential. He initiated road shows and videos to communicate his messages and strongly encouraged the national managers to follow his example.

Freymond's personality is in line with this culture, as he genuinely likes people and is a naturally charismatic communicator who is willing to share. However, Momentum 2000 rapidly turned into a disaster. As expected, resistance to change was strong. Top managers and talented employees left the company. Despite Freymond's communication skills, the objective of the change was unclear, thus creating feelings of insecurity.

By March 2000, half of the top management team had left the company and the remaining sales and former line managers felt they had lost power in the new structure.

Freymond then launched a road show through Switzerland, all the while feeling rather alone. He recalls this dramatic moment:

"I stood alone, with no team and no followers. The matrix was too complicated, people wanted a change, but not this change. The strategy was to become customer driven, but people didn't know how they could really contribute. They could not translate the objectives into operational tasks."

After two unsuccessful attempts to create a pilot team and his group's inability to renew contracts (which meant a great loss in revenues for the first quarter in the fiscal year 2000), the resultant sense of urgency finally gained the attention of the remaining management team. At this stage André Guyer, the appointed CRE for the finance sector, accepted ownership of the problem from a management perspective. He became an important actor in the change process, since his solid sales experience in the finance and IT industries gave him a clear understanding of business needs. He is a result-driven person, yet very focused on customer needs. One could regard him as quite an individualist, yet he understands the role and power of teamwork.

In June 2000, together with Freymond, he organized a workshop to gain a clear understanding of what had happened to the revenues and what could be done to improve the situation. The bottom line was that no one else besides them, the Swiss management team, could truly help. Basically it was decided that Unisys Switzerland's future depended exclusively on its employees and management. The motto *"we take our future into our hands"* was launched and an external management consultant was hired to serve as coach of the new change implementation process.

When Freymond met, Alain Neumann, the external consultant and a friend, he was questioning the whole attempt. Fortunately Neumann had the strength, skills, vision and the human touch to serve as a perfect coach in change management.

By October 2000, Freymond, Guyer and Neumann had together turned the situation around and put it on the track to success. As a first step, they organized an important two-day team-building workshop. Neumann and the top management were present in order to get the whole group to take ownership of the process and develop a clear vision on how to proceed to achieve better results and implement the organizational change.

"Taking the future into our hands"

From the outset it was clear that the group's success in leading the change program would depend on teamwork, leadership, communication and project ownership. To reach this state of mind, the managers had to overcome certain emotional barriers and resistance to change. They had to move from being quarrelsome managers to leaders who would create the synergies necessary for the change process.

Neumann's first mission was to identify the issues underlying the problem as well as the stakeholders. The outcome was the following:

- The global organization was there to stay.
- Everybody had to adapt locally.
- How do you merge the two positions?

Thereafter Alain Neumann assessed the situation and summarizes it in his own words:

"Dominique was the housekeeper of Switzerland! There was no team spirit, no Unisys Switzerland, just a "can't do this" culture. With some people, change is not possible, for instance all the Business Units Managers had to be replaced because of their attitude. Once this was done, 50% of the job was done."

The first issue was to get the managers to talk to one another rather than working at cross-purposes. Only then was it possible to view what had to be done, even if they had no other choice than to change.

Subsequently, competence centers had to be created to encourage innovative thinking and to reach the clients with a customer-oriented approach rather than a product-line approach. This logically implies structural and behavioral changes. As Neumann rightly puts it:

"Changes only happen with people who are willing to change. Strategy, tactics and process enable the implementation of change at all levels of the organization. Furthermore, one must lead the change process, not manage the change. It is equally important to provide emotional security through a methodical approach and clear communication of the objective. Finally, people leading the change must have a strong feeling of empathy."

Thanks to Alain Neumann's coaching and the team of Freymond and Guyer, the managers and CREs finally took ownership of the change project. Freymond received all the managers' commitment to jointly lead Unisys Switzerland into the future.

The next step was to urgently communicate, using different approaches, the shared vision to all employees, since 6 months had already been wasted.

Communication of the New Objectives

Thomas Huegli, the newly hired communication manager, had the immense task of finding creative ways to communicate the new objectives effectively. In October 2000, he launched a new road show to explain the bad results and remind the audience that there was no connection between the bad results and the new structure. The management also focused on the good points that could be developed. They addressed the staff, starting with the significant introduction: "We, the Swiss management team, are fully aware of the urgency implied by the current difficult situation. We are working hard, together and with total dedication to improve this." For the first time Unisys Switzerland was led by a truly united pilot team with a common goal. The new motto, "We take our future into our hands", was largely used to focus on the issue of ownership of the problems the branch was facing, so as to find solutions together and at all levels.

To communicate to the employees that the top management had a clear vision of the company's future and to demonstrate their unity, Huegli organized a new road show, called the "Kick-off tour 2001", that was conducted during February of that year. He was the one who had the insight to have the pilot team share their objectives while dressed as a football team. The new vision was: unify, reach common goals and dedication. He also suggested Freymond use a simplified organization chart instead of the complex matrix they had used before.

This symbolic experience largely contributed to creating a strong sense of belonging to Unisys Switzerland, a branch that had successfully integrated the new values and structure. Freymond and his team thus had a greater chance of reaching their goal and becoming a very profitable company – the number one technology platform provider and the best system integrator of Switzerland.

Strengthening a Culture Based on Communication

For Freymond, communication isn't only effective when conducting change. It is the foundation of a corporate culture based on trust, transparency and cooperation between all stakeholders of the company, including the HQ and the customers. Therefore Huegli, the communication manager, attends executive meetings, focuses on building trust and ensures that dialogue is favored at all time.

To stop rumors at an early stage and encourage bottom-up information, sessions of "talk to the CEO" have been introduced. Every 3 weeks Freymond meets the staff without other managers being present, and answers questions they may have.

He also envisaged the Unisys corner during which CREs together with their team and a customer organize a presentation of what they've been doing, and how this is done. This has proven to be extremely effective in building a sense of belonging.

Finally, in order to be very transparent, an intranet was constructed that contains valuable information on results, events, structure etc.

Questions

1. Discuss the concept of a "shadow organization" by referring to its nature and practice, and its resulting managerial challenges in at least three corporate organizations.

2. How should managers cope with the challenge of paradox in today's fast-changing environments, e.g. simultaneously being both adapters and shapers? Should all managers, and, for that matter, all individuals be able to handle paradox in their respective environments today?

3. How did Miller destabilize the state of equilibrium at Shell? Would these methods also be workable in other organizations? Why or why not?

4. Analyze the example of "managing chaos" at the Walt Disney Company by gathering their latest corporate information (see also their corporate website), and identifying what "simple rules" would be applicable for the purpose of coherence of activities.

5. What strategic management tools would be appropriate for each of the four levels of environmental uncertainty, and what managerial styles would be most relevant for each level?

6. Discuss the strategic leadership challenges that Unisys has been facing. How could Unisys' leadership make sense of the changes in the knowledge economy, and provide the necessary context to their organization?

References

Chapter 6: Managing the New Strategic Leadership Challenges

[1] Adapted from various authors, especially Youngblood, M.D. (1997), "Leadership at the Edge of Chaos", *Strategy and Leadership*, September-October, 8-14; and Tetenbaum, T.J. (1998), "Shifting Paradigms: From Newton to Chaos", *Organizational Dynamics*, Spring, 21-32.

[2] Adapted from Pascale, R.T. (1999), "Surfing at the Edge of Chaos", *Sloan Management Review*, Spring, 83-94.

[3] Anderson, P., "Seven Levers for Guiding the Evolving Enterprise", in Clippinger, J.H. (Editor) (1999), *The Biology of Business*, San Francisco: Jossey-Bass Publishers, 113-152.

[4] Eisenhardt, K.M. and Sull, D.N. (2001), "Strategy as Simple Rules", *Harvard Business Review*, January, 111.

[5] Eisenhardt, K.M. and Brown, S.L. (1998), *Competing on the Edge: Strategy as Structured Chaos*, Boston: Harvard Business School Press.

[6] Adapted from Pascale, R.T. (1999), *op. cit.*, 37.

[7] Beinhocker, E.D. (1997), "Strategy at the Edge of Chaos", *McKinsey Quarterly*, Number 1, 36.

[8] Beinhocker, E.D. (1997), *op. cit.*, 37.

[9] Courtney, H. (2001), *Crafting Strategy in an Uncertain World*, Boston: Harvard Business School Press.

[10] Beinhocker, E.D. (1999), "Robust Adaptive Strategies", *Sloan Management Review*, Spring, 95-106.

[11] Beinhocker, E.D. (1999), *op. cit.*

Understanding Organizational Sense Making

References

[1] Rene Tisse, et al. 2000. *The Knowledge Dividend*. Prentice Hall, London

[2] Manuel Castells, 1996. *The Rise of the Network Society*. Blackwell: Oxford

[3] David Snowden, 2002. Complex Acts of Knowing: Paradox and Descriptive Self-awareness. *Journal of Knowledge Management*, Vol 6/2

[4] Ralph D. Stacey, 2001. *Complex Responsive Processes in Organizations*. Routledge: London

[5] Gareth Morgan, 1997. *Images of Organization*. SAGE: London. See Chapter 8 in particular.

[6] Karl E. Weick, 1995. *Sensemaking in Organizations* SAGE: London

[7] Weick 1995, p. 70ff

[8] Vasant Dhar & Roger Stein, 1997. *Intelligent decision support methods – the science of knowledge work.* Prentice Hall:NJ (7 – 11). According to their taxonomy the levels of intelligence sophistication in any knowledge related event is as follows: data – access – scrubbing – integration – transformation – discovery – learning.

Further reading

Baumard, P. 1999. Tacit Knowledge in organisations. SAGE: London

Von Krogh, G. Ichijo, K. Nonaka, I, 2000. *Enabling Knowledge Creation.* Oxford University Press: Oxford

Mittleton-Kelly E. 2001. *Complex Systems and Evolutionary Perspectives of Organisations – The Application of Complexity Theory to Organisations.* Elsevier City

Written by

Authors and Contributors

Authors und Editors

Marius Leibold

is Professor in Strategy at Stellenbosch University (SU), South Africa, and also Professor of Strategy at the Business School Netherlands International. He has held visiting positions at North American and European universities. His research focuses on new business models for global competitiveness, incorporating complexity and fuzzy management approaches as applied in various industries such as financial services and the life sciences.
He can be contacted at: leibold@mweb.co.za

Gilbert J.B. Probst

is a Professor of Organizational Behavior and Management at the University of Geneva, where he also directs the MBA program. Prior to Geneva, he taught as a visiting faculty member at the Wharton School in Philadelphia. He received his Ph.D. from the University of St. Gallen. He is founder and chairman of the Geneva Knowledge Forum, comprising 20 multinationals, and co-author of *Managing Knowledge* (published by Wiley). He also serves as a board member of major companies and training institutions.
He can be contacted at: probst@hec.unige.ch

Michael Gibbert

is a doctoral candidate at the Institute for Leadership and Human Resource Management at the University of St. Gallen, Switzerland, and at Siemens AG in Munich, on leave at the Yale School of Management in 2002/3. His previous positions were at the Ludwig Maximilians University in Munich, the University of Stellenbosch, South Africa (visiting faculty member), and INSEAD, France (research associate). His research interests are the management of innovation in highly diversified firms, knowledge-based competitiveness, and the case-study research methodology.
He can be contacted at: michael.gibbert@unisg.ch

Article Authors

Eric Beinhocker

is a principal in McKinsey's Washington, DC, office.

Goran Carstedt

is a former Volvo and IKEA senior executive.

Vijay Govindarajan

is the Earl C. Daum 1924 Professor of International Business and director of the William F. Achtmeyer Center for Global Leadership at Dartmouth College in Hanover, New Hampshire.

Anil K. Gupta

a visiting professor at Stanford University at the time of this writing, is a distinguished scholar-teacher and a professor of strategy and global e-business at the University of Maryland in College Park.

Gary Hamel

is the Chairman of Strategos and Visiting Professor of Strategic management at London Business School.

Brian Huffman

is an assistant professor of management at the University of Wisconsin in River Falls.

Stefan Jenzowsky

is Vice President and Head of Business Innovation at Siemens Information and Communication Networks (ICN).

Claudia Jonczyk

is a research assistant at the University of Geneva.

W. Chan Kim

is the Boston Consulting Group Bruce D. Henderson Chair Professor of International Management at INSEAD in Fontainebleau, France.

Johann Kinghorn

is Director of the Programme in Value and Policy Studies, and Director of the Centre for Knowledge Dynamics and Decision-making at the University of Stellenbosch, South Africa.

Renée Mauborgne

is the INSEAD Distinguished Fellow and Affiliate Professor of Strategy and Management, and president of ITM Research in Fontainebleau.

James F. Moore

is president of GeoPartners Research Inc., a management consulting firm in Cambridge, Massachusetts that specializes in issues of business strategy and implementation.

Michael E. Porter

is the Bishop William Lawrence University Professor at Harvard University; he is based at Harvard Business School in Boston.

Peter Senge

is a senior lecturer at MIT Sloan School of Management and founding chair of the Society for Organizational Learning (SoL).

Michael Thiel

is doctoral candidate at Ludwigs-Maximilians-University in Munich.

Sven Völpel

is a Visiting Fellow at the Harvard Business School.

Mark D. Youngblood

is president and founder of Dallas-based Quay Alliance, Inc., an organizational change consulting firm.

Glossary of Major Terms

Ambidextrous management
A coupling of the word "ambivalent" (contrary properties) and "dexterous" (mentally deft) the term "ambidextrous" refers to the managerial ability to handle paradox and contrariness in mentally adroit ways.

Autopoiesis
Literally meaning "automatic production", i.e. "auto" = automatic, and "poiesis" = production. See the term "poised organization" for application in strategic management context.

Business ecosystem
Also termed "biocorporate system", it refers to an organization as a living organism within a larger system of business ecology, i.e. crossing a variety of industries and diversity of stakeholders and co-shaping organizations and their environments. A key characteristic of organizations in business ecosystems is their collaboration with competitors, thereby blurring the boundaries between "friend and fiend".

Business model
This refers to the particular business concept, or "way of doing business", of an organization. It includes the customer value proposition (product or service at the right place, price and time), the organization's choice of internal value chain (how it conceives and builds up the value proposition), and its particular external socio-cultural system linkages (e.g. supply chain, delivery chain) to provide customer value proposition(s).

Business socio-cultural system
A purposeful, voluntary group of organizations and their stakeholders within large societal networks, held together ("cohered") by common objectives, values and culture. While a business ecosystem (see above) focuses on information and coordination (genetic codes), a business socio-cultural system is knowledge and relationship bonded (cultural codes or "memes").

Co-evolution
Evolution is the study of how species (humans, animals, organizations) adapt, survive and expire over time. In an organizational context, this means that every organization changes over time due to internal and external adaptation, and in close relationships

with other organizations (competitors, as well customers and partner firms) and individuals. Co-evolution is not restricted to the business world (private sector), but involves the public and third sectors as well. It does not evolve by itself, but co-evolves with others (stakeholders, communities, and individuals) that co-shape its role, characteristics and behavior (see also business ecosystems, above).

Coherence
Coherence means to "stick together", remain united, or to be well knit and consistent. *Organizational coherence* points to application of techniques such as organizational values, purpose and culture to enable diverse organizational or network members to "stick together", without central direction, coordination and control. Coherence mechanisms enable unity to emerge from diversity.

Communities of Practice (COPs)
Groups of people informally bound together across traditional organizational or industry boundaries, by e.g. shared expertise, interests and passions (e.g. by email networks). COPs are self-governing and their life-span is limited, i.e. they are formed when the need for knowledge exchange arises and dissolve when a given project is completed – linkages between memebers, however, often remain and account for the formation and structure of new COPs.

Complexity management
A body of managerial techniques, including application of "simple rules", to guide and cohere seemingly chaotic, diverse and complex activities in organizations and business networks. It is based on complexity science, a body of knowledge focusing on purposeful co-evolution of systems via the influencing of underlying patterns of self-organizing behavior. A synonymous term is "chaos management", i.e. managing chaos by focusing on underlying pattern similarities.

Constructing/deconstructing/reconstructing value chains
Organizations and industries can be constructed, deconstructed and reconstructed according to the range and sequencing of value-adding activities. For example, traditional organizational structures are increasingly being deconstructed by removing bureaucratic layers of middle management, while many traditional industries are being reconstructed through technology (e.g. service call centers displacing branch offices in the insurance industry).

Customer competence
The competencies (i.e. knowledge, skills, capabilities) residing in customers, regarding products and services, and their utilization (see Customer Knowledge Management, below).

Customer Knowledge Management (CKM)
Managerial activities to develop and utilize the knowledge residing in customers for

purpose of enhancing the performance of socio-cultural business networks and their constituent organizations and individuals.

Cybernetics research
The field of study focusing on the optimization of relationships between machines and living systems – regarded as second-generation systems thinking (e.g. interdependency and self-organizing methods in living systems).

Dynamic capabilities
Residing especially in an organization's resources and processes, these are its abilities to configure and reconfigure internal and external competencies to appropriately address rapidly changing environments.

Enterprise Resource Management (ERM)
A logical extension of the concept of "Enterprise Resource Planning" (ERP) – while ERP focuses on the resources supply chain of an organization, ERM includes the management of all possible resources, including customers as potential sources of knowledge and co-developers of new value propositions.

Fitness landscape
The particular business landscape (e.g., an industry) in which an organization has chosen to play a role and evolve, and, consequently, in which it has to remain a "fit" player for continued success and survival (see also the related concepts of "knowledge landscape" and "organizational fitness").

Intermediation/Disintermediation/Reintermediation of industry role players
The types and numbers of industry role players (or intermediaries) in industry value systems can emerge or be deleted, adjusted or redefined, depending on the feasibility in changing conditions. For example, the Internet is causing the emergence of new role players in many industries, ranging from travel and tourism to grocery retailing and financial services.

Knowledge landscape
A particular business landscape (e.g. industry) in which an organization is not necessarily involved at present (but may decide to become involved in), characterized by specific knowledge and capability requirements. New knowledge landscapes continually arise, and pose new knowledge challenges and organizational fitness challenges. Being involved in various knowledge landscapes, with various fitness dimensions, displays an organization's robust strategic management capabilities.

Managing at the "edge of chaos"
The "edge of chaos" is a concept describing an area between order and chaos – just enough order and not too much chaos. If there is too much order, creativity is stifled; if there is too much chaos, there is self-destruction. Managing at the "edge of chaos"

indicates the appropriate utilization of complexity management techniques for optimization of innovation.

Networked incubators
The guided cultivation of innovative business start-ups through mechanisms that foster partnerships and other forms of linkages among a range of (potential) stakeholders.

Operations research
The field of study focusing on interdependency in the context of mechanistic systems (machine model of thinking, e.g. joint optimization of various production systems – regarded as "first-generation systems thinking").

Organizational fitness
Organizational fitness is a concept that transcends traditional profitability measures by including an organization's dynamic capabilities to be innovative for continuous organizational survival and prosperity. Organizational fitness can be measured in two ways:

First, looking *within* the organization
by its *ability to self-organize* internally quickly and effectively in the face of change. This ability ranges from (1) ineffective self-organization that freezes a business in place, through (2) an ability to keep pace with today's rapid rate of change but not to lead this change, and culminates in (3) an ability to reorganize much faster than others.

Second, looking *externally*
by the *adaptation* an entity exhibits within its *changing context*. The type and level of adaptation determine the success and, therefore, the continued life of the organization. Status in this area ranges from (1) being endangered due to total adaptation to a context that no longer exists through (2) being well suited to today's environment to (3) shaping the environment by creating major shifts in the business landscape.

Paradoxical management/leadership
A concept indicating the provision of managerial direction without being directive; being authoritative without being dominating; being strong while being open to influence and persuasion; enabling individuals and groups to develop and grow, without being manipulative; incentivizing and measuring performance without being controlling; sharing knowledge while also reserving key intellectual capital; and creating "new" knowledge while destroying/ unlearning "old" knowledge.

Poised organization
An organization that continuously and successfully changes in its knowledge landscape – a specifically chosen arena of business activity – by simultaneously balancing survival (effectiveness) and advancement (renewal) activities. It essentially means an ability to effectively rejuvenate itself (see autopoiesis, above)

Robust strategy

Strategy that provides organizational purpose, values and general direction, but without rigid policies, objectives, programs and control practices. Robustness indicates the ability to respond in several different modes (or strategic options), and the ability to be both proactive (first-mover; shaping) and reactive (late-mover; following), depending on the situation(s).

Self-organization

Collaboration and mutual activities that arise spontaneously through the interrelationships of a system's parts, without central control or direction, are termed "self-organization". A good example is the Internet, which evolves spontaneously over time without being centrally directed, coordinated or controlled.

Serious play

Imaginative techniques to enable "as-if" or "make believe" thinking among organizational and business network members. The purposeful "playing-around" with new ideas, concepts and applications engenders innovative strategies.

Shadow organization

An experimental business entity, separate from the conventional organization or business enterprise, which is utilized for the development and testing of a new business model.

Systemic Scorecard (SSC)

Derived from the well-known Balanced Scorecard (BSC), it refers to a measurement technique for overall fitness of a socio-cultural business system.

Systemic strategic management

The managerial activity of co-shaping viable customer value propositions by means of dynamic organizational and network capabilities in socio-cultural business systems to enable organizational fitness.

Systematic thinking

Logical, analytical, step-by-step thinking – often characterized by the approach of reducing large entities into smaller units for easier analysis and understanding.

Systemic thinking

Connective, holistic and pattern-like thinking – often characterized by the approach that "the whole is more than the sum of the parts".

Davenport, Tom; Probst, Gilbert (Editors)

Knowledge Management Case Book

Siemens Best Practises

With a Foreword by Dr. Heinrich von Pierer, President and CEO of Siemens AG

2nd revised and enlarged edition, 2002, 336 pages
ISBN 3-89578-181-9

This book provides a perspective on knowledge management at Siemens – according to an international benchmarking (MAKE) one of the "top ten KM companies world-wide" – by presenting the reader with the best of the corporation's practical applications and experiences. Davenport and Probst bring together instructive case studies from different areas that reflect the rich insights gained from years of experience in practising knowledge management.

Presenting applications from very different areas, this practice-orientated book is really outstanding in the broad field of KM literature.

"Perhaps the most revealing – and interesting – part of the cases in this book is not the analysis of the various knowledge management tools and processes, but the description of their development, of how they come about, of how commitment was gained, of how implementation was led."
   Yves Doz, The Timken Chaired Professor of Global Technology and Innovation at INSEAD, Fontainebleau

"This case book brings insights how our most valuable resource makes those tools happen. I found this book exciting reading, because it is, to my knowledge, the only book where a single company with a wide variety of knowledge management approaches accumulates years of experiences and lessons learned. Edited by two of the leading thinkers in the field of knowledge management, this book will show the way you practise knowledge management in your company."
   Heinz Fischer, Global Head of HR, Deutsche Bank AG

"This book is a rare and valuable description of a single company's knowledge management journey. Siemens has made impressive advances in becoming a knowledge-driven firm, and this volume details many of its directions and way-stations."
   Laurence Prusak, Executive Director, IBM Institute for Knowledge Management